{HERE}

Anthony DePalma

HERE

A

BIOGRAPHY

of

THE

NEW

AMERICAN

CONTINENT

BBS

PublicAffairs

New York

Book design by Jane Raese

Library of Congress Cataloging-in-Publication Data
DePalma, Anthony.
Here: a biography of the new American continent / by Anthony DePalma.
p.   cm.
Includes bibliographical references and index.
ISBN 1-891620-83-5
1. North America—Civilization.   2. Group identity—North America.
3. United States—Relations—Mexico.   4. United States—Relations—Canada.
5. Mexico—Relations—United States.   6. Canada—Relations—United States.
7. National characteristics, American.   8. National characteristics, Canadian.
9. National characteristics, Mexican.   I. Title.
E40.D46   2001
970—dc21
2001019371

FIRST EDITION

10 9 8 7 6 5 4 3 2 1

*For my father, Anthony,
who let me see the world,
and my mother, Phyllis,
who helped me feel it*

"No man is an island, entire of itself;
every man is a piece of the continent,
a part of the main."

John Donne
Devotions

CONTENTS

*

Preface xi

PREFACE

✳

Some time before I left the United States to live and work beyond the ends of America, I stumbled across a small treasure at an estate sale in old Newark, New Jersey. It was a thin book, just 158 pages long and bound in stiff red leather almost gone to brown. *The History of the United States Told in One-Syllable Words,* published in the 1920s, presented the magnificent sweep of the American conquest of a continent using only the simplest of words. A handwritten dedication in lacy script read "To Russell Jr., from Dad and Mother, Christmas 1924."

The confident tone of the book and its straightforward claim on history struck me as being thoroughly American. Though it was clearly meant for children like young Russell, I imagined that the book also had been read by immigrants who, like my grandfather, came to Newark, New York, and the other great American cities at the turn of the century. This simple text was an artifact of a classic American age when the only past that mattered was our past, and the only valid version of the future was the one that belonged to us. It was easy to picture newcomers struggling with the maddening inconsistencies of English and the exotic notion of limitless possibility embedded in the book. "God has led us through ways that have been strange, to reach the place where we now stand," the author, Josephine Pollard, wrote in her introduction. "The men of all the earth look on our land, and we are glad to have them call it the land of the free and the home of the brave."

Such pennywhistle patriotism seeps steadily through the book as it paints a vast landscape peopled with heroes any reader would want to emulate. Immigrants would have been led to see this continent as a place where noble ambitions imbued the air itself, a mythic land wholly different from the wretched Europe many had left behind and quite distinct from the America in which they cobbled together their new existence. The book was characteristically single-minded; it limned the essence of America while paying little heed to anything else that had happened on the continent since the Vikings briefly visited 1,000 years before. The ferocious war with France for control of the continent—all the rage of an epoch reduced to a few paragraphs. Britain's struggles after the American Revolution to control the border of what was left of its holdings in North America from Maine to Vancouver Island—quickly dismissed. And the book dispatched with little elaboration the fateful confrontation with Mexico that gave the United States its continental footing; the blame was all Mexico's because it had been "full of ill will" when Texas wanted to join the United States. No mention was made that Texas had belonged to Mexico.

In the six years I was away from home working as a correspondent for *The New York Times,* that one-syllable history of the United States came to mind many times. I thought of it when I met Canadians who did not love their own history and Mexicans who were afraid of theirs. It helped me realize just how we Americans use our history; we create it and control it and continually conform it to our liking. This custom-made history is then passed along, from parents to their children, from one generation of Americans to the next incoming wave of immigrants, until we have come up with a version of the life of this continent so much to our liking that our North American neighbors do not even recognize it.

My voyage beyond the ends of America quickly became a challenge to what I thought I knew about this most familiar of places. It became an emotional as well as an intellectual expedition as I moved with my family from one ring of the North American big top to another, beginning in Mexico, then pushing on to Canada, and finally returning full circle to the United States. I began with as many preconceptions as misperceptions, and not until some time had passed could I make the connections that led to the glimmer of understanding.

At first I was dismayed and then angered as I began to realize just how much my awareness of this continent matched the self-serving view presented in Pollard's one-syllable history, a view that I found most Americans shared. This is no accident of fate, nor a failing of my education. This is the way we Americans have used history since we became strong enough to control it. It is a familiar complaint in other countries. When it comes from our enemies, we dismiss it as blatant anti-Americanism; when it comes from our closest neighbors, we simply ignore it. We don't think much about Canada or Mexico at all, because they are too close, too common. But living under the sharper sunlight south of our border forced me to see our history from a new perspective. And then, when I leaped over the United States to settle under the solemn gray skies beyond our northern border, parallels of history and culture became unavoidable, and my compass needed resetting once again.

In time, my anger over the historical distortions I had inherited subsided and was replaced by a growing fascination with the intricate and innumerable ways in which what had happened here, in what became the United States, shaped what occurred in those wild lands that eventually came to be called Canada or Mexico. This personal reeducation came precisely when the continent itself was being reconceived in profound ways that would have been unthinkable just a few years before. The treaties, uprisings, murders, and elections that took place from 1993 to 2000 unveiled our shared destiny, just as they exposed our shared history. The future and the past were juxtaposed in a way that led to the most fundamental form of discovery—I began seeing what I thought I knew well in an entirely new way that changed it forever.

I came to realize that the familiar outlines of the three separate countries I had always known were beginning to recede and be replaced by the new American continent, of which I was a part. Like a genealogical treasure hunter, I traced our past across our borders and into other lands, just as I was crossing those borders to explore their unknown places for *The New York Times*. What I found transformed me. Humility and awe attended my realization that it was Canada that was obliquely referred to in the grievances listed in our Declaration of Independence; that it was the end of our Civil War that had helped Mexico win its freedom from European usurpers. I was laying claim to the history of the continent, and becoming, as John Donne had envisioned it, not an island but "a piece of the continent, a part of the main."

Living and working outside the United States made two things clear: Although we might want to ignore it, our history is thoroughly entangled with the history of our neighbors. And despite those shared roots, we have become very different societies. The European conquerors who created New France, New Spain, and New England, and who thus sowed the seeds of Canada, Mexico, and the United States, shared the old world from which they all came. Yet starting at roughly the same time in broadly the same place, the three countries that grew up on the continent created their own versions of a new world.

For half a millennium, these three universes existed side by side, sometimes warring with each other, often at peace, yet separated by boundaries and prejudices far stronger than any customs stations or border posts could ever be. Then as we entered the 1990s—almost exactly 500 years after Columbus stumbled into the new world—the harsh reality of a rapidly changing economic order, combined with the ineluctable tug of our past, began to transform profoundly the relationship among the three American nations. In order to compete in this rapidly globalizing world where European nations had formed a union and the Asian countries were acting like a bloc of their own, the nations of North America would have to draw closer together, whether they wanted to or not. A reluctant trinity took shape.

As a *New York Times* correspondent in Mexico and Canada at the time (and the first ever to report from both ends of America), I had a unique perspective from which to observe the momentous dawning of this uncertain new season in American history. I enjoyed a grandstand seat under the big top of this three-ring circus called North America, witnessing the remarkable revolution as it occurred from the high Arctic to the Chiapas highlands. In that brief period of sometimes explosive, sometimes evolutionary change, the North American continent itself assumed its own identity for the first time since Europeans began leaving footprints on this ancient and splendid land 500 years before.

This book represents one American's journey across North America, one American's pursuit of a northern passage connecting our past with a future taking shape before our eyes. It is the chronicle of the first years of a new American continent, a biography of a place with special meaning for all 400 million Americans who live in Canada, Mexico, and the United States. This book is also, in a sense, a biography of a single American—the grandson of immigrants who sought out America, son of a longshoreman who carried a piece of America on his back, husband to an immigrant who also came to look for America, and father to children who know foreign anthems as well as their own and who someday will want to know which America is theirs.

When I began to see things through this three-sided prism I have described, the world I knew began to change. I witnessed events in Mexico and Canada but inevitably compared or connected them to similar events here in the United States. Or the other way around. It was as if our borders were becoming mirrors, and when I looked across them, I saw not others but us, not "there" but "here." Our borders became reflections of who we are and, more important, of what we are becoming.

If we look at the places where America ends, we can see what the future holds for the United States: admiration and jealousy, as in the north, or an uncertain confrontation with the developing world, as on our southern flank. For all Americans, understanding this is to know better the essence of the sublime and perilous world we are entering.

In this book, I have tried to take readers on a similar journey of discovery. In each chapter, I portray some of the events and people, great and simple, that are shaping this evolutionary era of the new American continent. Wherever possible, I use that same three-sided prism to show what happened in one place from the perspective of another. I use the name "America" and, by extension, the phrase "the ends of America" to refer to the United States, because that is what I found the overwhelming majority of people on the continent do. For me to do otherwise would be pedantic and contrary to my goal of getting people to recognize the true dimensions of the place we call "here."

Like any other biography, this story rests in part on lives that came before. To ensure that we understand the countries with which we share this continent, I have sometimes had to present what might at first seem to be familiar history. But I have tried to open up the vista and portray those events in a continental context that reveals details and connections that may not have been apparent before. I follow a roughly chronological order, beginning in 1993, just months before the start of the momentous North American Free Trade Agreement, and ending with the dramatic triple elections in the year 2000 that sealed the genesis of this next new world. The sparks of discovery sometimes do not follow a regular pattern, and accurately relating this complex history at times meant embarking on short side trails. But I hope my approach brings invaluable insight, and in the end, a richer, more comprehensive map of the rediscovered American continent.

The details of my own rediscovery are interspersed through the broader American story, as are the lives of all Americans. In the end, this is a personal story, told from the heart, a discovery of something new in a world that is thought to be utterly familiar. My hope is that those who read *Here* will ever afterward find in that simple, powerful, one-syllable word all the makings of a new world.

On this long voyage, I have been helped by countless individuals, each with a personal vision of what America means. In particular I am indebted to *The New York Times* and the editors there who gave me my ticket for this magnificent opportunity, among them Bernie Gwertzman,

John Lee, Andy Rosenthal, Bill Stockton, and, in particular, Joe Lelyveld
and Bill Keller, two extraordinary correspondents and incessantly curious editors who have the knack of seeing things in a way they may
never have been seen before. I also am grateful to a colleague and
friend, Tom Friedman, who encouraged me to make my own journey
from Mexico City to Toronto. Stuart Krichevsky, my agent, believed in
the project from the moment it was presented to him, and helped bring
aboard Peter Osnos, Lisa Kaufman, and the other dedicated people at
PublicAffairs who agreed that North America matters. Two exacting
journalists, Chris Wilson of Reuters and *The Times*'s Dean Toda, read
early versions of the manuscript and made timely emendations. I had
many guides to help me on the other side of each border. In Mexico,
Gladys Boladeras, Ismael Villalobos, Jorge G. Castañeda, Homero Aridjis, Tim Golden, Tim Padgett, Keith Dannemiller, and Pepe and Debbie
Berdichevsky, among others, kept me from straying too far and made it
possible for me to keep my eyes on the right path. In Canada, I had
many native guides, but in particular Kalyani Vittala, Paul Knox, Lewis
Mitz, George Haynal, Chris Waddell, and Alain Dubuc. A fellow North
American *voyageur*, Professor John Wirth of the North American Institute, provided unflagging support and assistance, as did Professor
Stephen Blank of Pace University. Last, I want to thank Miriam, Aahren,
Laura Felice, and Andrés, all of them hearty souls who accompanied me
to the ends of America and beyond, and who helped me truly understand and appreciate the new American continent.

{HERE}

CHAPTER ONE

America Septentrional

✳

I have come to believe that this is a mighty continent
which was hitherto unknown.

Columbus's Journal of the Third Voyage
May 30–August 31, 1498

We can only imagine how the hearts of the early Spanish explorers raced and their imaginations ran wild as they first set foot on the mainland of North America in the early sixteenth century. They knew little about the mysterious place where they raised the flag of their king. Frightened Indians in Cuba had spoken only of a great and bountiful land nearby. This bolstered the Spaniards' belief that they could reach the forbidden shores of India or even China, which they had been searching for when they had set sail from Spain.

Nor can any person today know the keen disappointment the conquistadores felt as they came to the realization time after time that they still were far from their intended destination. No matter what opportunities and wonders presented by the new world they stumbled upon, their initial misunderstandings proved hard to correct. For decades to come, European maps of the mysterious continent badly miscalculated distances and misinterpreted the relationship of one land mass to another. Great portions of the maps were left blank, or were filled in with inland seas, gigantic offshore islands, and other fanciful features that were based more on imagination than fact. On a few of those inchoate maps, North America was simply called America Septentrional, an ancient Latin word referring to the seven stars of the Great Bear constellation, otherwise known as the Big Dipper, which mariners used to find the North Star that guided them across treacherous seas. Thus, for a time, the entire continent—or at least the part of it that was known—was treated as nothing more than a signpost.

At first the western world little understood or appreciated what had been discovered across the sea. For at least fifty years after Columbus's maiden voyage, North America was merely in the way. To the Admiral of the Ocean Sea, and the determined navigators who followed him, the undreamed-of continent was little more than an obstruction, an impediment to be circumvented on the way toward a more practical destination. Even when fragmentary reports of the continent's true breadth conflicted with earlier beliefs, myths were sustained. Well into the sixteenth century, European cartographers drew maps with India attached to Mexico. And California often was portrayed as an island for a century beyond that.

This continental confusion only marked the beginning of what would become a long history of misconceptions about North America, some of which persist today. In large measure, the mystery is due to the evanescent nature of the continent. Say Europe, and an idea comes to mind, a vision broad enough to encompass different languages and unique cultures, all connected by geography and history. Africa evokes a similar reaction. So too Asia, and South America. All of these continents, and all of the countries they contain, share borders that have at times been armed and hostile, and even these conflicts have helped create a sense of the broader place as a venue of war and a proscenium of power.

North America, as a notion, has not conveyed a single, strong image. We understand it is there, we know North America is a continent, and with scientific knowledge grounded in the observation and measurement of half a millennium, we know the boundaries of America Septentrional. But the way we have known it would, in Spanish, be defined by the verb *saber*, which refers to book learning or observation, and not *conocer*, which is used for those things we know intimately, as we know a friend or a special place like home. We know North America exists, but we do not know North America.

One reason for such enduring purblindness is that North America is a concept beyond geography, a shared set of values obscured for too long by political shortsightedness and cultural myopia. What binds together this centuries-old idea of America are not maps but ambitions, and the knowledge that we who live here have inherited the precious chance of starting afresh. What divides us are the different forms taken by this process of beginning anew. As will be seen later, Canada, Mexico, and the United States represent different versions of the new world, but each started with a break from tradition and an interruption of history lasting long enough to create a new history. That is the essence of what it has meant for every immigrant who came here, including my grandfather. After his three-and-a-half-week voyage across the Atlantic at the turn of the last century, he rarely talked about Italy. It was almost as though he had dumped his memories of the old country over the side of the great steel ship that had brought him here. When he touched the ground in this, his new land, he had only space enough in his heart for new memories. He left us two small photographs of himself and my grandmother, who came to America by his side, as proof of his beginnings. Little else physically connects that old world to this new one.

I never had the chance to ask my grandfather why he came to the United States, but I think I have an answer. In all likelihood, it may be as simple as this: I am an American because of pencils, cheap wooden pencils that replaced the vague dreams of a quiet man who left the only land he ever truly knew for some place he had only heard of, a place across the sea that offered him an opportunity to remake his life.

Let me explain. My grandfather was one of the 2 million Italians who fled their shacks and shanties in the poor south of Italy that is called the *mezzogiorno* and sailed for the United States between 1900 and 1910. Had he decided a bit earlier to leave his windy village of Molfetta, with its thirteenth-century seminary and its groves of gnarled olive trees on the sunny coast of the Adriatic, I might today be a different kind of American—a Brazilian, say, or an Argentine, because in the late nineteenth century, many desperate Italian immigrants favored those countries as destinations, not the United States. Had he hesitated and left after the peak years of American immigration, when Northeast cities were already packed solid and "wops" were not wanted even for digging ditches, he might have headed for Halifax's Pier 21 on Canada's Maritime coast, or the ancient port city of Veracruz in Mexico, and today I might see the world from a wholly different perspective.

But he left at a time when steamship lines stuffed so many of Europe's men and women into the dismal holds of their ships that they needed charge only the equivalent of $10 to cross the Atlantic, a time when a factory in Hoboken, New Jersey, in the shadow of Manhattan, was willing to hire greenhorns and put them to work assembling the wood, graphite, and paint of penny pencils. Hoboken, then a busy port city in

New York Harbor where the greatest ships of Europe docked, was already one of the most crowded spots on the continent, with more than 70,000 people squeezed into a single square mile. Most of its streets ended at the water's edge, as they did in Molfetta, and both cities drew their vitality from the sea. For many immigrants, Hoboken was their first stop in the new world, and their last. They elbowed their way in and, once they found work, stayed put. All that they sent back to Italy was word for others to follow.

My grandfather, Ignazio, had been a policeman in Italy and a one-time seminarian. He arrived in America with a new wife and no money. The American Lead Pencil Company on Willow Avenue and Fifth Street gave him a job, and he worked there long enough to earn a pin and a pat on the back when he retired. Although he lived in the United States for over fifty years, Ignazio never bought a house or became an American citizen. He sang in tinny operas in Hoboken's vaudeville theaters but never learned to speak English, and never gave up the snappy felt hats or the crooked black cigars that made him look for all the world as if he might still be promenading along the boulevard in Molfetta. I regret that I never asked him why he decided to give up everything and cross the ocean if, in the end, he was going to keep his new homeland at such a distance. But it was really just a mask he wore. Inside, he had abandoned Italy. After he set foot in America, he never went back, not once. His oldest son, my father Anthony, was born in Hoboken and lived there, beside the river, his whole life. He spoke Italian at home but English on the streets, and he went to work lugging coffee and bananas and bales of red chili pepper out of the dark bellies of ships that came to the Hudson River piers in Hoboken. He never went to Molfetta either.

I was the youngest of my father's four sons. In all, with two sisters, there were six of us. No one learned more than a few words of Italian at home, but neither did we ever have to battle winter's wrath from the frozen deck of a steel cargo ship. While I was still a child, I watched the pencil factory hammered to bits by a wrecking ball to make way for a middle-class housing project. And I saw Hoboken change from homey to seedy to chic after the shipping lines left and the historic piers rusted and gently collapsed into the brown waters of the Hudson. My father gave the Sisters of Charity responsibility for teaching me how to learn, and he sent me to study with the Christian Brothers, who introduced me to serious reading and purposeful writing. My father cleared the way for me to be the first in our family to go to college, and he saw me go on to become a foreign correspondent and bureau chief in Mexico and Canada for *The New York Times*.

I've been told that the journey from the pencil factory to *The New York Times* is a quintessential American tale, a concrete realization of the magnificent opportunity of the American continent. Maybe, but every American family I know has a similar story. We are a country of immigrants, in a continent of newcomers. All of us—Americans, Mexicans, Canadians—hail from someplace else. We are all descendants of people with vague dreams and unclear hopes of somehow making life better for those who came after them. The American continent gave Ignazio, and through him my father and me and my children, an opportunity he never would have had in Molfetta; that much is clear. But if it was because of the American Pencil Company that I am an American, then what has being American meant for what I have become?

To understand better, in 1998 I became the first in my family to see Molfetta since my grandfather turned his back on the city nearly a century before. A masonry shop on the waterfront still bears the name De-Palma, as does a local auto dealership, and more than 150 listings for the family name appear in the local telephone book, although I do not know any of these people. Before we had a chance to see any more of the town, another car rear-ended mine near the hospital when I slowed to let an old woman cross the street. I couldn't find anyone who spoke English. But the young man driving the new Ford Escort that rammed us called an uncle whose fluent Spanish—he had worked more than a decade in Venezuela—we were able to understand.

Amid the swearing and the cursing in Italian, which was easy to understand, the uncle explained that his nephew was in a lot of trouble. We resolved things amicably, but the accident forced me to consider how coincidental my tie to America had been. What if my grandfather had sailed for Venezuela, as had the other driver's uncle? What if he had heard that a textile plant in Montreal hired Italians? What if he had never left Molfetta?

I suppose that had Ignazio not crossed the Atlantic, Molfetta could still have provided a chance to succeed, but such success would likely have occurred within well-defined boundaries. Perhaps today I would have been chiseling away inside the DePalma masonry shop near the waterfront, or preparing to build a new apartment building on a few acres of olive groves my grandfather might have left us, the type of legacy many people in Molfetta seemed intent on leaving. My family probably would have changed its income but not its standing.

From this perspective, the ability to seize opportunity and be transformed by it is the factor that defines what being an American has meant for what I have become. Many things separate those of us in the United States from our North American neighbors—sometimes culture, sometimes language, and almost always worldview—but the one that has been most central to forming the characters of the three different nations in North America involves this most fundamental of North American traits. We share the desire to get ahead, but our opportunities for doing so differ markedly among these three nations that have for so long offered this path. I have met many successful people in Canada, the sons and daughters of immigrants from all over the world. But with few exceptions, Canada—despite its similarities to the United States—offered them only a remote degree of the bounty of opportunities they would have found had they lived in America. True to its British roots, Canada still puts great stock in having the proper training and the right connections, a club mentality that imposes rigid expectations of behavior and outcome. William Thorsell, longtime editor of *The Globe and Mail* in Toronto, posited that background, not merit, was what really mattered in Canada. "In New York they ask what you earn," he once wrote in an editorial-page column in *The Globe,* but in Toronto, "they ask where you live."[1] Canada's generic universities are not expected to transform students but to turn out graduates who are better-paid versions of their parents. Since the end of World War II, more than 60 percent of top Canadian executives have come from upper-class backgrounds, almost twice the percentage found among American executives. Similar figures are not available for Mexico, but the fact that a handful of families control the country's largest corporations makes clear that economic opportunity there is largely reserved for those who already have status and power.

Many values are not shared equally by the three American nations, as will be seen in a later chapter. But there once was a time when we were not so unlike each other. High-energy particle physics has a concept known as broken symmetry, which is useful to understanding the development of the American continent. At the start of the known universe, in the very first instant after the Big Bang fireball, a state of perfect symmetry existed in which everything looked alike and behaved the same way.

But as time passed, the raw material of the universe cooled and began to collect in different ways and with a great diversity of natural properties. The unifying symmetry that had briefly existed was lost.

A similar sequence of events took place on the North American continent. The landing by Columbus was the big bang that changed, instantaneously, the known world. At first, America was perceived as everything that Europe was not. But then the voyages of Jacques Cartier, John Smith, and the other explorers and all the settlers who followed them brought a range of horizons into view. The symmetry of America was finally broken when the Europeans, applying their own beliefs, attempted to change the nature of the continent. For five centuries, that process continued. Then, rather unexpectedly, officials from each country—each motivated by his own set of exigencies and responsibilities— took steps in the 1990s to begin the reintegration of the three nations of North America. And with it came an unprecedented wave of opportunity that washed across the continent. This shift changed the way we work in, live on, and think about the American continent. It also brought us into more frequent conflicts, the inevitable consequence of our intensified closeness. But overall, the people and events outlined in the following chapters have begun to restore some of the symmetry that was broken half a millennium ago. We are seeing that our most substantial differences—those based on the quality of the opportunity for transformation that living in North America provides—are leveling off. We are creating a new history.

✳

The power and importance of these changes do not, by themselves, ensure that we are aware of them. Like one of Mexico's earthquakes whose epicenters lie far from where they are felt most intensely, the forces shaping North America today gather strength largely out of our sight.

For all their closeness, Mexico and Canada are almost unknown to many of us. When *The Times* first sent me to Mexico in 1993 and then to Canada in 1996, my understanding of our neighbors was, I think, typical of most Americans' views. I had been across both borders, as have been many Americans, and I thought I knew all I needed to know about the nations that begin where America ends. During a trip across the United States in 1974, I stopped in El Paso and walked across the bridge to Ciudad Juárez, before that city had sunk completely into a hellhole of drugs and violence. I was twenty-two then, and I savored the day, poking my head into side streets and around strange corners. I haggled over the price of a striped blanket, certain I was being cheated, and ate in a cheap restaurant where I tasted the fire of Mexican chilies for the first time and knew I'd live to regret it. As an expedition to a foreign country, it wasn't much, but it was enough to allow me, like many other Americans, to say that I knew Mexico.

On another voyage across the continent a year later, with a new wife and a small dog, I drove west as far as our Volkswagen could carry us. When the wobbly VW met its match in the Rockies, we turned north into Canada and headed back east from there. We drove, often in stunned silence, across the empty expanses of a country far larger than we had ever imagined, a fragment of wilderness on our borders that reminded us of how recently we had all arrived. The roads and cars and even the faces of the people we met all seemed familiar. But every place-name was new, the money strangely colorful, and the gasoline then priced indecipherably in imperial gallons, all making us feel strangely at home yet at the same time quite out of sync with our surroundings. About Canada itself we knew almost as little as Mikhail Baryshnikov, who, less than a year before we were there, had defected in Toronto. "What did I know about Canada?" he wrote on the twenty-fifth anniversary of his fateful decision. "I have to be honest. I knew precisely three things: Canada had great hockey teams, it grew a lot of wheat because the bread we ate every winter was thanks to Canadian wheat, and Canada was where Glenn Gould lived and worked."[2]

One part of Canada I felt I did know well, and the place influenced my sentiments about the whole country and about North America. It was a small village on the banks of the St. Lawrence River that I had visited as a child. Every summer the family next door made the trip north, to the province of Quebec. One year we joined them. We drove an entire day in my father's black Buick to get to the village of Beaupré. There, beside the river, inside an enormous gray basilica dedicated to St. Anne, my neighbor Nicky pointed to a spot high up on one of the huge columns at the church's entrance. There hung the brace that he had strapped on every day after polio had sapped the strength from his legs. Doctors had told his parents he would never walk without it. His family took him to Canada seeking a miracle. They felt they had found one in Beaupré, and the tangle of leather and steel on the church column, the desperate materials of dreams and hopes that encircled it like some terrible ivy, was the proof.

Nicky lived next door to me, but he was far more than just a neighbor. In later years, well after he had begun to walk using only a cane, it became clear that his illness had shaped my life as profoundly as it had his. Our closeness meant I agreed to live within a world defined by his wheelchair and brace, while he tried to ride piggyback on my experience of the world. Often it was a compromise. We played baseball, but using the cards of a board game. I'd bounce Spaldings off the wall of the sweater factory across the street with a high enough arc to give him time to move his wheelchair to catch them. We spent a lot of time just talking, and we satisfied our curiosity with books that could transport us in ways that Nicky's wrecked legs could not. It was not at all a typical childhood in Hoboken, where the son of a longshoreman might have expected to follow his father and work on the docks or perhaps become a policeman or someone who worked with his hands, not someone who made his living with words. It was not the life Nicky and I had looked for. We lived the way we did simply because we had been thrown together by fate. Living side by side, whether we wanted to or not, had influenced the choices we made and the things we did. Being near each other made us more like each other.

In a similar way, when I arrived in Mexico and Canada, I looked for signs of how much living by our side had made our neighbors come to be like us. Again I was surprised. A Mexican taxi driver once remarked that Americans live in a fantasyland because they foolishly expect lines to be straight and laws to be obeyed, including traffic lights and stop signs. It didn't take long after I moved to Mexico to find out that precious little there sticks to plan. Like the great gray Metropolitan Cathedral in the heart of Mexico City that is sinking unevenly into the mud and occasionally has to be jacked up to keep from collapsing, Mexico seemed to be forever making adjustments to keep itself straight, although it was never quite clear just what Mexicans expected straight to be.

Resemblances were all I expected to find in Canada, but once there I detected differences in some of our most basic beliefs. There were pleasant surprises: The strong sense of public concern in Canadian life meant that I never saw in Toronto a vandalized subway car, vending machine, or public phone. Some differences were just unexpected: The Catholic schools in Ontario were publicly supported, and mail wasn't delivered on Saturday. And some differences were downright disconcerting: I had to worry about publication bans, closed-door meetings, and sky-high taxes to support a social safety network in which a hypochondriac could see five doctors in one day for a runny nose but somebody needing a heart bypass had to wait five months for the operation.

The United States, Mexico, and Canada were shaped by the same process of discovery, settlement, development, and eventual separation from the European powers that had given them life. The places from which most North Americans initially came—Spain, France, and England—shared a Western culture that was well defined and firmly established by the time the first explorers arrived. We not only share our history with Mexico and Canada—our history is their history, and theirs, ours. This reluctant continental trinity is both united and divided by our shared history, making each nation a part of the other and keeping each one unique. The factors that contributed to those dissimilarities were as numerous as the misconceptions we three nations have imposed on each other. But one difference stands out most prominently. New France was a creation of Versailles, run from Paris by those loyal to the crown. It held no attraction for dissenters, and neither did New Spain, which obediently stuffed the Spanish king's coffers for three centuries until Mexico shouted for and won its independence. From the beginning, the United States was settled by angry people who mistrusted the governments they had left behind in Europe and, at least initially, all governments. The colonists did not fight the American Revolution to win their freedom but rather to protect the freedom they already had won. On the way, they also managed to defeat the old world's attempt to recreate itself in North America.

The first modern nation is what Mexican poet Octavio Paz believed the thirteen rebellious American colonies managed to create, a state founded not on geography or language but on a powerful notion about individual rights and freedom that has provided an example for the world. But Paz also recognized contradictions and flaws that made America the seat of "a peculiar empire," one that struggles to reconcile its role as a democracy with that of conqueror, which is the way Mexicans still see us because of the Mexican-American War and the peace treaty that mutilated their country and appropriated the richest parts.[3]

The Canadians wrestle with the uncomfortable circumstances of what came to be their country, formed as it was not in the crucible of revolu-

tion but in the fine print of contract and legal arrangement. Their genesis has always seemed incomplete, which has left them struggling to define what Canada is and wondering what might have been had their
ancestors not backed the losing side in the struggle between Britain and
the colonies for control of a large part of North America. "We are a nation of losers," the Canadian historian Desmond Morton has said.[4] "After
all, losers have to go somewhere and that's not a bad thing. They've
been through a highly educational experience and they bring rather
more tolerance than people who believe they're winners." Defeat became one of the many layers in Canada's character. Like a set of nested
Russian dolls, inside the defeat of the British in the American Revolution is found the defeat of the French by the British in the Seven Years'
War. And inside that rests the defeat of the Huron and other native
tribes by the muskets of French settlers and the diseases that Jesuit missionaries carried with them across the ocean.

Defeat may have bred more tolerance in the Canadian character than
did victory in America's, but Canada's decision to remain loyal to the
British crown rather than join the rebels of the thirteen colonies in many
regards still defines Canada and is something Canadians find difficult to
see beyond. Their eyes are constantly on the United States. They can't
help it. Most of them—over 80 percent—live in a narrow band of fecund
earth and moderate temperatures extending to just 100 miles from the
U.S. border, so that it seems they have all just arrived from, or are about
to depart for, America. If Mexico had been settled in the same manner,
there might now be some 90 million Mexicans living within 100 miles of
the U.S. border, and that frontier would hardly have been left undefended for long. In the United States, most Americans rarely are conscious that they share this continent with anyone. Only about 5 percent
of Americans live close enough to the Canadian border to pick up Canadian radio or television broadcasts, and an equally small percentage of
the U.S. population lives sufficiently close to the Mexican border to experience the intense and sustained contact with foreign cultures that can
cause national loyalties to blur.

The American continent was built on the dreams and nightmares of
the millions of immigrants and slaves who followed Columbus and of
the descendants of the 10 million Native Americans thought to have
lived here before Europeans arrived. Our differences stem from the cultures all those wayfarers brought with them and the turns we have taken
through time. Mexico's concept of freedom does not match ours, and

Canadians put their own coloring on the distinction between individual choice and the common good. Today, similar events are seen in each country through a different lens—the idea of conquest is both central to each country yet entirely individual: Entering a free trade agreement caused tremors in each country, but the fears each nation felt were something different. For most of our history, we have remained co-cooned in our own lands, despite our proximities, and solitude has become perhaps the overarching theme in both of our neighbors. Canadian writers often used "The Two Solitudes," the title of a novel by the Canadian author Hugh MacLennan, as a shorthand way of describing the schizophrenia of their nation. Octavio Paz called his meditation on his homeland *The Labyrinth of Solitude*. And we in the United States—we know so little about our neighbors that we brag about it, wearing it as a sign of our independence and haughty power. That is our solitude.

"Every American should be forced to live outside the United States for a year or two," the novelist John Irving wrote in *A Prayer for Owen Meany*. Irving is an American who spends part of every year in Canada, a sojourn that obviously has changed the way he sees things. "Every country knows more about America than Americans know about themselves!" a character in the novel says, infuriated at bellicose American attitudes. "And Americans know absolutely nothing about any other country."[5]

Just three nations occupying a vast continent, the people of North America created in the new world a solitary realm where, against all logic, our closeness served to keep us distant from each other. This was not an affliction only of Americans, nor was it merely a symptom of the distant past. When Pierre Trudeau was prime minister of Canada, he tried to heal the wounds to his country's psyche in part by turning against its biggest ally. His government passed laws restricting the right of foreigners, mostly Americans, to invest in Canadian businesses, and he tried to hoard Canadian energy for Canada. "Living next to you is in some ways like sleeping with an elephant," a pugnacious Trudeau said in a speech at the National Press Building in Washington in 1969. "No matter how friendly and even-tempered the beast, one is affected by every twitch and grunt." The same need for distance was expressed by Carlos Salinas de Gortari when he was elected president of Mexico in 1988. He held out no hope that Mexico would ever drop its nationalistic defenses and join forces with its great oppressor, the United States, in a trade agreement. "I am not in favor of such a proposal," Salinas told the

Times's Larry Rohter a few weeks before taking office on December 1, 1988. "There is such a different economic level between the United States and Mexico that I don't believe such a common market would provide an advantage to either country."[6]

North America's borders were indeed hardening when, in the early 1990s, a monumental transformation got under way. The causes were varied but powerful enough to sweep away the prejudices of several centuries, a topic explored later. The transition was difficult. This embarkation forced Mexico through some of the most turbulent and telling moments in the ancient country's maze of history, a period marked by brutality, violence, and a glimmer of real democratic transition that at several points almost seemed to flicker out but stayed dimly lit and led, in a surprisingly brief time after those events, to what amounted to a revolution and Mexico's first peaceful transfer of power. As that process was playing out south of the U.S. border, on the north Canada was engaging in one of the most remarkable exercises in the history of democracy: Without generals or legions, it was forced to defend itself from domestic and external threats. Canada's attempt to rebuild its economy by drawing closer to the United States unleashed an assault on its borders and its national identity; at the same time, separatists threatened to tear Canada apart from within by fomenting independence for Quebec. The country was consumed with nothing less than a debate over its right to exist.

I had always seen the United States the way it tends to be presented in weather maps or academic illustrations—a free-floating, easily recognizable, well-defined shape with blank space to the north and south, a single block lifted out of a 3-D puzzle. Eventually I came to see it more the way satellite photos portray North America from the edge of space, stripped of political divisions that form three nations divided by two borders within one continent. These three neighbors had had far more to do with each other than simply exist side by side, something I think I recognized more quickly than others because of my personal experience and the way I had grown up. I could not deny that living next door to Nicky and his wheelchair when we were youths had changed both of us in ways that became clear only long afterward.

The United States, Mexico, and Canada also grew up together. They are three trees whose roots are growing more tangled, even as the trees themselves retain their own shape and stock. Despite America's dominance, the other two are clearly not moving toward becoming merely an elaborate version of the United States. Our closest neighbors are picking through our closets, taking what they like while hoping to leave the soiled jackets and torn slacks behind. Through these two neighbors and allies, the United States is shaping its own relationship with the rest of the world, a world in which we increasingly must deal with nations that are like us but sometimes resent us for our influence and power, and nations with whom we share very little and that resent us for what we have but they do not.

The reasons North America matters are evident every day, if we choose to see them. The drug trade, international trade, immigration, cultural exchange, mass communications, shared defense—all are linkages across our borders that are leading inevitably toward the integration of North America into a single, seamless entity. In the post–Cold War world, Mexico came to represent a strategic threat to the United States not because of any growing strength but precisely because of its weakness and the chance that internal divisions and the messy transition to true democracy could make it weaker still. "The border that separates the United States and Mexico is the only land border between the industrial and the non-industrial world, the so-called third world. And the United States had been fortunate in the twentieth century. Trouble in a country with such geographic proximity to America was something new," wrote former defense secretary Caspar Weinberger in *The Next War*, which outlined several scenarios for conflicts around the world that could involve the United States.[7] He hypothesized a bloody border conflict with Mexico in 2003 that would be triggered by drugs, illegal immigration, and unbridled domestic corruption, the three greatest concerns of both policymakers and the American public.

Weinberger's book was an intellectual exercise, not a call to arms. But over the course of my travels beyond the ends of America, it became clear to me that events occurring around us are of immense importance and historic significance that we need to understand for our own good. We have to be able to see through the haze of ignorance and distortion that has settled over the continent, just as the Spanish explorers could get nowhere until they understood what they had found. We must challenge our notions of what we thought we knew about the place where we live, and of our place in the world.

As should be clear by now, misunderstanding has been as common in North American history as have been immigrants and wars. In recent memory, there may be no more glaring example of mistaken identity than Mexico as it existed in late spring 1993. The rest of the world saw the ancient nation poised for great progress and a celebrated entrance into the first world. But in reality it was teetering on the edge of a period of violence and chaos like none it had suffered through since its own bloody revolution in 1910 had baptized the twentieth century.

That was the Mexico where my own journey began.

CHAPTER TWO

Stumbling into a New World

✳

It is your concern when your neighbor's wall is on fire.

Horace, *Epistles 18*

The white Grand Marquis slipped into a parking place outside the main terminal building as smoothly as an angel nestling on a cloud. Though Mexicans found it difficult to pronounce Grand Marquis (that hard-to-get-around Anglo-Saxon *d* in the first word combined with a pesky French ending in the second), the big cars were among the most sought after in a Mexico that in 1993 appeared to be hurtling into the first world, the cherished object of desire of chief executives, cardinals, and drug lords alike. The Grand Marquis was, above all, a symbol of power and status. Though more exotic cars now exist, the Grand Marquis was then the largest and most luxurious automobile assembled in Mexico, which still reserved the right to force automakers to build cars in Mexico if they planned to sell them there.

The Grand Marquis at the airport was turned out in a way intended to impress anyone who watched it glide by. The big car's windows were tinted black, shielding the interior from the intense Mexican sun but, more important, hiding the identity of the car's occupants and thus giving the car the chic look of a celebrity limousine. The car's exterior was the whitest white. For Mexicans, color remains a powerful instrument for conveying meaning, and white is imbued with connotations of racial purity that a people of mixed race regard as desirable, even essential, to the degree that it can be acquired. Mexicans are accustomed to seeing people with blond hair and blue eyes on television commercials, selling expensive cars, drinking the best brandy, smoking imported cigarettes. Since most of Mexico's 100 million people don't look like these beautiful television people they admire, the color white compensates for the black hair, dark eyes, and brown skin they inherited from their Indian ancestors. And a white Grand Marquis, with all the wealth and power the automobile symbolized, was as close to being white as many Mexicans could get.

Miguel Hidalgo International Airport in Guadalajara had become a symbol of a modern Mexico on the move, a place where, contrary to popular impressions, schedules were kept and things ran essentially as they were intended. Despite the celebration just the year before of the 450th anniversary of Guadalajara's founding, the colonial city was the very picture of the new Mexico, bustling with life and commerce, not unlike the dynamic cities of the American west. The squat airport terminal building, with stone floors that dark-skinned cleaning men and women seemed always to be mopping, had become well known to Americans who breezed through to begin a vacation there. Some hopped from Guadalajara to Acapulco, Zihuatanejo, or other Pacific Coast resorts where the water is warm and the margaritas are frozen. Canadian retirees weary of their country's chronic cold regularly used the airport too. A good number of them wintered in a select community in nearby Lake Chapala, and others, along with elderly Americans, eventually retired there permanently to enjoy favorable exchange rates and the great extravagance of paying someone else to scrub the toilets and wait all afternoon for the propane gas to be delivered.

The city of Guadalajara had recently succeeded in attracting major companies like IBM, which assembled computers and office equipment in hastily constructed industrial buildings that had none of the city's exuberant colonial style but were stylish enough for enterprises that turned a handsome profit and kept their American parent companies satisfied. In 1993 there were only a few portals through which American or Canadian businesses could enter the Mexican market and profit from the new Mexico. The *maquiladora* plants on the border constituted one lucrative area, Mexico City another, and Guadalajara a third. The Guadalajara airport had become one enormous, bustling reception hall for North American businessmen, and it was not at all uncommon to see limousines waiting for them just outside the terminal doors.

For a few minutes, the white Grand Marquis was still. The windows had not been lowered. No one had emerged. It was 3:30 on a scorching Monday afternoon. The usually crowded flight from Mexico City was about to arrive, and another would soon take off for Tijuana. Unnoticed, a car pulled up near the Grand Marquis; it was a less flashy green Buick. Then a blue and white GMC pickup truck rolled up to the waiting area. The occupants of the Grand Marquis may not even have paid attention to the vehicles as they awaited the arrival of the flight from the Mexican capital. But they probably turned their heads the moment another Buick came a whisker too close to the Grand Marquis. It tried to squeeze by but was blocked by the first Buick's rear door, which strangely had been left open.

At that instant, several Mexican men swaggered out of the shadows of the airport entrance. They leveled a battery of military-style assault rifles and sent a blaze of rapid fire toward the vehicles. They concentrated on two—the green Buick and the white Grand Marquis—opening fire from three angles at point-blank range. Several shots struck the Buick as it screeched away. The other car did not move. Glass shattered, and the Grand Marquis quivered as it was hit by the slugs from the AK-47s. The attack lasted no more than thirty seconds. Inside the car, two figures lay across the wide front seat, both leaning to the left as though they had tried to turn away from the bullets. Behind the steering wheel, the chauffeur, Pedro Pérez, lay still. His white shirt was studded with ten bloody holes. The other figure was dressed in black, an older man whose plumpness indicated a life not tested by either hunger or manual labor. He had been hit fourteen times across his chest and legs. Around his neck was a large gold crucifix on a thick braided gold chain, common accessories in Mexico for drug dealers. And for princes of the church.

I had arrived in Mexico two weeks earlier to begin a search for the new Mexico, a country perched on the dividing line between the developed north and the envious south, a country that was boldly attempting to open itself up to the modern world after decades of hiding behind protective walls and petulant politics. The Mexico that had installed young, dynamic, American-educated leaders in the highest and most important positions in the country, men who had won the respect and admiration of experts around the world for their liberal attitudes toward open economies and, to a lesser extent, democratic rule. The Mexico that had left behind its violent past and its heritage of corruption and lawlessness. The Mexico that was ripe for investment, ripe for democracy, ripe for inclusion in the ranks of modern nations.

By the time I flew to Guadalajara from Mexico City early the day after the shooting, I already knew something was tragically wrong with the new Mexico I had crossed the border to explore. The plump man in the Grand Marquis was Juan Jesús Posadas Ocampo, a Roman Catholic cardinal and the second-highest-ranking official of the Roman Catholic Church in Mexico. No one in Mexico could believe he had been gunned down in the middle of a Monday afternoon outside one of the busiest public places in the country. Worse, the shooters had casually flown back to their home base in Tijuana after the brutal attack. The dispatcher at the Guadalajara airport had held Aeromexico Flight 110 for twenty minutes because of what he called some disruption in the terminal building that was delaying passengers. Those already seated on the jet watched the gunmen put their bags in the overhead racks and calmly take their places, while outside, Mexico's dream of entering the modern world started to collapse.

Tourists were already pointing to the holes left in steel I-beams near the terminal entrance when I passed through the doors. The glass in the taxi dispatcher's booth was shattered, and there were gray lines painted in the parking lot to indicate the location of the Buick and the Grand Marquis, as well as the places where five people besides the cardinal and his driver had died.

Cardinal Posadas Ocampo headed the Catholic church in Guadalajara, a city of neighborhoods that are Spanish set pieces projecting a European sense of style far lovelier than the coarse stonework and dark palaces of colonial Mexico City. Guadalajara is filled with ancient churches, age-old plazas, and a reservoir of deep Spanish tradition that still deems it unacceptable for a young woman and her fiancé to sleep in the same house before they are married. The day I arrived, hundreds of people braved a relentless sun to wait in line for hours for a chance to get into the city's stern sixteenth-century cathedral and file past the coffin bearing the cardinal's body. I was taken in through a side door and led up toward the altar where the coffin rested. The bloody black robes had been replaced by ethereal gold vestments. The cardinal's hands were folded over his waist, and a large crucifix—perhaps the same one he had worn during the attack—had been placed on his chest, over his heart. An old woman barely tall enough to see over the edges of the polished wooden coffin reached in and touched the cardinal's hands, then kissed her fingers and touched him again. A clutch of tiny nuns dressed in black huddled nearby.

Outside, people waited all afternoon for their chance to see with their own eyes and feel with their hearts what had happened at the airport. They were still recovering from the shock, one deeply felt throughout Mexico. A prince of the church has special status in heavily Roman Catholic Mexican society, and people widely assumed that such status protects him from much of the random violence that other Mexicans routinely face. He was sitting in the supple seats of his luxurious Grand Marquis, accompanied by his chauffeur. He had a crucifix around his neck. If the fleshy pieces of someone with all the power of the church could be blasted onto the asphalt, what hope was there for those who had no status and no power, they wondered? Worse, what did the murder say about the Mexican system—the intricate network of class, influence, social commandments, and political realities that 100 million Mexicans lived by? The people waiting to get into the cathedral that day shielded themselves from the dry-season sun with newspapers that bore the headline *Justicia*. It was their silent supplication, and their demand. It was not just the cardinal's killer that Mexico wanted. As I was to find out in subsequent days, months, and years, the clamor for justice in every aspect of Mexican life was gathering force and building the momentum of a revolution.

✳

While I was preparing to move to Mexico in 1993, I assumed that my Catholic background would help me enter into and understand Mexican society, which has been shaped by Catholicism since the conquistador Hernán Cortés replaced the Aztec gods he found with his own. Aztec priests warned him that doing so would result in the whole empire rising up against him and his men. But Cortés would not be deterred. Soon after entering the Aztecs' capital, today's Mexico City, Cortés climbed Montezuma's great pyramid and zealously tried to smash the idol of Tlaloc, one of the Aztecs' most important deities, which he had found caked with inches of blackened blood and draped with skinned human heads. An eyewitness, Andrés de Tapia, said Cortés "gave a superhuman leap and balanced himself, taking the bar so that it hit the eyes of the idol and so removed the gold mask, saying: 'Something must be done for the Lord.'" Bewildered, Montezuma tried to stop Cortés and offered a compromise: Leave the Mexican gods on one side of the temple, and place the Christian images of the Virgin Mary and St. Christopher on the other. But Cortés turned him away and urged the emperor to give up his violent and angry gods. "They are only stone," he said. "Believe in our God who made heaven and earth and, by His works, you will know who the master is."[1]

The cardinal's murder seemed to be testimony to a bloody trail leading from the steps of the Aztecs' great pyramid to the cathedral in Guadalajara. From that day until the day I left Mexico, I never felt wholly comfortable in a Catholic church there. I think this was because I found in Mexico a cruder, more primitive religion than the one in which I had been raised. My church had been about restrained sermons and practiced prayers, about building on the faith of my father, and his father before him. For me, none of that was present in remote Mexico, in places like San Cristóbal de Las Casas in Chiapas, where the air inside the brooding yellow cathedral seemed still to bear the sound and earthy scent of Indians pushing in to hear the words of white men making incredible promises about paradise half a millennium ago. Instead, I felt intimidation there, and the fear that was used to convert simple people whose lives also were marked by violence. The statues inside Mexican churches are gruesome, dripping with plaster blood and jagged flesh so that even the Indians who spoke little or no Spanish would have been frightened into believing what the missionary priests said about the need for redemption. The most unsettling artifacts are the glass coffins that hold the waxy flesh of some holy priest or nun whose purity was so great that their bodies were believed to be incorruptible. They lie silently inside their glass cases, but their presence cannot be ignored, no more so than could the coffin that held Cardinal Posadas Ocampo in Guadalajara. The holy remains shouted to the Mexican faithful, shouted so fanatically that they often had to be protected by guards or signs begging that devout followers "Do Not Kiss the Glass."

The sanctified remains haunted only the more important cathedrals and basilicas. But inside nearly every small church in Mexico that I visited, I found a practice almost as unsettling. By tradition, the faithful cut hair from their own heads and offer it to the local priest to be placed with great ceremony and honor atop the statues of Christ and the saints. The tufts of hair, sometimes in long, luxurious braids, sit there turning dry and stiff until the offering is repeated by someone else whose hair is then placed on the venerated head. Seeing this made me wonder if Cortés's attempt to banish the Aztecs' bloody statue of Tlaloc had failed. It was as if Montezuma's compromise had been imposed and the Catholic saints and Aztec gods coexisted in the same space within the temple. Clearly, elements of sacrifice and devotion to plaster statues are not unique to Mexico. Catholicism put ample gore into the stories of the saints and martyrs. But as I struggled to understand Mexico in those early days of my stay, it seemed that these common elements shared by Catholicism and the Aztecs' beliefs had long ago been distorted to emphasize fear more than faith. Hundreds of years later, little appeared to have changed.

Still, faith held an important place in Mexico, and it was faith of a civic kind that the Mexican government seemed to be relying on when it made public its explanation of what happened to Cardinal Posadas Ocampo that afternoon at Guadalajara's airport. Investigators asked a skeptical Mexican people to believe that the cardinal's Grand Marquis had been mistaken for the car of a drug lord and was attacked by a rival drug gang. The real target, according to investigators, had been a gangster named Joaquín Guzmán Loera, whose alias was "El Chapo" or Shorty. El Chapo was a leader of one of Mexico's most vicious drug trafficking rings, the Sinaloa cartel. El Chapo paid police and government officials to look the other way while he moved millions of dollars worth of cocaine through Mexico and into the United States. That protection money kept him safe from official prosecution, but it did not guard him against rival gangs, which investigators said had been waiting at the airport to ambush him. When the assailants saw the cardinal's car, they attacked it, allowing El Chapo to escape in the green Buick.[2]

Mexican officials presented their evidence to incredulous reporters, then went on television and used computer graphics to re-create what they believed had happened at the airport. The graphics were intended to clarify the complicated sequence of events and calm the public, but their more immediate impact was to further undercut the officials' credibility; large segments of the Mexican public found the explanation no more believable than the video game the reenactment resembled. The attorney general of Mexico, Jorge Carpizo, a righteous former academic who had campaigned against corruption, looked shaken as he acknowledged that the assassins had received help from complicitous airport officials who had delayed the outgoing flight for Tijuana long enough for the assassins to escape. Carpizo pinned responsibility for the shooting on the rival Arellano Félix gang, but the central blame he assigned to "this monster of one thousand heads that is narcotrafficking."

Few Mexicans believed him; even the church hierarchy rejected the official version. Rumors started circulating as they always do in Mexico, a society that harbors a deep and abiding mistrust of officials. Although it was known for certain that the cardinal had gone to the airport to welcome Geronimo Prigione, the Italian-born papal nuncio—in effect, the Vatican's ambassador to Mexico—the reason was open to speculation. Prigione was a Machiavellian character, who flirted with Mexican politics and was rumored to keep unusual company. Eventually it would be confirmed that the Arellano Félix brothers, leaders of the rival Tijuana drug cartel believed to have been involved in the airport shoot-out, visited him at his residence in Mexico City. He intimated that they had come to make their confessions but he had not absolved them.

There were rumors too that the drug dealers had targeted Cardinal Posadas Ocampo because he had become too outspoken in his campaign against the illicit drug trade and the official corruption that allowed it to fester. If true, this would have been ironic, since many members of the cardinal's flock willingly worked to protect the gangsters and considered them heroes because they shared some of their fabulous wealth with the communities that harbored them from police. Some Mexicans even whispered that the cardinal had been murdered to send a message that real power in Mexico lay not with the government or the church, and certainly not with law enforcement, but with the gangs. No one, such a message would have made clear, was safe.

✳

This Mexico, swimming in blood and illicit drugs, was not the Mexico I had expected to cover in early spring 1993. The editors of *The New York Times* had begun to focus on the upcoming congressional vote on the North American Free Trade Agreement. We all assumed that if the trade pact passed, it would significantly alter bilateral relations between the United States and Mexico as well as create a new, if still undefined, sense of North American identity by bringing together Canada with Mexico and the United States in a formal way that could not be easily disrupted. Lowering tariffs to increase trade across the continent was important, even historic, but my editors believed that NAFTA would lead to more than that. If fully realized, it would mean that Mexico was committed to leaving the third world and entering the first, of putting distance between itself and the rest of Latin America and embracing the north. It would be the most far-reaching and momentous initiative between Mexico and the United States since the Marines landed at Veracruz in 1914.

The prelude to the agreement was already changing the way the *Times* treated Mexico. The newspaper's editors had not traditionally thought of Mexico as part of North America. In fact, the paper had paid very little attention to Mexico or, indeed, to the rest of Latin America once President Reagan's obsession with Nicaragua and El Salvador ended. When U.S. involvement in Central America lessened and Cold War tensions relaxed, the entire region returned to being as overlooked as before. "We know as much about Pakistan as we do about Mexico," Joe Lelyeld, the *Times*'s executive editor, told me when we first discussed the assignment. He felt the impending trade agreement dictated that the time had come to change that. One *Times* correspondent, Tim Golden, was already in the Mexico City office redirecting his extensive knowledge of Central America toward Mexico. And when I arrived, for the first time in memory, the *Times* had two correspondents exclusively dedicated to covering our most populous neighbor.

I did not make the trip alone. Miriam, my wife, our three children, the oldest then having just turned twelve, the younger two ten and seven, and a chubby cocker spaniel named Lucy accompanied me. I had lived my whole life in the northeastern United States, but Miriam is an inveterate traveler and, like my grandfather, an immigrant. She came from a small town across the harbor from Havana in 1961. Miriam was just a child when she arrived in the United States, but she had already watched many of her friends and neighbors in tightly packed streets of Guanabacoa tearfully leave for America. As the fat silver propeller planes roared out of the Havana airport, she watched them climb into the sky, thinking that this place called America must be up there, high above them. When her turn came to leave with her grandmother, she was allowed to take precious little more than a large doll, almost as tall as she was herself. At first they were not political refugees. They came to live in upper Manhattan with an aunt who had left Cuba years before the revolution to start a career. When Miriam's grandfather, who had stayed behind, became ill, they returned to Cuba briefly. But after they saw Fidel stand up before a huge crowd to defend communism, and after they heard gunshots ring throughout the night in the street near their house, they decided to leave Cuba for good.

Mexico, it quickly became apparent, was more like the old Cuba Miriam remembered than was the post-revolution, post-embargo, post-Soviet-pact Cuba that we had seen on the rare occasion when we were permitted to visit, or that we had heard about from family and friends. Despite the chaos that infused many aspects of life in Mexico, the formality and tradition that embellished even the most commonplace events and encounters bore a resemblance to old Havana. The man who tended the lawn and garden of the house we rented was called *Don* Florencio, a sign of respect. Every man above a certain age is referred to as Don. Mexicans do not use the term senior citizens but referred elegantly to *personas de la tercera edad*, persons of the third age in the sequence of infant, adult, and the elderly. Not only did Mexicans tell us *Mi casa es su casa*, which has become a cliché, but they seemed to give it real meaning. For instance, when they gave directions to their house they would say, without any affectation, "Your house is located at. . . ." Any sales clerk, in the largest department store to the smallest shop, invariably asked "How can I serve you?" and because salaries generally were low, no business ever seemed understaffed. The middle-class barbershop I went to contained a dozen chairs and so many barbers that if one took a break another jumped in and took care of the customer in the chair until the original barber returned. One man shined shoes, and two women could file, shape, and apply a clear gloss to the men's nails if they wanted. One young man's sole responsibility was to run down the street to buy bottles of Coke for the men who were being fussed over.

As I lived in Mexico, I learned that this system of deference, subservience, and respect that at first seemed so gentle and old-fashioned was in fact more like an elaborate fantasy. Using the honorific term *Don* for the gardener was not, as I had first thought, the reflection of a society blind to class differences or social asymmetry. Rather, it was an artifice of a society bent in large measure on preservation of the status quo. The respect and tradition were not authentic but in many circumstances intended merely to keep common Mexican men happy with the circumstances of their lives. For instance, the owner of the house we rented was a wealthy executive, well educated and a true gentleman. But he paid Don Florencio shockingly little, even though the gardener had been with him for many years, and rarely spoke to him except to give orders.

I, on the other hand, had accepted an invitation to Don Florencio's village for tamales on the Day of the Dead. When we showed up, we were honored guests, just as, a few months later, we were seated at the center of the banquet table after his granddaughter's baptism. I was the first served. Florencio beamed as he handed me a quivering piece of fat from a roasted pig wrapped in a tortilla. Only after I had been served did Florencio serve his own father.

The artificial gentility that Mexico's upper classes show toward those below is just one attempt among many to disguise a culture that has solidified into vastly unequal social strata. It reflects a European sensibility, similar to what probably existed in Molfetta at the time my grandfather left. The powerful oblige the powerless because doing so helps ensure the order of society—gardeners remain gardeners and so do their sons, while corporate vice presidents make their sons corporate vice presidents. Beyond that, we found that many of the clerks and bank tellers who professed to want to serve us didn't want to work at all, and some resented taking orders from gringos. The common terms of honor we heard everyday did not necessarily indicate that honor was involved, or that the different classes of society interacted in any but the most fundamental way. The class divide was very wide, we would soon see, and the role people were assigned was so difficult to break out of that it burdened even those Mexicans who dared dream of advancing themselves or their children.

In a short time I got to know a Mexican handyman named Marcos Cisneros who worked for a family in our neighborhood. Marcos took his son to the local public school at the same time that we brought our children to the bus stop. He had a bad leg and a silver tooth, and his son, also called Marcos, was then about the same age as my oldest boy. It pleased Marcos greatly to tell me his son had continued past the sixth grade, a point by which most Mexicans have ended their education for good. It also seemed to surprise him that I, a man he considered to have wealth and power, would take the time to talk to him.

What was his dream, I asked.

"That one day my boy can go to live and work, in Houston," he said.

And what would he do there? The answer Marcos gave made much clearer the difference between Mexico and the United States.

"Handyman, like me," Marcos said, "but in America."

Mexico is a large and diverse nation, and a great number of Mexicans have worked hard to achieve success, which they then pass along to their offspring. The division of class is quite severe, and those on the top are truly favored. Often they are perfectly bilingual in Spanish and English, sometimes with French or German added. They are superbly educated, benefiting from a rigorous succession of top-rank institutions beginning with private elementary and high schools, a top-flight Mexican university, then perhaps the Sorbonne followed by the Harvard Business School. They are given the chance to travel through Europe for a year or longer of social finishing. And, of major importance, they enjoy close contacts with other privileged people of their own generation. This network can remain intact for a lifetime. Some Mexicans do manage to exceed the achievements of their parents. But frequently they are either immigrants, who brought part of their fortunes with them from other countries, or criminals.

Sometimes the blame for reinforcing this stratification of society goes to the Catholic Church, because Catholicism is thought to keep believers from exercising control over or responsibility for their fate and their actions. God ordains, this line of thinking goes, God forgives, and Catholics expect to be cared for by the will of God. Mexico's Catholicism is deep, thorough, and maddeningly contradictory, producing not a moral outlook but, some argue, a debilitating ambiguity that has borne a wounded culture.

The Catholic Church's essential role in the formation of Mexican culture was clear right from the start. Conquistadores and missionaries often worked in tandem. Cortés used the stones of Aztec pyramids to build early churches. At the Museum of the Virreyes in Tepotzotlán, north of Mexico City, a historical map shows how the Dominicans, Franciscans, and other Catholic orders divided the territory of New Spain starting in the sixteenth century. The friars built a rich and complex system of missions that governed much of the country for centuries and made religion as integral an aspect of the structure of the nation as was the army. Even after the church was attacked and its vast holdings sacked in the late nineteenth century and then again in the 1930s, its influence has remained obvious and immediate in every corner of the country. Even the Sunday sermons of the former abbot of the Basilica of Guadalupe in Mexico City merited front-page headlines in the most important newspapers on Monday mornings.

To the harshest of Mexico's critics, Catholicism and the particular confessional culture that developed around it have left Mexico (and most of Latin America) roughly fifty years behind the United States and Canada in economic and moral development. Lawrence E. Harrison, a former official with the United States Agency for International Development, has argued that Catholicism forces Mexicans to focus on the pleasures of today and the glories of yesterday, at the expense of preparing for the future because they have entrusted their fate to God. Religious beliefs that rely on strict obedience pave the way for the rise of caudillos and an authoritarian system; trust in the cleansing power of confession makes it possible for wrongdoing to be wiped away in a confessional. Overall, Harrison argued, adherence to Catholicism makes Mexican society inherently conservative and orthodox. "There is no other satisfactory way to explain the sharply contrasting evolution of the North and the South in the Hemisphere than culture—the strikingly different values, attitude and institutions that have flowed from the Anglo-Protestant and Ibero-Catholic traditions."[3]

There is another view, one that at the very least explains the disparity in economic achievement between Mexico and the rest of North America. Peruvian economist Hernando de Soto, whose book *The Other Path* influenced the way many countries in the 1970s treated the poor, has conjectured that legal rights, not cultural values, allow capitalism to function well in some countries but not in others.[4] In particular, he has undertaken extensive studies in Peru and Egypt to show how the lack of well-defined property rights and the inability of the poor to control or benefit from the $9 trillion worth of property they occupy contributed mightily to social and economic stagnation in these countries.

When I spoke to de Soto in New York in 2000, he told me that Mexico suffers from the effects of the same legal impediments despite fairly recent constitutional changes. For most of the twentieth century, the poor in Mexico received land from the state, the fulfillment of Emiliano Zapata's revolutionary promise of *tierra y libertad*, "land and liberty." But though millions of acres of land were distributed, the number of Mexicans in poverty did not significantly decline. Much of the land was of poor quality; without irrigation it produced little more than the corn a family needed to feed itself. Under the constitutional system of land redistribution, the land actually was given to the community, or individuals called *ejidatarios* who held the land communally. Over time, the original parcels were subdivided into ever smaller farmsteads. This system provided succeeding generations with land but made it even less likely that the property could support them.

Such factors impede progress, but de Soto believes that restrictions on the use of the land most directly contribute to Mexico's poverty. By law, the peasants who received government land could not sell it, rent it, or mortgage it. The constitution was changed in 1991 to allow them to do so, but banks and lending institutions have been slow to accept such land titles in regular commercial exchanges. Thus the potential wealth represented by the millions of acres of property owned by peasants is locked up and unavailable for creating wealth.

✳

In recent years, the image of Mexico that Americans hold has been shaped by many factors, but few have had a more pervasive effect than the popularity of the piece of Mexican property known as Cancún. The Caribbean resort *is* Mexico for millions of Americans, and for a while that included our children. The summer before we knew we would leave the United States, we decided we could give the children a chance to use the Spanish they were learning at home and in school, so we booked a family vacation in Cancún. It turned out to be a fortuitous trip because a few months later I was assigned to Mexico. The day Miriam and I returned home from a house-hunting trip in Mexico, we talked to our children about living there, and their obvious enthusiasm for it surprised us. They had never moved before, but the idea of leaving home, school, and friends behind didn't seem to frighten them. Greatly encouraged, I left first, in May. A few weeks later, Miriam brought the children down for the long Memorial Day weekend to let them see what was to become their new home after the school year ended. They were glum. After a while we realized what was wrong: They had assumed that all of Mexico was like Cancún. They thought we would be living near a beach, with clear skies, high temperatures, and blue-green water all around.

Their disappointment was easy to understand. Why wouldn't they have believed that all of Mexico was like Cancún, since that was the only firsthand knowledge most people have outside of visiting a Taco Bell restaurant? The resort's superb beaches and cluttered hotel strip have made it one of the most popular tourist destinations in the world. But this is a fairly recent phenomenon. As recently as the mid-1960s, that part of the Yucatán peninsula where the resort has been built was inaccessible jungle, a sparsely populated paradise known to only a few. The first Spanish explorers undoubtedly sailed right by there, seeing it only as a dangerous shallow where they could run aground. For 500 years, it was visited by almost no one.

The Mexican government, desperate for foreign investment and a high-profile alternative to Acapulco and the other Pacific resorts, in 1967 ordered a computer survey of Mexico's topography to find the perfect place for a mega-resort that would attract hordes of vacationers, including great numbers of wealthy Americans. After Cancún was selected, work began immediately and has not stopped since. In the eyes of many Mexicans, Cancún is a fabulous success, a model for development that proves Mexico is capable of innovation and commitment to doing great things. To much of the rest of the world, however, it is proof that commercial excess isn't exclusively an American trait.

At the time the computer model selected the Yucatán coast, only visionaries pictured what could be built there. Today it is not easy to see beyond the long wall of hotels and imagine the site before the bulldozers arrived. But a few people remember, and they don't believe this symbol of modern Mexico is anything to be proud of. I searched out and found a man named Gabooch who was one of the few Mexicans who had lived on the place that became Cancún. When I met him, Gabooch still lived in a wooden shack. The resort developers had been forced to build around it, so at the time I visited, the little hut stood in the shadow of billion-dollar hotels. Gabooch lived as he always had—with a dirt floor and a hammock and little else in the way of personal possessions. His nod to modernity was a hot plate that worked on electricity pirated from a nearby construction site. He also said he no longer fed his dog lobster the way he used to when local waters were undisturbed and shellfish was plentiful.

Gabooch apologized to me for a house so humble that there was only one rickety chair to sit on. His broad nose, dark skin, and short stature belied the Mayan blood of his ancestors, but he also was a Mexican and so he offered me coffee. I had never tasted anything like it. Like so many other aspects of Mexican life, this coffee was a unique mixture of Indian and European cultures. Gabooch made coffee by pouring hot water over the crumbs of burnt tortillas. The Maya devised this alternative to coffee, which they usually can't afford, and have grown accustomed to its taste.

But many have never grown accustomed to the modern face of Mexico, nor have they ever felt a part of it. Gabooch spoke with the mixture of pride and sadness that many poor Mexicans display to strangers who take the time to listen to what they have to say. Speaking in his native Mayan tongue, he told me through a translator that he occasionally worked for one of the big resort projects. Once in a while he'd get a free meal if an official commemorating some date in the resort's frantic development took him to a civic ceremony. He didn't like playing the role of a living artifact, but he said attending the banquet afterward made it worth his while to go. Besides those few occasions, he said, Cancún had meant nothing good for him. All the success that had washed over the resort had simply rolled off his back and the backs of many Maya. He was silent for a moment, then he asked me to wait while he searched through a small box that he took from underneath his cooking table. He returned with a photograph wrapped in a paper towel. Carefully, he took out an old black-and-white snapshot that showed him standing on the same beach in Cancún that now is forested with high-rise hotels and flabby Americans. Everything had changed. Only the sea and the sand were the same. And Gabooch. But in the picture he is smiling.

"I know from when I was a child what it used to be like here," Gabooch told me. Soon, he feared, the hotels would cover everything and there would be no room for his shack or his hammock. No room for him at all.

"And then," he said, "what do I do?"

Of course, Cancún could not have prepared us for life in Mexico City. To our children's great disappointment, the largest city in North America had no beach, no open body of water—not even a river—and precious little green space. What it did have, in abundance, was people—some 26 million in the metropolitan area—and dreadfully polluted skies. The air was so contaminated that on most days the sky hung over the city like a threadbare theater curtain. I arrived in Mexico on May 10, but not until the second week in October did I see with my own eyes the giant twin volcanoes that photographs show looming over the city—pictures that, I later learned, were taken on clear days that occurred only once or twice a year.

We worried about the pollution, especially since a *Times* correspondent in the 1980s had demanded a transfer after one of his children contracted a serious illness that he attributed to Mexico's foul air. We wanted to avoid the worst of the contamination, and that influenced many of our decisions, including the selection of a school. We toured

the big American School downtown, but the old Tacubaya neighborhood was regularly smothered in fumes, and on days when the pollution
levels were too high, the school hoisted black flags and canceled outdoor gym. The school's staff proudly told us that construction would begin soon on a new building that would be air-conditioned, double
filtered, and totally self-contained. On high-alert days, they boasted, the
kids would never have to go outside.

We decided against the school, but not just because of the environment. It seemed foolish, even arrogant, to travel so far from home and
then keep ourselves apart from Mexican society. So we enrolled the kids
in a small Mexican school high on one of the mountains surrounding
the Valley of Mexico. We figured this would keep them above the pollution most days. Nearly all the classes were taught in Spanish, and they
would be the only Americans in the school. Just before I signed the final papers enrolling them, one of the school administrators told me she
had an important question to ask. "Would you mind," she began, and my
mind raced ahead to anticipate her question about stranding our kids
outside their language or their culture, "if there are only a few Catholics
in their classes?" Most of the children in the school were Jewish, the
sons and daughters of families that had immigrated to Mexico from
Syria, Lebanon, and other countries, some generations ago, others much
more recently. The school did not teach religion, but it did permit the
Jewish children to schedule bar mitzvah parties during the week, can-
celing school for the celebrant's entire class. One elaborate bar mitzvah
we attended was conducted in Hebrew, Spanish, English, and French,
and the tables set out for more than 150 guests were decorated with
cardboard cactus plants and black cowboy hats.

As a New Yorker, I was used to gargantuan cities, but even I found
Mexico City a municipal monstrosity, as unlikely a city as exists anywhere on earth. More people lived in the Federal District than in all of
the countries of Central America put together, yet it lies in an inland valley, more than 200 miles from either coast. It was built on the spongy
sediment of what, 500 years ago, had been a series of lakes. Most were
freshwater, but Texcoco, the only one that still exists, was filled with salt
water. The entire valley sits on the central Mexican plateau, which was
thrust more than 7,000 feet into the thin air by tectonic movements eons
ago.

Mexico's political, cultural, financial, and spiritual center is here because this is where the Aztecs built their capital, the wondrous Tenochti-

tlán. According to ancient legends, the Aztecs wandered from their home in northern Mexico until they found this spot, where they saw an eagle perched on a cactus with a serpent hanging from its beak. The image appears in the center of the modern Mexican flag. The first Europeans to see the city were Cortés and his exhausted men, who climbed to the rim of the surrounding mountains after a hard march from the sea in 1519. From that vantage point they saw a fabulous shimmering world. "We saw all those cities and villages built in the water, and other great towns on dry land, and that straight and level causeway leading to Mexico, and we were astounded," wrote one of Cortés's men, Bernal Díaz. "These great towns and *cues* and buildings rising from the water, all made of stone, seemed like an enchanted vision from the tale of Amadis. Indeed, some of our soldiers asked whether it was not all a dream."[5]

With trickery, subterfuge, and an uncanny ability to read and manipulate the emotions of the Indians he met on his march inland from Veracruz to the Valley of Mexico, Cortés was able to conquer one of the best organized and most warlike empires in Mesoamerica. The Indians who befriended Cortés did so because they hated the Aztecs. For ages, the ferocious Aztecs built their kingdom on conquest and sustained it through the exaction of constant tributes ranging from baskets of corn to the lives of slaves who eventually became human sacrifices. When the Tlaxcalans, a tribe that opposed the Aztecs, saw the Spanish guns, and when they cowered in front of the conquistadores' enormous horses (having never seen a horse, the Indians at first thought the animals were human because their riders spoke to them), they believed Cortés's audacious prediction that the mighty Aztecs could be defeated. By the time Cortés met Montezuma at the edge of Tenochtitlán, his army of scarcely 400 men was backed by a formidable Indian army of thousands hiding in the hills and waiting to exact sweet revenge.

The Spanish-Indian alliances permitted Cortés to lay siege to Tenochtitlán and, in a devastating battle that leveled great parts of the city, to strip the Aztecs of their king, their power, their empire, and their gods. The defeat was as complete and devastating as any people had ever suffered. But Cortés and his men were still vastly outnumbered by the native people, and other tribes outside the Valley of Mexico would resist the bearded newcomers unless they clearly demonstrated their powers. Cortés believed that building his capital atop the ruined Aztec city would leave no doubt about which society had prevailed and which had been vanquished. It was not the most logical decision to be taken by a commander thousands of miles from home, knowing that supplies from Spain would have to be carried to the valley from the coast. Nor was Tenochtitlán an ideal building site. It was a new-world Venice, a series of islands in the lakes that were connected by broad, straight causeways. Like the original Venice, flooding was a constant problem, and after the savage battle for control of the city, the waterways were rank with blood and rotting corpses. The pudding-like subsoil beneath the water could not support any substantial weight, a factor that has plagued the city throughout its history.

Mexico City is far older than any other city in North America, and its entire history is chronicled in its squares and under its streets. When the city government excavated the area in front of the Fine Arts Palace for an underground parking garage in the early 1990s, tons of artifacts were recovered in layers clearly corresponding to the epochs of the city's past. A person standing in front of the Great Temple of Montezuma, the base of which has been excavated and left open for the public, might imagine what Cortés saw in 1519. The conquistador wrote long reports back to the king of Spain, and he was accompanied by several chroniclers who left a detailed record of those very first encounters, often referring to place-names that still are commonly used today. I was always moved when I drove down the broad avenue called Puente de Alvarado to realize that I was tracing the same tracks as the Aztec causeway on which Cortés's lieutenant, Pedro de Alvarado, had fought during the fierce battle for that early American empire. Similarly, I was taken aback every time I realized that Mexico City's enormous central park, Chapultepec, had been named and enjoyed by the Aztecs, just as the park itself is the remnant of the gardens favored by Montezuma. Until well past Mexico's independence when it finally faded from view, a cliff there bore an Aztec warrior's stern visage that had been scratched into the rock before Cortés arrived.

The violent clash of Europeans and Aztecs is as close as mankind has ever come to an encounter with an alien world. Two advanced societies, each dominant in its own universe and ignorant of the other, were utterly changed the moment they collided. From that first instant, both sides knew that only one of their worlds could survive. The moment of recognition was followed by an immediate commitment to annihilation. This would become a pattern for the settlement of the new world whenever one society touched another, whether the destruction was caused by firearms or the mayhem of weapons like language and culture. In the continent's history, there has been only one notable exception—the French colony of Quebec, which the British conquered but for strategic reasons (discussed later) deliberately did not dismantle.

The clash between worlds in Mexico was total and unforgiving, and it left scars from which the people of Mexico are still trying to recover. In Mexico City, at the place called Tlatelolco where the last Aztec emperor surrendered the remnants of the Aztec empire to Cortés, there is a plaque that describes Mexico's struggle with the devils of its own history. "On August 13, 1521, heroically defended by Cuauhtémoc, Tlatelolco fell into the hands of Hernán Cortés. It was neither a triumph nor a defeat: it was the painful birth of the mestizo nation that is Mexico today."

Nearly 500 years later, this is the politically correct version of the epicenter of Mexico's past, but it contradicts much of the long, complicated, and often dark history of Mexico since that day. The Indians were defeated, and their defeat led them into centuries of subjugation, mistreatment, and marginalization that continue to this day. The elegant Paseo de la Reforma in Mexico City is adorned with an impressive sculpture of the Aztec emperors, but modern Mexico City also is home to the largest population of Indian people in Mexico, most of them poor, uneducated, and as completely marginalized as are the Indians on U.S. and Canadian reservations.

Along with the all-Mexican school we selected for the children, we decided at the outset to live in a community where most of our neighbors would be Mexican. Growing anticipation of NAFTA brought many Americans to Mexico City in 1993. Most were relocated corporate executives on two-year assignments, and most lived near each other in the wealthiest neighborhoods of Mexico City. They rented large houses from Mexican owners who had enough experience with past devaluations to demand their exorbitant rents in American dollars, although technically it was not legal to price anything in any currency other than the Mexican peso.

Mexico City is such a sprawling mess that it has been divided into sixteen boroughs (*delegaciones*) to help provide at least minimal municipal services. We rented a house in the *delegación* of Cuajimalpa, on the extreme western edge of the city, high up on one of the ridges that crown the Valley of Mexico. The area is the least developed part of the federal district and is high enough above the pollution that on most days I could, if I had time, go to an old pine forest and run with Mexican university athletes along a complex of dirt trails and marked courses. Cuajimalpa had once been a separate town. It still had its own small church, dating to the colonial era, and its own shopping areas where chickens were sold from the back of pickup trucks. Indians wandered in on the weekends to sell edible cactus and mushrooms from the woods. During Easter week, the main street was filled with creaky carnival rides that operated precariously close to each other. The Easter festival featured other amusements, including a canary that picked fortunes written on slips of papers packed tightly into a wooden box, and a freak show that anywhere else would have been considered politically incorrect. It cost a few pesos to enter the curtained-off area lined with deformed animals in glass jars. For a few pesos more, those who were more curious were ushered into a narrow hallway. A screen then would be pulled back to reveal what was purportedly a two-headed boy, from Chiapas, that clearly was two boys squeezed into a single stretched-out sweater.

Homero Aridjis, a Mexican poet, once told me that the differences between Mexicans and Americans are only slight in business, politics, and fine culture, such as classical music and opera. "But the divide is wide on the popular level where the U.S. doesn't penetrate into the psyche of Mexicans except in a vague and general way." For example, in Mexico City, America's presence can be so pervasive that billboards advertise a non-Mexican product like the Wonderbra in much in the way it is advertised north of the border, using the same models who clearly bear little resemblance to the stocky physique of mestizo women. In the countryside, though, traditions are still strong, and the United States is a more remote presence.

"In the pueblos," Aridjis said, "only Coca-Cola reveals the presence of the United States in any way."

We never encountered another American in Cuajimalpa, and as if to prove what Aridjis had said, no American retailer but Coke seemed to have any presence there at all. It provided a good tutorial for getting to know Mexican culture and the values of Mexicans not as expressed by officials but as lived in Mexico's innumerable towns and neighborhoods. The area's mixture of nearness to the city center and isolation from urban mores made it a perfect laboratory for testing Aridjis's observations about the influence of the United States—until I stumbled upon a split within a neighboring family that challenged his maxim.

Marcos the handyman worked for the Berdichevsky family. Debbie, whom we met first, had been born in the United States but was raised in Mexico. Her husband José, a dentist and entrepreneur whom everyone called Pepe, had lived in Mexico his whole life. Together they were an interesting sounding board for me because she considered herself to be American, and that colored her attitude toward things at the heart of Mexican culture, while he reflected the fundamental values of Mexican society. This was never clearer than the time the older of their two daughters turned sixteen and Debbie took her to the offices of the Cuajimalpa *delegación* to get her driver's permit. As always, a long line of people waited to conduct their business. All but Debbie and her daughter were working-class people, the people who made up most of Cuajimalpa. The *delegación* offices were notoriously inept and famously corrupt. Anyone who could afford to do so avoided waiting in line by finding a bureaucrat and asking if it wouldn't be possible to speed things up. A quick glance at the folded 50-peso bill lying on the counter made the transaction complete.

"I knew that, but I refused to go along," Debbie told me. In part, she said, it was because her American heritage taught her that rules are to be followed. And in part her Mexican upbringing made her resent the unfairness and injustice that most people suffered at the hands of the privileged and the powerful. She waited in line for well over an hour, and when there were but two or three people left in front of her, the clerk closed the window and went off for his long Mexican lunch. Frustrated, and out of time, Debbie went home.

That night, she told Pepe what had happened, and he merely shook his head. "You can't handle it that way," he told me, "not if you value your time." The next morning he went with his daughter to the *delegación* office. They did not wait in line. He found an accommodating clerk and explained that he was a dentist and couldn't be expected to wait interminably. Fifty pesos turned out to be quite adequate.

Pepe didn't gloat. He knew that almost anyone but his wife would have done the same. Debbie just said, "I couldn't."

✳

I was learning something fundamental about Mexican society. Like one of the Aztec pyramids, it was built of layers, one atop another. And no matter how far down the steps of the pyramid you looked, there always seemed to be one more step farther down. One's awareness of, and concern about, the levels beneath usually was more a matter of self-interest than altruism. The pattern was set right at the beginning. Within a generation after the conquistadores had flattened Tenochtitlán, disease, overwork, and neglect had so decimated the Indian population of central Mexico that even the conquerors were alarmed. Although they considered the Indians to be beings without souls, the conquistadores realized that without them it would be impossible to rebuild the shattered city or work the silver mines. The missionary priests, after consulting with Rome, were able to argue convincingly that the natives indeed could be saved if they accepted the true faith. The Castilians harbored doubts about the Indians' humanity, but they valued the willingness of the natives to bend to a strong ruler, a trait that obedience to the Aztec emperors had cultivated.

The leaders of the new world at first considered educating the sons of the Aztec nobles so that an indigenous ruling class, loyal to the Spanish throne, could be developed. Natives still greatly outnumbered the Europeans, and disciplined indigenous leaders could be of use in keeping crowds in check. A college was established, but funding was withdrawn when objections were raised to providing the natives such advantages. The college closed before it could change anything. Indians were to be considered lesser men, albeit with souls that could be saved through the missions. The Indians would be put to work in the mines and on the haciendas, and the enlightened Europeans would look after them. It was the beginning of a pattern of paternalistic treatment of Indians that has persisted in some form to this day, not just in Mexico but throughout North America.

An early manifestation of this mentality was the establishment of a *ciudad ideal* on the dry hillside just above the Valley of Mexico, in what is today Cuajimalpa. The city included a hospital, but it did much more than treat sicknesses. Fray Vasco de Quiroga, the cleric of fervent vision who founded the city, tended to the Indians, fed them, and taught them skills like knitting and weaving that he believed would better prepare them to survive under the new circumstances in which they lived. He treated them like children. He took away their independence and individual will, but by doing so he hoped to reshape their eternal souls. After establishing this city, he went on to found others in various parts of Mexico, including Santa Fe de la Laguna in Morelia, in the state of Michoacán, which has survived into the twenty-first century producing the same crafts Fray Quiroga himself taught to the first inhabitants.

In the early 1990s, Mexico City's government began work converting an abysmal municipal garbage dump near the site of Quiroga's first Santa Fe into a new city, the main street of which became Vasco de Quiroga Boulevard. The area once had been a sand quarry, and the top of the cliff was honeycombed with narrow tunnels dug by hand (most certainly Indian hands) during sixteenth-century mining operations. The new building sites were about 300 feet below that level, which made it possible to see both Mexico City's past, and its future, in a single glance.

Mexico City was being threatened by the chaos of centuries of haphazard development and the unchecked industrialization that had taken place after the revolution. Factories built in the 1920s and 1930s had never been replaced or even upgraded, and they spewed toxins into the city's dangerously polluted environment. When the weather changed and an inversion prevented smokestack emissions from escaping the atmosphere, the pollution reached such dangerous levels that the factories were forced to close temporarily. Greed and corruption had allowed building codes to be violated, with tragic consequences in the deadly 1985 earthquake. Most of the city's precious open space had been filled, and as the population grew and more water was withdrawn from the underground aquifer, officials discovered the city was sinking into the mud of the old lake bed on which it had been built.

The project represented an alternative future for Mexico City. City officials called it Santa Fe, after Fray Quiroga's vision of a utopian future. It was one of the largest commercial developments in Latin America at the time. It had the look of a suburban office project in the United States, with wide boulevards and flashy glass and steel office buildings. In scale and vision, it seemed to represent Mexico's entrance into the modern world and its willingness to embrace the free trade agreement, which city officials were betting would be approved. In their minds, Santa Fe and the trade pact would make Mexico City the business gateway to all of Latin America.

City officials eager to show me Santa Fe took me on a tour. At that time it was still too soon to tell whether NAFTA would be approved and what role the city would play in its implementation. But as I looked around the busy construction site, I thought that in at least one sense it did symbolize all of Mexico and the way the country squandered its abundant resources. I was led into one of the new office buildings, a three-story structure finished in yellow and purple stucco and surrounded by a forest of palm trees. As we entered, more than thirty-five Mexican laborers were pounding the floor with hammers. The stone tiles had a smooth finish, but the desired effect was mottled, a suggestion of age that was typical in many of the buildings in Mexico where even the new can look old. Each blow of the hammer pulverized a tiny bit of stone, but as the workers progressed from one section to another, the overall effect they created was of a gentle patina and a respectful aging. It wasn't the architectural effect that impressed me but rather the expenditure of labor. Officials told me the crews would work this way for days, progressing slowly through all the floors and stairways of the building, pounding and pounding until every stone was hand finished.

I was dazzled by the sheer extravagance of it: an army of workers paid for doing a task that might have been possible to achieve by machines at the quarry. But the salaries of the workers were so low—the minimum wage at the time was just over the equivalent of $4 a day—that it made sense to have them do it on-site. And most Mexicans officials and the leaders of the labor unions that were captive to the ruling party still believed in the concept of work being most valuable when it is shared by the greatest number of people. In other words, Mexico was still caught in the make-work era and had not yet felt the sting of unrestrained competition. But that was about to change.

CHAPTER THREE

Pyramids of Power

*

For all three countries, it [NAFTA] will force a re-examination
of national identity as the continental economic
restructuring process evolves.

Stephen J. Randall and Herman W. Konrad
NAFTA in Transition

Mexico's willingness to squander labor and resources was of concern to Mexicans who were serious about modernizing their country, men like Raúl Muñoz Leos, the president of Dupont of Mexico.[1] A keen businessman and careful observer of the Mexican scene, Raúl also was familiar with American ways, and he often proved to be the source of valuable insights into the heart of Mexican business and society. I met him about a month after I arrived in Mexico City. We were part of a group of executives and journalists who accompanied President Carlos Salinas de Gortari on a trip to the Yucatán peninsula. Salinas arrived in his preferred fashion—a flotilla of helicopters whisked him and all his invited guests (including Raúl and me) from the Chetumal airport on the coast to a rough rectangular landing field hacked out of the jungle a few days before. The downed chicle trees and dense underbrush that had been cleared away lined the edges of the road that also had been opened just for Salinas's visit.

Raúl and I, along with other journalists and invited Mexican and American guests, followed Salinas deep into the jungle. For me, the trip provided an unexpected opportunity to fulfill a lifelong dream. We drove to an active archaeological site, the ceremonial city of Calakmul in the state of Campeche. Part of the site had been cleared, but most was still encased in dense jungle vine. We were taken to pyramid number three, where only preliminary surveys had been done, and given free rein to clamber to the top. The base resembled nothing but a random pile of stones. As we climbed the pyramid, its great bulk and mystery still wrapped in centuries of obscurity, little sense of order, or even the presence of man, was evident. There was a small section of stones that seemed to form two or three steps; we saw a piece of porous white lime-stone with an angle too sharp to have been formed naturally. But then the trees thinned, the sky opened up, and we emerged into the sunlight at the peak of the pyramid, where our perspective of time and place changed dramatically. The vista that opened before me was undisturbed green for miles in every direction, with the flat Caribbean sky pale above it. Here and there I could pick out what appeared to be the tips of other pyramids poking through the canopy. In the world in which these structures had been created, there could have been no more powerful symbol of a people's might than this, the only point in this absolutely flat land from which it would have been possible to see all the people and at the same time feel close to heaven.

Exploring a raw, unexcavated archaeological site may not have been Raúl's dream, but he was moved nonetheless by what he saw and how it reflected on the modern Mexico he lived in. Surveying the work of dis-tant ancestors who had quarried the stone and brought it to this place without the help of any machine, placed the stones together in such a way that a thousand years later we could still stand on them and appre-ciate the same sense of majesty they had originally imparted, filled Raúl with understandable awe and a persistent melancholy for what had been lost.

"The difference is all in the act of building, which was the accomplish-ment back then," Raúl told me while we were still atop the pyramid. "To-day, work doesn't have the same meaning."

At that time, in 1993, work in Mexico had largely come to symbolize not personal accomplishment but political opportunity, particularly for President Salinas. He climbed pyramid three with us, a peasant hat shielding his bald head from the jungle sun. Resting at the summit, pos-sessing power as Mexico's president, the contemporary embodiment of the Maya rulers who built Calakmul, Salinas could reflect on the previ-ous five years of his administration. He had expended much of his en-ergy attempting to convert work into more than the perpetual labor of millions of poor Mexicans. The trip to Calakmul was part of a public acknowledgment of a project dear to the president's heart, a program he called Solidaridad (Solidarity). Under the program, public services, local empowerment, and welfare were brought together in an organized and overtly political way. Solidarity was public welfare with a component of public works administration, and it had been widely praised. But many critics were disturbed by the way it leached into political organizing. For a Solidarity project to be considered successful, it had to provide jobs, improve the quality of life in backwoods villages and isolated rural areas, and form the core of a political organization that came to have tendrils in rural communities around the country. By contributing their labor to a project, the peasants would have a real stake in the future of their communities. Salinas hoped they would also feel they had invested in Solidarity, in Mexico, and in him. Restricted by the Mexican constitution to a single six-year term, Salinas was thinking ahead to after he left office, when he might be able to control a huge, national, grassroots organization that would clamor for him to run again, even if it might mean changing the constitution or waiting six years.

After a brief ceremony in the forest to honor the environmental efforts of the chicle workers who surround the Calakmul site, Salinas and his entourage sped to the village of Xpujil in a convoy of Chevrolet Suburbans, as out of place in the dense forest as an oxcart would be in Times Square. Xpujil had been founded early in the 1900s by European entrepreneurs looking for mahogany and other jungle treasures. Salinas was there to celebrate the success of Solidarity, which had helped the community rebuild its corn flour mill and in so doing kept the forest from entirely reclaiming the settlement. Salinas was accompanied by his human services secretary Luis Donaldo Colosio and other officials. After a short speech in a corn shed, the president strode regally up Xpujil's single street as astonished residents stood outside houses that were barely more than shacks. Each house had been whitewashed the previous week. Nothing had changed inside—the floors were still made of dirt, the roofs leaked, and frayed hammocks hung limply from the rafters. But the facades gave the appearance that costly work had been done. This was a typical subterfuge of the Mexican government during these years. Solidarity's true mission was to create a political superstructure, not to pave streets or repair houses. Every time Salinas visited Washington or spoke with an American official, he mentioned Solidarity, and the help it provided communities like Xpujil, as proof that Mexicans were willing to work to help themselves.

Throughout 1993, Salinas was often in touch with Washington as he fought to win approval of the most important initiative of his administration. Mexico had been backed into a fiscal corner, and Salinas knew that only by taking a huge gamble could he help the nation escape economic calamity. The potential for catastrophe had been building for a long time. Since the revolution, Mexico's population had grown from 10 million to nearly 100 million. Recent efforts to introduce birth control had lowered the birthrate, but Mexico still needed to create one million new jobs a year just to keep pace with the number of young people entering the job market.

Old methods of stimulating the economy no longer worked. Such protectionist measures as high tariffs and import substitution had helped Mexico achieve solid growth from the 1940s through the 1960s. Competition had been kept out of Mexico, but so had innovation. Still, the absolute necessity for real change in the economy had been forestalled by the oil crisis of the early 1970s. Mexico, an oil exporter, reaped a windfall when oil prices soared. But when prices dropped in the early 1980s, Mexico was hurt so badly that it defaulted on its debt.

President Miguel de la Madrid, Salinas's immediate predecessor, was the first Mexican president to realize that the protectionist walls had to come down if Mexico was to attract investment. He pushed Mexico into joining the General Agreement on Tariffs and Trades (GATT) and becoming part of an international forum that required members to lower customs fees and lift nontariff barriers. Isolated no longer, Mexico looked for help from the outside world it had long shunned. And that included the United States. Treasury Secretary Nicholas Brady helped Mexico repackage its defaulted debt as Brady bonds, with incentives and safeguards that lured back leery international investors and launched the process of rebuilding the national economy.

One proven way for a developing nation of poor people to grow is by exporting products to more developed countries. Salinas, who had studied economics at Harvard University, knew this. The obvious market for Mexican exports was the United States. When Ronald Reagan campaigned in the 1980 presidential election, he had tossed out a vague proposal for increasing trade in the hemisphere. Under such an arrangement, each country agrees to lower or eliminate the tariffs it charges on goods that it imports from the other. In theory, everyone benefits as exports rise and employment is expanded. Working people can afford to purchase more goods, which leads to an increase in both imports and exports, and so on. Usually such deals are struck between countries whose economies are similar. No one had ever tried it between a highly advanced country like the United States, and one with great poverty and low wages like Mexico.

Salinas had already made it clear that he didn't think such a deal would work to Mexico's benefit—that despite their shared border, the two nations were too different, too unequal. But he also understood instinctively that his options were closing rapidly. He saw a bleak future for Mexico unless he could reverse seventy years of economic protectionism and continental mistrust. And so, on the day after he concluded the renegotiation of Mexico's debt in late 1989, he began work brokering just such a deal. His preferred trading partners were in Europe, and he traveled to the international economics forum in Davos, Switzerland, early in 1990 with an unspecific plan to strike up negotiations with the major European nations.

Salinas never had much chance of enticing the Europeans to the negotiating table; with Europe focused on the unraveling of the Soviet Union and the dissolution of the Soviet bloc, there was little interest in faraway Mexico or its problems. Mexico's commerce secretary, Jaime Serra Puche, had told Salinas that the Europeans were not going to respond favorably. And he doubted whether piecemeal negotiations with the United States for deals in individual sectors, such as furniture or beef, would ever be sufficient to raise the level of direct investment in Mexico.

"I thought we should be seeking something more comprehensive," Serra told me years later. But he knew that a more comprehensive deal with the United States would be packed with political tension. So nothing more was mentioned, and after a long, frustrating day at Davos, the Mexican team retired for the night to prepare for meetings the next day with the U.S. trade representative, Carla Hills. The Mexicans were lodged in tiny quarters inside a ski resort that had been taken over for the conference. Serra, exhausted, had started to doze off when there was a knock at the door. It was Salinas, who had come down from his room on a different floor in the hotel. Serra was startled to see the president at his door so late at night. "He said, 'Why don't you start exploring the idea about a comprehensive deal with Carla in the morning?'" Serra recalled. "And so I did."

Once Salinas received a positive affirmation that the United States was interested in striking some kind of deal, he made it the centerpiece of his economic policy and the keystone of the legacy he planned to leave when his administration ended. He was the deal's most outspoken proponent. "The key question is where do you want Mexicans to work, in Mexico or in the United States?" was the charged question Salinas asked American officials as he campaigned for passage of NAFTA in 1993. For himself, he would say, "I would rather export goods than labor." Salinas was most concerned about building support for the agreement in the United States, where there was substantial opposition to making Mexico a business partner. A powerful coalition was forming in the United States to oppose the agreement: Critics predicted jobs would be lost and factories closed, while low Mexican wages would inevitably have the effect of pushing down salaries for American workers. Salinas had nothing to worry about in Mexico. Although many Mexicans objected to what they saw as a surrender of sovereignty, Salinas and his party, the Partido Revolucionario Institucional (PRI, Institutional Revolutionary Party), had a solid lock on Congress, the legacy of more than sixty years of single-party rule. Whatever he decided on would become law. That didn't prevent opponents from trying to shout down the deal. Most of the criticism came from the left, primarily from academics and intellectuals, who in Mexico had long substituted for an effective opposition. The most outspoken was Jorge G. Castañeda, an academic and writer whose father had been foreign minister under the PRI (and who in 2000 would himself become foreign minister but for the opposition). Castañeda claimed that the trade agreement had little or nothing to do with trade. It was only, he said, an invitation for American investors to invade Mexico and a promise to protect them from any future expropriations—like the one in 1938 when Mexico had seized the oil fields of foreign companies from seventeen different nations, including the United States.

Robert A. Pastor, who had been Jimmy Carter's adviser on Latin America, visited Mexico often as the battle over NAFTA was raging. Once, over drinks at the Hotel Presidente in Mexico City, he told me how much he marveled at the changes that had made it possible for Mexico to abandon its recent history of anti-Americanism and negotiate a trade deal. In his view, the end of the Cold War had changed the relationship between the United States and Mexico because it "in effect replaces the strategic fears of America with the economic fears of competition with Germany and Japan." Just a few weeks before Congress was to vote on the trade agreement, he boiled it down to this:

"The real challenge for the Clinton administration is to convince the American people that Mexico is not a competitor but our partner in the competition with Germany and Japan."

Competition with the rest of the world had already forced American companies to shut hundred of factories in the United States and lay off legions of workers. American unions were in no mood to deal with Mexico. They did not buy the Clinton administration's argument that NAFTA would mean more exports and, eventually, more jobs. Instead, they predicted that American manufacturers enticed by Mexico's low wages would flock across the border. The deal inspired suspicion in Mexico as well, at least from those people who were aware of it. They feared Mexican industry could never compete with American companies and would quickly disappear. An opposition politician in Mexico, more outspoken than most, told me the agreement amounted to "economic annexation by the United States" and was another maneuver by the Salinas administration to convince the world that Mexico was undergoing a transformation when, in fact, it was only hiding behind a clever mask.

"The Mexican miracle is a new financial hoax," the politician, Israel Gallan, told me one day in Mexico City, "a hoax, but one that is excellently presented. I would give this government all the Academy Awards—best actor, best screenplay, best special effects—for what it has managed to accomplish."

Once Salinas had decided to overlook the centuries of mistrust that had developed between the two countries, he was not timid about making known what he wanted. Mexico discovered how effective lobbying can be in Washington. The Salinas government spent lavishly on its campaign for the free trade agreement. By some estimates, the whole effort cost $45 million, a third of that in the critical year 1993 when President Clinton had to work hard to convince Democrats in both the House and the Senate to approve the bill.

✳

Though I was little aware of it at the time, the NAFTA campaign also marked the beginning of genuine three-sided North American political maneuvering. Far north of Mexico, Canadians also argued over the strange new deal, but mostly because it reopened so many old wounds. Canada had gone through its own vicious battle in 1988 when Prime Minister Brian Mulroney acted for reasons similar to those that spurred

President Salinas five years later. Faced with surging deficits, raging unemployment, and a withering lack of investor confidence, Mulroney had dumped a century of deliberate economic isolation and in 1987 completed a deal for the Canada-U.S. Free Trade Agreement, which would lower the tariff wall that some Canadians felt was Canada's last line of national defense. A television commercial for the Liberal Party in the 1988 election showed two smartly dressed men at a table erasing the border with the United States after the free trade deal was signed. The trade agreement became the principal campaign issue in Canada—but went practically unnoticed in the United States that year. With the support of big business, which liked the deal, Mulroney won.

But Canadian nationalists crucified him for selling out the nation's sovereignty and putting Canada on the road to becoming an economic colony of the United States. Mulroney well understood how unpopular pushing the trade agreement had made him, but he was convinced that in the long run Canada stood to benefit handsomely. In the early 1990s, when he learned that the United States and Mexico were beginning to discuss entering a similar bilateral deal, he grew worried that Canada would be left out. Individually, both Canada and Mexico, with their separate deals, would be no match for the United States. But Mulroney believed that in a three-sided agreement, Mexico would be Canada's partner, not necessarily its competitor. Acting in common defense of their shared interests, the two smaller countries jointly would have more negotiating leverage at the table with the United States than either one would have separately.

Mulroney wisely decided not to run for reelection as his mandate neared an end in 1993. But when his successor as head of the Progressive Conservative Party and prime minister, Kim Campbell, called an election for October 1993, voters in Canada saw a chance to exact their revenge on Mulroney for the 1988 trade agreement.

Even though NAFTA would have changed little from the 1988 trade agreement, already into its fifth year, free trade became a divisive issue in the 1993 parliamentary elections. The Liberal Party of Jean Chrétien had campaigned hard against the 1988 free trade deal with the United States, and Chrétien himself was one of its harshest critics. Had he and the Liberal Party come out strongly against NAFTA in the 1993 election (which was held just over a month before the final NAFTA vote would be held in Washington), a reluctant U.S. Congress might have had sufficient reason to postpone the vote or kill the trade deal outright. Strong opposition from Chrétien would have made it difficult for President Clinton to go to Congress and the American people promoting a deal that our allies north of the border did not want.

The White House watched Canada's campaign with unusual interest in 1993. Mulroney and the Conservatives had been overtly pro-American, whereas Chrétien and the Liberals had been disconcertingly critical of the United States in the past. Anti-free-trade Democrats in the United States looked to Chrétien to bury the trade initiative. Ross Perot even got Chrétien on the phone and urged him to hit the NAFTA deal hard, then promised to build a monument to him in Texas when the pact died a sudden and violent death.

James J. Blanchard, then the U.S. ambassador to Canada, monitored the struggle from the American embassy in Ottawa, which was located right across the street from the Parliament buildings and directly in front of the prime minister's office. Blanchard, a former Michigan governor, fervently believed that NAFTA was important for border states like his that already relied on more than $100 billion in trade crossing the Ambassador Bridge from Detroit to Windsor each year. He met with Chrétien's chief advisers before the campaign and hammered at how critical their actions would be in the NAFTA debate. "If you want to kill NAFTA without leaving any fingerprints, I'm telling you now, as a fellow politician, you have a perfect way to do it," Blanchard remembered saying. "But I hope you won't."[2]

Chrétien saw a way to win support and reverse his position on the free trade that was pulling Canada out of recession. Canadians were so angry with Mulroney and the Conservatives for all their cronyism and arrogance that Chrétien was certain he could win votes by criticizing his predecessor. When it came to the NAFTA negotiations, many Canadians were still stung by the 1988 agreement, but they reluctantly conceded it could not be reversed. So, they reasoned, if NAFTA was inevitable, then they at least wanted to see it negotiated in a way that addressed their concerns. They were pleased that President Clinton had succumbed to late demands to attach side accords to strengthen the pact. These accords made it possible for the governments to take action against Mexico (or each other) if local environment and labor standards were not met. Canadians had also insisted on stronger protections in two areas they considered critical to Canada's interests: protecting its culture and preventing the dumping of products so cheaply that local industries could be destroyed. Washington eventually conceded enough ground on both issues to get Chrétien to tone down his opposition to the trade agreement.

When the Canadian election was held in October 1993, Canadian voters who were furious at Mulroney humbled his party by taking it from a ruling majority of 169 of Parliament's 292 seats to just 2 seats. It was one of the most devastating political reversals in Canadian history. Chrétien, as pragmatic a leader as Canada has produced in the past century, became prime minister and—obsessed with firing up the economy—a born-again advocate of free trade.

With the Canadian election over, the last step toward passage of NAFTA was the vote in the U.S. Congress. President Clinton prepared to use his personal skills of persuasion, and the perquisites of the presidency, to round up enough votes from both Democrats and Republicans to get the agreement passed. It was an extraordinary effort, at an extraordinarily sensitive time. In Mexico, President Salinas knew he couldn't lobby the members of Congress directly, but he was intent on avoiding any mishap that recalcitrant U.S. congressional members could use to defeat NAFTA. He had insisted that Mexico be on its best behavior for months, and he had quickly tried to undo the damage caused by the murder of Cardinal Posadas Ocampo with the quick explanations of investigators about mistaken identity.

However, although it was unknown at the time, an incident had occurred in the southern state of Chiapas two days before the cardinal's murder that might have derailed NAFTA had it become known. Salinas made sure it didn't. In May 1993, Mexican soldiers on patrol in Chiapas had literally stumbled on a group of armed men training in the dense forest of Mexico's most southern, most disadvantaged state. Staring at each other, both sides blinked. Shots were fired. At least one solider and one of the armed men died, and the army pursued the group deeper into the Chiapas jungle. The following day they found a rebel training base, which confirmed rumors that had circulated for months about an insurgent group planning an attack on the government. Such information, on the eve of the congressional vote, would have raised tough questions in the United States about the agreement and reinforced existing doubts about taking on Mexico as a partner. The news that Mexico harbored a rebel movement would have upset Salinas's carefully orchestrated campaign to assure the Americans that Mexico was a stable, modern nation that could be trusted.

Instead of tracking down the rebels, the Mexican army packed its gear and returned to base. A few months later, Salinas himself traveled to the heart of insurgent territory in Chiapas and dedicated an inordinately expensive clinic in the village of Guadalupe Tepeyac, believed to be an administrative center for the rebels. The modern concrete building towered over the wooden shacks and dirt roads of the village, an unmistakable reminder of the power of federal largesse that was intended to appease the people and keep them loyal. The army continued to receive reports of a general mobilization of the still-unknown rebel group but chose to ignore them while the debate in Washington reached its climax. On November 17, 1993, by a vote of 234 to 200, the House of Representatives approved NAFTA. Republicans supported the deal three to one, but the majority of members of President Clinton's own party lined up against it.

Salinas celebrated. Before the end of the same month in which he had pulled off the most far-reaching public policy initiative in Mexico since the revolution, he also consummated the single most important act of his presidential term, naming his successor. Early on a Sunday morning, Mexican reporters were tipped off by party officials that the PRI's candidate would be announced soon. The moment a Mexican president names his successor is simultaneously the peak of his power and the beginning of his powerlessness. The system had worked perfectly to transfer power from one PRI leader to another since the party had been founded, under a different name, in 1929. There had been no long series of primary elections around the country, nor even the pretense of a well-scripted nominating convention. This was a much more ancient type of ritual, based solely on a tradition that came as close to royal succession as occurs on the American continent.

The man Salinas picked as the PRI's candidate, and thus likely the next president of Mexico, was Luis Donaldo Colosio, the human services secretary who had accompanied him on the trip to Calakmul and Xpujil a few months before. Colosio had been a senator and president of the PRI. He shared Salinas's faith in competition and open markets, but he was considered to be a more aggressive political reformer than his mentor. Colosio was popular but not universally well-liked. Party stalwarts never forgave him for recognizing the opposition's electoral victory in the Baja California gubernatorial election in 1989.

But as soon as Colosio was named the PRI candidate, power and attention started transferring from Salinas to him. The system demands that all other contenders within the party put away their own ambition and support the official candidate. "We didn't treat Colosio as a candidate. We treated him as a king," Raymundo Riva Palacio, a Mexican journalist, told me. "On that Sunday, one king died and another king was born."

That evening, Colosio was officially presented to the party faithful at the PRI's enormous communist-style party headquarters in downtown Mexico City. It occupies an entire city block. The huge plaza in front of headquarters was mobbed by party faithful. All but one of the members of Salinas's inner cabinet had already called Colosio to pledge their support. The PRI had been busy. Only a few hours had passed since the official announcement, but the buildings were already draped with Colosio's name on enormous banners. Thousands of people had squeezed into the grounds trying to get into the hall where Colosio spoke. Only a few hundred made it inside, and they filled every inch of the room, leaving Colosio little more than a few inches of breathing space as he declared, "I belong to the generation of change, the generation headed by Carlos Salinas de Gortari."

That night should have marked the beginning of Salinas's slide into obscurity, but he believed he would continue to receive the accolades of the world, his accomplishments since 1988 secure. He was certain he would avoid the fate of other Mexican presidents who were reviled after they left office, a ritual of condemning the deposed leader that goes back to the Aztecs. Salinas also was sure that he would be the first president in a generation to leave office without the ignominy of a devaluation. His dream, well broadcast by the diminutive president and his allies, was to use this reputation for economic prowess to catapult himself to Geneva, where he hoped to make more Mexican history by becoming the first president of the fledgling World Trade Organization.

✳

Late the night of Colosio's ascension, I returned from PRI headquarters to our house in Cuajimalpa. It was late November, close to the end of our first remarkable year in Mexico. That night there was a full eclipse of the moon, almost as though to punctuate the events of the day, and the year. I woke my son Aahren and urged him to come outside to watch the sky. With sleepy eyes, he lay next to me on the damp grass. The moon was distant and small, and there was a chill in the air. As we waited for the moon to disappear, I thought back over all that had happened since

I had arrived in Mexico. I had not found the Mexico I had come looking for but instead had encountered a Mexico that was changing and had not existed before. I had come to savor the beauty of a place where flowers bloom all year and it is possible to stage a performance of Tchaikovsky's "Swan Lake" on the lake in Chapultepec Park, with live swans and horses, in the dead of winter. I had not been able to rely on those parts of myself that I hoped would help me understand Mexico, but I had learned from poets and pyramids how to see into the true heart of this closest of neighbors that sometimes seems so foreign. Mostly, though, I had stumbled through a particular period of history that was loaded with portents of mighty changes that were only taking shape. That night, atop the Valley of Mexico, as the earth's shadow covered the moon, as my impatient son fell asleep next to me, I could only guess that all I had witnessed over the previous year was but part of a much larger transformation just getting under way. It would take time to understand that 1993 had been only the beginning—of the torment of Mexico, the fading of borders, the integration of old enemies and the new American continent.

CHAPTER FOUR

Old Borders, New Politics

✳

Mexico. I rode a lot of ground down there. The first *ranchera*
you hear sung you understand the whole country. By the time
you've heard a hundred you don't know nothin'.
You never will.

Cormac McCarthy
Cities of the Plains

After the first day of January 1994, the national borders that for so
long had defined North America would never be the same. The
untested North American Free Trade Agreement that took effect
that day subtly began the process of transforming the frontiers from
lines separating the United States, Mexico, and Canada to seams binding
the three countries together. The trucks and trains and cars that cross
those borders in staggering numbers represent just one aspect of the
new relationship. Politics is another.

Few people realized this more clearly than Jean Chrétien, the crusty
political veteran from Quebec who had finally realized his dream of becoming prime minister a few months before the trade deal became reality. He didn't wait long to test the new continental waters. In March
1994, he arrived in Mexico City for his first official visit as prime minister, and the event was surrounded with all the primping and politics appropriate to the beginning of a new era.

Chrétien's advisers had encouraged him to make the trip to Mexico in
order to signal the importance of NAFTA to Canada, which was afraid,
as always, of being overshadowed by the United States. To Canada's way
of thinking, Mexico would make a good ally in future trilateral negotia-

tions. And if things worked out, Mexico could be cultivated as an important second outlet for Canadian exports, lessening Canada's life-support reliance on the American market. During the long round of negotiations leading to adoption of the trade deal, the Mexicans had shared similar hopes for the economic alliance, dreaming of the day when a united front with Canada would somehow counterbalance America's huge advantage. In a short time, however, they realized such a dream was unrealistic. "Mexico and Canada cannot possibly make a sandwich," a Mexican foreign minister, Manuel Tello Macías, once said. "There is too much meat in between."[1]

Still, the countries had pressed forward and ratified the trade deal, each for its own reasons. And now, a few months after NAFTA had been implemented, Chrétien was scheduled to preside over a huge Canadian trade fair in the Mexican capital to drum up business for Canadian and Mexican firms that were curious about the kinds of possibilities NAFTA had opened. His trip also had a less public but no less important mission. He was supposed to meet Luis Donaldo Colosio, who had recently launched his campaign as the ruling party's presidential candidate. In sixty-five years, Chrétien's advisers informed him, the PRI's candidate had never lost the presidential election. They didn't have to tell the prime minister that building a close relationship with the next president of Mexico was never more important.

Chrétien's trip marked the beginning of the process of merging the distant and separate worlds of Canada and Mexico into a new American continent. Although the two countries had established diplomatic relations nearly fifty years before, they had only rarely attempted to strike up any kind of significant relationship. What connected them also divided them, and the only camaraderie they felt was as small states that had to deal with the enormous power of the United States. The single exception to the disappointing history of Canada-Mexico relations had been during the later years of the long rule of Porfirio Díaz.

As the twentieth century began, Canadian companies, often acting as agents for the British, invested heavily in Mexican utilities—hydroelectric plants, telephone and telegraph companies—and together, Britain and Canada accounted for just over 29 percent of the foreign investment in Mexico when the revolution broke out in all its fury in 1910. With the violence that ensued, most of that investment ended, and for many years afterward, Canada's largest and most visible exports to Mexico were the sizable communities of Mennonites who had emigrated there in search of cheap farmland.

Changing that situation was very much on Chrétien's mind as his Canadian-built Challenger jet landed at the smoggy airport on the edge of Mexico City on Wednesday, March 24, 1994, at around the five-o'clock rush hour. He was driven through horrendous midweek traffic to the Hotel Presidente—an improbably tall building in a city infamous for the infirmity of its subsoil. There, he and his wife Aline were to get ready for that night's gala dinner that President Salinas had arranged in their honor. Ambassador David Winfield, nearing the end of a long and busy tenure in Mexico, was arranging the prime minister's itinerary. Coming so soon after the successful adoption of the trade agreement, the visit was a high point of Winfield's stay in Mexico and an auspicious beginning of a relationship that might somehow lead to an adjustment of North American power. In the economic sense, at least, Canada now had an ally in its battles against the insensitivity and arrogance of Washington.

At around seven o'clock, Winfield headed over to Los Pinos (the Pine Trees), an elegant mansion surrounded by a graceless necklace of office buildings that, taken as a whole, is to Mexico what the White House is to the United States. Most Mexicans have never been past the heavily armed gates, but many have seen at least some of the buildings and the fine grounds surrounding them because Los Pinos is located right off the city's primary ring road, the Periferico, six narrower-than-normal lanes of smoking, pollution-belching, industrial-grade traffic—a parking lot as much as a highway, where massive tie-ups occur at almost any time of the day or night.

The Periferico offered an early study into the character of Mexican society. I found it nearly impossible to drive there. The cars on either side of me seemed too close. At first I blamed the cars themselves, especially the old-fashioned Volkswagen Beetles that seemed to distort the space around them. After asking a few people, I learned it wasn't just me. Civil engineers had recently concluded that the roadway needed to be expanded. With much of the Periferico below street level as it passes through the heart of Mexico City, the cost of adding another lane was prohibitive. The solution was typical of how Mexican governments sometimes reduced problem solving to pettifoggery: Where there had been two lanes of traffic before, the engineers simply repainted all the lines and squeezed in three lanes. The resulting lanes are so narrow that there isn't room for three vehicles abreast to move at a good clip. Drivers have to keep extra distance from surrounding cars, as I had discovered. This spreads out traffic and ties up the highway more. Most times, however, traffic simply crawls, which may be what the engineers had in mind when they threw safety to the wind and created such narrow lanes. They figured that if Periferico traffic were cruising along, it could only be because there were not many cars on the road, and therefore with so little traffic, there would be no need for the vehicles to line up side by side by side.

As frustrated Mexican motorists sit in traffic on the Periferico, they get a bird's-eye view of Los Pinos. It is a delicious irony of Mexico that the seat of power in the power-crazy country is located where millions of Mexicans can see it but can never enter. Also, directly across the Periferico from Los Pinos sits an amusement park, with a pirate ship on a pendulum and a creaky wooden roller coaster that is regularly shut down when some unfortunate rider is thrown from one of the cars. After so many decades of one-party rule masquerading as democracy, Mexico became increasingly surrealistic, and it sometimes was hard to tell just where the amusement park ended and Los Pinos began.

✳

Many guests had already arrived at the Los Pinos banquet halls by the time Ambassador Winfield got there. Modern Mexicans can, with effort, adjust their free and flexible sense of time to accommodate northerners, and they know that events such as this, involving fastidious Canadians, will go off more or less on time. Winfield had spent much of the previous hour briefing the prime minister about the situation in Mexico. One question of concern was the likely impact of former Mexico City mayor Manuel Camacho Solís, who was threatening to upset the delicate balance of Mexican political peace by challenging Colosio within the structure of the PRI itself. Colosio also was facing opposition candidates, including Cuauhtémoc Cárdenas, who many people believed had won the 1988 election against Salinas but been denied the presidency by computer chicanery orchestrated by the PRI. But Cárdenas represented an insignificant threat compared with Camacho's raw grab for power.

Camacho was a key member of Salinas's inner group, a frenetic intellectual whose willingness to negotiate with opponents rather than to use his power to crush them had caused chaos in Mexico City. When protesters marched from city squares to the Periferico and caused havoc, Camacho would invite the demonstrators to city hall. Suspicions about his leadership had been raised within the party. Still, Camacho was convinced Salinas would pick him as the PRI's presidential candidate, and on the Sunday in November when he realized he was not Salinas's man, he broke with tradition and refused to congratulate Colosio. Later he resigned in protest and encouraged speculation that he intended to make some kind of end run around Colosio, turning the political scene on its head.

Chrétien wanted to know—as did analysts at the American embassy in Mexico City and back in Washington—as much as possible about Mexico's political struggles. The campaign turmoil was but one factor of concern. Also worrisome was the problem in Chiapas, which had erupted in violence on January 1, the very day—newscasters around the world had reported—NAFTA took effect. Scattered bombings, high-profile kidnappings, and political hostilities had created uncertainty in Mexico that hadn't been seen since the revolution. Camacho had forced a worried Salinas to send him to Chiapas as peace negotiator, and daily it seemed he was stealing the newspaper headlines that by tradition belonged to the Colosio campaign.

Mexico in early 1994 resonated with violence and intrigue, but for the visiting Canadians, the prospects NAFTA had opened overrode everything else. The huge trade fair they had organized was the largest Canada had ever mounted anywhere in the world. More than 450 Canadian companies were so fired up by the trade agreement and the possibilities it raised that they sent representatives on the trip to smoggy Mexico City with fervent hopes of returning with a deal in their pockets. Some 1,500 Canadian businessmen had crowded into a Mexico City hotel that morning to hear Winfield and the embassy staff talk about the new age that was dawning on the American continent, an era of increasing opportunity and prosperity stretching from the Yukon to the Yucatán.

The plan for the first evening of Chrétien's visit called for the prime minister and his wife to be greeted by Salinas and his wife Cecilia in the presidential residence at Los Pinos. From there, the two leaders would cross a gentle patio lined by pines and palm trees to one of the featureless halls that the Mexican government used for formal meetings and state dinners. Together, Chrétien and Salinas would welcome the guests—Canadians and Mexicans alike—and usher in the era of new relations between the two countries that shared a continent with the United States but did not know each other.

Under other circumstances, I might have covered Chrétien's visit, not so much because I expected anything significant to happen but because the assignment would have enabled me to highlight an aspect of continental relations—between Canada and Mexico—that had been largely ignored. However, I didn't plan to write about it because I had my hands full elsewhere. Since the beginning of the year, our office had been split between covering the uprising in Chiapas and monitoring the deteriorating political climate in Mexico City. One thread connecting the two was Manuel Camacho.

When Camacho resigned as mayor of Mexico in pique over Colosio's nomination, Salinas had tried to make amends by naming him foreign minister. Camacho accepted, but he clearly was not satisfied. After a rebel army attacked four cities in Chiapas in the first hours of the first day of 1994, Camacho threatened to resign his new post, saying he would refrain from doing so only if he was given a chance to defuse the Chiapas powder keg. Whether he already had planned to use Chiapas as a platform to challenge Colosio wasn't clear, but Salinas feared that a very public resignation by his foreign secretary would undermine confidence in his government throughout the rest of North America and the world. In the end, Salinas felt he had little choice but to send Camacho to Chiapas, despite the obvious problems this tack would cause for Colosio. He also decided to call off a weeklong counteroffensive that had unleashed Mexican fighter planes over Chiapas and triggered several deadly skirmishes between the Indian rebels and the Mexican army, which is largely composed of dark-skinned mestizos.

Little was known about the rebels in those first confusing days of January. They called themselves the Zapatista National Liberation Army, and their leader addressed stunned tourists and breathless reporters in the plaza at San Cristóbal de las Casas in Chiapas on New Year's Day. They claimed they were going to march on Mexico City and topple the Salinas government, thus ridding Mexico of the grotesque Western values the president embodied.[2] But a few days later, they seemed to switch causes and attacked the injustices suffered by Mexico's Indians. Subcomandante Marcos, a mestizo college professor from northern Mexico who led the rebels, wrote long, clever communiqués to leftist Mexican newspapers that published them in full. Marcos warned Mexico that when it agreed to join the United States in the trade agreement, it left behind its Indians, who represented the genuine soul of Mexico. The Zapatistas tried to make NAFTA a symbol of unfairness and inequality, calling it a "death sentence for Mexico's Indians." Marcos's powerful writing had a deep and immediate impact on the American continent. Just as some Americans saw NAFTA building bridges across the continent, others came to fear that the agreement was plowing a deep channel through Mexican, Canadian, and American societies. To critics, the trade agreement further separated the powerful from the defenseless, the rich from the working poor, the modern from the ancient. Only the rich would benefit because the agreement gave them a free hand to exploit workers. Some complained that the trade deal would lead to the rape of Mexican resources and labor, and then those same critics contradicted themselves by railing against the pact because the poor in states like Chiapas would not benefit from the jobs or economic growth generated by increased trade. Of course, the rest of Mexican society had ignored or exploited the Indians of southern Mexico for a long time before NAFTA came along. Focusing on the trade pact provided government leaders with a protective shield that deflected criticism away from them and onto NAFTA, permitting them to avoid taking direct responsibility for the deplorable conditions in Chiapas.

The controversy over NAFTA and the symbolism that its beginning bore for North America gave Camacho's exploits as peace commissioner great visibility. Through the first three months of 1994, he thoroughly overshadowed Colosio's stumbling campaign. His declarations made headlines on the front pages of Mexican newspapers; Colosio was confined to the inside pages. While everyone in Mexico was caught up in guessing the identity of Subcomandante Marcos, Camacho was regularly photographed talking to the masked rebel. Camacho held court with foreign correspondents in the hotels and restaurants of San Cristóbal, and his staff offered tequila and late-night chats "on deep background" to help reporters understand the peace commissioner's strategy. Indeed, they were creating the aura of a candidate whose campaign was not only historic but inevitable. Colosio, meanwhile, traveled through Mexico in the company of political hacks and colorless handlers, unable to project any of the confidence or authority Mexicans expect from a president, even an as-yet-unelected one.

Camacho never formally declared his candidacy, but as he negotiated with the Zapatista rebels, he subtly encouraged speculation that he would somehow replace Colosio. He argued that this strategy was valid because the impression that he might become a candidate gave him additional stature and greater leverage in talks with the Zapatistas—if they thought he was a potential future president with the power to enforce a peace deal, they would be more likely to listen to what he had to say.

The chaotic start of 1994 had created an uneasy feeling in Mexico, especially among the modern descendants of Montezuma's empire who still live throughout central Mexico—speaking the same language Cortés heard. Native peasants believe in a legend called *las cabañuelas*, according to which the first twelve days of the year dictate the fate and format of the entire year. Campesinos still commonly use *las cabañuelas* to determine when to plant corn and when to harvest it. It works this way: If it rains on the fourth day of January but is dry on the fifth, they are likely to sow their fields in April rather than May to take advantage of the rain.

A Mexican didn't have to believe in *las cabañuelas* to be shaken by the uprising in Chiapas, the related bombings in other parts of the country that were believed to be connected to the insurrection, and the political wrangling that had engulfed Los Pinos, all within the first twelve days of January. And what happened over the next twelve months proved to many that *las cabañuelas* still controlled destiny.

The fiery mix of insurgency and political brinkmanship that had savaged Mexico during the revolution appeared to have been set loose again, and the country, along with its neighbors, was shaken. The bottom had temporarily fallen out of the Mexican stock market, in which Americans and Canadians had invested heavily, and the queasiness that had upset American investors when Cardinal Posadas Ocampo was gunned down the previous May came back in full force. It was as though all of North America was riding the dips and curves of the roller coaster outside Los Pinos, wondering when Mexico's wild ride would end.

✳

The day before Chrétien's visit, Camacho seemed to put the brakes on his own roller-coaster ride. In a room at the same Hotel Presidente where Chrétien would ready himself for his first state dinner in Mexico, the urbane and erratic Camacho announced he was abandoning the candidacy that he had never formally declared. "Between seeking the presidency and contributing what I can to the process of peace in Chiapas, I choose peace," he said. I later rode down the escalator with him, with a huge mob of Mexican journalists in tow. He felt good about his decision, he said; it was the right thing to do. Later he told me he had picked this day of all days to make his announcement because he had learned that the foreign reserves of the Bank of Mexico were sufficient to protect the financial market if investors reacted negatively to the news, an indication of his dramatic sense of self-worth. He still wanted to be president, he said, but not at any cost. He would focus his attention on resolving the conflict in Chiapas and leave the campaigning to Colosio.

Camacho's maneuverings were the reason I had turned down an invitation to accompany Colosio on a campaign swing up to the border city of Tijuana that week. The trip marked Colosio's first visit as candidate to Baja California, one of the few states in Mexico not controlled by his party. The people of Baja California state remembered Colosio from his tenure as president of the PRI. In 1989 he had shocked them by announcing that after almost fifty frustrated years of trying to win a statewide election in any Mexican state, the conservative National Action Party had finally been allowed to succeed in Baja California. Colosio recognized the PAN victory over the objections of local politicians, who could not understand why that election should have been treated any differently from past elections in which the vote was merely a prop for the handoff of power from one PRI strongman to another.

The opposition had been permitted to win because Colosio, and his mentor Salinas, recognized that they had to appear to be straightening out Mexico's corrupt political system if they expected the country to accept the sweeping economic changes that Salinas planned to ram into place during his administration. Salinas knew he had to offer political reform to accompany his radical economic package, but he also knew that political freedoms that evolved too rapidly could cause chaos and revolution, as had happened with the dissolution of the Soviet bloc. Salinas pursued a process of gradual change, to be hinted at in his administration and developed further in that of his handpicked successor.

As Ambassador Winfield opened this window on Mexico for Chrétien, the new prime minister sympathized with Salinas's challenge. In the years since 1988, Canada too had found its old economic operating manual ripped to pieces and thrown into the air. That process of change had threatened Canada's well-being. Mexico's conflict had been internal;

Canada's was more complex because it meant overhauling its relationship with the United States, the part of the world more important to it than any other. The 1989 Canada-U.S. Free Trade Agreement was a seminal event that forced Canada to reset the bearing on its national compass.

For most of the previous century—in essence, most of Canada's existence as a separate, independent nation in North America—the basic orientation of the nation ran from east to west just as did the national railroads. These lines of steel stretched over 3,000 miles through the forest of Quebec and Ontario, through the unbroken plains, through the towering peaks of the Rocky Mountains, and into the drizzly coastal ports of British Columbia. But the country had deliberately kept the rails from crossing the border to far richer American markets. Mulroney had argued that Canada didn't have to throttle its trade in order to defend its national culture. Canada's identity, he vowed, was stronger than that.

Naturally, Canadians worried about being overwhelmed by the United States. As noted earlier, the electorate reacted to these changes by booting out Mulroney's party and bringing in Jean Chrétien and the Liberals. The 1993 election also marked the rise of political regionalism that was becoming as great a threat to Canada's national unity as the separatist movement in Quebec. In the west, the right-wing Reform Party gathered strength from the alienation Alberta and Saskatchewan traditionally felt toward the central government in Ottawa. Reform promised the west greater provincial autonomy, and the idea gained support across that part of the country. In Quebec, many former Mulroney supporters and Conservative Party defectors crossed over to the new Bloc Quebecois, enough of them so that in a remarkable twist of history, the Bloc—whose sole purpose was to oversee the separation of Quebec and the dismemberment of Canada—became the official opposition in Ottawa and the government-in-waiting.

✳

Shortly after he arrived at Los Pinos, Winfield got word that what was effectively Mexico's government-in-waiting had fallen. "A Mexican friend of mine came up to me and said, 'Did you hear? Luis Donaldo has been shot,'" Winfield recalled. A buzz quickly spread through the great hall as the thunderclap of news reverberated. "Everybody was saying *Lo escuchaste?* 'Did you hear?' People were shattered."

On that night, particularly in those first confusing moments after the shooting, Mexico trembled. All the horrible ghosts of its violent past seemed to have been unleashed yet again—Montezuma and his great temple, black and slick with blood; the conquistadores and the wanton slaughter they caused after the Aztecs welcomed them into grand Tenochtitlán; the fanatic generals who led Mexico into its wars with Spain, with France, with an aggressive United States, and in the revolution with Mexicans fighting Mexicans. All those demons howled through the streets again on the night Colosio was killed.

Sketchy details started to come in. Colosio had been shot twice while trying to make his way through a mob of supporters at the bottom of a dusty ravine in Tijuana. It was the kind of place—settled by the common people who were his most faithful supporters—where Colosio felt most comfortable. The first shot, captured on a mysterious police videotape that would be played over and over, like the Zapruder film of the Kennedy assassination, came from a steady hand that rose out of the tumult, pressed an old Brazilian pistol coldly against the back of the candidate's skull, and with a touch of the finger dispatched Mexico's future. The video does not show to whom the hand and pistol belonged. It was a disembodied arm, and because it belonged to no one, it belonged to everyone: The universality let the guilt settle on all of Mexican society that had allowed itself to be caught up so profoundly in the ancient rituals of blood and sacrifice. A second shot sealed the candidate's fate, and Mexico's, because it raised suspicions about conspiracy. (Evidence was so tainted, prosecutors could not prove that both bullets had been fired from the same pistol.)

Colosio died minutes later at the General Hospital in Tijuana. Several people were arrested at the scene, and there is little doubt that the person whose hand was seen on the trigger in the videotape was among them—a dazed, unemployed mechanic named Mario Aburto Martínez, a drifter who dreamed he was an Aztec warrior. In subsequent years, several different prosecutors, some from within party ranks, others brought in by an opposition party attorney general, investigated Colosio's murder but never could explain why Aburto had done it. They raised conspiracy theories, only to scuttle them time and again. Some speculated that the assassination had been intended to send the same message as the killing of Cardinal Posadas Ocampo—Tijuana drug dealers could not be controlled. There were suggestions that the killing had taken place in the state of Baja California because old-line politicians were upset that

Colosio had given it to the opposition in 1989. Others feared a split in the PRI itself, and a violent reaction by the traditionalists who felt betrayed when Salinas had picked another free-marketer, the third consecutive time the PRI's protectionist faction had been left waiting in the wings. But as in the murder of the cardinal ten months before, no explanation satisfied the Mexican people, who could not accept the notion that powerful people were just as vulnerable to violence as they were.

At the time of the assassination, Colosio was a candidate, not yet the president. Still, his death may have been more damaging to Mexico's psyche than had it occurred after he had been sworn into office. The shooting challenged the very system that had seemed to shield Mexico from so much of the violence that plagued Central and South America throughout the twentieth century. The system was driven by single-party rule. That party, the PRI, was so amorphous that it could encompass all the currents of Mexico. Through deft alternation from one ideology to another as the single, six-year term of each president started and ended, the system—one of the most original political innovations to come from Latin America yet one of the greatest obstacles to democracy—managed to keep the peace for almost sixty-five years.

At the head of the system was the president, who governed with nearly absolute autonomy. This was possible because the fine checks and balances in Mexico's revered constitution—honored with a national holiday each February—had been subordinated to the president's will. The legislative and judicial branches of government had been reduced to sounding boards. In image and in practice, the Mexican president was the spiritual descendant of the Aztec emperor who wore the skin of his enemies and could not be directly looked upon by commoners. The devious genius of the system was that real power belonged to the party, not to the men who occupied the presidency. *"El señor,"* which in Mexico refers both to the president and to God, ran every aspect of the country for six years. Then the system demanded he surrender power and willingly be replaced. That left the party in possession of the presidential chair. When he peered into the inner workings of this unique system, Peruvian novelist Mario Vargas Llosa marveled and called Mexico "the perfect dictatorship"—perfect because its totalitarian face was masked by the trappings of democracy. Six decades of uninterrupted rule by the same party—the greatest political winning streak in the world at that time—made evident the brutal truth of Vargas Llosa's claim.

Though it rarely appears to hold true, Mexico stands on essentially the same constitutional footing as the United States. Formally, the country is Los Estados Unidos Mexicanos, the United States of Mexico, and its constitution, now much altered, was modeled on America's when it was written in 1857, and again when it was rewritten in 1917 after the chaos of the revolution. Mexico's constitution takes an enlightened view of the country's violent origins, proclaiming Mexico a multiethnic society where Indians and mestizos all have full rights of citizenship. The streets of Mexico City where whole families of Indians live miserable lives is only one tragedy that proves otherwise. "The problem is that all these books of statutes are filled with the most wonderful laws and protections of any people anywhere in the world," a prominent Mexican lawyer and legislator, Santiago Creel, once told me over strong coffee in his Mexico City study. Creel pointed to the legal volumes that filled the shelves around us, impressively weighty tomes in sober coverings that suggested a firm adherence to order. The laws are based on the constitution, he said, which itself rests on an idealized view of a just and orderly world. But Creel knew the difference between theory and reality, between vague legal concepts and the application of law in a corrupt and autocratic society. "Out there in the streets," he said, nodding toward a window, "these books mean nothing."

Rumors about who was responsible for the Colosio killing began to circulate almost as soon as the shots were fired. As I scrambled to write the first-edition article on the shooting for *The Times*, I took a call from a Mexican political analyst whose judgment I valued. "Just think who stands to benefit from it," he said without hesitation. Colosio hadn't even been declared dead, and here was this analyst spinning a complicated conspiracy theory involving substitute candidates, constitutional restrictions, and palace intrigues revolving around Camacho, President Salinas himself, and Colosio's campaign manager, Ernesto Zedillo. One reason for all the speculation was a phrase in Mexico's constitution that prohibits public officials from running for president within six months of leaving office. With the presidential elections scheduled for August, every member of Salinas's cabinet who was still in office in March was eliminated from consideration. But Zedillo had resigned as secretary of education in November, when Colosio asked him to manage his campaign. The only other member of Salinas's inner circle not eliminated by the constitutional restriction was Camacho, who on becoming peace commissioner in Chiapas had insisted on receiving no salary, which meant he wasn't technically a public servant.

The Mexican capacity to invest in conspiracy theories is limitless. One of the most sinister at the time involved a personal rift between Colosio and Salinas, the man who only months before had selected Colosio as candidate and his likely successor. Though it challenged logic, many Mexicans believed that shortly after the first of January, with attention increasingly focused on Camacho and Chiapas, Colosio came to suspect the president's loyalty. According to the rumor, Salinas had put Camacho into such a prominent role to test Colosio's mettle. That had forced Colosio to move out from under Salinas's shadow. The candidate's speeches of that time can be read in such a way as to suggest a growing desperation as he attempted to establish his own identity as an independent man committed to real political change, putting him into direct conflict with Salinas. The president could no longer abide Colosio's straying from the fold, and when the rift between them grew too wide, the theory went, Salinas ordered the candidate killed.

No credible evidence was found to support this theory, nor was any apparent to the Canadians who were with Salinas on that night almost from the moment he received word of what had happened in Tijuana. Winfield saw a man who "was deeply wounded and affected" by Colosio's death. Salinas wore a dark business suit and his wife was dressed for the state dinner that had been scheduled to start in just a few moments. "You could tell the strain around their eyes, it was graphic," Winfield said. "Mrs. Salinas was with him, looking tragic." Winfield called the Hotel Presidente and notified the prime minister. Chrétien, though upset, insisted on being taken to Los Pinos. "We were the four of us as I recall, my wife and Mr. Salinas's wife," Chrétien told me in an interview in Ottawa years later. When President Salinas entered the room, "he was in shock," Chrétien said. "By that time he didn't know he [Colosio] had died. He had been shot, but we didn't know that he had died." Chrétien told Salinas that the state dinner should be canceled. The president gratefully agreed. "We decided that we would appear and shake hands with everybody. We walked from the residence to where this dinner was to be held. There was a big commotion in the crowd; people were crying. And everybody came to offer sympathy to the president and his wife."

The enormous, clumsy mechanism that is Mexico City continued to function the next day, but on every corner confusion, sadness, and anger reigned. I made my way through the crowds to PRI headquarters where Colosio's body had been taken for viewing. It was the same monumental space where just a few months before thousands had abruptly gathered to hail his selection as candidate. Ordinary Mexicans, thousands of them, pushed into the grim complex of party buildings. Another huge crowd waited at the Gayosso Funeral Home where Colosio's coffin was to be taken for a private service. Chrétien had seen Salinas at Los Pinos that morning for an abbreviated version of a scheduled bilateral meeting. They discussed ways Canadian election officials would help Mexico set the ground rules for the upcoming presidential elections in August. It was mostly protocol by then, with Salinas not wanting to abruptly dismiss the Canadian prime minister on this first important visit, and Chrétien not wanting to overstep the frail boundaries of their new relationship.

Later that day, Prime Minister Chrétien tried to make an appearance at the funeral home. Even with a sizable security detail, he could not make his way through the crowd to see Colosio's widow. On the advice of his security chief, he backed out when the mob seemed to turn angry, not yet aware who Chrétien was. At about the same time, Camacho arrived. In Chiapas, a military security detail had surrounded him as soon as news of the assassination was received, though it was not clear if the guards were there to protect him or arrest him. The crowd at Gayosso began to chant "murderer," intimating that Camacho's presidential ambitions had led him to undo Colosio's candidacy. As they pressed in to impede Camacho's way, Chrétien was caught in the pushing and shoving. When videotape of the incident appeared on Canadian television that night, it looked as if he had been roughed up by the Mexicans. It was an inauspicious start, even under such strange and tragic circumstances, to a new era in continental relations.

Camacho also tried to see Colosio's widow, but she refused to receive him. A political pariah, he returned to Chiapas, but a few months later, with the conflict there still unresolved, he quit as peace commissioner. "From the first days of the conflict in Chiapas, there was pressure on me because people said I was campaigning for the presidency, but all I was doing was working to get a peace settlement," Camacho told me in an interview.[3] He later left the PRI and helped found an independent party with other political outsiders. There is no doubt that his challenge to the system during the first months of 1994 contributed to the climate of tension and aggression that enveloped Mexico at the time. When Aburto was brought to Mexico City after the shooting, the first thing the alleged assassin reportedly said was "I want to see Camacho." The former mayor considered this version of events just another rumor started by the same people who were out to hurt him.

The truth about the assassination probably will never be known, and there probably will never be an answer that satisfies and is accepted by the Mexican people. Any investigation, no matter how thorough or independent, that concludes Aburto acted alone will be rejected. Only a conspiracy satisfactorily explains how the most powerful man in Mexico could be killed, and only that offers any comfort to all those who are themselves powerless. Yet any conspiracy theory can never be proved convincingly because so much of the evidence from the assassination has been tainted, so many mistakes have been made in the investigation, and so many witnesses have been intimidated. Even the scene has been compromised. A few years after the shooting, the ravine where it occurred was paved over and turned into a public plaza.

✳

The Colosio killing epitomized the difficulty of comprehending Mexico. Nothing about it made sense—not possible motives, not timing, not even the physics of the shooting itself. Three prosecutors concluded that the gunman had fired one shot that hit the right side of Colosio's head and then a second shot that struck the left side of his body. Their explanation? Colosio's body had spun around 180 degrees between shots, causing the disparate wounds. The killing was the most troubling mystery I had encountered but certainly not the only one. The multiple contradictions and ambiguities I had found since arriving had undercut my belief in what I thought I knew about Mexico and affected me both professionally and personally. In the school our children attended, a school named for Alexander Hamilton, the students spent several hours a day learning English, and nearly everyone loved listening to American pop music and wearing T-shirts with American trademarks. But the Mexican students constantly teased our kids for being American. I thought we could move into a place like Cuajimalpa to observe the lives of normal Mexicans, but I found that we were the ones being observed. Once the owner of our house sent a crew of workmen to replace the clay roof tiles, a slow process. They were with us a long time. We were warned to keep an eye on them, but it was impossible to ensure that one of us was always at home. One day they told us that while they had the front gate open our cocker spaniel Lucy had slipped outside. We scoured the streets for hours and tried to keep the kids from crying.

The next day Miriam went into the old center of Cuajimalpa to post lost-dog flyers. As she was doing so, a local policeman approached her. He said he thought he had seen the dog. If she told him where we lived, he could bring the dog to us if he saw it again. A few hours later, the policeman showed up with another man who held Lucy in his arms. "I found her wandering in the street," the man said. Miriam was relieved and heartened by what she thought was the basic decency of the people who lived around us. Lucy's rescuer even said that when he saw how frightened the dog was, he took her to a vet. We were happy to pay him the reward we had posted on the flyer. Before we could, he said that someone had offered to buy Lucy from him for ten times that much. "And I had to pay a lot at the vet too," he argued. The policeman, who had been standing at the man's side since they arrived, agreed. It was all lies, of course, and it became clear that rather than a rescue, this was a dognapping, a kind of ruse that also works on the Upper East Side of Manhattan. The difference was that the Cuajimalpa cop was in on the scam and planned to take his cut of whatever we might pay the con man. Miriam's initial admiration turned to anger, and she stood her ground. She got hold of Lucy and paid the original reward. Then she told the policeman and his accomplice that she knew someone in the president's office and would notify him if they didn't leave immediately.

They slunk away.

The petty thieves in our neighborhood knew we were foreigners and thus had marked us as easy prey. Many politicians in the Mexican government tried to do the same. They were solicitous toward foreign journalists from any American newspaper but especially *The New York Times*. When I thought they would object to requests for interviews, they went out of their way to get us whatever we asked for, although most Mexican officials rarely said anything of substance. They were taught always to defer to Los Pinos. For them, the relationship with the press was rather more like a social encounter; they were far more focused on building relationships than providing information. They wanted us to like them and couldn't understand it if we acted as though we didn't. The worst times were at Christmas when gifts poured into the office from government officials. It took us days to return them or to find charities that would accept the perishable food. We drafted notes explaining that we were not allowed to accept gifts, but we were careful to word the notes in such a way as not to insult the officials who sent them.

Around Christmas, many of our friends and acquaintances, Mexicans and Americans alike, joined a mass exodus from the smoggy capital for the holidays. For a few blessed days traffic subsided, and the general chaos of the city diminished. That in itself would have been reason to stay in Mexico, but there was another. A small traveling circus came to Cuajimalpa for the holidays. On Christmas Day, we sat in stiff folding chairs under a musty canvas big top and paid the equivalent of about three cents for a bag of popcorn to watch a ragtag collection of Mexican performers. There was an overweight archer with sore feet who fired arrows at heavily made-up show girls in torn tights standing just inches from us. There was a tiger trainer with sparkling silver caps on his teeth, and there were performing dogs dressed like bullfighters with filthy red capes. And in the single arena around which the chairs had been arranged, a thin old man who must have been eighty years old brought out a small performing elephant. We were close enough to the animal to see that its skin had turned a shade of green from lying in a dung-soiled cage too long. It was all a bit tawdry, but the poor working-class Mexicans around us loved it.

I came to see the circus—though not necessarily this one—as a fitting metaphor for North America. The process of approving and implementing NAFTA made it clear that Canada, Mexico, and the United States shared economic goals and undeniable philosophical links despite the deepest of political and historical differences. The Zapatista uprising and the Colosio assassination, coming so soon after the three nations joined hands, stopped the celebration and made everyone keenly aware of their shared stake in Mexico's future. North America's three nations remained three separate acts, but now they were performing in a three-ring circus under one big top, and what happened in one ring could be seen only in relation to what happened in the others.

✳

Continental politics in North America almost always has followed the same pattern: Only crises, wars, or natural and man-made disasters have made people in the three nations pay attention. Otherwise, North Americans have been content to ignore each other. They raised curtains on the frontiers to block the view and reinforce the common notion that all three countries—which face both the Atlantic and the Pacific Oceans—are independent island nations, separate and apart from the others. In part, this is a result of the three very different political traditions from which the countries evolved.

The underpinning of politics in modern Mexico is the need to have a strong central figure who can maintain order, as though chaos lay ready to pounce from around every corner. This tendency has been manifest in Mexican history from the Aztec emperors to the conquistadores and later the Spanish colonial rulers who were appointed by a king who never once set foot on Mexican soil. Even after Spanish claws were removed from New Spain in the early nineteenth century, this fundamental aspect of power did not change, nor was it challenged. This can't be explained as only the will of dictators. Rather it is a trait of the Mexican character, an elemental part of a society at turns both insular and suspicious.

Understanding Mexican history is more like unraveling a set of Christmas lights than following the course of a straight time line. Like the Aztec calendar that repeated a cycle of fifty-two years, time in Mexico seems circular. Loyalties change, heroes become villains, and enemies turn into allies, over and over and over. Mexico's fight for independence from Spain lasted from 1810 to 1821 and ended with the victory of forces led by a general who had once fought on the side of the Spaniards. After Spain conceded defeat, that same general, Agustín de Iturbide, was crowned emperor of Mexico. The premise behind this action seemed to be that to tolerate any other sharing of power for even the briefest time would invite revolution. Iturbide's empire lasted only one year, and the chaos that followed after he was deposed opened the way for Antonio López de Santa Anna to be welcomed as a hero to lead the country.

The imposition of a dictator to replace a deposed dictator occurred again in the twentieth century. The long reign of Porfirio Díaz, the war hero who helped defend Mexico against French invaders, finally ended with the first stirrings of the Mexican Revolution. The revolution began as a protest against antidemocratic rule but disintegrated into a brawl whose only clear goal seemed to be to return Mexico to a romantic, rural past.

Santa Anna, Iturbide, Díaz, the list of leaders who have fooled the Mexican people into believing they are something they are not, is so long and varied that it makes the mistrust of today's Mexicans comprehensible. This history is what makes reliance on the family a necessity in Mexico, and it is why masks and lies have become the defenses with which Mexicans protect themselves. They are reluctant to show themselves fully, for fear that being known so completely will make them vulnerable. By their reasoning, if you cannot trust the police, the government, the president, or even the church, hiding behind a mask may be the only effective way to protect yourself from lies.

✳

The political foundations of modern Canada were laid down in the eighteenth and nineteenth centuries, but those footings rest on even older systems left by one of the earliest empires to rise and fall on the American continent. After Samuel de Champlain began the systematic exploitation of the northern wilderness in the early 1600s, the French could not simply ignore or obliterate the Indian kingdoms they encountered. The French had not crossed the Atlantic to escape oppression or find the freedom to practice their own religion. Like the Spanish communities, their settlements in the new world were based in large measure not on creating a new society but on enriching the society that existed across the ocean. The desire for fur and the need to conduct trade with the Indians led the early French settlers to work with the Huron and other tribes, just as the Spaniards needed to deal with the Aztecs and other natives to ensure the mines had enough manpower to extract the king's silver and gold. But in New France, what had been originally conceived as a commercial relationship would become, over time, a political and military alliance that helped the empire survive as long as it did.

In all other ways, the French, like the Spanish, chose to create their new-world empire on the basis of exclusion. The French kings determined that their toehold in North America would be governed as a province of France, just like any other province. With rare exceptions, everyone who settled in New France was French, just as almost everyone who settled in New Spain was Spanish for the first three hundred years. The early inhabitants of New France were all loyal to the king, whose concept of an American north was restricted to a compact settlement accommodating the fur trade that so captivated the Paris aristocracy.

This model contrasted greatly with the pattern of settlement in the British colonies of North America. The British vigorously drove out claims of sovereignty by competing foreign powers wherever they found them. Then, once the British claim was secure, the conquered Dutch, Swedish, and even French settlers were allowed to participate in development of the colonies. This willingness to include diverse groups laid the groundwork for a society based on merit instead of origin. A conscientious blacksmith or skilled carpenter was welcome to set up shop no matter where he came from. But in New France and New Spain, foreigners were prohibited from receiving business charters and most other privileges. The most important positions were allotted by rank or nobility, not merit.

Settlers in the British colonies, except the slaves, controlled their own affairs and enjoyed personal, religious, and political freedoms unavailable in Europe. This was possible because Britain's government was the most liberal in Europe at the time. British farmers had begun to switch from small family plots to larger operations that were among the most advanced in Europe, creating a commercial consciousness far more developed than in other European societies. Ideas about individual rights and freedoms contained in the Magna Carta were transported across the Atlantic, though they were imperfectly applied. The Indians on whose land the settlers built their towns were denied inclusion. And slavery was considered economically essential and morally acceptable.

Spain believed its empire in America had to exclude outsiders. Few Spanish maps of North America were published in the 1500s and 1600s because Spain jealously kept to itself all the maritime information it had gathered. Not until the nineteenth century did an independent Mexico loosen its borders and welcome others, including a group of Americans who settled in Texas and quickly developed their own sense of nationhood. Americans fleeing the Civil War and its aftermath found refuge in Mexico, and in the twentieth century Mexico accepted refugees from Germany, the Middle East, and most other Latin American countries, as well as the United States. For a time it was a haven for political refugees from around the world, the most famous Leon Trotsky, the Russian revolutionary, who in 1940 was assassinated in Mexico City by Stalin's agents with the support of the Mexican communist party. The refugees' socialist ideology influenced the Mexican labor movement and hastened the rise of leftist politics that eventually threatened the ruling party's dominance.

Immigration helped shape the politics of Canada as well. After Britain finally won its long war with France and seized control of North America, Canada was opened to immigration. But the few British emigrants who went there were vastly outnumbered by the wave of newcomers who crossed into Canada after the American Revolution. Thousands of Empire loyalists who feared retribution for their support of the British monarch settled in Nova Scotia, Quebec, and what has become Ontario. Their resentment toward the rebellious colonial leaders laid the groundwork for the tenor of anti-Americanism that influenced Canadian politics for the next 200 years. In the late nineteenth and early twentieth centuries, Eastern Europeans settled in the sparsely populated western plains. They brought socialist ideals with them that made agricultural cooperatives acceptable and eventually helped develop the concept of publicly supported medical services, the forerunner of Canada's universal health care.

*

One of the goals Prime Minister Chrétien undoubtedly hoped to accomplish during his trip to Mexico was to make sure that Mexico's borders would be as open to Canadian products as Canada's borders would be to Mexican goods. After Colosio's assassination, he would have to wait for another chance to discuss that topic.

Such chances didn't come up often. Over time, as the borders of North America became less troublesome, boundary problems that cropped up were placed on a long list of international issues. But that wasn't always the case. During the first century of the existence of the United States, our borders were problems of the first order—contentious scars across the continent, points of ambition and violence over which Americans fought and died. For almost a century, Americans zealously pursued the vision of a continental empire running without limit across a majestic land whose bounty and wonders were still unfolding.

Nineteenth-century America's view of its borders was that they should be where America wanted them to be. Both the War of 1812 and the Mexican-American War that began in 1846 were, at least in part, battles over the borders and the expression of a particular time in American history. The interval between the two wars was so brief that one man played a major role in both. General Winfield Scott, a frumpy career soldier and frustrated politician, led troops along the Canadian border in the War of 1812 and, thirty years later, in the war against Mexico. The confrontation with Britain was one the young country had been picking for some time, and in the first years of its existence, the United States Congress heard many debates over the advantages of completely eliminating the British crown from North America.

At the time Scott led troops in the War of 1812, Canada was mostly wilderness, and far more French than British. Only about 75,000 settlers shivered through the unforgiving winter in what is now the province of Ontario; the bulk of the population—around 300,000 at the time—lived in the St. Lawrence valley and the long, narrow seigneurial farms laid out along the river by the French. Scott led attacks on British and Canadian troops on the Niagara frontier, the slender neck of land between Lakes Ontario and Erie. Scott focused on this area because he saw a weakly protected vantage point from which to push back the border. He also feared that an attack here by the British and their Indian allies would drive a wedge into the young American republic.

Difficult though it is to imagine today, at the beginning of the nineteenth century, this inconspicuous flatland near Niagara Falls, with its mild climate and fertile soil, was a hostile international border. Raids were launched on the British military barracks in York, now Toronto, and the decision by an American raiding party to attack the fort and set fire to the small civilian settlement around it led the British to retaliate by storming Washington and burning the White House. But those were among the few decisive actions in the first year of the war, which generally saw only failure, misstep, and incompetence.

At the beginning of 1814, when Scott was made brigadier general of the American army, he returned to western New York to take part in the Niagara campaign. The young officer led a small number of troops on several successful, though not conclusive, battles, including one at the Chippewa River where he was wounded. Small as it was, the victory lifted the spirits of the young country. "Everywhere bonfires blazed; bells rung out peals of joy; the big guns responded, and the pulse of Americans recovered a healthy beat," Scott wrote years afterward.[4]

In the end, the War of 1812 (sometimes known north of the border as the American Invasion) accomplished little but to sow suspicion along the boundary between the United States and the remnant of the British empire in North America. The fear of further American aggression, and the intrigues of American sympathizers in the British colonies who wanted to join the United States, kept parts of the border tense until well into the nineteenth century, and even today anxiety lingers, at least subconsciously, in the minds of some Canadians. When a water main burst under the streets of Hull, near Ottawa, early in 1999, creating a twenty-five-foot-deep crater into which a $450,000 fire truck fell nose first, a local resident exclaimed to a reporter from the *Ottawa Citizen*: "I thought the Americans had fired a cruise missile."[5]

After recovering from his wounds, Winfield Scott surfaced on the southern end of America. By the late 1830s, expansionists in the United States had fixed covetous glances on the weakened and chaotic new Mexican state that had been created after Spain granted independence in 1821. Unlike the Canadian colonies, which were still under the protective wing of Britain, Mexico had been left helpless by Spain. Three hundred years as a colony, governed exclusively by Spaniards who did not share Britain's ideas about individual rights or responsible government, had left New Spain without a trained managerial class, except for the clergy. In the chaos that followed more than a decade of fighting for independence, the Mexican people had merely exchanged one dictatorial power for another. Americans first in Texas, then in the White House, seized on these internal problems to realize long-held expansionist dreams.

After the Texans fought for and were granted independence, a series of expansionist U.S. presidents sought a pretense for "liberating" still more North American territory from Mexico. President James K. Polk, who had campaigned in 1844 on an expansionist platform, was intent on pushing America's borders all the way to the Pacific, even though the land was sovereign Mexican soil. In 1845, he sent an envoy to Mexico City with authorization to negotiate the purchase of Mexican land. The Mexican representatives sent the envoy packing. President Polk allowed the situation to simmer, and then, in March 1846, ordered troops to cross into Texas and advance to the Rio Grande. The Mexican army responded to the aggression and, after building up forces, crossed the river and attacked, killing or wounding sixteen Americans. Avenging the losses became the pretense under which Polk forced Congress to recognize that a state of war existed between the United States and Mexico.

General Scott, by now a powerful figure in Washington, was placed in command of a sizable invasion force. He landed at Veracruz and took the same route of conquest that Cortés used when he and his Indian allies routed the Aztecs 300 years before. Washington had difficulty defending the campaign as anything other than a land grab, and Scott knew this. He had already laid the groundwork for a favorable truce by the time he triumphantly entered Mexico City's Zocalo, the great plaza built atop the ruins of Montezuma's city. Scott wore a plumed hat and had the American military band play "Yankee Doodle." Acting on instructions from Washington, he boldly demanded what amounted to more than 40 percent of Mexico's national territory. In all, the treaty ceded to the United States 529,017 square miles of land—the current states of Arizona, California, Colorado, Nevada, and New Mexico, along with parts of Utah and Wyoming—in exchange for $15 million and the assumption of about $3 million worth of claims against Mexico from people living in these areas.[6]

For some Mexicans, the humiliation was absolute. Lucas Alamán, a historian and leading conservative of the time, put into words the thoughts of many Mexicans who observed Scott's victory, citing the memory of Cortés. "Who could ever have imagined that, three centuries after the death of the great conquistador, the city that he raised from its foundations would be occupied by an army from a nation that had then not even begun to exist."[7]

The unjust war was unpopular in the United States as well, especially since the conquered territory could potentially be opened to slavery. Thoreau combined his outrage against slavery with what he saw happening south of the border:

> When a sixth of the population of a nation which had undertaken to be the refuge of liberty are slave, and a whole country is unjustly overrun and conquered by a foreign army, and subject to military law, I think that it is not too soon for honest men to rebel and revolutionize. What makes this duty the more urgent is the fact that the country so overrun is not our own, but ours is the invading army.[8]

While his army occupied Mexico City, Scott was hard pressed to maintain the morale of his men, who were more concerned with getting paid than forging an empire. Gambling, prostitution, and desertion were problems he had to deal with during the nine-month occupation, for which the United States charged Mexico several million dollars. One measure Scott used to try to buck up his troops was to encourage publication of English-language newspapers. One of these newspapers was called the *North American*. Before he left Mexico, Scott was approached by a delegation of conservative Mexican leaders who encouraged him to declare himself dictator of Mexico, backed by the 15,000 American troops who became civilians as soon as the Treaty of Guadalupe Hidalgo was ratified. Scott, though flattered, said no.

In the 1860s, American ambition once more shadowed both borders. The remnants of both Mexico and British North America peered warily across the frontiers into a United States that was confronting its own demons. British Canada supported the Confederate states in the Civil War not only for commercial reasons but also because it believed that a victory by the South would stop, or at least weaken, expansionist aggression that might be directed at the northern border. The Mexicans, on the other hand, worried that a victorious South, with a mandate to continue slavery, would look for even more of Mexico's territory in which to expand its peculiar empire.

But Mexico could not focus too much on the Civil War because once again it was being convulsed by violence. The big European powers were keenly aware that America's internal conflict would render the Monroe Doctrine unenforceable and provide the cover that the old colonial powers—Britain, France, and Spain—needed to intervene in North America.

With the United States engaged in its own conflict, Napoleon III of France saw a chance to reestablish the new-world empire France had lost to the British a century before, as well as to extend France's influence over all of Latin America. Any aggression by France against Mexico would clearly violate the Monroe Doctrine, but Napoleon III gambled that the United States would be unable to respond while preoccupied with the Civil War. On a pretense of collecting on loans they had made to Mexico, France, Britain, and Spain landed troops at Veracruz. Within a few months, Britain and Spain withdrew, but France pushed on. Though the Mexicans managed some stirring victories, this invasion ended as had all previous invasions. The victorious French, with the help of Mexican conservatives like Alamán, who preferred dictatorial order to chaos, installed a Hapsburg prince named Maximilian as the emperor of Mexico.

Maximilian proved to be a surprisingly dedicated ruler, though astonishingly naive and hopelessly romantic. He introduced some genuine reforms to protect the Indians and to rebuild Mexico City so it resembled a European capital. The ephemeral regent, however, mostly deceived himself. He believed he was respected and well loved and had gained the loyalty of Mexico. None of that was true. He ignored warnings from his Hapsburg relatives in Europe. "They will murder you," one told him.

But as long as he had the support of France, Maximilian believed the empire would not perish.

The most fateful event of Maximilian's reign occurred not in Mexico or France but in Appomattox, Virginia, where on April 9, 1865, General Robert E. Lee surrendered to General Ulysses S. Grant, ending the American Civil War. Napoleon III reviewed his escapade in North America and had grave misgivings about continuing. Instead of the profitable enterprise he had hoped for, Mexico had turned out to be a drain on scarce resources. With war clouds gathering in Europe, Napoleon could not afford a confrontation with the reunified United States over Mexico. On January 15, 1866, he ordered all French forces to withdraw from Mexican soil. Without the protection of French troops, Maximilian's romantic adventure ended abruptly, and tragically. He was captured by troops loyal to the Mexican government in exile and was executed by a firing squad composed of the Mexicans he had believed loved him.

The end of the U.S. Civil War also triggered reactions in Canada. Canadians worried that the huge and victorious Union army might march north in revenge against the British for supporting the Confederacy. Canada was still only a handful of sparsely populated provinces that Britain—far more interested in the riches of India—was not eager to protect. A handful of Canadians believed that unity was the only defense and convoked a meeting of delegates from all the provinces to discuss a national plan. The rhetoric of their attacks on the United States was unrestrained: "They coveted Florida and seized it; they coveted Louisiana and purchased it; they coveted Texas and stole it and then they picked a fight with Mexico which ended up by their getting California," ranted D'Arcy McGee, a rabid supporter of confederation who went on to become one of the few Canadian politicians ever to be assassinated.[9] (He was shot by members of the Fenian Brotherhood, a fanatic group of Irish-American Civil War veterans from the Union army who planned to conquer Canada and hold it until Britain got out of Ireland.)

The delegates met first in Charlottetown, on Prince Edward Island, in 1864. They were a dispirited group without a common goal. The original proposal on the table was to unite the three old maritime provinces: Nova Scotia, New Brunswick, and Prince Edward Island. Later, the delegates considered a proposal to split the existing province of Canada into two provinces, Ontario and Quebec, each with its own language and its system of government. The Charlottetown meeting was held at the same time as performances of the Slaymaker's and Nichol's Olympic Circus, which had returned to the island for the first time in two decades. It was a rare attraction and generated far more interest at that time than the confederation debates.

After several meetings in a number of provinces, the delegates reached a compromise decision to create a largely self-governing nation. Their intention was to have a strong central government and comparatively weak provinces to avoid the kind of conflict that had torn apart the United States. They carved out areas of national responsibility for the federal government and set aside some areas, such as foreign affairs, that would continue to be handled by London, which would continue to provide military support. However, little effort was put into broadly defining a vision for what Canada, as a nation, was going to be. The process of compromise that led to confederation also, in great measure, planted the seed of contemporary Canada's painful search for identity. Today in Charlottetown, a lovely spot on the still largely unspoiled Prince Edward Island, the site where the delegates landed to launch their historic negotiations on forming a nation is marked by a gazebo and a number of plaques, one of which reads: "It was not actually an overwhelming desire for a new nation, but a combination of mutually threatening circumstances, that opened the door to the creation of the Canadian confederation."

The new country, composed of Nova Scotia, New Brunswick, Ontario, and Quebec, was formally established in 1867. Prince Edward Island, where the fathers of confederation had met, didn't agree to join until 1873. From the White House, President Andrew Johnson took note of developments beyond one end of America but was not among the foreign dignitaries to acknowledge the formation of a new nation in North America with so much as a congratulatory telegram.

✳

With his inaugural trip to Mexico in shambles, Prime Minister Chrétien tried to salvage what he could of his time there. Most of the scheduled events had been canceled, and the night of Colosio's funeral Chrétien attended a private dinner with the embassy staff at Ambassador Winfield's residence in Mexico City. He left for Canada the following morning without stopping to see President Salinas, who was already deeply involved in another extraordinary drama.

For the second time in less than six months, Salinas was engaged in the ritual of selecting a successor. This time, the pressures of containing rival factions within the ruling party and of calming a nervous and frightened country made his task immensely more difficult. He had far fewer candidates to choose from because of the constitutional restrictions on government officials becoming candidates. Still, it seemed that every prominent Mexican politician was pushing his favorite. Former president Luis Echeverría had burst into Los Pinos late on the night Colosio was killed to inform Salinas that he thought Emilio Gamboa, a PRI stalwart who had been secretary to President de la Madrid, ought to be the new candidate.[10] In subsequent days, many other PRI notables came forward, each with a name and a personal cheerleading squad.

During those days I was never far from PRI headquarters or the power struggle taking place inside. There were no briefings, no news conferences. This most important of decisions was being made in back rooms and over private telephone lines, and the people of Mexico could only wait and watch. Finally, not yet five full days after Colosio was murdered, PRI headquarters came alive in a different way. Ernesto Zedillo, Colosio's unsmiling campaign manager, was named the new candidate.

Zedillo met the constitutionally mandated time restraint for when public officials can run for office, making him the likely substitute candidate from the start. Even so, Zedillo didn't sit right with many people. He was smart, with an economics degree from Yale University, but he was stubborn and dour and had never run for office before in his life. Most important, he had not been cultivated for the presidency as had Colosio, or Salinas before him, or any of the others in the PRI's stable that had a stranglehold on Los Pinos. He had not had the chance to build up the cohorts of supporters that a PRI candidate traditionally calls on during the campaign. And this background was expected to be an important factor in view of Salinas's own narrow victory in 1988 and a resurgent left led once again by Cuauhtémoc Cárdenas.

Obviously, Zedillo had become candidate by an accident of fate, and he would be an accidental president as well. As I gathered up some biographical notes about Zedillo from the PRI staff at headquarters that day, it was easy to assume that he would become the next president of Mexico, since the PRI had not lost in sixty-five years.

There was no way to know what kind of president Zedillo would be. Nor could I have had much more than an inkling at that time that he would end up playing a transforming role in Mexico's history. Very quickly, events would make Zedillo a catalyst who brought together the three nations of North America in unexpected ways. And the first of these transforming events was already under way, though no one was aware of it at the time.

CHAPTER FIVE

The Crises That Bind

✳

Welcome to the nightmare.

Subcomandante Marcos
letter to President Zedillo, December 1994

U nlike other members of the Clinton administration who looked
stricken and acted uncomfortable whenever they were forced to
parachute into Mexico to respond to one emergency or another,
Lloyd Bentsen, the gangly Texan who was President Clinton's first secretary of the treasury, seemed at ease, even downright comfortable, south
of the border. He smiled like a cowboy and chatted amiably with the
Mexican officials over whom he towered. And even though dark clouds
were gathering on the border during his watch, he was perpetually positive and optimistic.

In September 1994, I met privately with Bentsen at the residence of
James R. Jones, the U.S. ambassador to Mexico. The rambling modern
house of glass and stone overlooks a ravine in the hills above Mexico
City. A quirk of fate has left the American residence sandwiched between the diplomatic compounds of Iran and Iraq. Mexico City officials
used to joke that their major worry was keeping these uneasy neighbors
on diplomats' row from throwing daggers at each other across the fences
that divide them.

Bentsen was on his second official visit to Mexico that year, and despite the troubles that had hung over Mexico at every turn since the first
minutes of 1994, he spoke with a Texan's confidence of the future of the
United States and the trading partner to which it was now bound by a

pact that was law. "This is a great time to be the Secretary of the Treasury of the United States," he had said at a news conference to announce some new cross-border tax information agreement with Mexico. Earlier that year, Bentsen had personally helped Mexico enter the Organization for Economic Cooperation and Development (OECD), which gave Mexico the right to brag that it had finally joined the club of industrialized nations. He praised the president-elect, Ernesto Zedillo, with whom he had dined the previous night, and believed he had paid him a compliment by noting the vigor and speed with which he had decided to adopt the economic policies of President Salinas. "I am encouraged by the continuation of good economic policies," Bentsen publicly declared.

But over tepid coffee served in the ambassador's personal china a short time later, I got Bentsen to reveal a different set of circumstances that he had not been so willing to share openly with reporters in America's new economic ally, a picture of what the new North American relationship was quickly coming to mean for the United States. America's primary strategic interest in Mexico for most of the twentieth century was to keep it stable and calm, and in the pivotal first year of NAFTA, the United States had already been forced to back up its commitment to Mexico's peace with money not once but three times.

President Salinas had bet his administration on NAFTA, and Bentsen acknowledged that the Clinton administration had worried about Mexico's economic future if the trade pact had been defeated. At the last moment before the crucial congressional vote in Washington, Bentsen helped pull together a $12 billion contingency plan to shore up the peso and support the entire Mexican economy if need be. Half the money would come from the United States, and the other half from a consortium of European banks.

The congressional vote in favor of NAFTA allowed Bentsen to shelve the financial life preserver he had been prepared to toss to Mexico. As a precaution, however, the legal papers authorizing the aid were kept up-to-date. It turned out to be a wise move. When Colosio was assassinated in March 1994, the rescue plans were dusted off and quickly shuttled to and from Washington and Mexico City for signatures by Bentsen and his Mexican counterpart, Pedro Aspe—a collector of classic Ford Mustangs who was the silver-haired symbol of Mexico's economic prowess. The fear—an overriding and real worry—was that the Colosio shooting would spook investors and strip the confidence they had only begun to have in Mexico. An incident like Colosio's death could trigger a run on Mexico's foreign reserves—which at the time were a well-guarded secret officially revealed only three times a year—as foreign investors turned in their pesos for dollars, marks, or yen.

Within hours of Colosio's death, Bentsen managed to make the $6 billion U.S. line of credit available to the Mexicans once again. The Europeans were slower to react, and their part of the original $12 billion package could not be revived immediately. In a surprising show of the strength of Mexico's financial institutions, and the high regard with which Aspe was then held by the global financial community, the economic disruption caused by the assassination was brief. Salinas declared a period of national mourning that allowed the banks to close for a few days. By the time they reopened, the panic had burned itself out.

Still, there was more trouble ahead. Mexico was moving nervously toward the national elections in August. The results would be an indication of how much damage had been done to Mexico's national psyche by the violence in Chiapas, the killing of Colosio, and the internal chaos within the PRI stemming from Manuel Camacho's renegade run for the presidency. Recalling how badly the 1981 Mexican debt crisis had hurt other markets, the European banks finally complied with their side of the original economic security package and authorized $6 billion in backup loans for Mexico in case the going got rough after the election. Together with the $6 billion line of credit the United States had put up in March, Mexico had a cushion of up to $12 billion to calm frightened investors and protect its economy.

Mexican intellectuals resented the U.S. aid. To them, Washington's repeated bailouts of Mexico showed how America propped up the corrupt ruling party and, by extension, the forces preventing Mexico from achieving true democracy. Sergio Aguayo, a security analyst at the Colegio de México and one of the country's most outspoken democracy activists, argued that without this kind of American support, the PRI would have crumbled once and for all, clearing the way for the democratic transition that had eluded Mexico for so long. America was widely perceived as the PRI's bodyguard, and when groups of campesinos came to Mexico City to protest anything from farm subsidies to land distribution policies, they marched in front of the American embassy.

The opposition charged fraud and interference in the 1994 election, but it did not seriously contest Zedillo's victory. The Mexican economy was unhurt, and the ritual of one ruling-party president passing his enormous power to another ruling-party president was about to be repeated. Bentsen carefully explained to me during our conversation that although it had been necessary to have economic life preservers ready again, none had been used. Not yet anyway.

Although he didn't tell me about it then, Bentsen had received memos from his staff warning that the Mexican peso was on shaky ground again, as it had been at the end of the previous two administrations. The weakness of the peso was a badly kept secret. Some economists, particularly Rudiger Dornbusch of MIT, were openly urging Mexico to devalue the peso, and they warned of catastrophic consequences if it delayed. Others recognized all the warning signs but hoped against hope that Mexico's economic team—the envy of the third world—would be able to pull off one more miracle, as had been the case so many times in the previous five years. On the streets of Mexico City, ordinary Mexicans were preparing for the worst. In their minds, the Bank of Mexico's plan to release large new bills of 200- and 500-peso denominations was a sign that the government planned to shrink the value of the peso.

Bentsen kept his optimistic public face right to the end. Two months after our conversation at Ambassador Jones's house, with just days to go before Zedillo took office, the Mexicans called on him to lend a hand to their campaign of confidence. Undersecretary of Treasury Lawrence Summers worked through the night with his Mexican counterpart, Guillermo Ortiz, to draft upbeat remarks Bentsen could make to show his support for the economic policies of the new Zedillo administration. In one of his final official acts as treasury secretary, Bentsen issued another confident statement about Mexico, but even his boundless optimism could not overcome the impact of the disturbing events that would evolve over the next few weeks. It would be up to Bentsen's successor, Robert Rubin, and Summers to guide efforts by the United States and Canada, along with other allies, to reinforce Mexico's financial system and manage one of the most significant economic crises in the twentieth century, a precursor to a frightening new cycle of global economic firestorms whose flames would whip almost instantaneously around the world and scorch the heartland of North America.

Bentsen was not the only public official who had failed to warn investors about what was coming, in part because so much had been riding on Mexico's continued success. NAFTA had become one of the few clear foreign policy achievements of the Clinton administration, and Washington did not want anything to interfere with its smooth implementation, even though by then people knew the trade deal had been so oversold that it could never live up to expectations. During the fractious debates preceding the congressional vote in 1993, the White House enthusiastically touted NAFTA's benefits whenever the legislation was challenged. In reaction, free trade opponents drastically hyped the dangers the deal represented, which led the White House to even more exaggeration about the expected benefits. The eleventh-hour addition of side agreements on labor and the environment placated opponents enough to get the bill through Congress, despite clear indications that the mechanisms they contained were not likely to protect much. NAFTA and the shadow it would cast on the U.S. economy had assumed monstrous proportions.

Most serious analysts predict that NAFTA will have to be in effect a decade or more before the real impact of the agreement can be measured. Even so, before the first year was out, businesses, unions, and civic activists in all three countries were complaining that NAFTA gave the other partners unfair advantages. Canadians griped about American imports, Americans criticized cheap Mexican labor, and Mexicans suspected the United States of unfairly dumping products and manipulating markets. I took these reactions as a sure sign that the agreement was working because it met the journalistic fairness test. If everyone mentioned in an article complains, and not just one side or the other, the writer can assume the article came close to hitting the truth.

That test still didn't fully explain matters. Wasn't NAFTA supposed to prevent such squabbling by eliminating *all* barriers to cross-border business? Of course, if NAFTA was supposed to do that, the agreement would have been one page long and simply stated that all trade could move unhindered across the borders. Instead, the text of the agreement filled volumes. Each country fought for and won concessions and special considerations. Mexico protected its farmers by winning a fifteen-year exemption from the tariff elimination schedule for corn, the most important part of the diet of most poor Mexicans, and the primary crop for the country's 1 million small family farms as well as the 1.5 million rural farmsteads on which campesinos usually could coax out just enough corn and beans to feed themselves. The corn exemption was designed to keep corn prices higher in Mexico than they are on the world market (sometimes as high as 70 percent above the world rate). Only the government pays the higher price because with few exceptions only the government buys Mexican corn. In effect, this means the corn exemption amounts to a continuing subsidy for the most impoverished parts of the Mexican economy, at least until American corn floods into Mexico.

The United States won important concessions for its tomato growers, and these protections have been constantly attacked by big farmers in northern Mexico whose capacity for producing and selling winter tomatoes is limited only by the agreement. Canadians thought they had wrested a firm commitment from the Americans to exclude culture from the free market, but early experience showed how differently the two nations see some things. The pact allows Canada to protect its culture industry by taking actions such as limiting the number and type of American magazines that cross the border. But when that happens, the United States has the right to retaliate, which it did when Washington challenged Canada's campaign against the Canadian edition of *Sports Illustrated* in 1996 and won.[1]

In economic terms, NAFTA would prove to be far more important for the two smaller countries than for the United States. A few years after NAFTA took effect, the American market accounted for more than 80 percent of Canada's export trade, but Canada made up only 20 percent of America's international business. Mexico sent more than 85 percent of its exports to the United States, but that represented only about 10 percent of the imports Americans bought. Overall, Canada's economy was only one-tenth the size of America's; Mexico's one-twentieth. More than half of all U.S. manufacturing exports to Canada and U.S. imports from Canada were produced by international companies, which meant that U.S. corporations benefited when the border was crossed in either direction. American corporations, particularly the auto companies, had a powerful presence in Mexico as well and reaped the benefit from any increases in exports or imports across the Rio Grande. Cross-continental commerce between Canada and Mexico was so small that it was assumed NAFTA could only help it grow.

The constant pounding that Mexico had taken at the beginning of 1994 eased unexpectedly that August just when it had been expected to peak because of the election. Deep in the forest of Chiapas, Mexico's newest romantic hero put on a star-studded show that brought down the house—but not the government that was its intended target.

The ragtag Zapatista army had turned from guns to shovels as they fought on with their most effective weapon, their self-created public image, which they had managed to distribute widely and effectively throughout North America and, indeed, around the world. Led by Subcomandante Marcos, the Zapatistas had not fired a shot since the first ten days of January, but they managed to taunt the Mexican army and to keep themselves on the world stage. Marcos had many more skills as a communicator than as a military commander. The government was not afraid of the Zapatistas' firepower, but it was taking a beating in world opinion because Marcos had so successfully portrayed his Indian followers as symbols of the struggle against free trade and globalization. His literary skills were exceeded only by his impeccable sense of timing, first displayed when he selected the first day of NAFTA (and one of the quietest news weeks of the year) to launch the uprising in Chiapas and catch the world's attention.

Marcos recognized that the greatest weakness of Mexico was its fragile image as a Latin American nation desperate to climb from the third world to the comfortable plateau already occupied by its new North American partners. Repeated Zapatista attacks on that image not only cost Mexico prestige and standing. They also curtailed the foreign investments that kept the economy going.

Indeed, Marcos understood Mexico's history and its psyche far better than did the people in Los Pinos who were determined to stop him. His real name was believed to be Rafael Sebastián Guillén, and before he went to the jungle, he was a radical 1980s university professor in Mexico City. His great success was creating a persona that gave him the kind of identity Mexicans had demanded of their leaders for ages. He clearly was leader of the Zapatista army, although he made a not terribly convincing show of claiming that he took orders from a committee of Indian elders. He hid his face behind an itchy black ski mask, recalling one of the most basic symbols of Mexico, a country where the truth is often hidden behind masks. (Masks also are cultural artifacts in Mexico, used in many ceremonies and on many holidays. We once visited a museum in the lovely colonial city of Zacatecas that contained nothing but hundreds of ceremonial masks.) With his mask, false name, and ambiguous title, Marcos could assume a universal Mexican character—the solitary rebel battling against the powerful on behalf of those who are powerless, the selfless hero who fights for everyone else under the banner "Everything for you, nothing for us." He became an Internet Zorro and a larger-than-life version of "The Saint," the masked wrestler who was a Mexican television and movie hero in the 1950s and 1960s. He was funny and unpredictable, learned and surrounded by myth, including the notion that women found him mysterious and irresistible. He was the perfect character in a movie script.

All of Chiapas was his movie set, but when that was not enough, he built his own stage. The site he picked for it was the dense tropical forest behind the Zapatista headquarters of Guadalupe Tepeyac (named for Mexico's patron saint, the Virgin of Guadalupe, who appeared to the dumbfounded Indian Juan Diego at a rocky outcropping called Tepeyac in the Valley of Mexico in 1531, just when the church in New Spain most needed a miracle). In Tepeyac, Marcos built a crude platform large enough to display Zapatista ideals and his growing persona. He rejected the terms of a peace settlement offered by the Mexican government, then announced that the Zapatistas would hold a preelection convention in Chiapas. He invited supporters of democracy to join the Maya in planning the future of Mexico. His scheme captured the popular imagination in Mexico as a kind of tropical Woodstock that would attract leftists, anarchists, and revolutionaries from throughout the hemisphere and around the globe.

Marcos had taken to calling the project his "Fitzcarraldo," after the Werner Herzog movie about a deranged visionary who futilely attempts to drag a large steamer, piece by piece, into an inland Peruvian lake. Marcos's main stage was a hillside outside Guadalupe Tepeyac, not far from the spot where a few months before the Zapatistas had released the seventy-year-old former governor of Chiapas, Absalón Castellaños Domínguez. The old man had been captured at his sprawling ranch during the first days of the uprising and was held captive until he was convicted by an Indian tribunal of crimes against the Maya. Marcos and his commanders had stripped the hillside of lush tropical vegetation and, while surrounded by heavily armed Mexican troops who had not returned to their barracks since the first days of 1994, had managed to terrace the slope and build row after row of crude benches to hold thousands of convention delegates. Over all of it they had draped a huge plastic awning made of tarps stitched together by the Maya. Some of the tarps had clearly been supplied by the government and bore the imprint on their undersides to prove it.

The army kept the Zapatistas encircled, but the government obviously was willing to help. How else could the high-intensity lights and heavy-duty generators have been hauled into the jungle without the army's knowledge? In addition, the long, tortuously rutted dirt road through the forest leading to Guadalupe Tepeyac had been leveled, widened, and repaired with heavy equipment that the Zapatistas certainly did not own.[2] The obvious question was why the state government, with a strong push from Los Pinos, would provide Marcos with such a platform after he had rejected offers for a negotiated peace. Part of Mexico City's strategy for dealing with the Zapatistas had been to encourage them to become political activists, perhaps even to form an opposition party. The Mexican government had many years of experience manipulating small opposition parties that existed primarily to give elections the appearance of democracy. Many of the parties received all their funding from the government, and were so captive to the PRI's power structure that they became little more than props convenient for showing election observers from other countries that Mexico tolerated different expressions of political will.

As Marcos craved a bigger and brighter spotlight, he grew more pragmatic. He accepted the government's assistance because it fit neatly into his scheme, and he never imagined he would be contaminated by it. Marcos also was stamping the Zapatista movement and the democratic convention with his concept of democracy. He ordered reporters to be screened, and he barred those from news organizations he considered hostile to the Zapatista cause. He rigidly controlled access to the site, which he called Aguascalientes, after a gathering convoked earlier in the century by the original Zapata and his revolutionaries. No private vehicles were allowed in the Zapatista territory. Every reporter and every delegate had to travel on buses chartered by Zapatista sympathizers. Amado Avendaño, editor of the small Chiapas newspaper *Tiempo*, had been put in charge of selling tickets. Avendaño had abandoned all journalistic objectivity after he became one of the first reporters to talk to Marcos. His newsroom became the conduit for Marcos's lengthy bulletins and the most reliable way to get messages to the rebel's jungle hideout. He embraced the Zapatistas so fully that he went on to become their candidate for governor of Chiapas. Even though Marcos blackballed many reporters, the bizarre caravan still totaled 170 buses. The first one pulled out of San Cristóbal at ten o'clock on a Sunday morning and rolled into Guadalupe Tepeyac—just ninety miles away—more than thirty hours later. Even the government bulldozers hadn't been able to make the winding dirt track much more than just passable.

For the government, the August convention was a blessed relief. Coming as it did two weeks before an election in which the PRI had good reason to fear that voters would blame the party for everything from the fighting in Chiapas to the assassination of Colosio, the gathering vented the frustration and tension that might otherwise have been expressed at the polls. There in the jungle, political struggles seemed a distant worry—armed Zapatista soldiers strolled through Aguascalientes, and music blared over the huge loudspeakers. The only commercial enterprise allowed into the convention grounds was an employee-owned bottling company that had Marcos's permission to sell boxes of tamarind, guava, and other tropical juices. The Zapatistas had even built a library in one hut made of sticks. They filled it with old books, including the nine volumes of the *Writings of Che Guevara*, all neatly organized and catalogued in the Dewey decimal system.

Finally, on Monday night, after interminable hours of Mexican *rancheras* and Zapatista speeches, I was behind Marcos's great stage when I caught sight of a small squadron of Zapatistas emerging from the forest. They walked single file ahead of one figure a good head taller than the rest. He wore what had become a familiar costume—the ragged khaki cap with three communist stars, the black ski mask, the bandoliers of large-caliber bullets. He had an unlit pipe between his lips. I rushed over and called to him from just inches away, but he was in a trance, like a rock star before a concert, blocking out everything but the stage.

This was his biggest audience. Although his visage had been flashed around the world, he had been living clandestinely in the forest for a decade and had never stood up before so many people. This night a few thousand supporters had come to his fortress in the rain forest to hear him speak. Displaying the bravado and a touch of the exhibitionism that would taunt Mexican officials for years to come, Marcos took the stage. Behind him, two enormous Mexican flags formed a dramatic backdrop, giant green and red wings that carried the aspirations of the Zapatistas and their followers. Marcos touched all the familiar themes—the corrupt government, the majestic integrity of the Indian people, the injustice of a system that fawned over foreign trade but turned its back on Mexico's profound poverty. Repeatedly he called for immediate change.

Marcos insisted that the National Democratic Convention would be a forum run by the delegates, not by him. But he was reluctant to give up the spotlight. After he finished his speech, he ordered a battalion of Zapatista soldiers to parade in front of the stage, stomping their boots on a pad of concrete that had been poured there to amplify the sound. Then he handed the gavel to Rosario Ibarra, a leftist member of congress whose son had years before been taken into custody by the government and never seen again, and left the stage. He didn't go far. He stood just below the dais, where he remained at the center of attention. The audience sent up gifts and many handwritten notes. He was a star, a figure larger than life. Finally, as thunder ominously shook the ground, he turned from the adoring crowd.

His timing was near-perfect. As he left, the skies over Aguascalientes rumbled and then ripped apart. It was the kind of summer tempest that everyone should have expected during the rainy season in Chiapas. As the rain hammered the huge tarp, people hurdled over the rows of benches to reach sturdier shelter. The tarp flapped and filled with rain, its bulbous underbelly inching closer to the people below. When one corner broke loose, rainwater gushed through and hit the electric lights. They sparked and short-circuited. Metal guy lines that held up the tarp began to snap. The people still left on the higher rows of the hillside benches had to push aside the tarp to keep from being smothered by it. It tore in pieces, and we all rushed the stage, looking for dry spots among the rough wooden timbers that supported Marcos's platform. Everyone and everything was soaked, and the rain continued to descend in curtains. The Zapatistas had built a few open-sided dormitories large enough to shelter about fifty people each, but everyone else scrambled for the tents they had brought with them on the buses. I made my way back in the dark to find my tent nearly covered by a mudslide. I grabbed a few dry notebooks from a bag and looked for a place to wait out the storm. I found room under the thatched roof of a juice stand with some other people. There, during an inundation almost biblical in its ferocity, I met a short, slight, soft-spoken Maya soldier whose name was Noé.

He was twenty-three, the father of three children. His new green uniform was drenched, as was the bandolier of shells he wore over his chest. When he came close, I could see they were .22 caliber, some already spent cartridges. His rifle was an old single-action .22 that he had painted green. Noé told me he had used the gun for hunting and scaring critters from his fields before he joined the Zapatistas two years before. The rifle's shoulder strap was a length of rope. He shivered so badly that he had disobeyed orders and popped into the juice stand to get out of the downpour. He took a cigarette. As he smoked he eyed the poncho a woman was wearing. "How much did that cost?" he said in the simple Spanish used by the Indians of Chiapas. They relied on the subjunctive tense because it was easiest to conjugate, even though doing so made them sound compliant and meek. I had on a rain jacket, but I also carried a poncho, which I gave him. He insisted on knowing the price, but when I told him just to take it, he let me slip it over his head.

As he warmed up we talked, and slowly he began to tell me about himself. He said he was from Las Margaritas, the last town the bus caravan had passed through before entering the rain forest. Like most other Indians in the area, he grew coffee for cash and corn and beans for subsistence. Over his two years in the Zapatista movement, he had returned home many times to tend the crops—a Maya minuteman. He said he sold his coffee for 3 pesos a kilo that summer, roughly 50 cents a pound, which was twice as much as he had received the year before but still barely enough to live on.

I later discovered that this failed commercial opportunity, more than NAFTA, was the source of some of the Indian outrage that fed the Zapatista movement. Noé's experience was a pattern repeated over and over among the Maya of Chiapas as they had tried to get their share of the benefits from the Mexican Revolution. Of course, the conflict stood for something far greater than coffee plants or yearly profits—it represented the abandonment of an entire people.

As the first great social movement of the twentieth century, the Mexican Revolution was notable for what it had promised—not a bright future but a return to a simple, agrarian past. It was not an ideological revolution so much as a reactionary one, triggered by pent-up frustrations against Porfirio Díaz's long, reckless march into modernization and the twentieth century. At first the man who led the opposition to Díaz, Francisco I. Madero, promised that the dictator would be replaced by democracy. Díaz, by then an old man, had been a hero in the patriotic war against French intervention in the mid-1800s. He recognized the extent of the feelings against him and stepped out of the way, leaving for exile in Paris—where he still is buried because Mexicans have repeatedly denied his descendants permission to bring back his remains.

Deposing the dictator was simply the first step in a contest for power. Madero, an upper-class hacienda owner educated in the United States who felt he had been chosen by God to lead the Mexican people, was arrested and murdered. The democratic ideals he stood for were replaced with a lust for power and a longing for simpler times. Strong men rose up in the north and the south with revolutionary aims of their own. Francisco Villa thundered out of the northern hills with a vague plan for power. Emiliano Zapata rose from Mexico's Indian south to restore the strong ties common Mexicans once had with their land, even if those ties were likely to keep Mexicans uneducated, unhealthy, and poor. They fought not to create the future but to redeem the past, the same dream that seemed to motivate Marcos. Eventually, as the struggle for power among the revolutionaries intensified, Zapata had to be eliminated, and the most conservative forces, led by another strong man, Venustiano Carranza, took control. Carranza was killed when he tried to flee Mexico, and Villa years later was assassinated too. Some of their idealistic aims survived in the 1917 constitution, particularly Zapata's themes of land and liberty. The government was empowered to confiscate large holdings from rich hacienda owners and distribute them to any peasant who asked for land.

By 1964, 25 percent of Mexico's national territory had been given away.[3] Very little of that land was productive, and almost none of it was in the state of Chiapas. Mexico's poorest and most remote state never enjoyed the freedom that had been promised by the revolution or the new constitution. Despite restrictive laws, some foreign owners had figured out how to maintain control of huge plantations, and kept for themselves the best bottomlands and most fertile soils of the state. As the land redistribution system exhausted the rest of the country, pressure for land grew in Chiapas. Finally, the government stepped in and announced it was breaking up the big plantations, expropriating farms and rich grazing land. To foil this attempt, many of the big landowners simply divided their ranches into many smaller parcels and registered them in the names of family members, feigning compliance with the law. The land distributed to peasants usually consisted of steep slopes in the highlands and practically inaccessible parcels deep in the forest near the border with Guatemala. Almost none of it was appropriate for settlement or farming without a great deal of public assistance. The government cut a few dirt roads through the underbrush and encouraged Indian settlers to plant coffee because prices were high at that time. A system of warehouses and itinerant buyers, called *coyotes,* sprang up haphazardly. But coffee prices collapsed, and the thin layer of topsoil in the forest was easily depleted. The Indians were left in a foreboding poverty that made many feel abandoned and worse off than before. Many other factors contributed to the rebellion, including the local Catholic diocese's espousal of liberation theology, which condoned activism—even violence—to right injustices against the poor and oppressed. But the crisis of land was one of the deepest wellsprings of dis-affection that Marcos tapped as he recruited followers, including people like Noé, who believed him when he said things would change.

Once the shooting started, for Noé and for many others the uprising became a struggle that would not be resolved by anything but a settle-ment that included Zapata's promised land and liberty. In Chiapas, lib-erty meant self-rule. "We don't want just any kind of peace," Noé told me as the rain dripped around us and the ground turned to fetid mud. He said there would have to be justice before the Zapatistas quit fighting for good. "We will never give up our weapons. Not me, not my friends, not Marcos." We talked for a while longer, and then he abruptly said it was time for him to leave. I offered him a sleeve of the crackers I had brought on the bus trip from San Cristóbal. He said he was hungry, but he put them in his shirt. Then he gave me an *abrazo,* a hesitant version of the embrace that Mexican men use to greet each other or say good-bye. He asked my name and I told him, twice, as if he had trouble be-lieving that our encounter was taking place. He then slipped off into the darkness, softly as he had come.

The remnants of Marcos's great tent clapped in the wind; the rain had stopped, but the trees continued to shower us with cold drops. The ground that only hours before had been dusty and hard had become a lake of mud as gooey as latex paint. The following day, Rosario Ibarra tried to rush the delegates through an abbreviated agenda, but the skies threatened to open up again. By late morning the historic gathering of leftists and democrats from around the world who were to have planned the future of the great nation of Mexico had to close gracelessly so the buses could get out before the rain began. Delegates were encouraged to leave behind their tents, sleeping bags, and anything the local people might use.

Among the last people to board the buses were twenty-seven Ameri-cans who had traveled to Chiapas for the convention. Cindy Arnold of El Paso, Texas, was one of them. She had spent the morning sorting through the garbage to separate recyclables from organic material. "The reason we came is we know that what happens in Mexico has a tremen-dous effect in the United States," she said with high spirits and firm con-victions. She felt a noble and worthy solidarity for the cause in which she said every American, by virtue of NAFTA, now had a larger stake. Cindy was physically and emotionally spent by the experience of being at Aguascalientes, but she also glowed with the kind of innocent and naive optimism that overcomes certain Americans and Canadians when dealing with Mexico. They have an emotional blind spot—bordering on paternalism—that prevents them from seeing the true complexity of events across the border. She surely returned to Texas to tell other supporters all that had happened in the jungle, greatly inflating an event that turned out to be more important for what it did not do—bring together a united opposition to challenge PRI hegemony—than what it managed to accomplish—prove Marcos's star quality. But to Cindy and many others, the Revolutionary Woodstock in Chiapas was "what the whole struggle in Mexico is about." And something about which Americans should care.

✳

The next time I saw Aguascalientes, snapped guy lines and shreds of canvas were all that remained of Marcos's Fitzcarraldo. The wooden benches were being reclaimed by the forest from which they had been cut. A Mexican general, fifty-five-year-old Ramón Arrieta, spoke to me and to other reporters near the stage where Marcos had told his adoring audience that he was willing to shed more blood and cause more deaths (at least 145 had already died on both sides) if that's what it took to bring democracy to Mexico. But by that time, in February 1995, General Arrieta was boasting that the government had Marcos on the run. The election was over, and Mexico had a new president, a new cabinet, and a new multiheaded crisis to be added to what Marcos called "the long nightmare known as the history of Mexico."

In the eyes of most Mexicans, Ernesto Zedillo had simply stumbled into the presidential chair after Colosio was murdered. He had campaigned with little enthusiasm but was seen as a safer alternative than any of the opposition candidates. Chiapas, Colosio, Camacho, and all the other crises unleashed at the beginning of 1994 had left Mexico wanting not change but stability, and the PRI offered constancy like no other party in the world. Zedillo took the oath of office on December 1 without having gained the confidence of the Mexican people. They considered him weak-kneed, and though he preached democracy and legality, Mexicans on the street clearly wanted someone to impose order.

It was an unpromising start, similar to the difficult beginning Salinas had faced in 1988 when it was widely believed that he had lost the election to Cárdenas but the PRI's computer chicanery turned it into a win, one of the party's most tainted and unpopular victories. To convert the people to his side, Salinas launched a dramatic offensive within a few weeks of taking office. He sent the army to arrest one of his personal nemeses, the corrupt leader of the oil workers union. By acting quickly and decisively, Salinas proved to the Mexican people his ability to take control.

Zedillo needed a strategy just as bold to establish himself, but before he could take any initiative, he was forced to chase the wily rabbit once more. Just a few weeks after Zedillo's inauguration, Marcos announced that Zapatista troops had broken out of the Mexican army's cordon and seized thirty-eight municipalities in Chiapas, declaring them all under the control of a rebel government led by the Zapatista high command and Amado Avendaño, the journalist from *Tiempo,* whom Marcos had made governor of the state in rebellion.

Marcos taunted Zedillo. "Welcome to the nightmare," he wrote in a December 1994 communiqué to Zedillo that *Tiempo* and every other Mexican newspaper published. It marked a drastic turnaround from the tranquil days of the democratic convention when it seemed that Mexico had played itself out on violence and rebellion. The latest Zapatista advance had more propaganda value than military merit, but it was enough to scare international investors who, anticipating major trouble, had already started taking their money out of Mexico.

Many factors contributed to the evolving financial crisis: Mexico's current account deficit was worsening as the government paid out more in debt and interest than it took in from direct foreign investment in the Mexican economy. Foreign reserves were dwindling. Burned in the last several changes of administration when both Presidents José López Portillo and Miguel de la Madrid had abruptly devalued the peso—despite repeated promises that they wouldn't—wary investors had already started looking for a safer haven. Indirectly, they were making the devaluation they feared almost inevitable. The sliding exchange rate established by Salinas had devalued the peso by about 10 percent, in an orderly, almost unnoticed fashion, since the beginning of the year, but because of all the other pressure on the economy, that wasn't enough. Still, Salinas insisted there would be no disruptive devaluation like the previous ones, not on his watch. He was determined to go down in history as a president who had not left behind a battered Mexico. With encouragement and offers of assistance from U.S. and Canadian politicians and officials, he also was lobbying for the presidency of the newly formed World Trade Organization, a position he believed would represent the ultimate recognition of his singular role in modernizing Mexico.

After Salinas rejected a plan for a devaluation in November, it was up to Zedillo and the new cabinet to handle the growing economic mess. Zedillo's view of the peso's vulnerability had changed substantially. During an interview the day after the election, Zedillo told me that the peso was rock solid. "Despite the difficult moments we experienced this year, the monetary policy functioned very well," he said. Zedillo discounted the need for change. "The evidence before us shows quite clearly that the exchange rate policy we have followed is the correct one."4 But by the time he met with Salinas in November, Zedillo strongly favored a devaluation. A key member of his economic team told me they had gambled that they could make it through the end of 1994 before making a major adjustment. One reason for their optimism was the peculiar payroll practice of many Mexican businesses. Most Mexicans are paid in cash at the beginning and middle of every month, the days known as *la quincena*. That not only was an invitation for thieves, but it also put pressure on cash reserves and caused a surge in buying, for which the stores prepared by stocking up on imports. After Zedillo took office, only one *quincena* remained before the new year, and most people were busy buying Christmas gifts, which the stores had imported long before. Zedillo's advisers thought that if Mexico's financial troubles hadn't cleared up early in the new year, the peso could be devalued then, when it was far less likely to cause disruption.

Mexico had limped through the first *quincena* of December, and there's no way of knowing what would have happened next had the Zapatistas not launched their offensive at the end of that month. The Mexican economy still suffered from many fundamental weaknesses, and I was in the American embassy talking about those soft spots and Mexico's outlook for 1995 when Marcos announced that the thirty-eight towns in Chiapas had been taken. It was a preposterous claim, given the sorry state of the Zapatista troops, but a nervous and frustrated Zedillo lost his patience and sent in the troops.

I left immediately for Chiapas, rented a jeep there, and, with Dudley Althaus of the *Houston Chronicle* and other correspondents, headed into the zone of conflict. We arrived at close to midnight to find the roads deserted and, as often happens in the Chiapas highlands, covered by dense fog that cast an eeriness on the newly erected banners declaring the area liberated Zapatista territory. We bypassed the rocks and tree stumps that had been placed in the road by the Zapatistas and pressed on toward Simojovel, one of the communities Marcos had allegedly taken and a place where we suspected Zapatista sympathies ran high. There were no other vehicles on the road, and no sign of life. As we neared Simojovel, the Zapatista fortifications grew more elaborate. A deep ditch, carved into the asphalt and backed by a barricade of logs and rocks, stopped us. Dudley, who'd been in Mexico longer than the rest of us, had a hunch about the roadblock. We got out of the jeep and slowly approached the trench, calling out that we were foreign reporters. From the darkness masked figures popped up. They had rifles, which they pointed at us, and they demanded that we turn around. Others, who apparently had been sleeping contentedly behind the barricade, roused themselves then and surrounded us. They were young, and it was obvious they had only recently bought their fashion jeans with U.S. labels in the store at Simojovel because they all looked new. But the young men had guns and a walkie-talkie that kept them in touch with Zapatista leaders, who ordered them not to let us pass. Not that night. We tried negotiating with them, but they were intent on following orders.

We turned back, stopping in other towns that had supposedly been captured but finding no one who had even seen a Zapatista. In Bochil we stayed at a cheap hotel on the main street; any military vehicles heading into the zone of conflict would have to pass the place. We spent what was left of the night there, and when the sun appeared the hotel manager made coffee. I had slept only a few hours, but what I heard when the manager turned on the television roused me immediately. Jaime Serra Puche, who had become President Zedillo's secretary of the treasury, was talking by telephone to a news anchor about an *ajuste técnico*—a "technical adjustment"—of about 15 percent, and I knew at once that the economic maneuvering we had been anticipating for weeks had occurred. Serra spoke calmly and insisted it was not really a devaluation, only a little fine-tuning to offset investors' negative reaction to the Zapatista offensive. But Serra was waving a red flag in front of currency speculators who immediately challenged the new exchange rate, forcing the Mexican government nearly to deplete its remaining foreign reserves defending the peso for little more than one additional day.

The newscast had barely ended when a long line of army personnel carriers and wheeled tanks rumbled past the hotel and into the territory Marcos had triumphantly claimed. We joined them and in a short time passed the spot where the young Zapatistas had stopped us the night before. It was abandoned, and Mexican troops had filled in the trench. By nightfall, the caravan rolled into Simojovel, where the local people lined the main street. Some cheered the arrival of government authority, but most stood silent as the convoy pulled in.

As the financial situation worsened, I returned to Mexico City. On the flight back, the jet had to detour around the smoking top of Popocate-petl, one of the two giant volcanoes on the city's outskirts, because it had started to spew columns of smoke and was threatening to erupt, which would have been a disastrous end to Mexico's year of disasters. I landed in a Mexico City whose people were panicked by the currency collapse—all except perhaps the cab driver who picked me up at the air-port. Calmly, he said he'd been through this kind of thing before and knew that nothing good would come of it. When he dropped me off, he said, he was going to a raffle drawing where a local newspaper was giv-ing away turkeys. He hoped to win one and to save it for when things got really bad.

This was the crisis Lloyd Bentsen and most American and Canadian officials had been unwilling to accept was on its way. The pacific summer and the orderly election had lulled observers who should have been more questioning. At this moment, just days before Christmas, several things were clear. The Zedillo administration had lost in its gamble of limping into the New Year. The conditions under which the reins of gov-ernment were handed over had been misstated and misunderstood. And the crisis that was engulfing Mexico was threatening to spread quickly to other developing economies, once more putting at risk the investments of Americans and Canadians who believed that Mexico had truly changed. A default in Mexico would trigger the kind of debt crisis that had spread throughout Latin America after Mexico's 1981 default. This time, however, the crisis would be global. Investing patterns had changed substantially, and now money moved with the speed of a long-distance telephone call across national boundaries. The profile of in-vestors had changed too. In 1981, the holders of defaulted Mexican bonds had primarily been banks. Now they were thousands of individual investors who would lose their money if Mexico defaulted. Containing a panic at that point would be nearly impossible. Mexico constituted a ma-jor portion of the emerging market portfolio, and trouble there would turn investors away from all emerging markets. Before they knew it, other developing nations would have trouble borrowing money and refi-nancing debt and could find themselves likewise on the brink of default.

By this time in the crisis, the preparations that Bentsen and the European banks had made earlier in the year were no more effective than buckets of sand at a match-factory fire. Far more capital than originally thought would be needed, and President Clinton had been advised by Treasury Secretary Rubin not to wait to extend a helping hand.

At first Clinton came up with a comparatively modest $18.5 billion package of aid, incorporating $9 billion from Washington, $5 billion from the Bank of International Settlements in Europe, $3 billion from international lenders, and $1.5 billion from Canada, to cover Mexico's debts and to help Zedillo get the country back on its feet. The help from the Chrétien government was not important in itself, but it was the kind of catalyst that Ottawa saw itself providing as a player of conscience on the world stage and, more important, within the western hemisphere. As the peso continued to hemorrhage, Clinton offered more help, saying, "It is in America's economic and strategic interests that Mexico succeeds."[5] The administration put together $40 billion in loan guarantees and had the support of both leaders of Congress. Even so, the package ran into fierce opposition in Congress, and as the situation in Mexico worsened, the Republicans in the House and Senate managed to kill it.

Washington was still bickering over Mexico when Zedillo finally made the opening gambit to establish the authority of his presidency. In early February 1995, he sent the army after Marcos. Zedillo also went on television to unmask Marcos, identifying him as a middle-class Mexico City professor, the son of a furniture salesman from the northern state of Tamaulipas, and a burned-out revolutionary from Mexico's student movement of the 1960s. Zedillo ordered army troops to capture him, and although they had not, they clearly had him on the run.

This was Zedillo's offensive, his chance to strike at his tormentor and to prove that this accidental president had the *pantalones* to run Mexico. Zedillo also needed to show a worried world that helping Mexico did not mean sending good money after bad. For this reason, the government insisted on letting only controlled news out of Chiapas. Blockades were established around the entire zone. There are so few roads that the army could keep a watchful eye on almost everything. At one point, I tried to force my way past an army blockade. With a group of Mexican reporters behind me, I argued that the Mexican constitution guaranteed free passage everywhere except in times of war. Had war been declared, I demanded to know, and if not, why couldn't we proceed? We thought the reasoning had worked on the soldiers and took a few steps forward.

Immediately, a Mexican soldier was holding the muzzle of his automatic rifle against my chest and warning me not to move any closer. I wrote about the blockade, and after the article appeared in *The Times*, the Mexican government, always worried about its image in the United States, agreed to lift the barricades.

The army went further than that. General Arrieta took me and eighteen Mexican reporters in three Bell 212 helicopters to the Zapatista stronghold of Guadalupe Tepeyac. It was the second time I got to see the Zapatistas' proud stage, where thousands had gathered a few months before for the National Democratic Convention. It now looked fragile and crude. One of the two huge flags that had formed such a dramatic backdrop behind Marcos was still there, the green and red bands thoroughly washed out by the jungle sun. The prized library was a shambles, the old books in disarray on tables and the dirt floor for General Arrieta to deride contemptuously. The calendar nailed to a post was opened to the date February 10, one day after President Zedillo had unmasked Marcos.

While the hunt for Marcos went on, Mexico's economy continued to melt down. The small middle class—estimated as just 10 to 20 percent of Mexico's population—was hit especially hard. They had believed Salinas when he promised to bring Mexico into the first world. But now they reeled as the stock market imploded, the default rate on bank loans soared, and interest on some mortgages and auto loans—calculated monthly—exceeded 100 percent.

The misery of the Mexican people was evident to the Clinton administration, and Washington was aware of the danger of not taking steps to help. Bypassing Senator Alphonse D'Amato of New York and other recalcitrant Republicans, President Clinton and Larry Summers went ahead with an alternative rescue plan. The president, in one of the most forceful foreign policy initiatives of his time in office, acted on the conviction that the economic future of the United States was tied to the health of the Mexican economy, and in that world of global trade and instantaneous currency trading, America did not have the option of sitting on its hands. The new package creatively tapped existing funds and did not require the approval of Congress. Using obscure sources such as the Treasury Department's exchange stabilization fund, and combining them with already available loan guarantees from international lenders and the International Monetary Fund (IMF, which agreed to increase its support from $7 billion in loan guarantees to a record $17.8 billion), the

Clinton administration offered a package that totaled just over $50 billion, about 25 percent more than the original deal. In exchange, Mexico agreed to the strict fiscal disciplines imposed by the IMF. It also had to put up future oil revenues as collateral. The terms of the deal were humiliating for the Mexicans to accept, but Zedillo made it clear that the country had no choice.

In subsequent years, through the Asian crisis, then the Russian crisis, and the Brazilian devaluation, Mexico's peso crisis of 1994–1995 was often cited as a warning of how quickly events can spin out of control in a globally linked economy. It came to be considered a defining moment for President Clinton, the point at which American foreign policy underwent a drastic transformation from Cold War diplomacy to the economics-driven foreign policy of the age of globalization. Clinton's rescue package also became an exemplar of enlightened self-interest when Mexico repaid the money, with interest, well in advance of its due date. The early repayment was possible in part because the U.S. economy had shifted into high gear, increasing demand for Mexican goods. But NAFTA had brought stability and a guarantee of steady economic policy that helped Mexico bounce back in months instead of years as was the case after the 1981 debacle. The Mexican crisis and Washington's response became catalysts for reforming the IMF and other global financial agencies, while also increasing pressure for the creation of a global emergency response team to head off future crises.

✳

Unwittingly, Salinas and Zedillo had jointly lit the fuse on one of the first crises of globalization and had ushered in a new era of international financial management. As I learned later, that was not an entirely new role for Mexico—or North America—to play. Mexico itself was created through a much earlier version of the same global commerce that has become such a dominant part of contemporary life. Columbus's letters home show that his voyage of discovery was not driven by science or the search for understanding but by the economics of trade and finance. "To speak only of what has been accomplished on this voyage, which was so hasty, their highnesses can see that I will give them as much gold as they may need, if their highnesses will render me very slight assistance," he reported back to Ferdinand and Isabella after his fateful first voyage, during which he for a time believed the north coast of Cuba to be mainland China.[6] New Spain functioned as a rigidly controlled trading bloc. The Spanish took great pains to protect their market by restricting the ability of the new-world colonies to produce any goods of value that might also be exported from Spain.

The gold and silver shipped back from Mexico to Spain and, through barter and trade, from Spain to all of Europe changed the world. The sudden wealth triggered a burst of capitalist activity, and suddenly merchandising—the buying and selling of manufactured goods, agricultural products, and commodities—swept across the European continent. Although gold was the most sought-after of the new world's treasures, other riches lured men across the ocean. Thousands of miles north of Mexico's mines, along the northeastern coast of what is now Canada, French and Portuguese sailors followed the route of Giovanni Caboto (John Cabot) to the rocky shores of Newfoundland, Labrador, and Quebec's Gaspé peninsula for the schools of silver cod so plentiful that they made the sea shine. Until the British conquest, the value of North American cod far surpassed all the beaver pelts and furs that had been sent to France.

In the early days of European contact with North America, historic discoveries and landfall claims could be enforced only by military might. For nearly a century, Spain alone had the resources to develop the new world. Excursions such as Caboto's landing in Newfoundland in 1497 and Jacques Cartier's exploration of the St. Lawrence River in 1534–1535 could not lead to colonies so long as Spain was more powerful than every other nation. King Philip II, intoxicated by the vast Spanish empire that had come under his control since Columbus's first voyage, was intent on becoming a "king of kings" and seeing his Catholic dominion extend throughout the known world. The British, French, and Dutch joined forces to counterbalance Spain's enormous and growing power. But when Philip tried to deliver his conquering blow in 1588, only to be foiled by a combination of weak strategy and horrible weather that sank most of the Spanish Armada before it reached the shores of England, Spain's hegemony over the American continent ended. The other European powers, freed from their paralyzing fear of Spain, began their own attempts to create empires in the new world.

For them all, the strange land across the ocean, filled with fantastic creatures and fearsome natives, represented a magnificent opportunity for re-creating their cultures and leaving behind the gravest faults of

European society. America became the splendid obsession of every nation that cast an eye toward its densely wooded shores. The Dutch, busy building their empire based on trade rather than military might, and the British, reaping the economies of scale of its farms as they consolidated and began producing excess food, were quick to establish commercial colonies, open to all, and based firmly on cross-Atlantic trade.

The French began with perhaps the greatest advantage, staking a claim that reached right into the heart of the mighty continent. The St. Lawrence River and its tributaries connected to the Great Lakes and from there through rivers and uncharted waterways that enabled French coureurs de bois to penetrate deep into the untouched regions of North America. The French empire ranged in a majestic arc from the Arctic to the Gulf of Mexico, while the Dutch and the British remained huddled on the Atlantic Coast, hemmed in by the Appalachian mountains.

But for many years, the French settlement was also burdened with the harshest climate and the narrowest vision. The weather limited the months of easy transit and placed great burdens on the early, reluctant settlers. Many of them arrived as indentured servants, often in debt to the French clergy. After serving their three years, they eagerly returned to France. The French king wanted the settlement to remain compact and thus easier to defend. The beaver trade could also be more effectively controlled if all furs had to pass through a single point managed by the crown.

With the Spanish empire in decline, competition escalated between England and France. Both saw North America as a prize in the contest for dominance. In many ways, their Seven Years' War from 1756 to 1763 was the first world war, fought across Europe and the fledgling colonies of North America. Although Americans know the fighting that took place in North America as the French and Indian War, at stake was the continued presence of France in the new world. The French held out long after they were outmanned and outgunned by the British. They believed their most important victories would come not on the battlefield but at the peace table, where a pen and diplomatic mastery could accomplish what cannons and soldiers could not. In the end, however, they managed to keep only two small islands off the coast of Newfoundland.

President Clinton realized that Mexico was linked to a global system of commerce just as tangibly as it had been in the sixteenth century. His audacious rescue kept the peso crisis from spreading to other countries, but it did not right Mexico's problems immediately. Pain was plentiful in all quarters as the country restructured its finances, cleaned up its debt, and tried to restore investor confidence. Mexico's strict economic diet was leaving many people hungry. I wanted to measure the impact of the crisis on ordinary Mexicans, and I was interested most in talking to the descendants of those same people who had been conquered by Cortés. I found them on a hillside at the edge of Mexico City, a few miles from our house in Cuajimalpa.

Near a park named Ocotal where I often went to run and clear my head, I had noticed an old woman sitting on one of the tiny, toy-sized, wooden stools that Mexicans enjoy using even if they look like children regardless of their age. She had put out a crudely lettered sign to let runners and picnickers know that parking was available in her field. She hoped to earn a few pesos by watching the cars so they were not stolen, although she could have done nothing to stop a thief.

Her name was Ricarda Martínez de Suárez. She was sixty years old, her husband Martín was eighty-three, and they lived on a pension the equivalent of U.S. $1 a day for both of them. When I asked what the devaluation meant for her, she shrugged. She grew her own vegetables in the dusty soil, so that wouldn't change a bit. She thought she would probably have to forgo the chicken backs and pieces of poultry skin she used to buy from the butchers who removed them when preparing an order for people like me and then sold to people like Ricarda for their dinners. All in all, she said she couldn't complain much because she had a house built by the woman who owned the land. Ricarda and her husband stayed there to watch things, a fairly common arrangement in Mexico that keeps certain squatters from becoming too well established.

We talked some more, and in time, as her trust in me grew, Ricarda started to lower the mask she had been hiding behind. Speaking slowly, twisting her gnarled fingers first on one hand, then the other, she told me she was most worried about Martín, who was sick and had to take a costly medication. "I don't know what we will do if the prices of medicine go up," she said. She shook her head, and her expression showed how close she was to destitution. Then the old woman surprised me. She leaned forward and took my hand. "If you really want to know how bad it is for some people, go back there, along that trail, and talk to the people who live there."

No matter how poor or disadvantaged they were, Mexicans almost always pointed out someone who was worse off. So I went in the direction that Ricarda had suggested. I traced a rough trail alongside the giant maguey cactus plants and the brush that grows up everywhere in Mexico City if it is not clipped back. I met a young man carrying an empty bucket. He lived in one of the shacks but was headed to a water spigot at the side of someone's house to get water for cooking and washing. He lived in the place Ricarda had mentioned and pointed me in that direction. By this point I was far from the road, on the edge of what might once have been a pasture but now was closing in with weeds. The trail opened up into the dry bed of a culvert. That morning it contained only garbage, flattened cardboard, bits of paper, and torn plastic bags.

Farther on, the garbage increased, and I saw several shacks. The first was little more than a few rough pieces of wood and a roof of laminated tar paper. I peeked inside but no one was there. I walked on to a kind of courtyard surrounded by four different shacks. Each was built of long sheets of the cardboard used to make juice boxes like the ones sold at the Zapatista convention. These had been discarded because of printing errors, but the wax coating made them a building material for many Mexicans. A few bits of scrap lumber made up the frame of the shack, and the cardboard was attached with rusty nails driven through bottle caps to keep them from ripping out in heavy winds. Overhead was the tar paper laminate that I'd seen in every part of Mexico. Electricity was pirated from nearby power lines, and inside one shack were a small television and a bare electric lightbulb. Each shack had beds, a table, and a stove that ran on kerosene. Three generations of the same family lived inside.

These people were not like the homeless I had written about while I worked in the United States, people with no income who live under the highway overpasses in Miami or in the abandoned city-owned buildings in Brooklyn. When these Mexican families pooled all their incomes, they had money to buy beds and dressers but not enough for a regular house. They paid rent for their huts but not to the unseen owner of the land who lived in the city. Instead, every month they paid the man who lived in the first wooden shack I'd come across. He had an arrangement with the owner to look out for things, just as Doña Ricarda did for the owner of her land nearby. All the families knew they could be forced out if the owner sold the land. But it was a risk worth taking for the opportunity to have a place of their own.

One twenty-five-year-old man who lived there, Miguel Angel García, who had only recently returned from serving in the Mexican army, was already dreaming about going dancing and maybe to a movie on Friday night with one of the girls who lived in Cuajimalpa, if he had the money. It all depended on whether the mason he helped had enough work and money to pay him.

To these people, living so close to the edge of Mexico's economy, the crisis that originated in government offices only a few miles away, and that was now sweeping around the globe, meant little. As bad as the peso crisis might make life elsewhere, conditions would be only negligibly worse than the harsh and difficult world in which most Mexicans lived all the time. That had not changed with the start of NAFTA or the initial steps President Salinas had taken to drag Mexico into the modern world. What had changed was that now we in the north had become closer to the people who had been hidden below our borders for so long. The self-interest that President Clinton had described in putting together the backdoor rescue package for Mexico meant that we now lived in an era when what happened to Ricarda Martínez and Miguel Angel García mattered to people in Canada and the United States far more directly than it had before because the Mexican market mattered far more directly than before. The people of North America might still be strangers to each other, but now they were strangers living in the same house, who had to help out in a crisis whether we wanted to or not.

Crises at every level were dragging all three countries together. Sometimes they occurred in the most desperate conditions, like the hillside in Cuajimalpa. Sometimes crisis hit elegant palaces of power like Los Pinos. And sometimes there was a crisis in the most unexpected of places, involving the most unexpected of people, as I was about to find out.

CHAPTER SIX

Goatsuckers, Mad Hatters, and Other Demons at Our Borders

✳

We are neighbors by fatality.

Carlos Salinas de Gortari
"Talking with David Frost," October 29, 1993

B rian Mulroney could not believe what he was seeing. Sitting in wintry Montreal watching television, the former prime minister stared at the image of a squat house of cinderblocks as grim and featureless as a million others throughout Mexico. But inside this particular house was the man with whom Mulroney, along with President George Bush, one hot Texas afternoon in 1992, had signed the agreement that eventually became NAFTA and changed the history of North America. Now, Carlos Salinas de Gortari had taken refuge in the dark of night inside the humble home of Rosa Coronado Flores, a local anti-poverty worker who lived on the outskirts of the northern Mexico city of Monterrey, the metropolis on the edge of the desert that was to have been Mexico's free trade showcase. There, just three months after stepping down as one of the most powerful presidents in Mexico's history, Salinas shocked everyone by announcing that he was going on a hunger strike to protest the way he and his family were being treated in Mexico.

If Mulroney shook his head in disbelief at the bizarre picture on his television screen, who would have blamed him? After bearing the bitter disappointment of his own fall from grace since leaving office two years before, the former prime minister was perplexed. The process of integrating the three nations of North America was progressing rapidly, yet both he and Salinas were paying a high price for such drastic change. Mulroney had retired prematurely from politics and had become a despised figure in much of Canada. And to judge by events in Monterrey, Salinas apparently was learning that the new era of continental relations had its own rules. One of the most important was for governments—and their leaders—to provide greater transparency and accountability. Such commandments hadn't been written into NAFTA, but the three nations involved considered openness a quid pro quo for entering the historic pact. In the thirteen months since the agreement took effect at the beginning of 1994, there had been little tolerance for the kind of secrets that were casually kept before. The first crisis of the new American continent—Mexico's bungled devaluation and the ensuing stampede of capital—had made it clear that the three partners must be fully informed about circumstances across North America's borders. Financial information had to become much easier to obtain than before. The new demand for openness also created a frenzy for uncovering corruption, and in these early days of March 1995, an intense spotlight had been focused on places, and people, that had never been touched by such light before.

Life after leaving government tends to be tougher for leaders in Canada and Mexico than in the United States, where reverence for the office of the president gives its former occupants a decent chance to rehabilitate their reputations (as Richard Nixon started to do before he died) or be gently forgotten (as Gerald Ford has managed to do). No such reverence attaches to the post of prime minister in Canada, which is not filled via a national vote that brings together the diverse regions and people of the country. Public feelings about the prime minister's office are generated by the personality controlling it, for however long or short a time that prime minister governs. This system leaves Canada strangely impersonal about the people who run the country. Canada has no national holiday to honor any of its leaders, except Queen Victoria, who ruled from across the ocean. Not even the first prime minister, Sir John A. Macdonald—who comes as close to a founding father as Canada has—is remembered with a national holiday.

Like most of his recent predecessors, Mulroney hadn't had an easy time of retirement since stepping down in 1993. During his nine years in office, the ambitious Mulroney had managed to infatuate or offend just about everyone in Canada, but voters seemed to remember only the offenses. Tales of influence peddling, favoritism, and corruption were woven into best-selling books and so many muckraking magazine articles that writing about Mulroney became a profitable industry for Canadian journalists. Scorned instead of sanctified, a wounded Mulroney was left to steam in the elegant office he occupied in a downtown Montreal law firm.

Still, nothing in Canada could compare with what was happening in Mexico, and Mulroney could be glad of that. Mexico was in upheaval, and his old *ami* Salinas was at the center of it. Salinas—who only a few months earlier had been heard bragging that Prime Minister Jean Chrétien would manage his campaign for the presidency of the World Trade Organization, who had successfully dragged Mexico into the modern economic world, who had ended six years in office with unparalleled popularity—was sitting on the edge of a small bed dressed in a white shirt and a leather bomber jacket with sheepskin collar that cradled his bald head like an egg in an Easter basket. Beneath a nearby end table was a box of bottled Evian water, which Salinas said was the only sustenance he would take while on his hunger strike.

A crowd of reporters gathered outside the Coronado Flores house seeking to talk to Salinas. I was among them. We were not sure of his intentions, but we had no doubt that this was the opening act in another bizarre Mexican drama, yet one more surprise like the death of the cardinal or the murder of Colosio that would engorge Mexico's complicated and damning history. It was important to place Salinas's actions in some kind of perspective, especially given the sensitive nature of the moment in North America's history. The peso crisis was still unfolding, and debate raged in Washington and Ottawa about the wisdom of having taken on Mexico, and its problems, in a partnership as permanent as the trade agreement. Another factor was at play: Raw political power in Mexico is wrapped up in the solitary figure of the president. At that moment, events in Monterrey likely would be an indicator of how Mexico itself was being transformed.

Hunger strikes are common in Mexico. They are the last resort of students, campesinos, and other powerless people for whom physically abusing their bodies is the only way left to counter injustice. No one in Mexico had ever seen someone of Salinas's prestige and stature try something like it. To appreciate what it represented for the people of Mexico, imagine Bill Clinton showing up in Harlem one day and vowing not to eat or drink anything but Perrier water until everyone in Washington stopped saying mean things about him and Hillary.

As Mulroney watched events unfold on television and in the newspapers, he was bothered by the way Salinas appeared to be letting his critics get the better of him. Mulroney's own thick skin had been among his most formidable defenses, and he hated seeing weakness in other leaders, especially those he had worked with and grown to like. I too found Salinas's condition disturbing, not so much because of the weakness it demonstrated, but because the vacant-eyed man in the Monterrey slum so contradicted the image of Salinas I had known since I arrived in Mexico.

Salinas was an unmistakable product of the Mexican class system. He had started his privileged life at the foot of his famous father Raúl, a powerful government minister of another generation who groomed his sons to rule. The future president grew up in a family of maids and servants, learned how to ride expensive horses, and was sent on an around-the-world tour that was the obligatory finishing touch to a Mexican aristocrat's education. He was awarded two master's degrees and a doctorate in political economy from the Kennedy School of Government at Harvard University. There he was befriended by economic experts and influential professors who thought the bright young man had a brilliant future and who would come to his rescue time and again.

The lives of privilege in Mexico have a disturbing side. The great wealth and influence of the upper class are accompanied by excess and domination over those beneath them. Rich Mexicans have always surrounded their homes with high walls, and they all share the fear that someday a mob will pound on the doors with their machetes and old hunting rifles, demanding to be let in. The only regular contact the wealthy have with the poor is through the servants they pay to live with them in small rooms on the roof of the house or beside the garage. The servants do the cooking and the washing; they rub shoulders with the other common people at the supermarket; they take the car to be repaired. It is common for even middle-class families to have a servant who can help run the house and be available for unscheduled deliveries of cooking gas and to wait for the telephone repairman. Although we felt uncomfortable about it at first, we too hired a maid. We interviewed several, and all told us they prefer working for American families rather than Mexican ones. They feel that gringos treat them better.

There are exceptions, of course. Some maids, drivers, and handymen who stay with a single Mexican family for decades are treated with respect and affection. In other families, though, long service makes the servants nearly invisible, or they become objects of suspicion and contempt. This is so common that it leaves a legacy of subservience. Vicki González, a stocky Mexican woman, cooked and cleaned and watched the children for us for more than a year. Then suddenly problems developed, and we had to let her go. She thanked us for having taken her in, and she asked us to say good-bye to the children for her because she would be gone before they returned from school. Before she left for the last time, she asked us if we wanted to check her room, which was beside the kitchen, to ensure that she had not stolen anything. Every Mexican she had ever worked for had insisted on checking. We hadn't even thought of it, and we surprised her when we said no.

Carlos Salinas's childhood home was filled with maids and manservants who responded without hesitation to any order from family members of any age. In an incident that became infamous in Mexico, a young Salinas and his older brother Raúl were playing a game involving imaginary scenes and guns, like any other boys. But the gun they used was real, and though the details are murky, the victim of this game was a Salinas maid, accidentally killed by a rifle shot fired by four-year-old Carlos.

The Salinas family did its best to hide the unfortunate incident, but it was revived during his 1988 campaign (and widely distributed in a booklet believed to have been financed by the head of the oil workers union whom Salinas had imprisoned). Salinas managed to overcome the criticism, and much more, and the Salinas I got to see in Los Pinos was a confident and complex figure. He always seemed to have another side that hadn't been revealed before. Just before his term in office ended, I accompanied him to San Pedro de las Colonias, the same town in Coahuila where outraged local residents had thrown sticks at him during the 1988 campaign. This time, the applause was fervent and, though not exactly spontaneous—for most events of this type in Mexico, the PRI bused in supporters—seemed to be mostly genuine.

I also had been with Salinas at a dinner on the patio of a private residence in Veracruz just months after the Colosio assassination and the start of the Chiapas uprising. He confidently slapped the back of Patricio Chirinos, the local PRI governor seated at his side, and dared the dinner table full of reporters to trip him up on a policy or political question. I had seen him motion casually to the uniformed military officer who stood behind his big leather armchair during interviews at Los Pinos and order a late afternoon cup of chamomile tea, drinking it with the saucer in one hand and the delicate china cup in another, his pinkie extended. On several of his weekly trips to rural Mexico, I had watched him stand in the wilting sun to receive the written petitions of peasant women and old men who would not entrust their supplication to the mail or to a presidential assistant. They believed that by placing it directly in the hand of *"El Señor,"* they ensured that their request would be acted upon. In such moments, a Mexican president resembles the Aztec emperor from whom his power descends, the individual man of ultimate power to whom the people prayed for assistance.

Now, in the dank house in Monterrey, Salinas looked like a vagrant and sounded like a mystic. I couldn't tell which Salinas was the real one. Was he now wearing a mask, or had he used one before that had made him look serious and honest? It wasn't the first time in Mexico that I looked directly into the eyes of someone I thought I knew well and could not be certain whether I was being lied to or not. The Mexican habit of hiding feelings behind a mask is a formidable defense. When Mexicans intentionally mislead, they do not always consider what they are doing to be a lie. Rather, they see it as a pragmatic treatment of the truth, which has a flexible form when it comes to what someone does and especially what someone says. Mexico is a society of declarations, which is why Mexican newspapers devote most of their news space to statements from the president and other officials. When I asked Mexican editors about this, they told me that the habit of placing so much importance on official declarations is a trait from Mexico's Indian past. The utterances of Aztec emperors were never challenged, and local caciques—tribal strongmen—wielded such incontestable power that their words immediately became law. I suppose the editors could be right, but the more likely explanation is that until recently, most of the newspapers were simply mouthpieces for the government.

When I finally managed to get into the house to speak to Salinas in Monterrey, I expected him to make declarations, but he was practically incoherent. His speech was slurred, his eyes glazed. Salinas recognized me and made some cryptic remarks. "You, more than anybody, know," he said. He tilted his head to look up at me and gave a thin, cynical smile. Before I could get him to explain what he meant, his assistants rushed me out. I knew, however, he was referring to an article about him that *The New York Times* had published recently. In it, sources in the Zedillo administration said they had evidence to show that Salinas had tried to interfere in the investigation into Colosio's assassination. They further implied that they believed he had somehow been involved in the murder, spectacularly reviving one of the rumors that had hung over Mexico in the days and months after the assassination.[1]

Years later, when Salinas finally agreed to talk to me again about these incidents, he said he had received information from within Zedillo's administration that the president planned to attack him personally. He believed Zedillo was ready to have him arrested and charged with destroying evidence relevant to the Colosio investigation, an accusation he denied absolutely. "I had told Mr. Zedillo then that I would not break the fast unless the attorney general himself produced a statement clearly stating that those allegations *The New York Times* had published were not true," he said during the interview in October 2000.

The line between tragedy and farce is thin in Mexico, and it often became a test of wills to keep them separated as the country bounced from tragedy to tragedy during those tumultuous years. Something had gone seriously wrong with Mexico and with Salinas, at least during those few days, but the scene itself was so peculiar that attention focused on what was happening rather than on why. Salinas came out of the house, and with dozens of tape recorders pushed to within inches of his face, he read a rambling statement about his love of Mexico and the campaign of mistruths being waged against him. In Mexico City, Antonio Lozano, the opposition party congressman Zedillo had named attorney general, released a statement saying only that investigators had no evidence linking Salinas to the Colosio assassination.

A steady stream of visitors came to see Salinas in Monterrey. Clearly they were trying to negotiate an end to what had become a historic confrontation between Salinas and Zedillo, a standoff between the Mexican political system of perpetuated power and the growing pressure for imposition of the rule of law. One intermediary was Arturo Warman, an old Salinas collaborator who had run the National Indigenous Institute at the time the Chiapas insurrection began. Zedillo then tapped him to head the department of agrarian reform, the byzantine bureaucracy that handled land claims from peasants under Article 27 of the constitution before it was amended. When Salinas stopped giving away land, more than 2.5 million Mexicans were still waiting to receive their parcel of promise. Warman's was a politically explosive position in a country where most poor people still believed that Zapata's revolution would provide them with free land, even though more than half the arable land in Mexico already had been given away.

Accustomed to negotiating intractable positions, Warman arrived in Monterrey with a message from Mexico City. He conceded later that he had told Zedillo he was prepared to resign from the cabinet if the president ordered him not to talk to Salinas. Zedillo acceded. By this time there was little doubt that Salinas would be forced into exile. The conflict involved the kind of melodramatic political intrigue that continually tugged Mexico toward the rest of Latin America and away from North America. Exile was a drastic solution to the power struggle between Salinas and Zedillo, but it was not without precedent in Mexico. In 1936, recently elected President Lázaro Cárdenas (father of Cuauhtémoc Cárdenas) rid himself of a meddlesome predecessor by forcing him to leave the country. Cárdenas accomplished this by first rousing working-class suspicions against former president Plutarco Elías Calles, who had continued to wield control over the Mexican system even after Cárdenas took office. Manipulating statements Calles had made in criticism of the labor movement, Cárdenas publicly challenged Calles, demanding to know why the former president had attacked, with "perverse intentions," the aspirations of Mexican workers.[2] Months later, after purging Calles's supporters from his cabinet and from the governorships of several states, Cárdenas had the satisfaction of watching Calles go into exile in the United States. A country where the president has absolute power has room for only one president.

Salinas told Warman that for the good of the country, he would be willing to end the hunger strike and possibly even leave Mexico. But he insisted that Zedillo first stop blaming him for Mexico's economic crisis. In addition to the attorney general's statement about the Colosio killing, Salinas wanted Zedillo to put an end to the rumors that Salinas had somehow been involved in the tragedy. Warman relayed the message to Mexico City. Zedillo said he could not control the thoughts of millions of Mexicans, but he could guarantee that neither he nor anyone in his administration would personally attack the Salinas clan. Zedillo knew it wouldn't be necessary for him to hound Salinas, because opposition parties, and other members of the PRI, would do the job for him.

Salinas's hunger strike lasted only a few days, and it ended in all the confusion with which it began. A Mexican photographer was invited to take a picture of the former president, still wearing his leather bomber, eating what he said was his first meal in days. Most Mexicans churlishly believed he had been eating all along. He made vague comments about an understanding that had been reached, and he implied that the circus could start afresh unless the commitments he had received from the Zedillo administration were honored. Then Salinas said good-bye to Mrs. Coronado Flores, climbed into a battered Dodge Dart with a cracked windshield, and drove off with Warman, leaving the pack of reporters dumbfounded.

He headed for Mexico City. Mulroney had called Salinas's office, and Salinas returned the call when he arrived. Both men told me they recollected the conversation that day, but their versions of it were totally different. Salinas remembered Mulroney being supportive and urging him to leave Mexico. "What I understood from what he told me was 'Don't stay there. Don't stay in Mexico. There are different ways of fighting back,'" Salinas told me years later. When I talked to Mulroney in Montreal in March 1999, his memory of the conversation was that he told Salinas to hang tough. "I said 'Carlos, you can't do this. If things go wrong, you stand there and you confront this stuff,'" Mulroney recalled. "You're the former president of Mexico. You deal with the problems." To Mulroney, the formerly unflappable Mexican president sounded harried. "You know, Brian," Mulroney remembered Salinas saying, "I'm going through a very rough time." It was a monumental understatement.

On March 10, 1995, Salinas left Mexico City aboard a private jet. The former president, who only weeks before had been a contender to head the WTO, who had believed he had secured his place in Mexico's thick history of heroes, turned his back on Mexico and slunk off to New York. When his U.S. visa expired, he flew to Montreal, where he lived in the Ritz Hotel and in an apartment building on Sherbrooke Street in downtown Montreal, just a few blocks from Mulroney's office.

Many Canadians believed the former prime minister had helped Salinas enter Canada—the natural extension of a good-neighbor policy to meet the exigencies of a new age of continental relations. According to Mulroney, the details of Salinas's entry into Canada were arranged by the Foreign Ministry without his input, since he was no longer in office. Salinas lived in Montreal for six months. Mulroney insisted he never saw Salinas in the city during that time, although the former president was seen shopping at exclusive stores not far from Mulroney's office. Salinas kept a low profile. But meetings of the Dow Jones company board of directors, which the former president had joined, couldn't be kept secret. Salinas-spotting became a popular sport in Mexican newspapers, which suddenly developed a great interest in the affairs of the Dow Jones board.

Mulroney acknowledged running into Salinas once on a flight from New York to Orlando. "We had a long chat," Mulroney said during an interview. "He was very ... I won't say depressed, but he was deeply concerned about what was going on. He was clearly troubled by it all, and not at all the Carlos Salinas that I had known in the halcyon days."

Subcomandante Marcos had mocked President Zedillo with the phrase "Welcome to the nightmare," but in 1995 it was Salinas who must have felt he was living in hell. The new Mexico he had personally created (and that I had come to explore) lay in shambles around him. The peso devaluation had ruined his economic legacy, along with his opportunity to ascend to the WTO presidency. His handpicked successor was dead. He was feuding with Zedillo. The Zapatista rebels had shown the Mexican miracle to be a hollow fraud.

As a final blow, the activities of his older brother Raúl were forcing the president's entire six-year administration to be judged anew. Just days before Salinas began his hunger strike, Raúl had been arrested and charged with involvement in the murder of his former brother-in-law, José Francisco Ruiz Massieu, a rising star in Mexican politics who was widely expected to become leader of the PRI delegation in the Chamber of Deputies, the lower house of congress, in Zedillo's administration.

Early one morning in late September 1994, Ruiz Massieu had attended a meeting with party officials in downtown Mexico City. Although he was usually accompanied by a chauffeur, that morning he drove his own car. Before he could pull out of his parking space on the street in front of the PRI committee room, a thin young man strode purposefully across the street, ripped a folded newspaper off his arm, and uncovered an automatic rifle. He pointed the gun at the driver's side window and shot Ruiz Massieu once in the neck. At first the killing looked like a professional hit—a lone gunman with a sophisticated weapon. But as details emerged, the hit took on a far more ominous dimension.

The gunman's rifle had jammed after the first shot went off, though the single shot was enough to kill Ruiz Massieu. The gunman then ran toward the Paseo de la Reforma where a getaway car waited. On the way, he collided with a bank guard.

An unfamiliar feature for Americans new to Mexico City is the sight of armed guards outside every bank. Their effectiveness is suspect, since they are poorly trained and woefully equipped with ancient shotguns and well-worn rifles. Most commonly, they are found chatting with girlfriends or chewing greasy tacos. That morning, by some design of fate, the bank guard across the street from the PRI meeting managed to block the way of the fleeing gunman, knocking him to the ground long enough for backup to arrive and arrest him.

The story then took twists and turns that a pulp murder mystery could rarely match—family intrigues, a missing congressman, crusading investigators who tortured, bribed, and abused witnesses. The final touch in this tragedy of brothers was Ruiz Massieu's own brother Mario—a drug-busting deputy attorney general—who took over the investigation and vowed revenge, only to be charged later with attempting to obstruct his own investigation by concealing the identity of the real mastermind—Raúl Salinas de Gortari.

Lozano, the attorney general, had a tough decision to make. No former president or member of his family had ever been held responsible for the political or criminal abuses that had occurred during his administration. But Zedillo had vowed that no one would be above the law, and the Republicans in the U.S. Congress who had opposed President Clinton's rescue package would be ready in an instant to attack any suggestion of laxity toward corruption on Zedillo's watch. Undoubtedly, Lozano was also influenced by the bad blood between Zedillo and Salinas over who was to blame for the peso crisis. In late February, Lozano sent an elite unit to arrest Raúl. A few days later, Carlos Salinas began his hunger strike, though he always insisted that it had nothing to do with Raúl.

As the authorities investigated Raúl, more became known about the full range of his activities during the six years his brother had been in office. Questions were continuously raised in Washington and Ottawa about how much their officials had known about what was happening in Mexico. Raúl maintained a huge account with Citibank, an institution with a privileged place in Mexican history because it remained open and active after every other foreign bank—including the Bank of Montreal—had been scared off by the revolution. Citibank would be investigated by American authorities for taking Raúl's millions without checking the source of the fortune. Although he was only a middle-level manager of a food commodities program, Raúl had amassed upward of $100 million, most of which passed through Citibank and ended up in Swiss bank accounts under fictitious names. Raúl said the money was an investment fund made up of contributions from several powerful friends, at least one of whom publicly corroborated the unlikely story. Suspicious Swiss authorities seized the money, claiming it had come from drug deals and money-laundering operations.

The incidents inevitably came back to haunt former president Salinas. In countless commentaries and articles in Mexican newspapers, the proof of Carlos Salinas's guilt came down to this one point: How could the president, who controlled everything in Mexico, not know what his brother was doing? Salinas has always denied being aware of the extent of his older brother's activities, but when I talked to key members of his administration, they said the president regularly was briefed on Raúl's most outrageous exploits. Graft and kickbacks were not uncommon, but they warned the president that Raúl was getting too greedy. For a time, Raúl left Mexico and moved to California, where he spent several months doing academic research at the University of California in San Diego. He clearly was no academic, but the fellowship removed him from Mexico during a critical period of his brother's term. Still, he returned before the end of President Salinas's six-year administration and resumed his activities with even more vigor.

Raúl's prosecution became a way for Mexico to channel all its growing resentment, even hatred, of the former president toward one target. Raúl's excesses were matched by the excesses of the government prosecutors. Witnesses were bribed and tortured. A special prosecutor known as the Elliot Ness of Mexico called reporters out to Raúl's ranch in Cuajimalpa when forensic experts unearthed a skeleton—supposedly that of the missing Mexican congressman alleged to have helped Raúl arrange the murder of Ruiz Massieu. The skeleton turned out to be the remains of a relative of a fortune teller on the prosecutor's payroll who had planted it on Raúl's property and then led investigators there.

Eventually, in 1999, Raúl was convicted of masterminding the Ruiz Massieu murder and was sentenced to fifty years in prison, which later was reduced to twenty-seven and a half years. Prosecutors never offered a convincing motive for the killing, although most Mexicans thought jealousy and family hatred had played a role. Raúl maintained his innocence and claimed his prosecution was politically motivated by his brothers' enemies.

Raúl's arrest represented a bold attempt by the wobbly Zedillo administration to reestablish itself after the chaos of the Colosio assassination that brought it to power and the peso devaluation that threatened to undo its authority. Breaking with the covenant of presidential untouchability by going after a target as visible as the president's brother cleared the way for a torrent of corruption investigations that shook Mexico's most important institutions, including the army. Inevitably, perhaps, forcing corruption into the open this way seemed to magnify Mexico's lawlessness. The country appeared to be corrupt to the core, and essentially unchanged despite what had been promised during the NAFTA debate. The string of revelations about Raúl and his cronies, the millions hidden in Switzerland, the influence peddling and—most damaging of all—the suspected links to drug gangs seemed never-ending. Mexico may have entered a new era of cooperation with its neighbors in North America, but the country and its political system appeared to be fundamentally and unchangeably corrupt.

As outrage over the corruption grew, Washington and Ottawa were called to account for what was known about Mexico, and when it had been known. Officials in both countries insisted they had no solid proof indicating any reason to worry about President Salinas's integrity. "We were not asleep at the wheel," an American diplomat assured me. In subsequent months I reviewed U.S. government documents indicating that during the Salinas presidency and in the early years of Zedillo's administration, Drug Enforcement Agency informants had linked Raúl to the top drug traffickers in Mexico. However, they never got hard proof that Raúl was in league with the drug lords. Some of the memos in the files referred to news reports about such rumors as proof the rumors were real. Former ambassador Jones told me he believed President Salinas had been fundamentally honest. While Jones was in Mexico City, he said, the inability of U.S. intelligence to nail down wrongdoing by Salinas had led him to urge reporters to be cautious about making unsubstantiated statements. For Jones, a former congressman and chief of staff to President Lyndon Johnson, it was a strange reversal of roles. "During Vietnam, reporters doubted every bit of information about the war and the way it was going," Jones told me years after he had left the diplomatic corps. "In Mexico it was just the opposite. I found myself telling reporters not to believe everything in the files because the information wasn't always reliable. But they went with it anyway."

Canadians had less at stake in Mexico than did Americans, but intelligence had kept Canadian officials only generally informed about what was happening there. "Not once in all the briefings did a report ever say 'Look, Salinas's family is greatly involved in corruption,'" Mulroney told me in 1999. Reports prepared by the Foreign Ministry, the Canadian Security Intelligence Service, and the Royal Canadian Mounted Police all gave Salinas a nearly clean bill of health. "Salinas was always perceived by the government of Canada and clearly by the government of the United States as having been clean, personally clean, with no involvement of any kind in anything untoward," Mulroney said.

In Mexico, however, people saw things differently. By mid-1995, they had transformed Salinas into a demon who could be blamed for nearly everything wrong with the country. And at that point, as always in the tortured history of the Mexican state, much was indeed wrong with Mexico. "I will guarantee peace and stability through the law," Salinas had said in his triumphant state of the nation address in 1993, when his visage rippled from banners flying over thousands of streets in the capital. Now his face was reproduced in crude rubber masks that street kids hawked at busy intersections throughout Mexico City. Whenever traffic stalled along Paseo de la Reforma or Avenida Chapultepec in downtown Mexico City, we watched tiny Mexican street kids, some no more than four or five years old, with their faces made up as clowns and balloons in the seat of their pants, do an exquisitely timed pantomime. The skits lasted just as long as it took for the traffic light to change. Sometimes one boy would hop on the shoulders of another, then another on top of him, and one more above. When all had come into alignment, they pirouetted and shook their bulbous bottoms. The laugh line came when the smallest one, from atop the column, put on a rubber mask mocking the man who may well have been the most powerful president in Mexican history, then thrust out his hands demanding money.

During this time, Salinas became the devil figure in traditional Easter plays. When a weird story came out of Puerto Rico reporting a mysterious night creature called the *chupacabra*—the goatsucker—that drained the blood out of the island's goats, it was Salinas who, in Mexico, became known on the streets and on T-shirts sold at El Tepito and other street markets as the *chupatodo*—the one who sucks up everything.

✳

Salinas was not the only North American leader to be demonized. After Mulroney left office, he was blamed for almost everything that was wrong with Canada, though masks showing his prominent chin tended to be sold only at Halloween. He became the central character of a savagely biting café theater production in Toronto called "The Life and Times of Brian Mulroney," the final installment in a fifteen-year series of satirical plays about Canadian history. Mulroney was portrayed as a boot-licking acolyte of Ronald Reagan and George Bush who obsequiously warbled "Give us twenty years and you won't recognize this country." The mere mention of Mulroney's name enraged sensible Canadians for years after he left office. For a time, though, this same man was the single most popular political leader in Canada, an agile persuader who enjoyed spectacular success despite a background without privilege or social status.

Mulroney grew up in a poor part of Quebec, which always had attracted Irish Catholic immigrants who felt more comfortable dealing with the Catholic church in Quebec than with the Protestant society in English Canada. Through dint of his strong personality and ambition, Mulroney worked his way up the ladder—a feat much more common in America, where ideals of success and self-improvement reigned, than in Canada, where being a self-made man was less commonly regarded as an advantage for a politician. Mulroney openly admired the United States and American ways of doing things. He was, to an extent, an American. And in large measure that leaning turned the Canadian people against him.

After Mulroney left office in 1993, resentment against him resurfaced whenever Canadians bought anything and had to pay a hefty goods and services tax that reminded them how Mulroney had changed Canada. Mulroney had said the country needed a broad-based consumption tax to replace a hidden 13.5 percent manufacturer's tax on domestic goods and exports that made Canadian-manufactured goods uncompetitive in the open North American market created by the free trade agreements. He believed that Canadians wanted transparency, and a way to start paying off the crushing federal deficit he had inherited from the Liberals (and which his government prolonged). Perhaps, but they certainly did not want this tax, and they blamed Mulroney for it every time they looked at a sales receipt.

Even we had problems adjusting to this constant sticker shock during our time living in Toronto. Along with a provincial consumption tax, the levy on most purchases in the province of Ontario was a hefty 15 percent. When the tax was combined with the generally higher prices we found on goods (due to the smaller size of Canada's market), the tax wiped out the advantage we had hoped for from the exchange-rate difference between the U.S. dollar and the weak Canadian dollar (called a loonie because it bears the image of Canada's most common waterfowl). Until I got more accustomed to Canada, I would routinely ask sales clerks to recheck their figures because they always seemed too high. Later, that temptation lessened, but I came to associate the tax with Mulroney as routinely as any Canadian.

Canadians were also incensed by cronyism in the Mulroney government, and as time went on they grew increasingly embarrassed and outright defensive about what they saw as Mulroney's mawkish pro-Americanism. No moment was more galling for Canadians than the evening in 1985 when President Ronald Reagan visited Quebec City and the prime minister pulled him on stage for a fawning duet of "When Irish Eyes Are Smiling."

The most damaging accusation against Mulroney came, as it had for Raúl Salinas in Mexico, by way of Swiss authorities. In a letter asking the Swiss for assistance with a corruption investigation, the Mounties had mentioned that they were checking a former official who might have received kickbacks. In the letter, the Mounties said the investigation "is of special importance to the Canadian Government because criminal activities carried out by the former Prime Minister are involved," leaving no doubt that they had targeted Mulroney. The contents of the letter were leaked to a Canadian reporter. Mulroney and several associates were suspected of having influenced a $1.8 billion contract given to Airbus Industrie for the purchase of thirty-four passenger jets by Air Canada, then owned by the Canadian government. Mulroney completely denied the charges. The Mounties had started the investigation in 1989 but lacked evidence and put it on hold. The flood of negative books and articles about Mulroney during Jean Chrétien's government caused the Mounties to reopen the investigation. After the request for assistance from Swiss authorities was revealed, Mulroney, who had readily advised Salinas to stand up to his tormentors, stood up for himself. He sued the Canadian government for libel and asked for $36.5 million in damages, along with a public apology. It was akin to Salinas's hunger strike—a confrontation between a former leader and his successor. This time, in at least this one instance, power remained with the ousted leader. A day before Mulroney's libel trial was scheduled to begin in January 1997, Chrétien backed down. The federal government and the Mounties issued an apology for the letter to Swiss authorities that had mentioned the former prime minister. The government also agreed to pay about $1 million (Canadian) for Mulroney's legal fees.

✳

As NAFTA neared the end of its second full year in 1995, its impact was being felt across the continent but still in a mostly negative way. In the United States, labor unions and Ralph Nader's Public Citizen advocacy group were busy keeping track of every factory closing and of every job that was shipped off to Mexico. The pace of U.S. exports to Mexico had not yet increased in the way the Clinton administration had promised— the devaluation of the peso had caused a recession in Mexico that was holding down wages and putting a damper on spending. In Canada, Jean Chrétien and the Liberal Party were cutting deeply into the country's intricate web of public welfare and social programs to wrestle down the budget deficit. Unhappiness was apparent across North America, which helped open the way for another demon to raise its head on our borders, this one an old nightmare from Canada's past that represented a strategic concern right where America ends.

The demon took the shape of a portly silver-haired man in a formal vest crossed by the chain of a pocket watch. In private, he spoke with an accent straight from a leather-bound British club, but in public his pronouncements were delivered in a flowery, fiery French that incited a good many people in La Belle Province of Quebec to do what they repeatedly told public opinion surveys they did not readily want to do: vote to separate Quebec from the rest of Canada.

NAFTA had given Jacques Parizeau, premier of the province of Quebec, more ammunition with which to defend Quebec's claim to independence. The province had long seen free trade as a liberating force and had outspokenly favored both the Canada-U.S. Free Trade Agreement in 1988 and NAFTA in 1993. Parizeau's mantra was that belonging to Canada no longer made sense for Quebec, and the free trade agreement proved that was so. Free trade meant there would be no difference in commercial terms between the U.S. border with Canada and the borders of an independent Quebec. "Sooner or later, and probably sooner, we're going to get the votes for independence," Parizeau commented to

James J. Blanchard, who was making his first visit to Quebec as U.S. ambassador to Canada. It was October 1993, and Congress had not yet voted on NAFTA, but Parizeau had already worked the pact into his grand vision of the Quebec nation. "Unlike those anti-American guys in Ottawa, we're free traders," he told Blanchard. "That, by itself, should qualify us for NAFTA, whatever the law says."[3]

In the ensuing two years, Parizeau carefully laid the groundwork for Quebec's second public referendum on secession, using Chrétien and his budget cutting to stir up resentment against Ottawa. The provincial vote was scheduled for fall 1995, and polls predicted an extremely close result. Events on America's northern border were almost as difficult to understand as the presidential joust between Zedillo and Salinas in Mexico, and showed the degree to which arrogance about the role of the United States in the world shortened our vision. The breakup of Canada seemed unthinkable; therefore we could ignore it. Which we did, until it seemed almost about to happen.

In the weeks leading up to the referendum, currency traders around the globe tracked opinion polls as they attempted to predict the outcome and its likely effect on the Canadian dollar. Some foreign exchange companies in Washington state stopped accepting Canadian dollars. Panicky calls flooded telephone lines at the American consulates in the province as people sought ways to protect themselves and their money in case the separatists won.

As a leader who inspired strong reactions, Parizeau belonged in the same league as Mulroney and Salinas. But in 1995, the two signers of NAFTA were already private citizens, undergoing ordeals that were a form of retribution for their errors in office. Parizeau was still premier of Quebec. Throughout the 1995 referendum campaign, he was caricatured in English Canada as the Mad Hatter from Disney's *Alice in Wonderland,* to whom he bore a resemblance in both character and physical demeanor. Chrétien once described him as having "the manner of an English lord and no apparent acquaintance with humility."[4] Parizeau acted as though the referendum itself was merely an appetizer to be dispensed with as quickly as possible before getting to the main course, Quebec sovereignty. He sent notices to the commanders of Canadian Defense Forces in Quebec inviting them to bring themselves, and their jets, tanks, and other military hardware, to join the new Quebec legion of defense, a treasonable act for which he might have been arrested—or hanged—in other countries. He was so sure the separatist side would win that he secretly recorded a victory speech the afternoon of the referendum. He had devised a plan to use $20 billion from the provincial treasury, the publicly owned utility, Hydro Quebec, and the Quebec public employees pension fund to stabilize the Canadian dollar and Quebec government bonds after a yes vote shook the financial markets. He obviously had drawn no lesson from the fallout at the other end of America when Mexico wasted more than $20 billion in foreign reserves desperately trying to save the peso.

Washington has always been careful to keep its distance and allow the Quebec issue to be settled internally. But at least one group in Washington openly studied the possibilities presented by Quebec's nationalist dream and clearly laid out the consequences. The Center for Strategic and International Studies (CSIS) analyzed whether an independent Quebec would automatically be admitted to NAFTA because Canada was a member. As Parizeau had made clear, this was a key issue in Quebec's plans to secede. Separatists had no doubt that Quebec would be allowed to join NAFTA after the breakup with Canada. They hoped that with the NAFTA mantle, Quebec would be better able to absorb the economic shock of separation. Quebec's role in NAFTA also was an important question for the United States, since trade with Quebec was so great—in excess of $35 billion a year—that an independent Quebec would be America's eighth- or ninth-largest trading partner. (Even without Quebec, Canada would account for more trade with America than would any other nation.) After reviewing the history of NAFTA and the rules governing it, the CSIS concluded that a separate Quebec would not automatically be accepted into NAFTA.[5] Nor could an independent Quebec be assured of taking its place alongside Canada in other crucial agreements such as the auto pact, which has eliminated many barriers to continental automobile manufacturing since 1965. Under U.S. and international laws, participation in such agreements or pacts could not be unilaterally extended to new states. A petition for membership would be preceded by review, which would open the possibility of amending existing regulations and adding new ones, which neither Canada nor Quebec would necessarily want.

After tense weeks of campaigning, capped by a huge pro-Canada demonstration in Montreal, the referendum on Quebec separation was held October 30, 1995. I was in Mexico the day the people of Quebec decided Canada's fate, but when I moved to Canada a year later, I found injuries from that painful encounter still evident. Only Quebecers could vote, but many Canadians recounted the night spent watching returns on the Canadian Broadcasting Corporation. As the votes trickled in to CBC studios, their hearts sank with the realization that the nightmare they had spent a lifetime avoiding might actually come to be. By the end of the night, the vote was narrowly against Quebec's secession, but the outcome rested on the votes of just a few urban blocks in Montreal; changing 30,000 votes from no to yes would have sent one of the world's most successful countries into a black hole of uncertainty. The final tally showed that the separatist side had garnered just over 49 percent of the vote; those rejecting the separatists' plan came to just over 50 percent, led by Montreal, the eastern townships bordering the United States, and the aboriginal north.

After the narrow decision, Canadians soberly reflected on what had happened. Politicians from Chrétien on down were rethinking their strategies and vowing never again to let Canada come so close to self-destructing. Disaster had been close enough to sniff, but few realized how precarious matters had become until the very end. These were not the thoughts of victors but rather the ruminations of survivors of a near-fatal crash, those who have been shaken by how close they came to oblivion and who cannot claim that anything but luck prevented a disaster. They realized that Parizeau and a few others had come in through an unlocked side door and nearly made off with their country.

It later became known that the separatist government used misleading propaganda, questionable electoral practices, and a public question so unclear that many people did not even understand what they were voting for or against. It also was evident that Parizeau and the radical wing of Quebec separatists had planned to use a referendum victory not in the way they had stated—to begin negotiations on a sovereignty association with the rest of Canada—but to launch a new nation. Forming a sovereignty association would have meant that Quebec and the rest of Canada would share a common currency, retain open trade, and enjoy fairly open borders. Each side would have its own laws and its own government. According to the stated plan, if an agreement could not be reached within a year on the technical issues of sovereignty association—such as splitting the debt and reapportioning the army—Quebec would declare its independence.

The one-year timetable for negotiations was patently unrealistic—it took a year of preparation and eighteen months of tough bargaining just to get the NAFTA deal on the table, and the agreement could be rescinded at any time with six months' notice. Parizeau apparently had no intention of adhering to the schedule once election night had passed. His plan, revealed afterward in the French-language magazine *L'Actualité,* was to conclude quickly after a separatist victory that negotiations with Canada were hopeless. Quebec would then sue for independence, which Parizeau assumed would be promptly recognized by France and, shortly thereafter, the United States. Former Ambassador Blanchard called Parizeau a wishful thinker whose plans for becoming father of an independent nation of Quebec were divorced from reality.[6]

After the stinging defeat in the referendum (the separatists' second in almost thirty years), Parizeau let slip what was widely considered a side of his character that until then he had kept hidden. "It's true we've been defeated, but by what?" he asked a crowd of supporters on the night of the referendum, "By money and the ethnic vote." This was a crude broadside at Jews and immigrants in Montreal who overwhelmingly voted against the separatists, and the remark seemed to confirm some of the worst fears about Parizeau and the radical wing of the separatist movement he represented. He was forced to resign and was replaced by Lucien Bouchard, who had served in Mulroney's cabinet and represented Canada as ambassador to France. After a falling-out with Mulroney, Bouchard had switched to the separatist cause. He became revered in Quebec for his fiery character, his rigorous intellect, and the mythical story of his life. Struck by a rapidly advancing case of flesh-eating disease, he had been forced to have one of his legs amputated. Shortly after he left the hospital, he took over the flagging referendum campaign and almost carried it to victory. After replacing Parizeau as premier of Quebec, Saint Lucien, cane in hand, vowed to hold another referendum. Next time, he promised, he would not lose.

The reaction of the rest of North America to the dramatic events in Canada was based on two conflicting views: One held that after thirty years of threatening to break away, Quebec never really intended to do so. That meant that each referendum and the constitutional debate that preceded and followed the vote were nothing more than the idle shop talk of a nation of quibblers and nitpickers. But from the other perspective, the referendum, whether or not it passed, reflected the same tribalism that the United States was trying to halt in Bosnia and other unstable parts of the world. "In a world darkened by ethnic conflicts that literally tear nations apart, Canada has stood for all of us as a model of how people of different cultures can live and work together in peace, prosperity, and respect," President Clinton had told the Canadian Parliament in Ottawa several months before the vote on secession. It was the strongest statement advocating Canadian unity from an American president in many years, and it reflected the feeling that a united Canada was a model for the rest of the world, but a Canada that could not keep from breaking up would send a dangerous message to an already troubled world. The leaders of some foreign countries even resented Ottawa's willingness to permit the separatists' referendum to be held, because they feared the example would encourage similar movements on their own troubled soil.

Most Americans simply paid little attention. Chrétien's government itself did not focus on Quebec until the campaign's final days. The prime minister believed that dealing directly with the separatists only gave them credibility they did not deserve. Chrétien's opponents accused him of sleepwalking into a near disaster. He replied that separatists would portray any counteroffensive as a sign that Ottawa was preparing for secession. Chrétien's caution was warranted, given separatist doublespeak and the facility with which Parizeau twisted facts to his own purposes. But the decision to publicly ignore this most divisive of issues until it was almost too late seemed a peculiarly Canadian approach. Even when the provincial government of Ontario did conduct its own assessment of the impact Quebec separation would have on Ontario's economy, provincial leaders refused to make it public until they were sued by *The Globe and Mail* and forced to release the documents. The study predicted a severe financial crisis and found the potential existed for the federal government to resort to using national defense forces to protect federal buildings and keep the peace.

Canada's close call left many in North America wondering about the country's future. Charles F. Doran, a Canada expert at Johns Hopkins University, doubted that Canada could survive as a sovereign nation if Quebec ever held another referendum and did vote to secede. Quebec's departure could loosen the comparatively weak bonds holding together Canada's entire uneven federation of provinces and territories, Doran argued, and a regional centrifugal force would tear what was left of the country to pieces. The Atlantic provinces, suddenly cut off from the rest of Canada, would grow restless. Worried about the significantly enlarged power of Ontario, they might decide to form their own union, or look south to the United States. Similarly, western Canada—British Columbia, Alberta, and the prairie provinces—would find itself under pressure to reorganize, either in conjunction with each other or with the United States. Quebec itself could end up broken into smaller pieces, creating homelands for the Cree Indians in the north and for conservative Anglo voters on the island of Montreal.

"Eventually, North America could look more like the former Soviet Union," Doran wrote, "with one large state at the center, the United States, edged by a series of small, isolated, weak entities along its northern border." The prospect, chilling though seemingly remote, became more believable after Parizeau's antics in the last referendum and could change the way North Americans viewed the American continent. "Long accustomed to contemplating North America as a secure continental island untouched by the turmoil affecting other world regions, the United States may find that on the threshold of the 21st century, its relations with Canada are far from exceptional."[7]

✳

By bringing together North America's three nations in a close commercial partnership, NAFTA and the ongoing process of integration were accelerating the pace of change and forcing Americans to be more intently aware of events occurring across their neighbors' fences. Initially, much of the attention was focused on the obvious—jobs, factory closings, corruption, and the leading proponents of change. Both Salinas and Mulroney were casualties of this process of integration, just as Jacques Parizeau was a casualty of contrary forces, those that would tear the continent apart.

As the process of coming together proceeded in early 1996, it became clearer that economics was but one aspect of what was at stake. Significant societal fronts were making their way across the continent like cold weather from Canada or moist air rising from the Gulf of Mexico. These great movements reached everywhere from the corridors of power down to the dwellings of some of the simplest citizens of North America. At those lowest levels was evidence of the parallel nations that had long existed in North America, even though most Americans might not have been aware of them. As I traveled among the direct descendants of the native people of North America at this time, listening to their stories and trying to portray their struggles, I realized that another America would have to be explored if the American continent truly was to be rediscovered.

CHAPTER SEVEN

From Conquest to National Character

✳

Positively, there are whites somewhere to the southwest
and they have wood sawn into boards, they too use boats,
and their animals are strange to us.

**Two Cree Indians from the Lake of the Woods region
speaking to a French explorer in 1720 about New Spain**

The foothills of the Sierra Madre, where the forbidding central plain of the Chihuahua desert suddenly hardens and thrusts upward in jagged, thirsty peaks, is where I met Sebastián Gloria. The old man thought he was about ninety years old; he didn't know for sure and neither did anyone else. Age in and of itself is not all that important among the timeless cliffs and changeless skies of northern Mexico's Indian country. Bowed over almost double, but still wiry and tough, Sebastián had lived his whole life in and around a shallow cave in much the same way his Tarahumara ancestors had lived since the conquistadores arrived in the new world. His cave was located about 1,000 miles north of Mexico City and less than 250 miles from the U.S. border. The old man knew little about Mexico, and nothing of America.

Sebastián called me *chabochi*, the word the Tarahumara Indians use for all outsiders. In their lyrical language it means "one with spider webs on his face." That is what the Tarahumara called the bearded conquistadores who tried but failed to control these fiercely independent tribesmen. As the Spaniards advanced into Mexico's northern reaches, the Tarahumara retreated into the hostile Sierra Madre. To hear the old man call me *chabochi* because of my full beard was to feel as though I had arrived in these dry hills of stone and cactus just a few days after Hernán Cortés, rather than nearly five centuries later.

But much time clearly had passed—time as we measure it, but not the Tarahumara. The roof of Sebastián's cave and most of the dry sloping walls were coated with a thick layer of campfire soot, an accumulation that, like the fingerprints of children and old people along a house's stairwell, gave blackened proof of the many lives lived within. The cave held little else—a few simple cribs made from sticks to hold corn and beans and a couple of green chili peppers, and a rickety wooden table without chairs. Just outside the cave a small area was fenced off and covered with a mat of straw. This was an important place, for it was where Sebastián curled up when he felt weak, and where the goat slept.

I had gone into the Sierra Madre to document a brutal drought that had sucked all the arroyos dry and stunted the Tarahumara corn until the ears were little bigger than eggs. I was shocked, of course, at the dozens of Tarahumara children who had died of malnutrition in the San Teresita clinic in the mountain town of Creel, but I was even more dismayed at how people like Sebastián and his son Luis, who was forty-six, took such hardships as utterly normal. The only way Sebastián and Luis would speak to me was through my guide, Ismael Villalobos, a mestizo who had known the Tarahumara since he was a child and who I knew cried at their misery. We had approached Sebastián's cave and others like it in the region shouting *chicón, chicón,* words of indeterminate origin and meaning but which the Indians associated with Ismael and the food he brought. Sebastián was grateful when Ismael handed him a sack of beans and some corn flour for making tortillas. The old man led us to the food supplies he and Luís had put away until the next harvest, six months away. These consisted of less than a pound of beans, a few pounds of peppers, and some shrunken ears of corn that would last less than a month. But his biggest worry, he said, was that he did not have enough food for the goat, the family's storehouse of milk and, eventually, meat.

That initial encounter with Sebastián was the first of many trips I took to the land of the Tarahumara, and each time I returned I once again was stunned by how little the events occurring around them had changed them. One time Luciano, a Tarahumara elder, asked me how many cattle roamed the streets of Mexico City, which he had heard was a large pueblo. Another time the Tarahumara took me to a ledge from which I could see across seven valleys and, it seemed then, a part of infinity. The wall of the ledge was covered in ancient red pictographs, haunting, magical human figures that danced and floated with the mysteries of dark summer nights and unexplained stars. They allowed me to see the burial area where the bones of their ancestors are laid high up a steep canyon wall, along with remnants of clothing and the few treasured items left with the dead for their trip to the next life. All that surrounds the Tarahumara is a reflection of their philosophy, which is as irreducible as they are themselves. They believe in no God, no forces of good or evil. They divide the world into two spheres: that which is useful, and therefore, in our Western system of concepts, what we would call good; and that which serves no useful purpose, what we would consider to be bad, or evil. In all the time I was with them, I never saw or heard any indication that this fundamental classification fell short of putting all the order they needed into their world. Neither did I ever sense that they felt impoverished or deprived; even during the terrible drought that was killing their babies, they did not complain. Little government help arrived to assist them—but little help was sought. Long ago, the Tarahumara had decided not to live in the new land created by the *chabochis*. And they still did not.

Another time, Ismael and I drove far back to the almost unreachable valley of Rituchi in the mountains near the moldering Jesuit settlement of Sisoguichi, one of many missions the order abandoned when it was evicted from New Spain in 1767. We visited Rubén Mendoza Hierro, talking for more than an hour with the thirty-two-year-old farmer who was dressed in the traditional Tarahumara toga and sandals that laced to his bare knees. Finally, he gently asked a favor. He needed help with the funeral of his younger brother, Francisco, who had been killed and nearly cut in half only a day before while riding his bicycle blind drunk on the railroad tracks through a town several hours away. Rubén changed into a colorful new shirt and sat in the back of Ismael's pickup as we bounced for miles over boulders and along a dirt track into town. We arrived just as Tarahumara women were making the last tortillas for the funeral. The women cooked on a small woodfire stove in the same bare concrete room where Francisco's coffin, draped in purple chenille, was propped on wooden sawhorses. Rubén said nothing as he walked to the coffin and peered into the glass window that exposed his brother's face, with pieces of straw still in his beard and on the ragged sweater he wore. Ismael and I helped Rubén load the coffin onto the back of the pickup and take it first to the church and then the cemetery. After Rubén and other Tarahumara lowered the coffin into the grave, they set the tortillas on top of it, to help Francisco in his journey to the afterlife. I heard no wailing, no prayers or mystic incantations. That would not be useful. The Tarahumara are practiced at death, and the many graves around us then, some marked with rough crosses, others only pine boughs, provided ample proof that they had consigned many tortillas to the dirt. Rubén invited us back to town for *tesquino,* a home-brewed corn beer they said would help them forget how Francisco's face had looked in the coffin window. I had trouble understanding that this was happening in North America until I noticed that the new shirt Rubén wore had been sewn from cotton material printed with the image of the Teenage Mutant Ninja Turtles.

✳

Less than a year later, I stood with the icy waters of the North Atlantic at my back, on a beach of hard brown sand laced with fingers of ice. A dead seal had washed up overnight, its body still supple as it lay among the plastic bottles and other debris that floated in on the waters just off Davis Inlet, an island community of Canada's Innu, an ancient Indian people who have lived in the stony and foreboding landscape of northern Labrador for thousands of years. The sky was frigid with approaching winter as I picked my way through the trash to a cemetery just up from the beach. The gravesites there were not much different from those I had seen in Mexico. Some were marked only with pine boughs. On others there was a wooden cross.

Six graves were laid out near the Davis Inlet beach. They belonged to children who had died in a single fire a few years before. Their parents had gone out drinking and left them alone. When the adults stumbled back in the black of northern night, they stood helplessly as the house was engulfed by flames, listening to their children's terrified screams for help. Three of the children had been buried side by side, their crosses united like a gap-toothed picket fence. A single cross-piece connected the uprights, just as this one tragedy in 1992 had pierced the heart of every member of the Davis Inlet community. At the foot of the cross I found the sandy ground covered with children's things: a small soccer ball, some pencils and pens, a frilly hat turned gray by the sun, and a Webster "Pocket Pal" dictionary. It was a childish and simple display, and it was tragically familiar. The graves of the Tarahumara too were encrusted with the most precious possessions of the dead.

I then climbed to the place where the tragic fire had occurred, an empty lot on the top of a hill where the wind howled in from the inlet, whistling through stunted pine trees. The inlet was not the reassuring blue shown in big-screen movies about the north. These waters seemed hard as steel, and just as cold. They formed a barrier that had trapped the Innu since they were moved to the island in 1967 by a federal government that thought it knew best but could never even get the plumbing right.

James Pasteen, an Innu elder who spoke to me in his native language while his grandson translated, called Davis "an evil place" that caused tragedies like the fire. I sought him out after I saw him using a scaffolding made of young pine trunks outside his house to cure caribou meat in the old way of his people, one of the last nomadic tribes in Canada. In Pasteen's youth, he and the other Innu roamed the gray and inhospitable Labrador countryside tracking caribou and hunting seals. They lived in canvas tents, heated by small tin stoves, and they built rafters of pine to keep the meat from the dogs while it dried.

Since 1967, the Innu have no longer hunted the caribou because Daniel Rattle—the turbulent waters separating the island of Davis Inlet from the mainland—is choked with ice for much of the year and all but impassable. The Innu settled reluctantly into their new world because the government promised to take care of them if they sent their children to the school run by whites. Davis turned out to be a wretched place of leaky wooden bungalows, sugary pies from the post store, and bootleg whiskey. When the elders decided it was too dangerous to allow any more whiskey to come in with the bush pilots or the containership that docked once a year, the Innu learned to make their own "home brew," the Innu's *tesquino*. I saw the white plastic pails used as stills in a corner of every bungalow I entered, except for James Pasteen's. He kept a picture of Jesus on the wall. The teenagers and young adults who had never lived with the caribou the way Pasteen had only knew the boredom of their bleak island and they, like their parents, had discovered their own excitement. They drained the gasoline from their wrecked snowmobiles into plastic garbage bags. Then they would get a wicked high by sticking their heads into the bags and breathing the vapors until they nearly passed out. Everyone in the village knew the gas destroyed brain cells—and the future. They sniffed anyway.

The fire that killed the six children made it impossible for the rest of Canada to ignore the truth about the "evil place"—that the helping hand of white government had only deepened the despair of the Innu. Moving them to Davis had isolated them in a poverty far worse than anything they had suffered while following the caribou. Alcoholism raged through the community, consuming more than 90 percent of the adults. Unemployment was practically universal, and without the prospect of a job, few Innu saw any reason to stay in school. Gas sniffing was an epidemic, and the suicide rate at Davis Inlet and the only other Innu community, Sheshatshiu, just outside Happy Valley–Goose Bay in central Labrador, was identified as the highest in the world.

In 1996, nearly thirty years after the Innu community had been transplanted from the mainland to Davis Inlet, the Canadian government admitted its mistake and agreed to spend $62 million to move the Innu back on shore. When that finally happens, the Innu will try to isolate themselves from the contemporary American continent as completely as do some of the Tarahumara. Chief Katie Rich told me she was certain that the only way for her people to keep from disappearing was to return to the land, and to the past. In only sixty years of contact with the modern world, Innu history had been ravaged. Like immigrants, they had left behind everything they knew. But unlike other immigrants to the new world, they had not replaced that history with a new one. Rich felt that moving on shore would do that. With a second chance, they will put as much distance as they can between the irretrievable past and the dismal present that had engulfed them. That would leave them free to create their own future.

✳

In their respective settlements on opposite ends of North America, the Innu and the Tarahumara struggle against the new order they never sought, just as we in the rest of North America try to understand the new world that is forming around us whether we want it to or not. On occasion, the volatile mix of modern and ancient that the native people live with explodes into violence, as it did in Chiapas. More often, though, they smolder with resentment as their communities are ravaged by the worst—and, ironically, what others often consider to be the best—aspects of modern life. Most North Americans see little of this tension, unless a particularly violent incident brings out the news vans. But as I traveled the continent, I sought out these worn-down places and thread-bare lives again and again. I came to realize that by reexamining the conditions under which some Native Americans live, I might better understand the way in which societies react to events of great consequence over which they have little or no control. How these far-flung native communities adapted to certain changes, and flatly rejected others, might serve as a guide for helping us deal with the forces that today are altering the shape of North America.

The first transformation of the splendidly isolated domain the natives of North America had inhabited for untold ages happened in what amounts to a historical heartbeat, and the aftershock was felt throughout the world. We have always deemed the encounter of Europeans with the original inhabitants of the new world as either a discovery or a conquest, but both descriptions fall short of the truth. There may be a different approach, one more relevant to the world in which we live. What if, as Rafael Tovar y de Teresa, the president of Mexico's National Council for Culture and the Arts, once suggested during a meeting in Ottawa, we were to view Europe's conquest of the new world as history's first attempt at globalization? He posited that because the energy behind much of the settlement of the American continent—whether from the Spanish, the French, or the English—was drawn from the desire to expand trade, the conquest was a situation not unlike our own today. Of course, the sixteenth century made for an unruly globalization governed only by the brutal laws of an open market. People were exploited and natural resources depleted, factors that also suggest parallels to today.

And as is true today, the native people of what now are Mexico, Canada, and the United States shared some basic principles. When Europeans began settling here, the indigenous people of North America all used fire, they all understood the basic practices of agriculture, they all had developed and had time to practice some concepts of religion that helped explain the world around them, and they all possessed some sense of stewardship of the bountiful land in which they lived. But their cultures were so different one from the other that an Aztec would have had great difficulty finding any common ground with an Iroquois. Similarly, the people of North America today all draw from the same well of modernity—rampant globalization, advanced telecommunications, and a belief that science can be bent into useful technology—but their individual lives continue to reflect separate cultures and systems of belief.

One trait is shared universally in North America: The soul of a voyager is inside each one of us, because every one of us, or our ancestors, lived through the experience of arriving here and beginning over. That is the wayfarer's essence, and it infused every individual who dared to cross the frozen Bering Strait. It was inside every immigrant who tried not to sneak one last look at home before setting out for the new world. Even those who did not come here voluntarily but were brought in chains were cruelly forced to develop a voyager's ability to begin history anew if they were to survive.

Having arrived here so much earlier than the Europeans made the natives believe they had been in North America since time began. The landings of the newcomers sometimes frightened them, which was understandable given the consequences of such encounters. But often the advent of strangers seemed to trigger some subconscious appreciation for the shared experience of arriving at a new place. When that happened, the natives rejoiced, believing that the strange visitors were actually long-lost spirits of gods returning home. The first Indians Columbus met thought he had come from heaven. East coast Indians believed the ships of the Europeans were huge birds carrying heavenly spirits to them. West coast Indians called the explorers children of the moon because their strange wooden ships traveled on moonbeams reflecting off the ocean.

Voyages such as these embody the essence of the American continent, and make the people of Canada, Mexico, and the United States Americans all. But the continent cannot be categorized so broadly as to use the term "American" the way the term "European" is used to describe French, Germans, Italians, and other nationalities of the old continent. The commercial culture of the United States is too overpowering, the reach of Hollywood myth-making too great, for the term "American" to be used to describe anyone but the people of the United States (which is the way I use it in this book). That presents a quandary for someone wanting to describe the strong links that exist among the three countries that together make up the North American continent. Even the term "North American" is inadequate, because that is how Mexicans refer to Yankees and Canadians. Corporations use "North America" as shorthand for the two large northern markets, which delights Canadians because they can use the term "North American presence" to describe a much wider market than their own. Few if any northerners would call Mexicans North Americans, and no Mexicans I ever met were willing to describe themselves as such.

How, then, to refer to the more than 400 million people who live on the territory known since the sixteenth century as North America? The theory of broken symmetry enabled us to see North America as a unitary place before the settlers left their imprints on the territory that became Canada, Mexico, and the United States. With a common background as voyagers to a wild, new land, the people of all three nations could all be considered Newlanders—the progeny of people changed by the very process of moving from one place to another. Motivated by dreams and shaped by opportunities taken, or lost, Newlanders have taught the world much. From Mexico has come the dynamic of racial synthesis, the blending of different people to create a new race. Mexico's patron saint, the Virgin of Guadalupe, is portrayed on the old Indian shawl that is still on display in Mexico City as a brown-skinned mestizo woman who appeared to Juan Diego in 1531. The apparition is considered a great miracle in Mexico and throughout Latin America. What surely is miraculous is that the woman is said to have appeared only ten years after the Spanish conquest, a time when it was unlikely that Mexico could have had any women of mixed race. With Indians far outnumbering the men of Cortés's army, however, that racial blending was the inevitable direction of society in New Spain. The Virgin's *mestizaje*—the mixing of races that before the conquest had been unknown, and unthinkable, in the Western world—presaged the racial alchemy that has become the inevitable future for the rest of North America, and most of mankind.

Another concept born from this new land was the supremacy of ideas. The rejected and persecuted colonists of British North America channeled their rage against an unjust monarch into a new nation. In the process, they proved for the first time that to be a nation, people needed not necessarily allegiance to a throne but rather loyalty to a concept, in this case the dignity of the individual. That abstract idea on which the American Revolution was raised has taken root wherever people join together to demand their rights.

And although Canada is the American continent's youngest modern state, it was built on the foundations of some of the continent's oldest societies, including the native people without whose assistance the French settlers would not have survived, not even the first winter. When the disparate segments of British North America drew together in the mid-nineteenth century to negotiate confederation of the Dominion of Canada, the world had to bear witness that it was possible to create a great nation without going to war.

Newlanders share a common taproot of history, but since shortly after Europeans arrived on the continent, Canada, Mexico, and the United States—the part of the Western Hemisphere we might consider our "hereisphere"—have not been thought of in any common context but geography. Even that creates confusion. Does Mexico rightly belong in North America, especially since its economic alignment through NAFTA planted it squarely with Canada and the United States? Or should it remain with the Spanish-speaking neighbors in Central and South America with which it has traditionally been associated? The course of rivers and the breadth of mountains unmistakably link Mexico to the north. Monarch butterflies, migrating from Mexico to Canada and then, in later generations, back along the same route to Mexico, instinctively know that. In most factors important to contemporary society, economically and even culturally, the nation's compass points north, where Mexico's future lies, and not south, which connects it to Latin America and its past. Some of Mexico's Latin neighbors have already made clear that they think Mexico is drifting away from them, and they resent it. "I don't know if the Mexicans wanted to put a distance between themselves and us . . . and left us in the poor neighborhood," Fidel Castro said in an uncommon attack on Mexico in late 1998 that expressed the view of many Latinos. "They left us in a house of misery and moved to an aristocratic quarter."[1]

The American continent to which Mexico now seems eager to belong has always been a place of great contrasts, an immense land that mixes north and south, mountain and desert, arctic and tropic, rich and poor, European and Indian, new world and old. It is at the same time the oldest part of the earth—the rocks in the vast sea of impenetrable stone that covers much of Canada are 3.96 billion years old—and among the last major land areas to be settled by man. Whether that settlement occurred 10,000 years ago, or 30,000 as some more recent evidence suggests, it was a magnificent achievement, "the hugest migration known to man," wrote Mexican novelist Carlos Fuentes, "from Alaska to Patagonia, lands baptised by migration."[2]

This shared history of scattered native settlements represents the beginning of the still-ongoing process of North American entanglement. Despite the vast cultural differences among Indian nations, archaeologists have found evidence of complex trade relationships that brought goods from settlements in the Mississippi Valley up through the Canadian plains, and from British Columbia almost down to what now is Mexico. The museum at the Minneapolis Institute of Arts has documented a trade network that regularly brought goods from the Valley of Mexico as far north as the modern city of Red Wing, Minnesota. Around 1300 A.D., the transcontinental influence was so great that Red Wing was a ceremonial center with its own earthen pyramids resembling the flat-topped structures built by the ancient peoples in Mexico.

Whether across the Bering Strait or, as has recently been suggested, simultaneously at various points in North and South America with seagoing vessels capable of crossing the Pacific, the peopling of America was a unique moment in human history. It was propelled entirely by man's curiosity and, as Carlos Fuentes imagined it, "accompanied by flights and images, metaphors and metamorphoses that make the going bearable, that save the peoples from fatigue, discouragement, distance, time, the centuries necessary to travel America from pole to pole."[3]

At no time in history was there ever an invasion on the scale of the one that struck the American continent in the sixteenth and seventeenth centuries. Conquerors, no matter from where they hailed, set foot on the shores of the mighty continent and claimed it for their own, often with the local natives gazing on in wonderment. The Indians who welcomed the strange men from the sea provided invaluable assistance that indirectly led to their own downfall. Cortés sailed from Cuba in 1519; after making landfall on the Yucatán peninsula, he heard from the natives that other strange bearded men had lived among them for years. Cortés eventually found two fellow Spaniards who had been shipwrecked since 1511. One, Jerónimo de Aguilar, had learned to speak Mayan and readily agreed to depart with Cortés for Mexico. But the other, Gonzalo Guerrero, had tattooed his face, taken a wife, and had a family. When he saw the Castilians and heard Cortés speak of conquest and gold, he rejected his countrymen and returned to the jungle, perhaps anticipating in some way what was to come of Cortés's mission. Aguilar's ability to translate proved invaluable to Cortés, especially after he landed in the region of current-day Tabasco and there found a beguiling Indian woman called Malinche, the daughter of a local Aztec chieftain. Beautiful Malinche, whom Cortés called Marina, could speak both Mayan and Nahuatl, the language of the Aztecs. Through both Aguilar and Malinche, Cortés gained the incalculable advantage of being able to communicate with, and therefore deceive, Montezuma himself. The importance of communication to the settlement of the new world presents another parallel to today's globalization.

Seventeen years after Cortés's fateful trip, the French explorer Jacques Cartier encountered Indians living in villages scattered along the St. Lawrence River. They, like La Malinche, proved to be the key to conquest. Cartier came for gold but found only fool's gold. A devastating winter threatened to kill off his dispirited men by starvation or sickness. Donnacona, the Iroquois chief, showed Cartier how to use the boiled needles of an evergreen tree to stave off the scurvy that had laid low his crew. That first-aid assistance enabled Cartier to return to France with his staked claim to the new continent and eventually open the way for the settlement of New France.

Many years after Cartier's arrival, Indians told the French about the Dutch traders in Fort Orange (Albany) and the Spanish explorers they met where the Mississippi River flowed into the Gulf of Mexico. Their renderings of the rocks and rivers helped explorers fill in areas of North America that European mapmakers had left blank. And the Indians of the Iroquois Confederacy showed that united, the five tribes were far stronger than any one of them individually, which provided the jealous and bickering British colonies with an inspiration for a new kind of nation. The Iroquois also provided an early lesson in trading. When the French refused to sell them rifles, thinking it too dangerous, the Indians struck a deal with the less concerned Dutch, and got the guns they wanted.

A review of the stormy period that followed the initial encounters between natives and Europeans in the new world reveals the shared beginnings of the three nations of North America as well as the fundamental differences that would distinguish them in time to come. Modern perceptions of those beginnings underscore how powerfully history has shaped national character. In Mexico, the sad saga of the arrival of the Spanish is referred to as "la conquista." No people have ever lost so much so fast. Within a few years after they first warily welcomed these strange men with beards into Tenochtitlán, thinking they were gods making a long-awaited return, the Aztecs had lost their homes, their emperor, and their gods.

But the Aztecs did not disappear. The Spaniards—who had come to plunder, not to colonize—needed them to work in the silver mines, on the huge landholdings, even to rebuild ruined Tenochtitlán. Spanish men outnumbered women ten to one, and thus the seeds were planted for the mixed race of most modern Mexicans. Nine out of ten Mexicans today are mestizo, and in them the Indian past is forever struggling with concepts derived from their inherited European values. The remaining 10 million Mexicans are full-blooded Indians whose first language is an indigenous one.

Mexicans and their country are torn between the twin poles of their identities, trying to be modern but falling back on ancient ways of work, courtesy, and corruption. They are proud of their Indian roots, but no number of statues of the warrior king Cuauhtémoc or other Indian heroes can hide their shameful treatment of today's descendants of the Aztecs. I saw this firsthand when a friend, Henry McDonald, an American real estate executive in Mexico City, told me of his experience when he tried to take his family to dinner at an expensive restaurant in Mexico City not far from the monument to Mexico's Indian past. They were turned away because he had brought along his dark-skinned Indian housekeeper. It wasn't a sophisticated rejection, nor a veiled objection. The maître' d simply told Henry that no tables were available at that time. Henry kept an American schedule in Mexico and arrived at the restaurant at about 7 P.M., when it was practically empty. Mario Padilla, the restaurant manager, later told me quite openly that the restaurant never allowed servants or chauffeurs into the main dining room. This policy was for the benefit of patrons, he said, most of whom have servants but would never bring them along. However, some people "lack discretion," he said, obviously referring to Americans like Henry who wouldn't know not to bring a maid to dinner at a fine restaurant. For that reason, rules had to be enforced. It was not a racist policy, Padilla assured me. "We're just trying to protect the image of the restaurant."

Whenever the subject of racism in Mexico is discussed, the name of Benito Juárez is invoked and the question is asked, "How can Mexico be racist if it had an Indian president?" Juárez, the most revered of Mexican leaders, was a Zapotec Indian from Oaxaca who left his isolated mountain village when he was twelve and was taken in by a Spanish-speaking family in the city of Oaxaca who helped him get an education and become a lawyer. He belonged to a group of liberal-minded intellectuals opposed to the disastrous rule of Santa Anna, the hoary hero turned dictator. Exiled in Louisiana, Juárez and the other liberals devised a plan to overthrow the old caudillo. The reformers instituted new laws, which touched off a civil war with conservatives. The liberals won and elected

Juárez president, but the war had emptied the national treasury. Juárez, facing what would become the recurring nightmare of Mexican leaders, was forced to declare a moratorium on debt repayments. That opened the way for France, a principal lender, to start the war that installed Maximilian on the throne of an imaginary Mexican empire. Juárez went into hiding in the United States but returned and eventually triumphed over Maximilian, ordering his execution.

Juárez had indeed been Mexico's president, but for nearly 150 years since then the country's ruling elite has been composed of light-skinned Mexicans with European features. In recent years, presidents have been careful to bring in at least one dark-skinned member of the cabinet to accompany the president on his day trips into ethnic parts of the country, but rarely does that official have any real power or authority. Mexicans are always conscious of skin color, even if the more sophisticated never mention it by name but instead touch their forearm to indicate that the person's skin was dark, and therefore less acceptable than a light-skinned person would be. In the local marketplace we frequented when we lived in Cuajimalpa, the shopkeepers and the hawkers never called us gringos. But they would shout out "Hey, *güero*," or "Come look at what I have for you today, *güera*" which is like saying "blondie" or "whitey." The unspoken assumption was that a light-skinned person was more likely to have money, and made a better potential customer, than someone with dark skin.

Mexico is struggling with the incompatibility of its Indian past and the economic and social realities of contemporary North America, where it has decided its future lies. It was no accident that the leaders of the Zapatista uprising in Chiapas fired their first shots the day NAFTA took effect, which was also the day the government had promised Mexico would fully enter the modern world.

That dual character of Mexican society is reflected in the twin names given to many Mexican pueblos, which have a saint's name combined with an Indian word. San Juan Chamula in Chiapas, Santa Rosa Jáuregui in Queretaro, San Antonio Techalote in Tlaxcala, are among hundreds like them across the country where Mexico's European and Indian roots mingle. European and Indian currents flow together to make up contemporary Mexico's character, and sometimes cause turbulence. Indian concepts have entered the national psyche in Mexico far more deeply than have Indian influences in the United States or Canada, and this tension presents an unresolved conflict for Mexico. Indian ideas about education and health, the economy, the environment, and religion differ markedly from the views held by the rest of Mexican society. The majority of Mexican mestizos constantly struggle to balance these contradictions within themselves.

When forced to confront an American's notion of democracy, or a Canadian's concept of time, Mexicans have to react on two fronts—as Europeans and as Indians. As a result, they often are left feeling they can only lose. In 1996, Mexico adopted daylight saving time, moving clocks ahead an hour in spring and back in the fall. This disrupted the lives of millions of rural Mexicans, but it brought the country closer to the schedules kept in NAFTA's other two members. Still, defining time and applying it in a universal way remained a challenge. A Canadian executive working in Mexico once told me that giving the simplest instructions in the plant he ran posed difficulties because of these fundamental differences. For example, he said, the idea of an absolute deadline can be foreign to many Mexicans, even those he thought should have known better. "The Mexicans see it more as a guideline and not a deadline," said Louis-Jean Chartier, a twenty-seven-year-old financial officer of Bombardier Transportation's Ciudad Sahagún plant in central Mexico. He was not talking only about the semiskilled men and women on the assembly line. Rather, he meant the clerks and secretaries in the company's head office, members of Mexico's white-collar class. In Bombardier's Montreal headquarters, requests for a same-day turnaround on a report are standard. But Chartier said that in Mexico most efforts to get such a report done in one day inevitably fail, not because of laziness but because immediacy resonates differently there than in Montreal. "They just couldn't understand that a report done in the office here in Ciudad Sahagún could be at all important for the top-level management in Canada," Chartier said. "It was just a misunderstanding, but there were misunderstandings every day." Jorge G. Castañeda, the Mexican intellectual, once suggested that the reasons for this type of behavior go far deeper than personal perception. Living in Mexico's unvarying climate, without the regular cadence of changing seasons that reflect an orderly progression of time throughout the year, has created a fluid concept of time in Indian people. Castañeda said this approach to time has been inherited by modern Mexicans and makes them less vulnerable to the dictates of deadlines.

Living in Mexico, I found that misunderstandings based on cultural dissimilarities were common. The problem typically arose when dealing with domestic help. Despite our discomfort with the idea of keeping a maid, and our best efforts to treat each one with respect, the need to lay out directions in such great detail invariably resulted in a patronizing tone we had wanted to avoid. Even so, there were disagreements, disappointments, and disputes that poisoned our relationship with them. After our first maid quit, we went through two others (including one who did steal from us) before having the very good fortune of meeting a remarkable young woman named Graciela Díaz, a full-blooded Zapotec Indian who, like Juárez, came from a small village in the Oaxaca hills.

Slight and usually silent, Graciela came into our home cautiously. It was her first job with an American family, her first time away from home, and she didn't know what to expect. She wanted to help her father, a campesino, and planned to send most of her pay to him. Her sincerity and intelligence were apparent immediately, and we encouraged her to return to school, which she had left years before. She resisted at first, but eventually agreed when we offered to give her time to attend adult classes at a city school to complete her middle school education, which the majority of Mexicans, and almost all Indians, never finish. Living with us, she gradually gained confidence and began to stand her ground with the service men and vendors with whom she dealt. We asked her to eat with us at the dinner table, and she did, on occasion. But usually she said she preferred to eat in the kitchen, sitting on a stool and studying her schoolbooks.

Graciela disproved some of the more facile generalizations about Mexicans, and more specifically about Mexico's Indians. Her understanding of time and responsibility was close to ours, yet we were not at all the same. We were always much impressed with her humility, her good nature in the face of great hardship, and her willingness to learn. She studied all the required subjects of middle school, and in addition she studied us. She wanted to learn more English than was in her books. She wanted to know what our lives had been like in the United States, which she of course had never seen except in movies. She watched us when we went to mass on Sundays, and when we helped the children with their homework. Occasionally, we would reverse roles and ask her about her life in Oaxaca, only to come face to face with the gap between us. Her father had no support except for the land he controlled and the help his sons and daughters provided. The village she lived in had only one telephone. Occasionally, one of her brothers called, and she would be embarrassed if I had answered the phone and had to summon her. One night when she finished one of these calls, she came back crying and told us one of her brothers had been killed in a fight with drug traffickers. We asked her if she wanted to go home, and she said no. She'd deal with it when she returned at Christmas. By then, other problems had arisen. As I explain later, they almost always do.

One of the greatest American misconceptions about Mexico is that the towering civilizations of the Maya and the Aztecs have completely disappeared. That could not be further from the truth. Modern Maya were responsible for the uprising in Chiapas, and over 1.4 million Mexican descendants of the Aztecs today continue to speak their indigenous language, Nahuatl. The Mexican government has tried to focus more attention on publishing textbooks in Nahuatl and training teachers who speak indigenous languages, an effort that is long overdue. In 1995, Miriam and I spent a few days with Nahuatl-speaking Indians in the state of Guerrero, southwest of Mexico City. They lived in a dusty village on the Rio Balsas with the twin Catholic-Indian name of San Juan Totolzintla. The saint name, San Juan, was bestowed by the Augustinian missionaries who arrived soon after the Spanish conquistadores; the original name, Totolzintla, came from the Indians and has been preserved by their descendants. When we made the long trip there along a dirt road that hugged the river, we stopped at a recently built schoolhouse. The construction had been so shoddy that the building couldn't be used. Instead, classes were held in an old house farther from the river, near the entrance to the village. In a covered patio with a smooth concrete floor, a Spanish-speaking teacher sent from Mexico City taught history from a comic book written in Spanish, which most of the dozen small Nahuatl-speaking children there barely understood. The subject of the lesson was the heroic life of Benito Juárez.

I visited many villages in Mexico like this one, each without any sign of economic viability, each one smelling of smoke, sweat, and shit. Few, however, seemed as totally defeated as San Juan Totolzintla. Baked by the sun day after day until its streets were as dry and cracked as the floor of a ceramics kiln, the town offered its residents only two ways to earn a living: working for the government or robbing the graves of their own Indian ancestors.

As I accompanied townsmen down a dung-covered path, they explained that after the defeat of Montezuma and the Aztec empire, the Spaniards rode out from Tenochtitlán in search of more gold. In Totolzintla, about 145 miles south of Mexico City, local inhabitants grew frightened as the Spaniards approached. The strange bearded men were thought to be half animal because they came on the backs of horses, which the Indians had never seen. They were also considered magicians, since they whispered to the horses, which these Indians thought were huge deer. The elders gathered up the community's most valuable treasures, took them to a spot across the Rio Balsas, and buried them among the graves of their ancestors.

Five hundred years later, the men of Totolzintla wade across the fast-flowing but shallow river carrying a shovel and *coa*, a digging tool used by the Aztecs, to search through the sacred ground for pieces of silver jewelry or exquisitely turned precious stone. Everything they find except for bones is ripped from the ground and sold to a man "from the city" who claims to be buying artifacts for a chain of hotels. The Indians know this looting is reprehensible. When they disturb a grave, they light a candle and leave it in the hole to appease the offended spirits until the grave can be closed again. But the men of San Juan Totolzintla know they are offending even more their own dignity and self-worth.

Although Mexico still has by far the largest indigenous population in North America, its Indians remain the most isolated and economically marginalized of all those in the continent. Mexico's splendid constitution extends to them thorough protections, but as with most other aspects of Mexican constitutional law, the safeguards are mostly theoretical, a contradiction at the heart of the Chiapas uprising. One of the demands of the Tzeltal, Tzotzil, and Tojolabal Maya who took up arms in Chiapas was the right to use their traditions in elections, as do some Oaxaca pueblos. When the Indians in San Andrés Larrainzar in Chiapas tried to hold elections according to their custom of discussing a candidate's history and then calling for a show of hands, the state and federal governments protested. The irony escaped most Mexicans. The Mexican government, so well known for trampling on democratic rights and organizing voter fraud through marked ballots or the intimidation of voters, challenged the elections because the votes were not cast by secret ballot. Similarly, the Zapatistas wanted the right to self-government in certain regions of the state of Chiapas, but federal officials refused, claiming that to cede control over any portion of Mexican territory would undermine Mexican sovereignty by creating a state within a state.

Poverty hangs like wood smoke over the lives of most Indian families and gives everything about them the stink of desperation, which in turn attracts corruption. Graciela once told us matter-of-factly that her father had voted for the PRI candidate in the last election even though he knew the man was corrupt. He had been won over by the PRI's promise of a new machete in exchange for his vote. "He needed the machete," was the explanation she gave, and in that moment, for her, it was as valid as any discourse on democracy would have been. When possessions are reduced to so few, everything assumes great value.

And for Indians in Mexico, nothing is more valuable than land. The quest for *tierra* is as old as Mexico, and as violent. For more than a decade, Graciela's father was involved in a savage dispute over his small, parched parcel of land in Oaxaca, and the threat of violence never diminished. Any question in Mexico involving land is never simple, and is always surrounded by great suspicion, even when goodwill motivated the question. We found that out in early 1996, when my son Aahren proposed creating a public hiking trail in Mexico City as his project to earn the Eagle Scout badge in Boy Scouts. He decided to lay out and construct the trail in the Ajusco mountains, a huge tract of parkland above Mexico City. He thought that because the land was publicly owned, he could avoid complicated negotiations with private owners. He explained his project to city officials, and was surprised to be told that he needed permission from the community of Indians and mestizos in the *ejido* of Santo Tomás who had been given ownership of the mountaintop under Article 27 of the Mexican constitution.

Aahren had to find Don Gabriel Nava Pasalagua, the local Indian leader, and try to get him to stand still long enough to hear his proposal. The Boy Scouts were willing to do all the work to clear and mark a trail to the top of La Cruz de Márquez for use by the people of Mexico City, where public hiking trails had not existed before. Don Gabriel's suspicions were not easy to allay. He kept asking how much it was going to cost; the concept of community service was as foreign to him as a computer program might have been. At last, Aahren's honesty and good intentions convinced him to say yes. Don Gabriel became an unabashed supporter, bounding up the side of the hill to show us that the best way to climb the peak was to use the route the villagers take to get to the huge cross they had erected there in the clouds. Until the trail was completed, though, he harbored the belief that there would be money to be made from it, and that his community had the right to share in the proceeds.

✳

"The conquest" is also mentioned in the textbooks of Canadian schools, but unlike Mexico's great clash of civilizations, "conquest" in this instance does not refer to native people. The British crown had negotiated treaties (except in British Columbia and a few other areas) that laid the groundwork for centuries of paternalistic treatment and led to tragedies like Davis Inlet. Still, the "conquest" is just as painful a central fact of the nation's founding, and as difficult for Canada to embrace, as is the defeat of the Aztecs for Mexico. In Canadian terms, the conquest refers to the defeat of the French army in North America by the British. It is encapsulated by the year 1759, and the long, bloody siege of Quebec, the walled capital city of New France. The British assault on Quebec came to an effective end with a short and inglorious battle on open fields just outside Quebec. The fields had been cleared by a local farmer, Abraham Martin, and have ever since kept his name—the Plains of Abraham. The fall of Quebec was a decisive victory for the British that took the lives of the commanders of both sides. It helped bring the Seven Years' War to an end and resolved what historian Francis Parkman called "the most momentous and far-reaching question ever brought to issue on this continent" by bringing to a close France's doomed dreams in North America. Historians sometimes consider this same battle the opening shot of the American Revolution.

In Canada, as in Mexico, native people were not seen as simply an impediment to European expansion. Rather, from the start, they were acknowledged to be indispensable to the settlement of the wild and untamed lands the Spanish and the French had claimed. The primary enterprises of New France were cod fishing and fur trading. The fishermen worked alone, but the traders needed outposts and contact with a large network of trappers who knew the country and the best ways of traveling through it. European manpower or ingenuity was not required because natives not only would do the work but were far more skilled at it than the French. This reservoir of talent obviated the need for large numbers of European settlers. The St. Lawrence and Ottawa Rivers offered an easy link to the Great Lakes and the Mississippi River, opening up a vast inland empire. Alliances with the Indians meant France could not only claim the continent but also defend it.

The natives of the northern part of the continent became crucial allies for both France and England. As Cortés had done in conquering the Aztecs, the European powers sought to exploit long-standing rivalries between native groups and turn the Indians' aggressions to their own advantage. The natives proved frighteningly effective allies in defense of New France in the French and Indian War and again in the War of 1812, when it was Britain's turn to defend Canada. But the real losers in that war were the Indians on both sides of the border, because as soon as American expansionist designs on Canada were blocked, attention was shifted to the west and the ancestral lands of the Indians the French had protected.

Westward expansion took place in Canada too, and although the pressure on Indian tribes was less intense than in the United States, it was clear that the native groups would not be permitted to live as the free and independent people they had once been. The rebellion of 1885 in Manitoba, and the later uprising led by a French-Indian half-breed named Louis Riel in what became Saskatchewan, marked the point at which there no longer was any doubt about the fate of Indians in British North America. Officials began to assemble the system of Indian reserves and special Indian status that would cause so much pain, and shame, for Canada.

Despite that difficult beginning, Canada was where the struggle for native rights would head in the most innovative direction in North America. But that was still years off.

There is no simple parallel in the United States to Canada's conquest or Mexico's *conquista,* although historical similarities abound. America's Indians were soundly defeated, as were those in Mexico, and so were the European powers, as were the French in Canada and the Spanish in Mexico. But instead of scarring America's soul, the victory over native Indians and the expulsion of colonial powers became an elixir that invigorated the American myth. Instead of "la conquista," we call our conquest of the native tribes "How the West Was Won," and have added it to the lexicon of our manifest continental destiny. It is some measure of national maturity that the slaughter of the Indians has been reduced in the mythology of our society from thrilling adventure to sad, but unavoidable, tragedy.

Even so, American attempts to grab territory from Mexico and Canada in the eighteenth and nineteenth centuries are still so thoroughly cloaked in heroics that most Americans do not think of them as aggressions against the Indian people who lived there. Rather, they are viewed as manifestations of the destiny of the American people, universally celebrated even by our one-time enemies and now-pliant neighbors.

※

Taken together, these three vastly different accounts of "conquest" among North America's three nations go not only to their roots but also some of their most fundamental differences. The manner in which we interpret and incorporate the difficult aspects of our past influences our national character. The United States has always been an ideological nation, composed of culturally different people bound by a strong vision summed up by the opening words of the Constitution, "We the people." Ideology, not history, is the foundation.

Canada is essentially a historical nation, conceived in a political compact triggered not by resolution of the conflict between French and English but by a commitment to resist annexation by the United States. Canada is still stuck somewhere in that historical swamp, advancing only with great difficulty. The survival of Quebec, along with the idea of two founding nations—the French and English—is a historical concept, and not a very flexible one. That idea came into conflict with the new constitution that Canada adopted in 1981–1982 and its first Charter of Rights and Freedoms, which guaranteed "the right to life, liberty and security of the person," and made all Canadians "equal before and under the law"—ideas considered very American and therefore potentially subversive. The dual-nation pedigree is not just a historical oddity commemorated over the doorways flanking the main entrance to the House of Commons, where one side bears symbols of Canada's French roots and the other its British heritage. Rather, the concept of two founding nations courses through Canadian existence, with the result, in contemporary times, of ensuring that some Canadians are more equal than others.

The disparity is evident in matters of religion. For much of Canadian history, the terms "French" and "English" became substitutes for "Catholic" and "Protestant," and the religious conflict between the two groups was as fierce as any based on language or national origin. The political compromise that brought French and English together in confederation has resulted in certain anomalies. For example, Catholics in Ontario have the right to attend religious schools supported with public funds, the legacy of protections extended to the French. However, French speakers are a shrinking minority in Ontario, yet Jews, Sikhs, and members of other religions that traditionally run religious schools have been denied any public funds. Adherence to these distant historical origins also helps explain why, even though huge groups of East Indians, Chinese, and other immigrants have come to Canada, safety instructions on a Canadian Airlines DC-10 I took from Vancouver to Toronto—with 95 percent of passengers speaking Chinese, Arabic, or some other language—were given in French and English.

Mexico is neither purely ideological nor single-mindedly historical. It is, above all else, a cultural nation. Mexico draws from history and expresses itself through politics, but at the most basic level it reflects the cultural values of the descendants of *la conquista*. By any measure, it is a complex and precarious self-view, especially as North America's borders start to blur. Mexicans can be filled with contradictory feelings of *malinchismo,* or self-loathing for having sublimated themselves to powerful outsiders as La Malinche did—and as some would put it, as Salinas did too in signing NAFTA. Clinging to a noble and inscrutable past can help relieve some of the pain of a chaotic history filled with defeat. But it also raises contradictions. These contradictions are expressed widely across Mexico, but the clearest example I saw was at the old Spanish fortress of San Juan de Ulúa in the harbor of Veracruz. Plaques inside the ancient fortification bear the full name of the important seaport that was the landing spot of Cortés and the conquistadores, as well as of conquering French and American armies in succeeding centuries right up to the twentieth. Although the full name is rarely invoked outside of ceremonies and historical documents, Veracruz is formally called "The Three Times Heroic City of Veracruz," even though the three occasions cited were Mexican defeats.

The strength of Mexico is the incredible kaleidoscope of its culture, an endlessly changing and fascinating spectrum of sights, sounds, and tastes, most of them uniquely Mexican. But embedded even in such a distinctive culture are the anchors of universality, and therefore the possibilities of connection. I saw this one winter when I spent a week with the Tarahumara and an extraordinary American named Romayne Wheeler. Romayne was a classically trained pianist and a classically restless soul searching for fulfillment. By the time I got to know him, he had abandoned a promising musical career to live with and play the piano for the Tarahumara. They were suspicious of him at first, and told him his feet were so white they looked like milk that the dogs would want to lick. Little by little, this gentle man was able to break down the enormous barriers that separated him from the Tarahumara. He learned their language and could read meaning into their sometimes cryptic remarks. For example, if a Tarahumara said, "Yesterday evening I dreamed a wonderful word that I would like to give to you. Don't drop it," it meant he was trying to convey some thought or idea he'd had, the way we pass along a message to a friend. Wheeler honored their customs, wore their clothes, and ate their food. But his most effective way of reaching them was through his music, even though it came from outside the universe of the Tarahumara. Many of them had never before heard classical music or seen a piano.

Eventually, his piano so endeared Wheeler to the Indians that they hauled it to the edge of an imposing cliff and built a stone house there to protect it, and him. They also carved a lookout for him on the promontory. I slept there on a stone bench during this stay with the Tarahumara, there at the edge of the Batopilas canyon, with vistas of several vast canyons beyond that. I slept beneath a sky as black as the mouth of a cave, pricked by tiny points of starlight and a slender crescent moon. The cold of night was as intense as the heat of day. It woke me, and I lay there beneath the moon staring out at the darkened canyons long after Wheeler had finished playing the piano and the only music was the wind. I thought of Sebastián Gloria and the sooty cave where he lived and probably would die. From the edge of the Tarahumara's ancient land, the enormous history of the continent, this epic story of mankind's greatest opportunity, seemed to be compressed into one moment that I could touch right there, where the Tarahumara had learned to tame time. Although I've traveled very much farther than that cliff, I never felt more distant from my home in the United States than I did at that moment, and never closer to the soul of America.

This was a dream the Tarahumara had given me and one I didn't want to drop, at the very least not until I'd had the chance to follow it to the other end of America. I could feel my perspective changing as I grew more accustomed to looking at North America as our "hereisphere," as one common ground rather than three separate countries. As I began examining the other sides of America, but from my vantage point in Mexico, I ran into inevitable comparisons that made everything more complex and infinitely more encompassing. I couldn't use the Tarahumara's simple division of the world into useful and useless things. But to keep perspective, I tried whenever possible to ground my observations of the continent in real people, and to see the extraordinary story of North America in the unique lives of individual Newlanders, both the powerful few like the Tortilla King, and the many who had almost no real power but their own convictions, like the men aboard Canadian Airlines flight 1079.

CHAPTER EIGHT

Hell of a Transition

✳

If history is theater, our country's history has been
a masquerade interrupted time and again
by explosions, riots and revolts.

Octavio Paz
"The Philanthropic Ogre," in *The Labyrinth of Solitude*

The day I crossed two borders with seventy Mexican farmworkers
to watch President Zedillo of Mexico stand side by side with
Prime Minister Chrétien of Canada to denounce American aggression was the day I began truly to appreciate the connections building beyond the ends of America.

This continental revelation commenced one evening in June 1996, after I had made my way to the contained chaos that is Benito Juárez International Airport on the edge of Mexico City. Canadian Airlines flight
1079 to Toronto was scheduled to leave at 11:59. I hadn't expected to
find many people boarding the big 737 so late at night, but the waiting
room was quite busy. It didn't immediately register, but soon I realized
that except for a few business-class passengers in suits, the people taking the plane were dark-skinned men wearing the muddy boots, straw
hats, and plaid workshirts of the countryside. This most basic of Mexican costumes is seen everywhere in the country except for the capital
and especially not at the airport. Even the poorest Mexicans do a fair bit
of traveling around their country, visiting far-flung family or investigating money-making schemes, but flying is far too expensive for them.
They ride Mexico's decrepit passenger trains, and they are the masters

of the battered and belching behemoths that leave from every small-town bus stop and crawl across Mexican highways for the equivalent in pesos of pennies per mile.

These men were definitely dressed like bus travelers, but here they were in the waiting room at the Mexico City airport. Under his arm, each man hugged a pouch. I went over to talk to one of them, who told me he was from the central state of Guanajuato, not one of Mexico's poorest states but traditionally a source of illegal migrant workers to the United States.

"Canada," he answered when I asked where they were all going. "To work in the fields."

One man with a silver front tooth who said this was not his first trip north cautiously offered a few details. It cost him about $400 for the ticket to Canada, he said, and another $100 for a work visa from the Canadian government, which ran the guest worker program that contracts for and then transports thousands of Mexican workers each year.

"*El padrón* pays the rest and then takes it out of our money," said the man with the silver tooth, referring to the contracting Canadian farmer, who also is required to provide housing and transportation for the workers while they are in Canada. "I guess it's a lot, but it's definitely worth it," he told me. Others standing around him, suddenly shy and unwilling to look me directly in the eye, nodded in agreement. One of them patted the thin plastic pouch under his arm.

"We have documents and all the papers we need. That means we're legal. Everyone knows we're legal, and they have to treat us with respect. The farmers have to pay us what they promise they'll pay, and we don't have to worry about *la migra* because we've got the papers," he said, again touching the pouch as though it were a shield.

By then nearly all the men had gathered around me—not sure who I was but with typical Mexican fatalism worried I might keep them from leaving.

"How many of you have crossed the border into the United States to work?" I asked in Spanish. Their eyes avoided mine, and everyone said no, they hadn't ever crossed over, but I was sure they weren't being truthful. The path to the border is well worn in Mexico. Typically, a worker like any one of these men from Guanajuato, or from Oaxaca or Hidalgo or almost any other Mexican state, buys a cheap bus ticket to the border, where he pays a local gangster to help him cross illegally into America. If the workers are lucky enough to slip by the border guards, who use motion detectors, patrol dogs, and infrared night scopes, they might spend a year or two wandering through the United States, following the crops as the seasons change and finally returning to Mexico just before Christmas with little more in their pockets than when they left. One man finally said he wished the United States had a program similar to Canada's, but he thought it was unlikely given the hard feelings along the border. During World War II, the United States began legally bringing in about 200,000 Mexican workers a year through the bracero program, but subsequently it became cheaper for American farmers to hire undocumented Mexicans who would not complain they were being worked too hard or paid too little. Mexicans quickly realized they didn't need a contract to get work on American farms, and in 1964 the program ended. By the mid-1990s, the flow of legal and illegal immigrants across the border had saddled the southwestern United States with a resident population of as many as 5 million Mexicans, and a festering international sore point.

A few years after the plane trip with the farmworkers, when I had taken over as bureau chief in Toronto, I visited several of the migrant labor camps in Canada and talked to the men who crossed both borders each year to work in Ontario's farm belt. To a man, and even the few women who had begun making the transcontinental voyage, all said the same thing: The documents they carried guaranteed they would be treated fairly. They did not mind living in old farmhouses, with sheets draped across the windows and greasy stoves in the kitchen. They did not complain about being almost totally isolated on the farms with only minimal contact with surrounding communities or, occasionally, a representative from the office of the Mexican consulate in Toronto. They had no delusion about settling in Canada permanently; they were strictly forbidden to stay, and besides, most planned to return home with the $3,000 to $4,000 they'd be able to save during a single season to build a house, buy a satellite television dish, pay for a child's education, or otherwise get ahead. "We'd rather stay in Mexico, to be near our families and our own fields, but Mexico doesn't have enough work for us," Lorenzo Márquez told me one rainy summer day out in the fields of the Niagara peninsula, once America's frontier.

The money all these migrants, legal and otherwise, send back from Canada and the United States to small-town Mexico is estimated to exceed $4.5 billion a year—more than $10 million a day. It represents a government-sponsored, transcontinental opportunity transfer, a rare glimpse at what might have happened to Mexico had its people been given more chances to succeed. All the men I spoke to were convinced they could improve their lives and give their children the opportunity to do something other than to follow them into the fields. This was a clear departure from the typical resignation about the future I had encountered in Mexico, and what sometimes seemed to be Mexico's inability to get ahead. I remembered an American border official bluntly telling me that if the 1848 treaty with Mexico had given the United States control of the Colorado River delta atop the Sea of Cortez, a major city like New Orleans or St. Louis would be there today, not the muddy wasteland that Mexico has allowed it to remain.

When I heard about the government's program, it seemed that the way Canada treated its guest workers from Mexico reinforced the idea that Canadians are simply more civil and infinitely more compassionate than Americans. After visiting a few Ontario farms where the migrants worked, I wasn't so sure. I saw no gross violations—no toddlers picking cucumbers, no workers showered in pesticides as the fields were being sprayed. This was not legal slavery. But the work was just as tough, the same old yellow school buses were the only shelter in the fields, the workers themselves were just as confused and badly informed as in California or Ohio, and I heard similar complaints about the lack of sanitation, overly long hours, and malfunctioning machinery that caused accidents. The distance from Mexico would always keep most Mexicans from making the journey to Canada—unless a government agency organized it for them or a private company was allowed to make a profit. The Canadian farmers seemed as hard pressed to make ends meet as are small farmers in the United States. I heard the same argument about wages being higher than prices that I had heard from farmers in Ohio, Michigan, and California when they discussed farm labor issues. Given the opportunity to hire from an unlimited pool of illegal workers, Canadian farmers might have been as willing to do so as Americans, if a few thousand miles hadn't stood in the way. And if Canada ever acquired Mexican farmworkers proportionate in number to those in the Southwest, Canadian voters might very well be reluctant to extend these outsiders the same health care available to Canadians who pay taxes all year long.

The Mexicans on flight 1079 were like many other Mexicans I have known, willing to accept stunning hardship while expecting little in return. That is the legacy of a system that excluded so many people for so long, that boasted of taking care of workers when in fact it conspired to keep the minimum wage at $3–$4 a day. It is the legacy of an era when government agencies worked to take care of a privileged few while giving only the impression of helping the vast majority of others. The viewpoint has filtered deep down inside the Mexican people, and it colors the way they see every part of the world. The best shoeshine I ever had was in Mexico City, where the man who ran the stand near the American embassy downtown on the Paseo de la Reforma spent fifteen minutes shining my old Florsheims until they could blind a dog and then say that the cost was "whatever you think, *mi jefe.*" Some of the migrant workers on my flight, flying for the first time, were genuinely surprised to find that the food the stewardesses brought on their carts was free.

Time after time, I heard Mexicans express how little they had come to expect from their government, no matter who was in office. "They come and go, but for us it is always the same," one of the men at the airport told me. "They promise everything during their campaigns, everything, and then they don't deliver anything. It doesn't matter what party they belong to." In Mazatlán, on Mexico's Pacific coast, I had heard the same despair about government from widows of shrimp fishermen swallowed by a hurricane. Because the widows didn't expect anything more than tiny pensions, they had come up with their own plan of survival: They bought a small fleet of fishing boats that had been confiscated from drug dealers and managed the shrimp business themselves, a bold initiative in a country where women, especially rural women, have little chance to take control of their lives. Most simply let fate take its course.

When we touched down on the runway at Toronto's Lester B. Pearson International Airport—clean, orderly, in some ways sterile, and in most ways the precise opposite of the airport in Mexico City—the farmworkers were kept in their seats as the rest of the passengers deplaned. When those in the rows closest to the front of the cabin saw me leave, they waved good-bye. That image was going through my mind a few hours later when, after a brief flight east to Ottawa, I sat at one of the ornate wooden desks in the Canadian Parliament's House of Commons waiting for President Zedillo to speak.

The occasion was one of the initial summits of the new North American era, Zedillo's first formal state visit to Ottawa. He intended to spread the news that Mexico was increasingly able to overcome economic catastrophes. The message was directed at everyone who remembered the first Mexican financial crisis, the one triggered by the government's default on its debt obligations in the early 1980s. That incident cost Mexico, and most of Latin America, an entire decade of well-being. The most recent Mexican fiasco, the 1994–1995 peso crisis, had spread around the globe like the flu in a kindergarten classroom. But by this time, in June 1996, Mexico was already well on the road to recovery, led mostly by surging exports to the United States. Moreover, Zedillo would solemnly declare to the earnest Canadian parliamentarians who came to hear him, Mexico's ability to bounce back so quickly had been aided immensely by the new trade agreement with Canada and the United States.

When Prime Minister Chrétien welcomed Zedillo to the joint session of Parliament, he took a few minutes to recall a little continental history. In summer 1861, he said, several years before Canada's formation as a country, a trade mission left the port of Montreal bound for Veracruz. The merchants and officials landed at the historic city just a few weeks after the arrival of the French troops who would install Maximilian on the jury-rigged throne of the new Mexican empire. The struggles between French and Mexican troops, between conservative and liberal politicians, between Maximilian and Benito Juárez, were too much for the Canadians, Chrétien said. The trade delegations from Montreal hurriedly packed up and headed for Brazil.

The first official Canadian trade mission to Mexico didn't take place until 1905, Chrétien explained. The long reign of Porfirio Díaz gave Mexico "peace, order, and prosperity," which to the Canadians sounded quite similar to the "peace, order, and good government" pledged in the constitution Canada had inherited from Britain. Chrétien recalled that he had been part of a more recent trade mission, in March 1994, that had been disrupted by the Colosio assassination. "There were some who feared for Mexico at the time," Chrétien said, referring to the dark days he spent in Mexico at the time of the murder. "I did not." Then Chrétien pinpointed precisely the billboard message of the visit. "Canada and Mexico have more in common than many people realize," he said. Both are proud of their indigenous pasts as well as the contributions of their European ancestors. And, he declared, they share a border with a large and powerful neighbor. They were partners, not competitors, and given the right circumstances, they could be allies. He encouraged Zedillo to use his visit to explore the vastness of Canada, and "to look at our common future."

Finally, Zedillo rose to spirited applause before the assembled parliamentarians and began to speak about the promise of Mexico. "Mexico sees Canada as a country in which we share a vision of a hemisphere filled with enormous potential," Zedillo said. Unwittingly, he had repeated the same sentiment I had heard expressed by the seventy farmworkers who, at that moment, were probably leaving the Toronto airport to take their places in Canada, glad for the chance to find work and opportunity—North America's promise—thousands of miles of unfamiliar territory away from their homes.

The day after his address to Parliament, Zedillo himself was in Toronto, talking to a room full of Canadian impresarios. He ran through a long list of business deals that had recently been consummated in Mexico, and he talked up Mexico's potential as a good place for Canadians to invest. Only near the end of his speech at the luxurious King Edward Hotel did Zedillo dare acknowledge the obvious. "An unacceptable number of Mexican people are living in poverty," he said. He promised to improve education, health care, and housing during his six-year administration, but, he said, even those steps could have only limited effect. "Advancement of our society cannot be assured only by economic policy and structural reform." Electoral reform, new investigatory powers for congress, and a strengthened justice system were among the markers of progress Zedillo promised to deliver. What he wanted, in essence what he and all Mexicans were striving for, was the transformation of their country into something more truthfully replicating what he said was "the tolerance, civility, and democracy" of Canada and the United States.

But he was not praising civility when he stood beside Chrétien in Parliament's Railway Conference Room to denounce American aggression toward Mexico's old ally Cuba. A few months earlier, in February 1996, Cuban MiGs had shot down two civilian planes carrying Cuban-Americans who had taken off from Florida intent on provoking an international incident. Prodded by the powerful Cuban-American lobby in south Florida—whose support President Clinton needed to win reelection later that year—Clinton decided to punish Cuba for Castro's intransigence. He signed the Helms-Burton law, which imposed severe penalties on business people who had taken over property in Cuba that once belonged to American companies such as ITT and Boise Cascade. Entrepreneurs from many countries were liable to be targeted, but the first to be put on formal notice—and, more important, to be barred from entering the United States—were Canadian executives with the Sherritt International mining company and the Mexican entrepreneurs from Monterrey who had purchased part of the Cuban telephone company.

Chrétien often called the three NAFTA partners the "three amigos" and liked to say that Canada, Mexico, and the United States were part of a *"gran familia"* within North America. On this day in Ottawa, however, there apparently had been a not-so-friendly spat within the family, and only two of the three amigos were talking to each other.

✳

In terms of international relations around the world, this split between the United States and its neighbors was minor. But in terms of North American relations, it signified a new dynamic. It is rare in history for a continent to be divided by so few borders as is North America. It may be rarer still for a great nation to hold the comparative advantage over its smaller, less powerful neighbors that the United States has enjoyed for so long. This combination of continental factors has afforded the United States a position of splendid isolation, which at times has become an irresistible temptation to turn our backs on the rest of the world. Although America's presence in distant lands is often criticized, an isolationist America scares contemporary society more.

America's continental breadth is what makes an isolationist path so enticing. With only pliant neighbors on our borders, Americans have fully embraced the perception of their nation as an untouchable colossus stretching from sea to sea. There was a time, though, when confidence was not so abundant. English settlers did not venture deep into the continent but remained huddled on the east coast, their backs snuggled protectively against the barrier of the Appalachians. There were many reasons for the original colonies to want to remain small. Plutarch's notion that when republics grow too large they tear apart still had not been disproved by any nation or state. Even when its size is limited, it was believed, a republic had to be based on military might, like Sparta, to maintain its integrity. Bigness was a quality the colonists feared for a century and a half following the first settlements in the new world, and entangling alliances seemed the natural accompaniment to such worries. Even the early reports of expeditions to the west and the marvels of the continent that explorers uncovered did little at first to fire the imagination or create a westward push.[1]

Those attitudes changed gradually after the young republic gained full possession of the western lands granted through the Treaty of Paris in 1783. Early in the nineteenth century, the successful settlement of Louisiana made fears about bigness being incompatible with democracy seem outdated. By 1845, the number of states had grown to twenty-seven, and the population of hardy souls west of the Appalachians had increased from just a quarter million in 1790 to more than 2 million. In that year, a newspaperman, John L. O'Sullivan, expressed in print a sentiment that was to guide the young nation's developing sense of itself. He declared that the United States had a "manifest destiny to over-spread the continent allotted by Providence."[2]

The immensely popular reports of the exploits and discoveries of John Charles Fremont in the 1840s glorified the American west and encouraged the expansionists who coveted Mexico's California coast and the Oregon country, which was then under the tentative control of Great Britain. This continental vista fed America's independent spirit and fired its confidence. Most immigrants by the late 1800s had come from Europe, where borders were unavoidable realities, both advantageous and ruinous. The new Americans tried not to have borders, and turned inward from those they could not avoid. Most of their descendants, contemporary Americans, are similarly parochial. Many Americans feel no need to learn another language, they do not sense that events in the rest of the world—or even in the rest of North America—have much to do with them. Only 18 percent of Americans have enough curiosity about other countries to bother getting a passport to visit them, and every Congress has a few members who boast that they are such genuine Americans that they've never held a passport. Canadians are more active citizens of the world, but not much more. Just over 22 percent of them hold valid passports, and that includes the Hong Kong businessmen who legally bought Canadian citizenship because they were afraid the Chinese takeover of Hong Kong would ruin their businesses. In Mexico, of course, poverty keeps most people from taking vacations anywhere. Only 6 percent of Mexicans hold valid passports.[3] But poverty is also the great motivator that sends an endless stream of illegal immigrants across the U.S. border in search of the opportunity they cannot find in Mexico.

The only experience most Americans have with a foreign country comes from crossing over into either Canada or Mexico. If we understand so little about our only neighbors, what can we know of the world that we, now, are supposed to lead? The signing of NAFTA raised awareness in the United States of events beyond our borders and provided a refresher course on what it means to lead. A strange dynamic was at work, however, a process outlined by Robert A. Pastor, the Latin America expert.[4] In this "Newtonian conundrum," each action to open up or free America's borders is met by an opposite, though not always equal, reaction to shut it down. For example, as the trade pact lowered tariffs and made the passage of goods across the border easier, resistance increased to the free passage of many goods, such as winter vegetables coming from Mexico and wheat coming from Canada. As illegal immigration from Mexico to the United States increased, California passed Proposition 187, stripping illegal immigrants of government-funded social benefits. NAFTA made it easier for some professionals to cross the border, but Congress gave border agents sweeping new powers to summarily expel Mexicans—and Canadians—for slight infractions of immigration rules. The transition of North America was progressing, but movement wasn't always pointed forward.

NAFTA put new emphasis on America's neighbors, especially Mexico, but to critics almost nothing that came across the borders made the trade pact worthwhile. The unions that had helped elect President Clinton blamed the free trade agreement, and Clinton himself, for factory closings and job losses every time a company announced it was moving north or south of the border. Led by Senator Alphonse D'Amato, Republicans tried to pour water over President Clinton's handling of the peso crisis. In combative hearings in Washington, D'Amato tried to show—and won many converts to his side—that Bentsen and Summers had known more about Mexico's precarious economics than they had let on, and their sleight of hand had cost American taxpayers billions for a rescue package that he was sure would not be repaid. (He didn't apologize when he was proved wrong and Mexico repaid the money.)

Not only were Americans incensed by their neighbors. The Mexicans were still smarting from the battle to get NAFTA through the U.S. Congress. They had been forced to accept many insults, but some of the harshest came in the 1993 television debate between Vice President Al Gore and Texas billionaire Ross Perot. Besides famously predicting "a giant sucking sound" of jobs from the United States to Mexico, Perot said at one point in the debate that American hogs "have a better life than good, decent, hard-working Mexicans." The fact that Mexican diplomats did not continually throw such comments into the faces of their American counterparts didn't mean the sting had worn off. For the Canadians, even though the trade pact was turning out to be lucrative, labor unions and groups like the Council of Canadians complained that unless something changed, in a short time Canada would be nothing more than an economic appendage of the United States.

Given that infected atmosphere, it was not surprising that officials from the American embassy in Ottawa squirmed during Zedillo's visit. They watched the two closest and most often offended neighbors of the United States join hands and vow to deflect or undermine the Helms-Burton law. Canada had been instrumental in organizing a recent vote in the usually docile Organization of American States criticizing the extraterritorial reach of the American law. Canada had also rushed its own law into the statute books to prevent local companies from complying with the American legislation. The "two amigos" had raised their fists and were taking angry swipes at their common problem.

✳

The businessmen and investors Zedillo went to Canada to woo during his first visit were impressed by his obvious grasp of economic realities and his willingness to discuss frankly some of the failings of the Mexican system. They appreciated his graduate degree in economics from Yale and the very serviceable—if stiff—English he was willing to use to speak to them. They told me later that they were concerned about Mexico's spotty record on human rights—which had received much attention in Canada and the United States during the conflict in Chiapas—but were not about to make business decisions based on that issue. No, from almost every point of view, the door to greater investment in a new, transforming, more democratic Mexico seemed to be wide open.

Only one thing kept them away, they said, and that was the stink of corruption that seemed to be rising wherever Mexican soil was turned. From the downtown office suites of big businesses in Canada, where rules and laws are routinely and predictably followed, corruption appeared to hover over every street in Mexico. This was nothing new, but the rules by which the game was played had changed.

With the ascent of Zedillo and his refusal to enforce the ruling party's system of control, expectations had risen that corruption would finally be diminished, though no one expected it to disappear entirely. In fact, the changes made to weaken the authoritarian structure of Mexico had seemingly left no one in charge at all. There were no rules, no limits, no internal system of balances to hold the greediest parts of Mexican society in check. Mexico City was becoming an increasingly dangerous place where executives were regularly assaulted, robbed, or kidnapped. Under the old regime, the city's police force—which never generated much confidence—had at least been able to restrain the gangsters by insisting that the cops got their cut too. Now that system had unraveled. The police no longer were freely allowed to extort money without fear of getting caught. Subsequently, they stopped regulating the criminals and were no more willing to arrest them than before. That created a vacuum into which the criminals—some of them cops—naturally expanded.

It became clear to many people in the city that the benefit to be gained from even a small-scale kidnapping far outweighed the diminishing risk of being caught. The economics were simple. Hijacking the car of a company manager and forcing him to use his automated teller machine card to withdraw the maximum allowed from several machines could bring in far more money than any job an uneducated campesino might land in Mexico's new economy. On the other hand, the chance of being caught and punished was negligible. The same equation held true for the police, which led to an increase in police corruption. Even the army, which had been dragged into the national fight against the illegal drug trade, had been corrupted through the exposure to obscene amounts of money offered by the drug kings for protection. In addition to the rising level of corruption, there seemed to be no end to official incompetence, which became more appalling as the days wore on. A nadir was reached when a prominent Mexico City judge was found dead in his office with *two* bullet wounds to the chest, and police declared it a suicide.

To Canadian eyes, Mexico was a tableau of evils and depradations like a canvas by Hieronymous Bosch. The gangsters and drug traffickers appeared to have been left on their own. The pack of special prosecutors who tried to solve the murders of Colosio, Ruiz Massieu, and Cardinal Posadas Ocampo each contradicted the other. At one point, all three cases were given to a single investigator, who so bungled everything that he too was forced to go into hiding. Venality, incompetence, and greed soiled every aspect of Mexican life, even something as basic and incorruptible as the tortillas made of corn that every Mexican eats every day.

Tortillas are Mexico. The round, unleavened flat cakes are made of native corn that must be boiled, shelled, ground into a dough, patted flat, and then cooked. The process is laborious, like life in Mexico, but the product is delicious and lusty, just like Mexican life. Tortillas sustained the Aztecs, and today they remain the staple food of all Mexicans, from Mexico's wealthiest man, Carlos Slim Helú, to the Tarahumara Indians, who told me they knew the *chabochis* don't respect them because when Tarahumara have to rest at their homes, they are offered day-old tortillas. A Tarahumara would always offer a stranger the last fresh tortilla off the grill and save the stale one for himself.

Until the early 1950s, making tortillas was the single most important domestic task of Mexican women, and it occupied them from morning to night. In Mexico City and a few other large urban areas, it was possible to buy handmade tortillas prepared by women who spent their days slapping the corn dough in their hands. The *palmeadoras* had their own union, and the price of tortillas was tightly controlled so that every Mexican would have something to eat, although often it wasn't much more than a tortilla, salt, and a few beans.

To ensure every Mexican access to this most basic food required a complicated system of subsidy and support that dangerously exposed the heart of Mexican business and the soul of Mexican government. The tortilla makers received a subsidy through the low-cost corn they bought from the federal government. The government in turn tried to subsidize farmers by paying more than the market price for corn. In this way, each of the millions of tortillas churned out daily received a double subsidy that reduced the price for anyone who bought them. All Mexicans, from the Indian servant who worked for a millionaire to the millionaire himself, paid the same below-market price for tortillas. Officials maintained that any system that tried to restrict the subsidy to those who truly needed it would be corrupted immediately.

Tortillas, and the corn of which they are made, are gifts to the rest of the American continent from the ancestors of modern Mexico. The cultivation of corn began in Mexico 5,000 years ago and moved north through the continent. There was no more important element in ancient life than corn. The people who built the imposing pyramids at Teotihuacán, north of Mexico City, paid homage to a corn god. I once visited a church in Amecameca, near the base of the Popocatepetl volcano, where a centuries-old Christ figure made of corn husks was kept in a glass case above the altar. When villagers feared the volcano would erupt, they removed the corn figure of Christ and carried it in a sacred procession through the village. In Texcoco, near Mexico City, I once toured the Center for Investigation and Improvement of Corn, one of the most technologically advanced agricultural research stations in the world, which also maintains the world's largest storage bank of corn seed. The genetic material from wild plants is sometimes blended with different varieties of corn to create stronger, more disease-resistant stock. Even Mexican society has been pollinated by corn and has incorporated some of its traits. In areas of torrential seasonal rain, the corn stalks must be bent double and tied down to keep the constant moisture from causing a mold to form on the ears. So too, Mexicans reason, it is the way of life that men must be bent over and burdened if they are to survive.

In the 1950s, Mexican entrepreneurs experimented with different ways of making tortillas, using a central operation to cook and grind the corn into flour that could then be packaged and sold in stores. At first it was a rough and inefficient operation, but one man with close contacts to the Salinas family capitalized on the simple technology and changed the way the eleventh most populous nation in the world eats. Starting from a small operation in Nuevo León, the northern state that also is the ancestral home of the Salinas clan, an industrious local businessman named Roberto González Barrera exploited technological advances and his friendship with the Salinas family. Some marketing genius also was involved. His company, Maseca, knew how to package the corn flour and, through advertising, convince millions of Mexican women to abandon traditional methods for something new and easy that smacked of American consumer convenience.

González Barrera claimed that Maseca flour made cheaper and more nutritious tortillas. But to this day most Mexicans will swear that tortillas made from fresh dough, called *nixtamal,* and slapped out by hand are infinitely preferable to those made from store-bought packaged corn flour. "For us, when you don't get a good tortilla in a restaurant, it is taken as a very good indication of a deterioration of the quality of life," Homero Aridjis, the Mexican poet, once told me. "It is like in France if you don't get a good baguette. It means that something serious has happened."

Maseca's tortillas might not have been as tasty as homemade ones, but they were more convenient, so people bought them—a classic lesson of American marketing. González Barrera had more than marketing know-how to help him become so successful. Raúl Salinas de Lozano, the father of Carlos Salinas, was a secretary of the department of trade and industry from 1958 to 1964, and many people thought he had the chance to be a PRI presidential candidate. Salinas's department lent González Barrera money and provided special permits to expand. In a series of aggressive moves, González Barrera purchased the companies that made the new tortilla cooking machines, and insisted that local tortilla makers use his brand of corn flour instead of the fresh-mixed *nixtamal.* Competition was keen. Then, in 1990, the government of Carlos Salinas—son of Don Raúl—threw the match to Maseca, limiting the amount of corn the *nixtamaleros* would receive from government stores and ordering that any additional demand for tortillas be met by using corn flour, which was produced only by the state, and by Maseca.

Maseca grew to control 90 percent of the flour tortilla market, and González Barrera exulted in being known as the "Tortilla King." His good fortune wasn't restricted to tortillas. He put in a successful bid for one of the banks the Salinas administration privatized in the early 1990s. He worked closely with Conasupo, the government commodities program that distributed millions of sacks of Maseca flour. Raúl Salinas, the president's brother, was the agency's director of planning from 1988 to 1992.

Although favors, like compliments, are expected to be returned in Mexico, González Barrera insisted he never received special treatment from Salinas. Maseca's success, he said, was the result of hard work and smart investments. Yet he was known as one of the PRI's most generous supporters, contributing millions to the party and its campaigns. And despite repeated denials, González Barrera was widely believed to have been among the Mexican businessmen who gave Raúl Salinas the $100 million discovered in his Swiss bank account.

To many, the rise and reign of the Tortilla King seemed an overt example of the kind of coziness between Salinas and Mexican business that was later to cause Mexico such grief. "He's one guy who got rich on taxpayer money," an American official told me, "but most businessmen in Mexico got rich the same way." A newly independent press, and a lower house of congress that had been given unprecedented autonomy, began investigating the more egregious misconduct of the Salinas years. The PRI still maintained its majority in Congress, but since the opposition had gained considerably in the same election that brought Zedillo to Los Pinos, he was forced to share power with Congress and the members of other parties.

One of the biggest thorns in Zedillo's side was Adolfo Aguilar Zinser, a smart Mexican lawyer I had first met in the 1994 presidential campaign of Cuauhtémoc Cárdenas. Aguilar Zinser had gone on to become an independent member of Congress, although it was clear where his sympathies lay. He got himself named to the new Congress's first investigatory commission—a departure for a legislative body that traditionally had been so powerless. Formal meeting rooms had not even been included in the plans when the ponderous legislative chambers, the Palace of Saint Lazarus, were constructed in the early 1980s. Nobody had thought to include them because committees rarely ever met, except for publicly funded dinners. All legislation came directly from the president's office, usually with the congressional approval required by the constitution already clipped to its underside.

Back in the presidential campaign of 1994, when I had accompanied Cárdenas on a campaign swing through Monterrey, Aguilar Zinser first warned me that Raúl Salinas had plundered Mexico with a level of greed and gluttony to which few living Mexicans could find an equivalent. Raúl was still very much in his brother's shadow then. But one night as the campaign's Chevrolet Suburban rattled along a dark highway, Aguilar Zinser told me an incredible story about Raúl's huge ranches and expensive horses. He talked about dirty business deals and audacious attempts by Raúl to blackmail and extort money from an unending stream of businessmen and local officials. Less than a year after Aguilar Zinser told me about Raúl's unsavory character, the president's brother was arrested on murder charges.

The committee Aguilar Zinser sat on in the new Congress had been empowered to investigate Conasupo during the years Raúl was there. It was a historic development, the initial stirrings of an independent legislature that could bring the kind of oversight and accountability that Mexico's North American partners were demanding. But the committee was also flawed for several reasons. Although the opposition was represented by members like Aguilar Zinser, the PRI maintained its majority and therefore controlled the chairmanship of the committee, just as it did for almost every other important committee. There was no chance the entire committee would work diligently to root out corruption in the Salinas administration. The only way for such a committee to pry seriously into the PRI's past was to do it without the party's input.

Aguilar Zinser began by confiscating a warehouse of records. As news photographers recorded the boxes being stacked on the back of a truck, Aguilar Zinser publicly vowed to search them all for proof that the agency had been misused by Raúl and compliant PRI officials. Leaks started to come from the commission's offices, giving details of crooked deals to buy corn that had been designated as animal feed but was used for humans, of sweetheart deals for local businessmen who bought corn flour plants the government was privatizing, and of the distribution of a shipment of powdered milk from Ireland that had been contaminated by radioactive fallout from the Chernobyl nuclear power plant.

Aguilar Zinser also came across documents hinting that González Barrera and Maseca had received special treatment from Conasupo, including some peculiar handling of a $7 million payment in 1989. The money had supposedly been meant to cover damages caused when the government couldn't make a timely payment for corn flour it had purchased from Maseca. Conasupo's own records showed the payment had repeatedly been disallowed by government auditors. Their judgment had been overturned by officials at the highest level, including the secretary of budget and planning, Ernesto Zedillo.

Aguilar Zinser knew he was on dangerous ground. There was precedent for attacking the family of a former president, but no one had ever denounced the man sitting in Los Pinos with the red, white, and green presidential sash still across his chest. But the congressman felt he had convincing proof that Zedillo had not stopped the questionable deal, despite the objections of government auditors. Aguilar Zinser was obviously politically motivated. Although an independent, he hated the PRI and would be delighted to tarnish Zedillo's reputation.

The investigation showed how far Mexico had come, and also how far the country still had to go to reach true democracy. Whereas pesky legislative committees routinely made life miserable for Washington politicians or parliamentarians in Ottawa, Mexican congressmen had always acted like sheep. After Aguilar Zinser found evidence indicating that Conasupo seemed to have bent over backward for Maseca, he knew he couldn't just bring it to the attention of the committee chairman, a PRI leader. He wanted to go directly to the public, but he believed no one in the Mexican press would be willing to question a sitting president. So he called me.

I had talked to Aguilar Zinser several times for an earlier article on González Barrera at the beginning of 1996. After that article was published, the congressman dropped the first hint that there was much more to tell. A few months later he agreed to let me see the records. I pored over hundreds of pages of documents involving Conasupo and the 1989 payment to Maseca. The records were clear: Several government auditors had concluded Maseca was not owed any money and shouldn't be paid. But a succession of officials who took over as President Salinas assumed office pushed through the payment anyway. Salinas's commerce secretary, Jaime Serra Puche, as ex-officio head of the board overseeing Conasupo operations, believed the payment was justified and overrode the auditors' recommendations. The authorization papers then went to Zedillo's office for release of the funds, and there too the payment was approved.

Aguilar Zinser's point was that although comparatively little money was involved—\$7 million—the way the payment had been forced through the government showed the hubris of the PRI and its coziness with powerful interests. The payment also drew Zedillo into the Salinas circle at a time when the new president was trying to distance himself from his predecessor.

By this time, late June 1996, I had already accepted the position as bureau chief in Canada and was preparing to move to Toronto. Miriam and I planned to leave Mexico just after the school year ended, which coincided with Aguilar Zinser's schedule for presenting his report to Congress. I did not alert him to my impending departure because I did not want to influence his timing. The day before the report was to be presented to Congress and published in *The New York Times,* I called Carlos Almada, President Zedillo's spokesman. I laid out the evidence I had and got an official response of denial to include in the published article. I knew the administration would be upset, but I had no clue how strong their reaction would be.

That night, after editing the article with the New York office, I returned home, from which the movers had already taken most of the furniture. Two of our children were visiting friends in the United States. Our youngest son, Andrés, was sleeping on the floor near our bed, which the movers had left until last. Without a television or radio, I was unaware of just how quickly Los Pinos had reacted. It wasn't until after we had gone to sleep and the phone jolted me awake that I knew just how rattled Los Pinos was. "Did you get arrested?" asked Vin O'Brien, late man on *The Times*'s foreign desk. Los Pinos had apparently obtained the early edition of *The Times,* which is published in New York the night before the regular edition is distributed. O'Brien told me that according to a news wire report, the government had denounced the article, and me individually, and hinted that I had been deported. I assured him we were all right and promised to call if there was any trouble. We then waited uneasily for daylight, when the extent of the government's anger would quickly become clear.

I found out that Zedillo's office had gone to Jacobo Zabludovsky, anchor of the main national newscast for decades and captive to the PRI establishment, to express the president's discontent. "The article contains calumnious insinuations about the actions of the directors of the agency," the president's spokesman had written in a statement read word for word on the televised national news program. Even though I had included the government's response to Aguilar Zinser's report, Zedillo's men were furious, especially with the headline "Corruption Commission in Mexico Ties Zedillo to Disputed Payment." The statement from Los Pinos declared that the government would take "whatever legal actions are necessary to deal with the lamentable act," intimating that deportation and arrest were possible. Aguilar Zinser was branded a traitor for having taken the affair to the foreign press, and the next day all the Mexican newspapers seemed to validate the concerns he had harbored about the local press by attacking him and me.

It took no time at all for the PRI majority on the corruption commission to disavow Aguilar Zinser's report without offering a plausible explanation of why Serra and Zedillo had disregarded the auditors' findings. I officially became persona non grata, and my imminent departure for Canada fueled speculation that I had been deported.

That last night in Mexico we stayed in a downtown hotel. By the time we arrived in the United States and were reunited with our oldest son, Aahren, the government's attacks on me were being reported in U.S. newspapers. Aahren had one in his pocket when he greeted us at the airport in Dallas, and said he had worried that I had been jailed.

A few months later, the PRI majority in Congress pulled the rug out from under Aguilar Zinser. The Conasupo investigation was shut down, and Aguilar Zinser's committee was terminated. However, after the PRI lost its majority in the June 1997 midterm elections, the Conasupo investigation committee was reestablished, this time without a PRI majority. The committee concluded that the payment to Maseca had been illegal and recommended that those responsible be punished. But in April 1999, the Zedillo administration liquidated Conasupo, effectively closing the book on the entire affair and letting everyone off the hook.[5]

✳

Transitions rarely are easy and predictable. In the summer of 1996, it was obvious that the process of change that was under way on the American continent was not going to be free of complications. The forces of integration within North America worked full-time to bring the three amigos together, but likewise other forces, namely corruption and suspicion, worked mightily to tear them apart. More time would be needed to know which side would be dominant. In the meantime, I had a unique opportunity to pursue a new continental vision. I had been given tantalizing hints of what the new era in continental relations would look like, and what it would imply for all the people living here. For the first time, *The Times* was transferring its bureau chief from one end of America to the other. This meant that I'd have to head northward across the United States and reverse my perspective once more. In Mexico, the United States had been above us, and I searched out areas where these two very different societies were similar, or were becoming more alike because of the commercial and cultural connections that had been forming rapidly since 1994. In Canada, the United States would be below us, and my goal would be to look for those aspects of life where these two most similar societies were different, especially since the trade agreement and globalization had been drawing us closer together than ever before. Besides this spatial perspective, time would also be a point of comparison. Where Mexico had been four-square dealing with its place in the future, the Canada I moved to in 1996 was struggling mightily with its past. On a personal level, for me and my family, moving again meant facing the challenges of another new transition, and another assault on our assumptions, about ourselves and our place here. And the first assault took place not long after we arrived.

CHAPTER NINE

A Border Like
No Other

✳

That country must be ours.

Robert Morris
a member of the first Continental Congress, regarding Canada

Habits usually die hard. During the years we lived in Mexico, I grew accustomed to carrying my passport in my computer case and keeping handy all the immigration documents that Mexican guards, soldiers, and police could demand at any time. This wariness came with the wayfarer's sense that I developed there, an awareness of being a foreigner moving temporarily inside someone else's country. When we made preparations to leave Mexico and move to Canada, this sense was still deeply ingrained in me. We applied for visas while in Mexico, underwent the physical exams Canada requires, and meticulously complied with all the other requirements imposed by Citizenship and Immigration Canada. The day we landed in Toronto for the first time, we went directly to the immigration offices at Pearson Airport to have all of us, including the dog, registered as incoming immigrants. I'm not sure if we would have been so obsessive about meeting details had we merely been coming to Toronto from New Jersey. But the trip from Mexico across two frontiers made me feel more like a stranger in a foreign land than an American in Canada.

During the next four weeks in Canada, our children started school, our household belongings were delivered, and we passed through the bureaucratic gauntlet of initiating phone service and procuring driver's licenses with surprising ease. The experience so lulled me into feeling I had returned home that I got caught up in a trap of my own making the very first time I left Canada and crossed the border back into the United States. I was booked on a flight to New York to check in with *The Times*'s main office. Only after I arrived at the airport and the ticket agent asked to see my passport did I realize that I hadn't brought it along. Obviously, I knew without any question that I couldn't fly to New York without a passport—or at least a birth certificate. But I hadn't brought along my computer, and when I left the house I had simply overlooked the fact that I was leaving the country. The caution and the defensiveness about the border that I had developed in Mexico had quickly evaporated in Toronto, and in my mind that morning I was already home and therefore no longer a foreigner. My mistake caused only a minor inconvenience; I missed one flight while waiting for Miriam to send a Toronto cab driver who dutifully drove an empty cab to the airport and handed me the passport. But it was a surprising acknowledgment of the differences in the imaginative hold of the northern border over the one on the southern end of America.

That was only my first lesson in understanding the line separating Canada and the United States. In time, I came to appreciate that the northern border is so complex because of its ubiquitously dual nature. For Americans the border is almost invisible, whereas Canadians are painfully conscious of it all the time (and, as I learned, would never have made the same mistake I made in forgetting my passport). We see the border as joining Canada to the United States. For Canadians it is the last line separating us from them. We look at the way the border meanders around Quebec and the Maritimes and wonder what to make of the curious lines around Maine, Vermont, and New York. Then we lose hope of understanding why the border seems to have been blown off course in there among the Great Lakes where it dips down to Detroit. Canadians read the boundary line the way a historian reads a battle map, instinctively wary of every little advance, every surrendered mile, every section where the defensive line didn't hold.

We saw another dimension of Canada's border, and Mexico's character, when we tried to fulfill a promise we had made to bring Graciela, our housekeeper in Mexico, to Canada. Graciela had continued to attend her high school equivalency classes and was making halting progress with English, with the help of our children and their music. We had grown quite fond of her, and had offered to arrange for her to accompany us during the years we were going to live in Canada. She had never been to Canada and didn't know much about it except that it was "like America," which she had never seen either. We carefully filled out her visa application too, and were dealing with the Canadian embassy in Mexico City over the requirements for her visa when everything came to a sudden stop. She came home crying one day and locked herself in her room. When she finally came out, she told Miriam she was pregnant. She had no idea how to locate the father, a man she had met at Chapultepec Park one Sunday. Even if she could find him again at the park, she doubted he would ever accept any responsibility for the child.

Getting Graciela into Canada had already proved to be more difficult than we imagined. We initially thought Canada would embrace any immigrants willing to face the cold. But immigration officials put severe restrictions on domestic helpers like Graciela. She had to have completed high school, speak English fluently enough to use the telephone, and have a job waiting for her the moment she arrived in Canada. We assured officials at the Canadian embassy in Mexico City that she did indeed have a guaranteed job with us in Toronto, but we argued that if Graciela possessed all the credentials they asked of her, she would never leave Mexico because she would be one of the country's elites. They shrugged. We were in the middle of trying to make other arrangements when Graciela's unexpected pregnancy ended any chance we might have had of fulfilling our promise to her.

The best we could do for Graciela was to pay her way to Toronto so she could join us for the duration of a visitor's six-month visa once she had given birth to her baby. She finally arrived in Toronto one Sunday in January. Miriam waited for her at Pearson Airport, but after the final passenger from the Mexico City flight came through the gates, Graciela still was nowhere to be found. We later discovered that she was being detained by suspicious immigration officers who refused to believe her story—which she told in a rough and quavering English—that an American family had paid her way and was waiting outside to pick her up. Sensing that something had gone wrong, Miriam argued with the immigration authorities and finally convinced them to allow her into the holding area. She found Graciela alone, frightened and mistrustful of the new country we had told her had been declared one of the best places in the world to live. She came home with us that night but decided to stay at our house for only six weeks. In Toronto, she took English classes that we paid for (only official immigrants could attend for free) and romped in snow for the very first time. Before long, she felt comfortable enough to buy her own subway tokens and travel downtown on Sunday afternoon, almost as if she were back in Mexico City. She wasn't, and she missed her baby. Graciela did not like being a foreigner.

Much more so than in other countries, the border is a part of Canada's genetic makeup: It determines what Canada is and contributes chromosomes to the nation's identity. As much as the heavy whiteness of the frozen north or the rugged majesty of the western mountains, the border tells Canadians who they are and clearly defines who they are not. Life wasn't always that way; it was once quite clear who the Canadians were—French-speaking Roman Catholic settlers hacking out a flimsy existence along the St. Lawrence River. From this starting point, they intended to oversee an empire that stretched south to the Gulf of Mexico and west into wild regions that would not be charted except by Indians for another 100 years. They hoped to discover a northern passage to the Orient, or a rich new land to rival Spain's El Dorado, but the French were continually disappointed by their new world. They put down few roots in North America before the beginning of the seventeenth century when Samuel de Champlain arrived with plans for a settlement at an impressive promontory on the St. Lawrence that became the city of Quebec. Champlain's interest in the new world had been inspired by the fabulous riches he first saw on a visit to New Spain.

"A more beautiful country could not be seen or desired than the kingdom of New Spain," Champlain wrote of his visit to Mexico. "The soil is very fertile, producing corn twice in the year, and in as great abundance as one could desire, and, whatever season it may be, there is always very good fresh fruit on the trees."[1] He was astounded by everything he saw, but nothing fired his imagination more than Mexico City itself. "All the contentment I felt at the sight of things so pleasing was but little in regard to what I experienced when I beheld that beautiful city of Mexico, which I had not supposed to be so superbly constructed of splendid temples, palaces and fine houses."

Champlain dreamed of building a city as great as Mexico. After repeated attempts to win support for the venture, he began work at Quebec in 1608, the same year John Smith was appointed governor of Jamestown, the first permanent English settlement in the new world. Champlain arrived to find the banks of the St. Lawrence deserted; the Indian encampments he had marveled at on earlier trips had been abandoned during his absence. Still, the French were far outnumbered by natives, and the first Catholic missionaries unloaded their chalices and crucifixes not long after Champlain's arrival and began their proselytizing in 1615. In 1635 the Jesuits opened a school, the Jesuit College in Quebec City, which became the American continent's first institution of higher learning north of Mexico (the University of Mexico had been founded in 1551, Harvard in 1636). Fearless Jesuits waded into the threatening worlds of the Huron, the Mohawks, and the Algonquin, but often tested was their faith and not that of the natives. Before long, both the savagery of the Indians and the martyrdom of the Jesuits were woven into the tale of Canada's beginnings.

Although not as unsettling as the bloody Christs that stared at me from the walls and ceilings of Mexican churches, the painted tableaux of the torture of Jean de Brébeuf and the other Jesuit martyrs that hide in the shadows of the Basilica of Mary Queen of the World in Montreal also kept me at a distance from my religion. Those scenes of skin being ripped from the living victims and fingers hacked from their hands did not convey the heroism or inspiration that the artist might have intended; rather, I recoiled at the violent clash they represented, the monumental misunderstanding that had marked those first encounters. The intolerance and fanaticism of the old world had accompanied the missionaries—like some Norwegian rat in the hold of a seafaring ship—to the new world.

Few in number but with their access to the great Indian trade routes and waterways, the early French settlers had a disproportionate impact on the development of the American continent. Still, those hearty souls could not provide the royal court in Paris with the kind of riches of which the king had dreamed—precious metals, exotic spices, rare and wondrous animals—the new-world cornucopia that the French had enviously watched enrich the rival kingdom of Spain. The North American settlers shipped back furs and fish, more valuable than gold over time but a great disappointment to the overworked imaginations of the French courtiers. Champlain worked hard to convince Paris to provide the resources that would enable him to create a permanent settlement in the wild new land. In 1663, Louis XIV assumed control of New France and ruled it as another province of the motherland, which it remained throughout its existence. For the ancien régime, the vast territory's greatest value was as a bargaining chip in the quest for domination in Europe. When the Seven Years' War with England began in 1756, France knew the battlefield would include North America but kept most of its army in Europe. The French hoped to hold out long enough to negotiate a treaty in which its North American land could be bartered for territory in Europe or the Caribbean that would prove to be more valuable.

The British left no doubt of their intent to change the balance of power in Europe with a victory in North America. British troops sent across the Atlantic outnumbered all the inhabitants of New France. Quebec fell first, then Montreal. The Treaty of Paris in 1763 recognized the British victory and set the new borders of Quebec. But it did not settle the fate of roughly 60,000 French-speaking people who, in the preceding 150 years, had established towns and roads and the roots of a society in North America, nor did it fix the social charter that would become Canada. That would be decided by demands on another front. Just as the Spanish conquest had left the Aztecs vanquished, the British conquest stripped the French Canadians of their empire, their king, and their God, since Catholicism had not been recognized at the outset of the occupation and many clergy left the new world. But the tables were turned when the conquerors sought the help of the conquered.

Seeing that assimilation would be impossible to achieve quickly because the French majority was simply too large, and with eyes on another, more pressing problem in its own colonies, Britain offered the people of New France a deal in 1774. The restrictions and English law imposed after the war ended would be lifted. The French would be allowed to retain their language, their Roman civil code, and their religion. The British also promised to expand Quebec's borders to include vast western areas that the Americans coveted. In exchange, the French needed only refrain from joining the American colonists' intensifying spirit of rebellion.

England's victory over the French altered the equilibrium in North America. The colonists "would not fail to shake off their dependence the moment Canada should be ceded," wrote France's foreign minister, Duc de Choiseul, in a letter to Paris from North America.[2] Accustomed to governing themselves, and no longer needing the protection of the British army to hold off the French, the American colonists forgot their infighting and overlooked bitter jealousies to attack Britain's rule in North America. United in this cause, they built a case for independence based on the violation of human rights, unfair taxation, religious persecution, and wanton cruelty. Britain's recent record of mistreating the people of the territory that had been New France became a grievance mentioned in the Declaration of Independence. The signers condemned King George for "abolishing the free system of English laws in a neighboring province, establishing therein an arbitrary government, and enlarging its boundaries, so as to render it at once an example and fit instrument for introducing the same absolute rule into these colonies."

After the Seven Years' War settled the French question in North America, the American colonists had tried their best to convince the Canadians—orphaned by France, beaten by Britain—to fight by their side against England. They believed the French would not refuse to join the Revolutionary forces. The logic of the New Englanders was as clear as new ice on a shallow pond: The French in Quebec would no more want to be ruled by the British, their former enemies, than the American colonists were willing to tolerate King George's excesses. The cagey New Englanders also had another motive for wanting Canada on their side. They did not worry about defending themselves against the Canadian forces. Boston merchants had tested the mettle of the French already, having mounted a naval force that sacked the mighty fortress at Louisbourg on Cape Breton Island in 1745. But the French regained control in the subsequent treaty negotiations in 1749, the same year the British founded the city of Halifax on Nova Scotia to counterbalance the French on Cape Breton. The American colonists feared that if they were not joined by the settlers of all of what had previously been New France—the people against whom the colonists had savagely fought for more than a generation—the British would use the northern border to attack the American colonies.

When the first Continental Congress met in Philadelphia in 1774, the delegates resolved to take Canada by force. After the first unsuccessful attacks on Quebec and Montreal in 1774, the delegates' will wavered. War hawks insisted on pressing the attacks; moderates feared that further provocations would surely draw in the British. In 1775, the congress called off the actions against Canada. But the confrontation at Bunker Hill a few days later roused war sentiment in the Continental Congress so effectively that the resolution blocking incursions against Canada was dropped.

"The unanimous voice of the Continent is 'Canada must be ours; Quebec must be taken,'" was future president John Adams's blunt view of the relationship with Britain's other colonies in North America. On May 27, 1775, the Continental Congress sent an open letter directly to the people of Canada. "We yet entertain hopes of your uniting with us in defense of common liberty," it said. But factors working against the colonists were too strong. The Quebec Act's leniency toward the Catholicism of the French was more tolerable to the people of Canada than was the fierce Protestantism of the New Englanders. The French even believed that the Continental Congress's opposition to the Quebec Act was itself another sign of the Americans' anti-Catholic feelings. The rowdy behavior of American soldiers while in Canada did little to convince the fearful French that the Americans' promise to mount a common defense of liberty was sincere.

Still, the Americans persisted, believing that the overwhelming righteousness of their cause would eventually convince the French to join them. At one point, rebel leaders, including Benjamin Franklin, were so sure their revolution was democracy's true voice that they were all flame and fire for recruiting other North American colonies to join the Continental Congress. Besides French Canada, this included Newfoundland, Nova Scotia, Georgia, East and West Florida, and, for a time, even Ireland. Franklin eventually headed a delegation to Montreal to convince the Canadians to join the revolt. Accompanying him were Charles Carroll, a Catholic, and Carroll's brother John, a Catholic priest, whose presence was intended to mollify the still-suspicious French. Franklin knew the chances of success were small, especially with no more than 400 English Protestants living in Montreal at the time.[3] Yet he persisted, and to get his message across, he helped start an English-language newspaper in the province. (That newspaper, the Montreal *Gazette,* is still published.) But Montreal rejected Franklin's entreaties and sided instead with the British. More than 220 years later, during a debate on national television in the 1997 elections, Jean Chrétien referred to this alliance when he said that "without Quebec, there wouldn't be a Canada."

After Franklin returned from Montreal, the Continental Congress planned another invasion of Canada, this one led by the Marquis de Lafayette, but it never occurred. In the end, the Articles of Confederation, the precursor to the Constitution that was ratified in 1781, put into words the feelings of many Americans then—and perhaps also now—toward the eventual inclusion of Canada in the American union. Welcoming Canada into the fold was treated as simply a matter of time and was, in essence, preapproved in a way that applied uniquely to it. Article XI reads: "Canada acceding to this confederation and joining in the measures of the United States, shall be admitted into, and entitled to all the advantages of this union, but no other colony shall be admitted into the same, unless such admission be agreed to by nine states."

The unlikely alliance of French North America and Britain against the American colonists was shaped by global politics and domestic necessities. The arrangement was driven by exigencies, not by common cause, and its complicated and difficult legacy persists today with an immediacy that few people outside Canada can ever understand. I had just arrived in Canada in September 1996 when *The Globe and Mail* newspaper carried an advertisement for a new cereal by Kellogg's of Canada called Just Right. "The Quintessentially Canadian Cereal," was the ad's pitch, with just the right amount of grains and nuts, a balanced blend, like the country itself. "Americans are known to be aggressive among other things," the Kellogg's ad said. "The Brits are known to be reserved. Canadians? Besides the obvious exceptions, we're known for being, well, moderate. Let's just say, in the world of cereals, Kellogg's Just Right is pretty much in the same boat."

The cereal campaign fizzled when French-speakers in Quebec, dredging up ancient rivalries, objected. Kellogg's message of happy coexistence was portrayed in French newspapers as an attempt at "planting a small Canadian flag in our cereal bowl and I wonder what gives them the right," wrote a columnist for *La Presse*, Montreal's largest French daily newspaper. Company officials said they never intended to get in the middle of the unending debate over Canadian unity. "We were just looking for an analogy of what the cereal is," Christine Lowry, Kellogg's director of corporate affairs told me. "Just, you know, a little of this and a little of that, a bit of everything in this nice mosaic."

The ads were pulled. Just Right abandoned all patriotic embellishments and became just another cereal.

✳

America's borders are not marked by unscalable mountains, raging rivers, or other intimidating physical barriers. In contemporary North America, national boundaries more accurately represent conceptual divisions, especially since they increasingly join the same three nations of North America they are supposed to keep separate. As an abstraction, the southern border with Mexico is subject to a variety of interpretations, depending on which side of the line one is standing.

Stretches of our touchy border with Mexico are split by rusting steel walls tall enough to leave some streets in Mexico darkened at times by the shadow of the United States, a metaphor sharp enough to resonate with most Mexicans. These barriers have become such powerful symbols of the mistrust that exists between the two nations that many Americans assume the entire border must be like this. But such in-your-face fortifications are scattered only lightly across the border—in Tijuana, Mexicali, and a few other places. Taken together, the segments of armored border—created from army-surplus landing strip material—total no more than 55.5 miles, a tiny percentage of the entire frontier. The great majority of the international boundary line—which stretches 1,952 miles from Texas to the sandy beaches south of San Diego—is sporadically marked, flimsily defended, and to a large extent indistinguishable as to exactly where America ends and Mexico begins. So much so that once, when I went looking for the edge of America, I couldn't find it.

In most places, the physical frontier is a pulsing point near the middle of the muddy trickle that is now the Rio Grande (the Rio Bravo in Mexico.) In some spots, it is just a sign warning desperate Mexicans that poisonous snakes are waiting in the desert for anyone who might try to cross the lunar landscape that the United States has deliberately left on its frontier to discourage Mexicans from entering illegally. But in no place is the border less distinct than along the quirky twenty-four miles between Arizona and the Mexican state of Baja California—the only stretch of our southern border that runs north-south. Mostly, though, the border is nothing more than a conceptual barricade dividing two distinct worlds, on one side the orderliness of the United States, on the other Mexico's unruliness.

On a sweltering afternoon in 1996, I took a walk with Alton Goff, a chief of the International Boundary and Water Commission, across the Morales Dam over the Colorado River to where the American border was supposed to be. But Goff, a voluble desert rat who cherishes life in the southwest, turned sheepish when I asked him to point out the precise spot where Mexico began. He couldn't, he explained, because in 1993 floods on the Gila River that flows into the Colorado had altered the main channel and with it the exact bearings of the border. He ventured a guess as to where it had ended up, but when I asked Alfredo Martínez Orantes, Goff's counterpart on the Mexican side, to show me where he thought the border was, he indicated a spot at least 100 yards away from Goff's. Later we flew over the twenty-four miles of border in a small plane. From a few hundred feet above the desert, all we could

make out was the broad, undulating, footprint of the Colorado River after the 1993 flood had pounded the officially designated border into a
diplomatic memory. We tried one more time to find the border. After
landing we scrambled past the adobe sheds and the overheated streets
on the Mexican side, sliding down through wind-blown debris to the
banks of the Colorado, source of legend and life for a great swath of
North America. What had once been a raging river had been sucked
bone dry by diversions that channeled the sweet currents into the All-
American Canal and other public works that spirited the precious water
to California and put the lie to laissez-faire in the great American west
by demonstrating how reliant big-sky country is on big government.

We searched hard for a sign of the Continental Divide, a point to determine on which side lay the promise of America and on which the
tragedy of Mexico, but we found nothing but fine white sand, as powdery as the tourist beaches in faraway Cancún and just as incapable of
conveying any sense of Mexico. Goff paced out a calculated number of
strides and, where he stopped, looked around for a familiar point.

"It's here, more or less," he said, tracing with his boot in the sand. One
side America. The other Mexico.

More or less.

Delineated by steel wall or a warning, the border always separated
and rarely joined Mexico and the United States. Except for the mapmaker's oddity that Al Goff ruled over, and a few other diversions, the
United States is always north, always above Mexico, a great power towering over an impoverished land that can never forget who is on top. For
most Mexicans, the simple geography of the border condemns their
homeland to a position somewhere between inferiority and submission.
This attitude became clearest to me when, using a translator, I returned
to Mexico City one summer and interviewed a number of deaf mutes.
Several other deaf Mexicans had recently been found begging on the
New York City subway and living in squalid conditions under the control of a family of slick manipulators, Mexicans all, in Queens. The sign
language these Mexicans use is not an international standard but a
homegrown communication unique to Mexico, which makes it a powerful scope into Mexico's innermost feelings. In particular, the sign the
deaf mutes use to represent the United States in conversation explains
how Mexicans perceive the relationship with their neighbor to the
north. The sign is fairly simple—the right hand, palm up, laid over the
top of the left hand, which is held palm down. The symbolism couldn't

be clearer—one part is always subservient to the other, one always on top, the other always kept underneath. Forming the sign also makes these individuals look as if they are in handcuffs, which may be another subconscious message about the United States.

Across America's other border, the sign-language symbol for the United States also suggests the essence of the cross-border relationship. In Canada, the fingers of both hands are intertwined and moved up and down in front of the speaker's heart. The reality of the border is not always so heartfelt. Canadians say "south" as a way of referring to the U.S. border when what they really want to say is that the north—Canada—is superior, somehow above the garish excesses of America's Hollywood culture. It is one-upmanship with roots that go back to the shared beginnings of both countries, and the eternal feeling of relief, or regret, among Canadians for not having joined our revolution. Stretching 4,010 miles—and with Alaska included, add another 1,548 miles—the border splits what for little more than twenty years in the eighteenth century had been Britain's unified North American kingdom, the raw material from which the English throne started to assemble its global empire. Raw and blustery Newfoundland, where Cabot landed in 1497—just five years after Columbus's voyage—was Britain's first overseas colony and provided the basis for England's legal claim on North America, as well as being the wellspring for the pair of Anglo-Saxon nations that developed here. When Queen Elizabeth visited in 1997 to commemorate the 500th anniversary of Cabot's voyage, I heard her declare Newfoundland "the geographical and intellectual beginning of North America."

No part of the Canada-U.S. border has walls along it to match those in Mexico; it is usually guarded by no force more powerful than the shared abstractions of justice and law. This border is reinforced by neither impassable natural impediments nor, for most of its length, the linguistic barriers that usually separate nations. It is an unusual situation, by all accounts, and perhaps unique in history. "The long frontier from the Atlantic to the Pacific Oceans, guarded only by neighborly respect and honorable obligations, is an example to every country and a pattern for the future of the world," Winston Churchill said in the dark days of 1939.[4] That international harmony is no accident of geography, for if it were merely proximity that created peace, the centuries of conflict in Europe would never have happened, and the southern border with Mexico—certainly as close to the United States as is Canada—would not be sown with such suspicion and mistrust. Much more was involved, something John F. Kennedy recognized when he spoke about the many dimensions of the relationship between the United States and Canada. "Geography has made us neighbors. History has made us friends. Economics has made us partners, and necessity has made us allies."[5]

An elegant white arch now stands on the international boundary line between British Columbia and Washington State. It is a rather indiscreet monument to an extraordinary historical reality. Stand on one side of the arch and you are in Canada, then take two steps through and come out in the United States. It stands just a few feet away from the offices of the Immigration and Naturalization Service on the U.S. side, Canada Customs on the other, and most travelers don't even notice it. But when the stream of cars and trucks over the border backs up, leaving travelers in slow-moving traffic, it is possible to read the words etched there in the concrete above the arch. Canada and the United States, the monument dating from 1921 proclaims in sentiments not so easily expressed today, are "children of a common mother."

England's parentage is clearly evident all along America's northern border. It is the foundation on which both the United States and English-speaking Canada stand, and is the deepest part of the breach that separates the United States from Mexico and, to some extent, French Canada. Britain's notions of individual rights and freedoms were among the most liberal in Europe and were the foundation of the new American Republic. Because France did not embrace those ideas until the end of the eighteenth century, New France began with conservative roots. Spain had soundly rejected the principles of the perfectibility of man that came with the Enlightenment, and as a result, Mexico—Spain's stepchild—was the captive of almost 300 years of colonial rule. That profoundly conservative outlook did not keep Spain from achieving greatness, albeit a flawed greatness. Its cities were the most developed on the American continent, and its cathedrals by far the most splendid. By the late eighteenth century, New Spain represented the first world, whereas the British colonies and New France would have been considered unstable, third world, developing nations.

After the American Revolution, the young United States and the British provinces of Upper and Lower Canada developed along similar paths. In each country, settlements clung to the water's edge along lakes, rivers, and the seacoast, relying on trade with Europe for most manufactured goods. The international border between them was still contentious, and in 1812 they tumbled into a war that had little lasting impact except to determine the color of the White House, which had to be repainted after British troops burned it in revenge for the sacking of Fort York in what is now the city of Toronto. That fort still stands, hemmed in by rusting railroad tracks and an elevated highway along Toronto's waterfront. In the summer, it is the site of beer festivals, and people picnic on the grounds dedicated to the British and Canadian regulars who died defending Canada from the Americans. The fort remains a subtle reminder of our differences.

Although the fighting in that war ceased in 1814, the hostilities between the United States and Britain continued. America's push into the western territories it won in the war, as well as those it had acquired from France in the Louisiana Purchase, kept Britain nervous. Continuous squabbling over the Oregon territory, which stretched from California to the tip of Alaska, made a showdown between the United States and Great Britain appear inevitable. Worse, America also felt England was meddling in Mexico, where British banks had generously lent money to the newly independent nation and were gaining a great deal of influence on America's southern flank. American businessmen considered Britain the only foreign obstacle in the way of American ambitions to absorb the great potential of Mexico's Pacific coast, including the biggest prize of all, California.

Britain was still very much in charge of its remaining North American colonies. After the American colonies broke away, it had no intention of creating another nation on the continent. Rather, it presumed that the virtues of an orderly British settlement in the conquered territory of New France would show the wayward colonists the errors of their ways and reunite the fractured British North America. British leaders rejected representative government in favor of an appointed governor who could keep things tightly under control, for the British were finding it hard to tame the north. The English-speaking population in Canada then consisted largely of the families and descendants of about 50,000 Americans loyal to the crown. They fled the colonies after the Revolutionary War, but their sympathy for the British had dimmed. Many had turned their backs on America's rebellion because they had been promised 100 acres and free tools in Canada. They settled in a strip of land below the St. Lawrence River (today's eastern townships in Quebec) and through a thin arc along Lakes Erie and Ontario that became a wedge driven into American territory. Included among the Loyalists were some of the most conservative members of American society: well-to-do merchants, lawyers, and the clergy. They imposed their ideas and values on Canada. They were indeed an unhappy minority, fearful of an attack from the revolutionaries they had left in the United States, and also afraid of being overwhelmed by the French within whose territory they lived.

Despite their shared lineage, the United States and Canada were, by the 1820s, moving in different directions. America was brashly transforming itself from infant democracy to potent world contender. It surpassed in almost every respect the remains of New France, which was still decades from coalescing into a nation, and the stagnant and decaying power of New Spain, which had become the independent and chaotic new nation of Mexico. Any lingering fear of a large republic's incompatibility with democracy had been vanquished by the successful settlement of Louisiana and the Ohio Valley. The entrance into the union of fourteen new states brought the United States to a fever pitch of expansion. The perceived threat of competition from Britain, and the evident weakness of the Mexican state under Santa Anna, helped turn the fever into blood lust.

The veil over the American drama at this time was slavery. Expansionists used it as justification for more conquests, promising that new territory could help ease current tensions by providing ample space for the adherents of both sides of the slavery issue. Such explanations also would help assuage any feelings of guilt for the way the new land would have to be gained. Robert J. Walker, a Mississippi senator who went on to become secretary of the treasury in the 1840s, argued for the annexation of the independent republic of Texas because the land would serve as a safety valve for the Deep South's growing population of slaves. Even more audaciously, Walker foresaw the day when freed black slaves would settle in parts of old Mexico, ridding the United States of that particular problem.[6]

Before the 1840s were over, the United States had taken nearly half of Mexico, although American textbooks rarely put it that way. The Treaty of Guadalupe Hidalgo gave Americans access not only to the Pacific ports but also to California's gold, discovered nine days after the treaty was signed. America's push westward created economic and nationalistic opportunities undreamed of even a few decades before, but the slavery issue droned through every development and pitched the young United States into a civil war.

The civil conflict in America sent powerful shock waves across both its borders. Mexico's misadventure with Maximilian, which was halted abruptly after the end of the U.S. Civil War revived the Monroe Doctrine, helped bring to power Porfirio Díaz, whose long reign set off the Mexican Revolution. Canada's accelerated drive for confederation was motivated in part by fear of being annexed by the victorious Union army. The new nation initially was called the Kingdom of Canada, making clear the provinces' rejection of the American way and their continued loyalty to Britain. Many in the United States were displeased by the continued presence of a foreign monarch and his representatives in this hemisphere. The Maine legislature formally opposed Canada's designation as a kingdom, and the issue was discussed in Congress, which left no doubt that flaunting the British throne would be considered a provocation. Once again, Canadians sought a compromise. At one of the conferences, the stiff-necked and devoutly religious premier of New Brunswick, Leonard Tilley, offered a way to express the would-be nation's optimism without offending anyone. He quoted the Bible: "And he shall have dominion from sea even unto sea and from the river to the ends of the earth." The allusion gave the new nation the classification of dominion, which for 100 years would cause confusion about how independent a nation the Dominion of Canada had become.

On July 1, 1867, ninety-one years after the Declaration of Independence was signed and more than three centuries after the conquistadores laid the cornerstones of the new city of Mexico, North America's youngest nation came into being. Queen Victoria had decided that the capital should be built on the dividing line between the contentious provinces of Upper Canada and Lower Canada, an inhospitably cold lumber post on the Ottawa River that was supposed to bridge the two poles of the new nation's past and, symbolically at least, resolve the conflicts between French and English, Catholic and Protestant, old world and new, that had festered in the north since the conquest. Queen Victoria also preferred Ottawa because it was farther than Montreal or Toronto from the U.S. border. The legal declaration of Canada's sovereignty had been handled in the House of Commons in London with unusual dispatch a few months earlier by a British government that had far loftier imperial goals than beaver and buckskin. The vote was affirmative, and debate moved on quickly to the next order of business, the issuance of dog licenses, which evoked far stronger emotions than Canada's independence, much to the dismay of the Canadians.[7]

There had been no declaration of independence, and there were few shouts of joy for finally achieving freedom. Canada's national anthem,

"O Canada," contains no historical references as do the anthems of the United States or Mexico; the nation's birth was a legal arrangement conducted by parliamentary debaters over the course of weeks of nuanced argument. The nation was built not with bullets and patriotic zeal but with the practical and political compromise necessary to make the French in Quebec happy and keep the Americans south of the border at bay. In some respects, Canada's sovereignty was not so much declared as implied, and that ambivalence has contributed to the nation's character ever since. "Other nations fought their way onto the world's map by revolution or by winning or losing a war," former prime minister Joe Clark wrote in 1994. "We are a nation by agreement. That is how we started, how we function, how we succeed or fail."[8]

Canada came into being as a ward of the British throne, a confederation that recognized both the democratic will of the people and the continued loyalty to the crown. The parliamentarians in London saw a more lucrative future in other colonies and were willing to grant outright independence. They were surprised when Canadian delegates did not press for it. But with the British North America Act, through which the Dominion of Canada was created, the dispute between the United States and Britain for control of North America ended. In exchange for accepting a Canadian nation that stretched from ocean to ocean, including the Pacific coast regions expansionists once coveted, America could lay to rest its fears about any further conflict with Britain. The United States would be spared the expense of defending its borders on the ground, focusing instead on other issues. The border arrangement with Britain turned out to be a satisfactory quid pro quo for the moment. Had Canada pressed for outright independence at that point, it might not have been able to strike as equitable a bargain.

When Canada threw itself a hugely expensive centennial exposition in Montreal in 1967 to celebrate this rare and gentle process of nation building, it had acquired most, but not all, of the essential elements of statehood. It had finally turned its back on its past and adopted its own flag in 1965 after having used a British ensign since 1867 (the province of Ontario later adopted the ensign as its banner). Typically, the red maple leaf design of the new flag was the product of compromise and was adopted—with explanations but no history—after six months of debate that had paralyzed Parliament. But Canada still had no constitution establishing its sovereignty. The country continued to be governed by the British North America Act, the same law of the British Parliament that had created the dominion in 1867. The law could be amended only by a Canadian delegation in London and a majority vote of the British Parliament.

Attempts to wrest that final control from London and establish Canada's sovereignty on its own soil had been ongoing since 1927 but always were stymied by the provinces. They were willing to accede to a new constitution only if the document strengthened their powers and further limited the central government's authority, a reversal of the founders' goals. The fathers of confederation wanted to preserve both the French and English nationalities within a single confederation, but after seeing how states' rights had nearly torn America apart, they deliberately chose to have a strong central government and weaker provinces. The goals were contradictory: Appeasing Quebec's special interests boosted the powers of all provinces but weakened Ottawa so much that Canada came to be regarded as one of the most decentralized federations in the world.

After an unsuccessful attempt by Quebec to separate legally via a public referendum in 1980, Prime Minister Pierre Trudeau tried standing up to the provinces. Constitutional reform had become one of his driving ambitions. He prodded and threatened the provinces, and finally, in 1982, after brokering several secret deals that enraged the separatist leaders of his home province of Quebec, Trudeau struck a deal with the other provinces and the British Parliament for Canada to adopt its own constitution and charter of rights and freedoms—in essence, a Canadian bill of rights. The struggle for power between the provinces and the central government was intense, and the arrogant Trudeau, certain he was right, minced no words. "If there was not the will in the country to be constitutionally independent 115 years after Canada stopped being a colony, that would have meant there was no national will at all," he recalled in his memoirs, "and therefore no country worthy of the name."9

The provinces finally accepted the proposal after Trudeau threw in some sweeteners, including one he detested. Perhaps unique in national constitutions, Canada's permits the legislature of a local province temporarily to bypass or ignore a clause of the constitution with which it disagrees. "Mealy mouthed," Trudeau called this exit clause, but he accepted it in order to appease the leaders of the English-speaking provinces who insisted on the loophole to preserve their power against any possible attempt by Ottawa, or the newly fortified Supreme Court of Canada, to overstep provincial authority. Only Quebec crossed its arms

and refused to sign the new constitution, later accusing Trudeau of trea-
son. Quebec still has not formally accepted Canada's constitution, but
that hasn't stopped provincial leaders from occasionally raising constitutional objections to proposals from Ottawa.

The day the nine provincial leaders finally signed the new constitution, Trudeau delivered a previously scheduled speech in Philadelphia.
"I reminded the American audience that in their city more than 200
years earlier the United States had declared its independence and written its constitution," he noted in his memoirs. "In Canada," he told the
Americans, "we did it this morning."

Trudeau also stressed the similarities between our histories, without
mentioning the striking differences that remained. Adding a charter of
rights and freedoms to the constitution had made Canada a "society
where all people are equal and where they share some fundamental values based on freedom," Trudeau said. But equality is a volatile notion in
a country born of two founding nations, a country that pampers those
who speak English and French but not those who speak dozens of other
languages. And despite the constitution and the charter of rights and
freedoms, the monarchy and Parliament remain what Thomas Jefferson
called the "safe depository of the ultimate powers of society," not the abstract will of the Canadian people. On the day that sovereignty over the
world's second-largest country finally passed to Canada's own parliament in Ottawa on April 17, 1982, it was Queen Elizabeth II who signed
the formal document. To this day, she remains the Queen of Canada to
whom Canadians swear allegiance in their oath of citizenship. The day
of the signing started with bright sunshine but ended in a downpour,
which to Trudeau was an omen of things to come for Canada.

Despite Trudeau's efforts to keep Canada well separated from the
United States, it has acquired U.S. characteristics through the supremacy
of individual rights in the new charter and the jurisdiction of the courts
in interpreting the constitution. The justices of Canada's supreme court
have become ambitious interpreters of the charter, using it to uphold a
range of individual rights. Conservative Canadians, especially those in
the western provinces, soon were condemning "judge-made law," sometimes more bluntly called "creeping Americanism." These critics became
upset when the justices took on native Indian rights and accepted oral
histories and Indian blanket dances as legal evidence in treaty claims.
They were furious when the justices supported gay rights. And as time

went on, they saw a conspiracy against the established order in Canada by a court willing to rewrite basic law without consulting Parliament. This was vividly brought out by one case involving a woman who appealed her deportation order even though her visa to visit Canada had expired eighteen years before. She appealed on the basis of the human rights guarantee inherent in the charter, citing the fact that she had given birth to children while in Canada. An immigration department official rejected the claim, but after the case received attention in the Toronto newspapers, Liberal Party leaders sought a way around the laws governing immigration. The case went before the Supreme Court, which decided not to strike down the immigration act but to hold that the charter of rights and freedoms, along with the fundamental values of Canadian society, required that the woman and her children not be deported, even if that was what the law dictated.

In late 1996, I attended a dinner in Toronto with Seymour Martin Lipset, a sociologist and veteran observer of Canada and the United States. He predicted that adoption of the charter of rights and freedoms and the way the Supreme Court interprets it would tear down the consensus principles on which Canada's history has rested for a century and replace them with the same type of individual rights embodied in the American constitution, beginning with the first words "We the people. . . ."

A few months after that dinner, I discovered that Canada sometimes has a peculiar sense of individual rights, or at least one that contradicts what is contained in the charter. It was a brutal December day on which a frigid winter wind whipped the Manitoba prairie. I was in the gray provincial capital, Winnipeg, to ask the head of the Canadian Wheat Board why Canadian farmers who opposed the agency's monopoly on wheat and barley sales had been sent to jail. From the moment I arrived at the board's headquarters on Main Street in Winnipeg, I could sense the immense power and central role that this organization has played in the development of the Canadian west. Its limestone facade was ornately carved with sheaves of wheat and agricultural scenes—humble images discordant with the imperious architecture they adorned.

The chief commissioner of the board, Lorne F. Hehn, was a former farmer himself, the type of man who though dressed in a suit exhibits the girth and gait of someone used to working outside. He was generous with his time, telling me how the isolated farmers of depression-era Canada had been at a great disadvantage in not knowing the going price for wheat and other grains before bringing their harvests to market. By setting pool prices, guaranteeing to buy all the wheat that was produced, and then marketing it for the best price available around the world, the board had succeeded admirably in raising incomes within the entire industry. Its yearly sales exceeded $4.5 billion, and through the board's efforts, Canada was able to export 80 percent of its grain harvest to more than seventy countries, including Russia and the United States. Another significant achievement, he said, was implanting blessed dependability in a business traditionally whipsawed by weather, overstocks, and transportation problems.

"Canadians built one hell of a country by working together," Hehn told me. He rejected the recent demands of farmers who, backed by the instantly accessible market prices now on the Internet, wanted participation in the board's sales programs to be optional. If they could get a better price for wheat or barley outside the pool, they wanted the freedom to exploit that opportunity. The heart of Hehn's argument was that individual rights sometimes have to be subordinated to the good of the community, an echo of the social-democratic views that Eastern European immigrants brought with them to the Canadian west when they settled there. Hehn said an optional system would never work. "In good years, with rising prices, we wouldn't get enough wheat to meet our customer demands," he told me, "and in bad years, when prices decline, we'd get it all."

Hehn had reacted angrily to recent attempts by Canadian farmers to bust the system, and had wholeheartedly supported the jailing of several farmers who broke the laws. He said he had no sympathy for them, even though he had once been a farmer himself. He said he understood that it might be hard for me, an American, to understand this, but Canadians really do believe it's worthwhile to give up their right to sell grain at higher spot prices if that means more farmers will get higher prices most of the time. That attitude sprouts like spring wheat not just on the prairies but throughout Canadian culture, despite the charter of rights and freedoms. It is the basis for law enforcement, environmental protection, health care, and other aspects of Canadian society that differ from ours. "In society we are seeing more and more of this attitude of 'give me choice,'" he said, making clear that he was talking about the United States and about American influences on Canada. "In the long run, if that happens, we end up giving up the strengths and advantages that we gain by working together."

From Winnipeg, I drove about 300 miles southwest toward the rural community of Lyleton near the American border. Along a snow-covered stretch of flatland, to the side of a road that ran straight south two miles to the border, in an old trailer that smelled of wet woolen socks and was tilted enough to make walking difficult for a visitor not accustomed to the weird angle, I met Andy McMechan. Andy had just been released from the Brandon Correctional Institution penitentiary after serving 155 days on charges that he sold a couple bushels of barley across the border in the United States without going through the Wheat Board.

Andy was born to be a farmer. Tough as a tractor, he loathed only a few things—wearing neckties, spending too much of the day under a roof, and being forced to follow senseless rules just because they were rules. He married an American girl named Pamela and decided to build his homestead amid the golden glow of wheat on the flat prairie lands of Manitoba. Pamela's family had left her 640 acres in Antler, North Dakota, near the border, and Andy farmed both that tract and nearly 1,000 acres of his own land in Lyleton—crossing the border so regularly he'd almost forgotten it was there. One Sunday he hooked up his tractor and ventured off to Antler to push some snow from the driveway. "I figured if I was going down anyway, I might as well bring some barley," he said. He had already been warned against selling his own grain and had been told not to come to within one-half mile of the border. But Andy was agitating for change, and he knew he had the support of lots of other farmers who had contacted him through a group called Farmers for Justice.

It was a Sunday, and crossing over the silent border checkpoint in Lyleton was no problem. But hours later, when he returned to the Canadian side, customs officers stopped him. "They told me 'We're seizing your tractor,' just like that," Andy said. He was surprised to see Mounties at the border too. The system was going to make an example of him for the growing ranks of farmers who also challenged the Wheat Board's monopoly, farmers like Russ Barrows of Coutts, Alberta, who had been fined $4,000 for trying to sell one bag of Canadian wheat that normally would fetch about $5. But Andy had decided that if going to jail was necessary to stand up for his rights, he would do it in a way that let other Canadians know what was happening in their country. American farmers also knew what was going on in Manitoba, but Andy was no hero to them, nor did they support the Canadian Wheat Board. The American farmers were angry at the board for shipping Canadian wheat across the border at uncompetitive prices, and as I found out when they called me to complain, they saw Andy not as a fellow farmer, or a Canadian, but only as a competitor.

But in parts of the vast Canadian prairies, Andy had become a sympathetic figure of rebellion. When he was brought into court for a bail hearing, the jailers shackled his wrists and ankles. His offense was not murder or larceny, but only, he said, trying to sell his own grain, which he had grown with his own hands. "I was quite aware of how other people were going to respond, so when they came to put on the shackles, I made sure my pants were tucked inside them so they'd really show up," he said. Photographs of Andy in chains became an instantly recognized symbol of the farmers' fight. He was kept in prison with petty thieves and wife beaters and was allowed into the prison yard for only a half hour a day.

"They preach about it, and all I hear is that this is a free country, but if that's so, why don't they let me go and sell my grain?" Andy said. "If not, then tell us that this is not a free country. Who are they trying to kid?" When I checked in with him a few years later, he still was fighting mad. "It's only gotten worse," he said.

Pamela said she sometimes feels like an outsider in Lyleton, even though she's lived there since she married Andy many years ago. She grew up in Antler only seven miles from the border but never crossed over into Canada until Andy proposed to her and brought her north, the fourth of five McMechan brothers to marry an American girl. "When we first got married, people at home used to ask me how I liked living in Canada," Pamela said. "I used to tell them I didn't think the border existed. But after all this trouble with Andy I think differently."

On Andy McMechan's farm, where the fields run off into the horizon, I had found that some of the starkest differences between the United States and Canada arose from contrasting notions about individual rights. Although the two nations once were so close that the United States left an expansion clause especially for Canada to join the union, they had diverged on the concept of individual rights. And even though it seemed obvious that the American-style charter of rights would continually challenge Canada's customary belief that society is more important than the individual, fundamental differences would remain. In a way I had never understood before, the Canadian concept of self was substantially different from ours, and it affected the way Canadians perceived the rest of the world. Commentators have said the U.S.-Canada relationship is guided not by the small issues on which we disagree but by the many things we have in common. That is a good approach, because some of our differences have been great irritants in the past, and of all contemporary points of conflict, nothing has been more corrosive for a longer time than Canada's dealings with one other country in the hemisphere—Cuba.

CHAPTER TEN

Affairs Too Foreign

✴

The first piece of advice I give you is this:
Be friends with the United States—the Canadian people
like the Americans—but don't be subservient to the
American government, because Canadians
are very proud people.

Pierre Elliott Trudeau
to incoming Prime Minister Brian Mulroney in 1984

Neat and efficient, like the image of itself Canada sometimes savors, the snow-white Challenger jet took off from an icy runway at the Ottawa airport and eased into a flight pattern that took it over the United States en route to a destination that few American jets ever reach. Although a military jet, this Canadian-built Challenger screamed power executive—it was outfitted with two pairs of leather recliners face-to-face across small tables, and twin banquettes that lined the cabin walls beneath the jet's small windows. In all, there was room aboard for nine people. The carpet was plush, the cabin quiet, and the Canadian Forces crew stood ready to offer Lloyd Axworthy, Canada's bookish foreign minister, anything he needed as he prepared to stir up a diplomatic hornet's nest of trouble with American officials. Even though Washington was still a bit hung over from the excesses of President Clinton's second inaugural celebration, many reddened eyes were focused that day in January 1997 on Axworthy and his intention to become the first high-ranking representative of an American ally in many years to shake hands with Fidel Castro in Havana.

Axworthy, a stout prairie statesman who idolized Lester B. Pearson, Canada's Nobel Prize–winning foreign secretary and, later, prime minister, had long ago grown accustomed to the trials of Canada's winter. He knew, as do most Canadians, that to keep one's sanity through the country's cruelest season, it is sometimes necessary to get away. Florida, Jamaica, Bermuda, Mexico, any place where parkas are never worn and tires are never chained is a suitable refuge. A trip to Havana could be taken any time of the year, but was there a better time than a congealed January day? The fine wool overcoat Axworthy wore as he boarded the Challenger would be wholly out of place in Havana, but not nearly as much so as Axworthy himself. Even though the Canadians had never completely broken off relations with Cuba after Castro took over, it had been more than twenty years since a senior Canadian official had so openly defied American wishes by setting foot in forbidden Havana. Axworthy, who had recently become foreign minister, intended to change that.

Settling in for the flight, he carefully removed the coat, then took off his suit jacket and rolled up his shirtsleeves, ready to get to work putting the finishing touches to remarks he would use to defend his dash to Cuba. The purpose of the thirty-six-hour trip, he told me as he made himself comfortable and started on a generous Canadian lunch, was not to badger Castro about Cuba's dismal human rights record or to press the Cuban leader into holding truly democratic elections. He wasn't going to stick his thumb in Uncle Sam's eye over the Helms-Burton law that Jean Chrétien and Ernesto Zedillo had denounced a few months earlier. Rather, Axworthy said, he was going to get a firsthand look at the flattened wreck of communism in the Americas that Cuba had become. He wanted to see for himself the potential Caribbean powerhouse that Canadian investors were so excited about. And he wanted to assess the way Cuba's return to the bosom of democracy someday would mark a new era for the Western Hemisphere, an era of sweeping democracy that Axworthy believed would belong to Canada. In Axworthy's vision, a Canada that was unhindered by a colonial past, and unscarred by embargoes, invasions, and interventions, could fill the shoes of the United States and assume a leadership role in the Americas that the United States seemed reluctant to take.

That was the public explanation Axworthy and his small team of advisers used. But it was clear his motives went far deeper than just taking inventory. For thirty-five years, through the administrations of seven frustrated American presidents, Canada's embrace of Cuba had been a blaring note of dissonance in the generally harmonic set piece that is bilateral relations between the United States and its closest ally. Washington accepted as inevitable that Canada would take a contrary view on some issues if only to prove the independence of its foreign policy. On the matter of promoting the democratic transition of communism's remaining toehold in the West, however, Washington was annoyed by a front that was splintered. Most irksome to Washington was that the Canadians never just disagreed outright; they presented their ambitions in Cuba as essentially being the same as the Americans'—democracy, human rights, representative government. But whereas Washington had imposed and enforced its economic embargo against Cuba, Canada had from the beginning decided to embrace the island. It engaged Castro in diplomatic negotiations and maintained economic relations as it would have with any friendly nation. Generations of U.S. House and Senate members saw this as coddling Castro. But because it was Canada, the lawmakers rarely bothered to do or say anything about it.

That changed when an increasingly desperate Castro, marooned by the dissolution of the Soviet Union, decided to exploit the island's surviving economic opportunities. Canadian entrepreneurs eagerly brokered lucrative deals that the embargo kept off-limits to Americans. Suddenly more than democratic discipline was at stake. This was a significant economic opportunity in what was thought could someday become the hottest market in the Caribbean, and American businesses had to stand by and watch Canadians, along with Mexicans, Italians, and others, grab all the spoils. The trigger-happy Cuban-American lobby in south Florida questioned Canadian motives, and American resentment toward Canada's coziness with Cuba boiled over.

For Canada, doing business with Cuba has meant more than building hotels and running exclusive tourist packages, although those enterprises have been immensely rewarding and have left the avenues of Toronto, Montreal, and other winter-bound Canadian cities blanketed with billboard advertisements luring Canadians to serene Cuban beaches that most Americans cannot enjoy. "We know who our friends are," Canada's then ambassador to the United States, Raymond Chrétien, told me one day over lunch at the Royal York Hotel in Toronto, "but we also want to be able to go to the beaches of Cuba."

Defying Washington's embargo was the home-run swing of Canadian politics, the one sure way for Canada's leaders to prove that despite the resemblance between the two countries, Canada could pursue its own international agenda. In practical terms, chasing Cuba had been a safe gambit for Ottawa. The rest of the Canada-U.S. relationship was far too important for either side to let Castro endanger it. Even when Canadian investments on the island reached their peak in the mid-1990s, and more than 150,000 Canadians a year tanned themselves on Cuban beaches, it all amounted to a drop in the bucket compared with the commerce that crossed the U.S.-Canada border. When two-way trade between Cuba and Canada reached just over $400 million a year, it still amounted to less than half of what Canada and the United States traded in a single day.

Standing up to Washington has played well in Canada since the time it was George Washington the Canadians rebuffed after he invited them to join the thirteen colonies in ditching Britain. But few northerners have more successfully thumbed their noses at the United States than Lloyd Axworthy. As a member of the opposition during the pro-American Mulroney years, Axworthy lashed out at American economic and cultural imperialism. Time and again, he ranted about the dangers of entering into free trade agreements with a country so single-mindedly focused on taking advantage of its neighbors. But when his own Liberal Party came to power in 1993, both the party and Axworthy stopped preaching about Canada's need to resist the lure of the United States. In a short time, the Liberals were cozying up to Washington on almost every issue for which they had criticized Mulroney's Conservatives. They eagerly signed NAFTA, jumped to the front to volunteer for peacekeeping duties to support America's operations in Haiti, opened up Canadian skies to rigorous American airline competition in 1995, and in countless other ways agreed to do Washington's bidding. Canada and the United States might be holding hands now across the border, but Axworthy knew how important it was to show they still slept in separate beds.

"We are different countries and we do things in different ways," Axworthy told me in his clipped manner of speaking—like frozen peas tumbling out of a bag. He was dumbstruck by the vicious reaction to his trip that came out of Washington, where Canada had already been accused of "rewarding a dictator in our hemisphere" because Axworthy had been invited to dine with Castro at the Palace of the Revolution in Havana. "There is no way for one country to tell another country what to do," he sniffed, sounding what has been the constant drumbeat of bilateral relations between these two closest of neighbors. The complex

Canadian view of U.S. policy—at times wholeheartedly supporting
Washington's objectives, at other times using its special relationship to
spearhead effective opposition to American initiatives—certainly had not
been devised by Axworthy. It had developed over many years and came
from many wellsprings. Until World War II, Canada's ties with Britain
kept it firmly in the European orbit, and often that aligned it against
U.S. policy.

During the war, Canada had played a small but important role with
the Allies, and usually was content, under Prime Minister William Lyon
Mackenzie King, to go along rather than go ahead. A reminder of that
subordinate relationship came as recently as 1998, when the Quebec
government dedicated a public monument depicting the historic meetings between Churchill and Roosevelt in the misty, walled city in 1943
and 1944. Statues of the West's two great wartime leaders were shown in
heroic poses, but Canada's own prime minister was not included. Some
considered the omission another French-Canadian slap at English
Canada, but the Quebecois government argued that King was left out
not because of separatist pique but because he had played an insignificant role in the conferences. The reasoning was generally correct. After
the flashbulbs popped during the photo sessions with the wartime leaders in 1943, King essentially disappeared from the scene and had no role
in the negotiations but to play host.[1]

Canadian sensitivity to what it considered American bullying in diplomatic affairs intensified rapidly in the 1950s and 1960s for clear reasons.
Canada's ties with Britain were fraying, even though a substantial number of Canadians continued to support the monarchy. Britain had come
out of the war victorious but battered and nearly broke, its influence in
the world greatly diminished. By contrast, the home fronts in the United
States and Canada were untouched by the war. Canada, in fact, emerged
from the conflict stronger and more stable than when the war had broken out. Britain no longer had the economic stamina to support its former colony through trade and finance. Canada had to find new markets,
which led the country into the ready arms of a prosperous and aggressive United States. In the postwar years, it became evident that although
Canada's long and noble past lay across the Atlantic Ocean, its future
could most certainly be found on the other side of Lake Ontario. In a
speech before a Toronto audience in 1951, when he was foreign minister, Lester Pearson declared that Canada and the United States shared
"destinies, economic and political."[2]

The new North American alliance soon showed signs of strain. U.S. strategy in Korea was too aggressive for Canada's tastes. Overall, Canada felt uncomfortable with the Cold War standoff that was developing between the United States and the Soviet Union, in great part because it forced Canada to worry about defending its arctic border, which it had never worried about before. If hostilities broke out between the United States and the Soviet Union, nuclear missiles were likely to fly over the North Pole and Canada's arctic territories. In March 1955, U.S. Secretary of State John Foster Dulles told Pearson that "if war came ... it would start by communist air strikes on North America," and Pearson clearly understood that Canada was all that separated the two great superpowers.[3]

When the United States proposed building a far northern defensive system with American nuclear weapons stationed in Canada, most Canadians regarded the proposal as a threat to Canadian sovereignty and the opening gambit in an era of bad feelings. "The days of relatively easy and automatic relations with our neighbor are, I think, over," Pearson said at the time.[4] For many years, prickliness replaced amicability across the border. Conservative Prime Minister John Diefenbaker antagonized President Kennedy with his extreme defensiveness about Canadian sovereignty, and an impatient Richard Nixon grew weary of dealing with Pierre Trudeau's obstinate resistance to American hegemony. Nixon was heard on the Watergate tapes snarling "that asshole Trudeau."[5]

Canada's ambiguous relationship with the United States thereafter intensified, and Lloyd Axworthy personified that ambiguity. His attraction to and admiration for the United States was substantial. He attended graduate school at Princeton University and even became a diehard New York Knicks basketball fan in the 1960s. But he never accepted the view that Canada should blindly follow the United States, nor did he agree with Secretary of State Madeleine Albright's declaration in 1996 that America is the "indispensable nation." Axworthy stated many times that it was certainly better to have the United States supporting an initiative than opposing it, but important things could happen without America's participation. Because of him, Canada was among the first nations to support formally the citizens' campaign to ban land mines. Canada sponsored and helped get adopted the 1997 international treaty banning land mines; only a few nations had refused to sign the treaty, but prominent among them was the United States. Axworthy campaigned for the international criminal tribunal that Washington opposed, and spoke openly against NATO's refusal to disavow the first use of nuclear weapons, again despite stiff opposition from the United States.

Often rumpled and uncomfortable performing the ceremonial duties of a foreign minister, Axworthy nonetheless seemed totally at ease in Havana. Even when the Cubans spirited him and his entourage off to the fabulous beach at Varadero to tour the exclusive resort properties of Canadian investors, he talked freely to reporters about "opportunities of engagement," the term Canadians used to describe their approach to handling Cuba's recalcitrance. The only discomfort Axworthy showed came when he was taken by bus to a place not far from the Varadero beach where the air stank of oil. The Cubans wanted to highlight a project to reopen shallow oil wells that had been abandoned when the Russians pulled out. It was yet another investment by Sherritt International, the Canadian company the U.S. Department of State had identified as a violator of the Helms-Burton law. Besides the oil field, Sherritt operated an old nickel mine that had belonged to an American company, Freeport-McMoran, before Castro seized it without paying adequate compensation in the 1960s. Helms-Burton made it possible for foreign companies using property formerly owned by Americans to be sued for compensation in American courts, an extraordinary extension of American jurisdiction that all American allies, including Canada, rejected. Still, it was law (although implementation of that particular provision involving extraterritorial lawsuits was continually delayed by President Clinton) and raised indelicate questions for Canadians in Cuba. The mud pumps and other heavy equipment at the oil field Axworthy visited were clearly marked as made in the United States and were owned by Sherritt. When this was pointed out, Cuban officials said the equipment proved the futility of the U.S. embargo. Axworthy ignored the questions and rushed off to another beach.

While Sherritt managers offered half-hearted explanations for the presence of the American equipment, the head of Sherritt, Ian Delaney, was nowhere to be seen. Delaney is that rarest of North American creatures—a boastful Canadian. Enactment of the Helms-Burton law made him choose carefully what he said and did in public, but in earlier days little more than a glimpse of a reporter's notebook would get him talking about his expanding international empire. He was profiled in Canadian magazines as "Castro's Favorite Capitalist" and the "Canadian in Cuba" who was beating the Americans at their own game. When officials sent a letter warning Delaney, his family, and officials of his company not to set foot in the United States because he was in violation of the Helms-Burton law, he framed the letter and hung it on the wall of his office at Sherritt headquarters in Toronto's exclusive Rosedale neighborhood. Delaney wasn't the only Canadian I met who wore a reprimand from Washington as a badge of honor. George Burne, an executive of the Canadian office of the international diamond company DeBeers, also had been warned not to enter the United States because of a long-standing Justice Department investigation into price fixing by the DeBeers diamond cartel. "In Canada, anything hinting of standing up to the United States leaves you smelling like a hero," Burne boasted.

Axworthy joined Castro for dinner at the Palace of the Revolution. The menu included lobster and baby lamb chops, along with a vegetable soup Axworthy commented on to be polite. Despite earlier statements to the contrary, the Canadian was impatient to move the conversation to human rights. He had to sit through a long-winded discussion of how Castro himself had provided the recipe for the soup, supervised the planting and harvesting of the vegetables, and overseen their preparation in the kitchen. Axworthy left Cuba the next day, and he did not depart empty-handed. He had won no concessions from Castro on the rights issues that were at the top of Canada's agenda, but the comandante sent Axworthy the recipe for his vegetable soup. "I went to Cuba to talk to Castro about human rights and democracy," Axworthy told friends in 2001 when Princeton University presented him with an award, "and all I came back with was a recipe for vegetable soup."

A little over a year after Axworthy's Cold War recipe swap, Prime Minister Chrétien took his own trip there. He stood alongside Castro on the tarmac at Havana's Jose Martí Airport while the Cuban leader berated the United States, claiming at one point that the U.S. embargo was the equivalent of genocide. Chrétien did not counter anything Castro said against the United States but defended Canada's policy of engagement with Cuba, which had included financing and building a new airport terminal. Later the prime minister told reporters that he thought he could accomplish more with a soft touch than by assaulting the Cubans with rhetoric. Although he believed that Canada's special relationship with Cuba made Castro listen to him, he did not demand much of the Cuban leader during the visit. He asked for just one specific act—the release of four dissidents, including one woman, Beatríz Roque, who had serious health problems. Castro acknowledged that he had received the list of names from Chrétien and would take it under consideration.

Chrétien's trip was no more successful than Axworthy's had been. Castro put the dissidents on trial anyway, and when they were convicted of antirevolutionary crimes, he allowed them to be sentenced to up to five years in prison. This stirred in Chrétien and Axworthy a measure of the frustration with Castro that had bedeviled American presidents since 1960. A vexed and annoyed Axworthy announced that Canada's Cuba policy would be completely rethought, and in the meantime all new projects that were not humanitarian aid would be blocked. Castro's insult had been especially hurtful to the foreign minister, who had risked his prestige by going to Cuba. As far back at least as Pearson's day, it had been galling for Canadian officials to feel they were being ignored when they stepped up to take a role in world events.

The Helms-Burton law was not changing Cuban politics, but it was proving effective in altering the way principal U.S. trade partners invested in Cuba. Delaney was forced to reexamine Sherritt International's position in Cuba, not for moral reasons but because his Cuban investments simply were not performing as well as expected and Helms-Burton made financing hard to obtain. Another North American company that had received a Helms-Burton warning from Washington was the Mexican firm Grupo Domos, a small but well-connected investment group from Monterrey that had, with help from the Salinas administration, bought a large share of Cuba's decrepit telephone system. Grupo Domos agreed to pay $750 million for 49 percent of the nationalized telephone company, a creaking collection of Czechoslovakian line switching equipment paired with balky Soviet electronics and heavy black handsets left over from the late 1950s when the system was owned and operated by International Telephone and Telegraph.

ITT had since been broken up, but one of the surviving divisions still had a $130 million claim before an international settlements board on the property confiscated in Cuba. Grupo Domos violated the Helms-Burton law by taking over the lines and switches of the old system, even though the firm was careful not to install its offices in the creaking tower in Old Havana that ITT had used for its Cuban operations. That building itself was a remnant of the Cold War, the physical embodiment of a time of mistrust and drawn swords that turned even the slightest differences into flashpoints. The cornice of the old building was coming apart when I went to see it, and the sidewalk was cordoned off to keep passersby from being injured by falling masonry. But anyone who bent underneath the rope, as I did, and risked walking up to the side of the building could read the bronze plaque commemorating the day the "onerous concession of the telephone monopoly was seized" in August 1960 by resolution number one of the new revolutionary government.

The day I visited Mexico's largest beachhead in Cuba, the Grupo Domos executives were comfortably settled into a gracious old structure never owned by Americans. The colonial-era building was located near a park not far from the Plaza de Armas and the glass pavilion that was built around the *Granma*, the fishing boat that had taken Fidel, Ché Guevara, and a few other revolutionaries from their exile in Mexico back to Cuba to begin their victorious revolutionary push in the late 1950s.

With more gumption than telecommunications know-how, the executives of Grupo Domos told me over sweetened coffee that they were going to rebuild the old system, taking advantage of Cuba's rapidly expanding need for communication with the rest of the world. But without Salinas or his backers in Los Pinos, the Mexicans' deal had to survive on its own merits, which it could not, especially not after the peso crisis. Grupo Domos executives said the warning the company had received from the State Department regarding Helms-Burton violations made it difficult to arrange the private financing they needed to keep the enterprise going. The law also was interfering with the firm's plan to expand in Texas and other parts of the southwestern United States, which were off-limits to all company executives as long as they controlled the investment in Cuba.

Within a few years, the combination of pressure from Helms-Burton and a business plan that wasn't working as planned led Grupo Domos to withdraw completely from the Cuban telephone market. The group sold its stake to the Italian phone company, which had less to fear from Washington since it had no direct business dealings with the United States. The Italians tried to protect themselves anyway by signing a deal to compensate ITT for the use of confiscated property.

The Cuban opportunities that American businesses resented losing never became as lucrative as the Canadians and Mexicans who grabbed them had hoped. Nonetheless, the Cuban government's embrace of the U.S. dollar had transformed the island since Miriam and I first visited in the late 1970s. In that brief interval of good relations under President Jimmy Carter, we had applied for Cuban visas—she as a Cuban national who had left the island with her grandmother at age ten, and I not as a journalist then but as her spouse. Her grandmother came too, even though she was almost eighty. It was their first visit to the island since 1962, when Miriam was a cheery little girl under the care of the stern, old-world grandmother. Miriam returned in 1978 as a newly married woman, a college graduate pursuing a teaching career, and, to the stepbrothers and stepsisters who had known her only by the black-and-white photograph her father kept atop the Russian-made television set in the plankboard hut they lived in, an angel with perfumed hair and clothes that were softer than anything they had ever felt. Miriam was torn between the joy of being reunited with her father and the sadness of realizing how politics had disrupted their world.

When I flew to Cuba from Mexico and Canada from 1996 through 1998, the old buildings were as rundown as before, but at least one aspect of Cuba had undergone incredible change. The old signs "Socialism or death" still were visible over the tunnel leading to the tonier residential areas outside the city, but not far away were billboards for new luxury hotels and Adidas shoes. Dollars were accepted everywhere, and we heard English being spoken in the major hotels because so many Canadian and clandestine American businesspeople stayed there. Cuba even offered comfortable exile to President Salinas after his American and Canadian visas had expired, and once I went looking for him there. I knocked on the doors of private villas in an exclusive biological reserve that Castro had built in the Cuban interior to attract tourist dollars. Salinas had been there but had gone back into hiding by the time I arrived.

It was possible for us to visit Cuba from both Mexico and Canada, and to reopen old wounds caused by the U.S. embargo and the separation from family and history it had imposed on Miriam. Seeing billboards all over Toronto and hearing radio announcements offering the island's *calor inolvidable*—unforgettable warmth—triggered memories and forced upon us regrets for all that Canadians had but that we had missed because we were Americans. On a personal level, we wanted Canada's approach of engagement to work. When I called the Cuban consulate in Toronto and heard the electronic instructions to "press four if you want to start a business in Cuba," the U.S. embargo seemed impossibly outdated, a Cold War relic intended to spite Castro but that punished the Cuban people and Americans like us. And yet, when I had the chance to talk to a few independent Cuban journalists who had neither typewriters nor carbon paper to work with, who had been arrested, interrogated, threatened, beaten, jailed, and harassed for doing what I do freely and openly every working day, my store of sympathy for Castro's regime, and for Canada's relaxed relations with Castro, was depleted.

On another trip to Cuba, I visited an important archaeological site where Canadian experts from the Royal Ontario Museum were excavating a Taíno Indian village that had been preserved in a mysterious mud. It was a metaphor, I thought, for the Cuba that had been closed off from the rest of the world and preserved as it had been long ago while the rest of the world changed in myriad ways. During that same trip, I stopped by the Cementerio de Colón to lay flowers near the stone angel on Miriam's family crypt. The cemetery was as elaborately gaudy and bone-white as it had always been, row after row of fantastic monuments to death, and life, pressed together like sheep in a pen. But even here something fundamental had changed.

At the entrance to the cemetery, my driver, Hector Castaños, a Cuban gentleman with a reliable car, was stopped by a skinny attendant dressed in shorts and a sleeveless top. She sauntered over from a tiny guardhouse, her thin slippers clacking on the gravel. She looked into the car and, seeing me, started yelling at Hector. She berated him for trying to sneak by. "You know that tourists now have to pay to see the cemetery," she said in Spanish, not knowing I understood, "and they have to pay in American dollars."

✳

Cuba may be the deepest and longest-festering wound in U.S.-Canada diplomatic relations, but it isn't the only one that has left a scar. Since the end of World War II, Canada and the United States have undergone several cycles of distancing and rapprochement triggered by political differences in Ottawa and Washington. When Canada, under Trudeau, moved to formally recognize Red China, the United States was furious, even though Nixon himself would travel to Beijing shortly thereafter. Mutual-defense issues and disputes over handling an arctic radar warning system and the North American Air Defense Command (NORAD) caused regular schisms during the Cold War. Very little common cause existed between the two neighbors over Vietnam going back to the earliest days of the war, when Canada was one of the three neutral members of the International Commission for Supervision and Control overseeing the French pullout from Saigon. As the United States got involved in the conflict, Canada's opposition to the war hardened, and eventually up to 125,000 American draft dodgers crossed the border. Once again, the border provided a portal to political asylum that allowed statesmen to air their differences without harming the important underlying relationships between the two nations.

In large measure, Canada and the United States saw the world in dissimilar ways because they saw it from positions that were as different as chalk from cheese. Washington was at the center of world events. Ottawa often was at the same events but relegated to a seat on the sidelines. Canada's positions often represented a conciliatory stance based on moral grounds and an alternative view to the hardened positions of the superpowers. But to Washington, Canada sometimes appeared to act without regard to the immediate or long-term consequences of the actions involved. Or, at times, Canada seemed simply to be contrary. Prime Minister Chrétien may have inadvertently revealed Canada's feelings about tweaking the United States when he was accidentally caught speaking in front of an open microphone in 1997. He was attending a NATO meeting in Madrid and was annoyed because President Clinton was late for a photo opportunity with all the NATO leaders. Chatting with the equally impatient European leaders, the prime minister, who called his 1985 memoirs *Straight from the Heart*, gave a candid assessment of Canada's big neighbor, sharply criticizing President Clinton on everything from Cuba to the military intervention in Haiti.

"I like to stand up to the Americans. It's popular," he boasted before the other NATO leaders and the open microphone. "But you have to be very careful because they're our friends."

In his memoirs, written before he became prime minister, Chrétien also had talked tough about standing up to America. "Although Canada is an ally and a relatively small player, it's ridiculous to assume our only role is to applaud every act of the United States government. Canada should develop its own positions after careful study and feel free, if necessary, to disagree with the Americans in the same way we would disagree with the British or the Germans or even the Russians. That is a sign of a mature nation."[6]

Such disagreements had their limits, of course, even under a leader as focused on the symbols of sovereignty as Chrétien. Although there were many instances when the two countries legitimately disagreed, the power and closeness of the United States, and the countless ways

Canada's economic, social, and national defense realities depended on Washington, sometimes constrained the ability of Canadian leaders to act. This made it more difficult for Canadian leaders to pursue their— and possibly the nation's—objectives. In some ways, Canada's views about society were closer to those of Norway and the other Scandinavian countries than those of the United States. In a different setting where it did not share borders with such an ideologically rigid state, Canada's slide toward the Scandinavian type of socialism after World War II might have been much steeper. But internal political divisions and Canada's growing dependence on American investments and trade meant that such inclinations had to be checked. In addition to taking the political pulse of the provinces, with all their own clashes and contradictions, Canadian officials took Washington's reaction into account before making policy decisions. Even though joining the Organization of Petroleum Exporting Countries might have made sense for an oil-exporting country like Canada (or Mexico, for that matter), the split between the oil-producing regions of the west and the oil-consuming parts of eastern Canada, along with Washington's anticipated opposition to such a move, made the question of joining OPEC moot.

Despite the obvious importance of Washington to Canada's affairs, Axworthy and others were convinced that Canada could take on a larger and more independent international role for itself. On the flight back from Havana in 1997, Axworthy told me that even though Canada's dependence on American investments had become greater than ever before because of NAFTA, Canada's view of the world, and particularly the Western Hemisphere, had changed. Canada could exert influence that the United States couldn't and could help further democratic and economic development of the Americas. Axworthy was typical of the Canadians who longed to rebuild Canadian influence, although they were not fooled into thinking Canada could return to the stature it had achieved in World War II, when Canadian troops were assigned their own beach in the Allied invasion of Europe on D-Day.

Canada's postwar role as an important world player did not last long, but it used its unique prestige effectively. In the wreckage of the postwar world, Canada, with its large military force, abundant resources, and undamaged industrial plant was a small country punching far above its weight. It was a solid member of the British Commonwealth, it operated freely alongside the United States, and it also dealt openly with the third world and with nonaligned nations. It was likable, relatively harmless, and welcomed around the world—a Danny Kaye of sovereign nations. Canadians also came to be seen as "experts on interpreting America," as Norman Jewison once told my assistant, Kalyani Vittala. In the postwar period, Canada assumed a mediating role between London—and more generally all of Western Europe—and Washington. It had the closeness necessary to approach Washington with a European proposal, and to report back on Washington's reaction. And the border it shared gave Canada the right to say no to Washington, which it did often, but not when it counted most. As recently as 1976, President Ford and Henry Kissinger made it possible for Canada to join the Group of 7 (G-7), the exclusive club of the most industrialized and important economic powers in the world. There was little doubt at the time—and even less today—that Canada's $750 billion economy was out of its league in the G-7, alongside industrial giants like Britain, Germany, and Japan, while substantial economic powers such as Brazil and China were left out. But when the group was formed in the mid-1970s, membership was limited to industrialized democracies, which did not then include either Brazil or China. By its nature, Canada's economy was more akin to Italy's than Britain's or America's. Ford and Kissinger wanted Canada in the group to counterbalance the Europeans. They believed Canada would generally understand American needs and vote for American interests, even if it did not always share the American point of view.

Canada's reputation as a peace-loving nation started to develop with the strong stand it took against nuclear weapons, even though the government was eager to develop Canada's own commercial nuclear power industry. Using technology developed through Canada's supportive role in the Manhattan Project during the war, scientists developed small heavy-water nuclear reactors that functioned without enriched uranium, which meant they would not be dependent on the United States, then its only supplier. Canadian officials believed the reactors could be used to strengthen the economic capabilities of smaller countries and tie them to Canada. It planned to make the reactors readily available, starting with India, a fellow member of the British Commonwealth, with which Canada felt a special kinship. In 1956, under a foreign aid program, Canada gave India a CIRUS research reactor worth about $10 million. Canada also helped India construct two CANDU nuclear reactors in 1963 and 1967.[7] When Trudeau found out that Indira Gandhi had used the reactors to develop India's nuclear weapons program, which became frighteningly public when India conducted a nuclear test in 1974, Trudeau felt he had been taken advantage of.[8] Realizing Canada's mistake, Trudeau went to the United Nations and proposed a comprehensive nuclear test ban treaty. Like a prodigal son, Trudeau claimed that Canada knew the dangers of the nuclear age better than other nations. When he said Canada was "not only the first country in the world with the capacity to produce nuclear weapons that chose not to do so, but we are also the first nuclear-armed country to have chosen to divest itself of nuclear weapons," he was referring to American nuclear missiles.[9] Two decades after Lester Pearson had allowed them to be stationed in Canada, Trudeau forced Washington to remove them.[10]

Canada was eager to continue being the kind of peacekeeper that Pearson had developed, but an unwillingness to pay the bill for keeping Canadian forces in trouble spots inhibited Canada's ability to act as a global peace officer. Canada spends about 1.5 percent of its gross domestic product on defense, the smallest percentage of any NATO member. Continual budget cuts reduced troop strength and left Canadian forces operating helicopters, tanks, and other equipment that often were older than the soldiers themselves. When violence erupted in East Timor in 1999, Canada offered to send peacekeepers, but three times the planes that were supposed to carry them there failed. Canada built what may be the world's first heroic monument to peacekeepers on a small triangle of land near the new American embassy in Ottawa, but in time it learned that Pearson's concept of peacekeeping had changed radically. He envisioned the blue helmets of U.N. peacekeepers placed between opposing forces while both sides negotiated a lasting peace. In an increasingly complex world where most conflicts erupted not between warring states but among factions within a single state, peacekeeping became peacemaking, which Canadian General Lewis W. MacKenzie, who served as overall commander of U.N. peacekeeping forces in Sarajevo, had discovered was the far more dangerous role.

One winter afternoon, MacKenzie relaxed over coffee in the drafty living room of a nineteenth-century farmhouse he and his wife restored in Ontario cottage country, where he ran unsuccessfully for Parliament in 1997. The general agreed with American officials who were constantly telling Canada that it couldn't continue to hide behind American tanks and would have to spend more money on defense. Canadian forces had been allowed to deteriorate to the point that Canada was in danger of becoming the first NATO ally incapable of fielding a modern army, a point picked up some time later by *Jane's Fighting Ships,* which rated the firepower of Canada's navy behind that of countries like Mexico and Chile. MacKenzie warned that Canada would soon be unable to fight even a limited war or keep the peace. Using Canadian forces in peace-making roles without providing them the proper training and modern weapons was a risky operation, MacKenzie argued, and one that put the soldiers at unacceptable risk.

Defense spending didn't increase under Chrétien, and although Canada didn't shy away from peacemaking efforts, it was forced to ac-cept limitations on its involvement in foreign crises. Increasingly, it fo-cused on its own hemisphere, where exerting influence would not be nearly as costly as global missions to make peace. Instead of patrolling trouble spots in armored personnel carriers, Canada would help the na-tions of the Americas—including Cuba—develop open markets and democracy. Axworthy jiggered with the Foreign Affairs Ministry to cre-ate a separate division of the Americas.

The first head of the division, Michael Kergin, became Chrétien's chief foreign policy adviser and accompanied the prime minister to Cuba, before eventually becoming ambassador in Washington. He was replaced in the ambassador's post by Canada's former consul general in New York, George Haynal. Haynal believed there was room on the world stage for a middle power like Canada, whose principled stands sometimes conflicted with American aims but still merited respect. The benefits to Canada of seeing the world in terms of a larger community of the Americas reflected some of the changes in the contemporary world. Sometime after Canada's reshuffling, the U.S. Department of State followed suit, removing Canada from the old European section where it had been bunched, with Britain, for many years. A new Bureau of Western Hemispheric Affairs was created to cover American interests from the Canadian arctic to the pampas of Argentina.

In many ways, the differences between Canada and the United States—stark though they sometimes may have been—were less impor-tant than the way the two countries were able to complement each other. "When our interests converge with the U.S., Canada's best role is as a lead-off batter in a baseball game—smaller, more sprightly, able to get things started," Haynal told me during a conference in Ottawa. "That way we can set things up for the clean-up hitter, which in most cases will be the United States."

Canada showed it also would try to score runs on its own, and the first such effort came with Chile. I was in the Auditorio Nacional in Mexico City in late 1993 when Vice President Al Gore proposed the first summit of the Western Hemisphere's thirty-four democratic nations and singled out Chile as the next Latin country after Mexico to be admitted into NAFTA. Four years later, I was in Toronto when Canada's trade minister welcomed Chilean President Eduardo Frei for the signing ceremony of a bilateral trade agreement between Canada and Chile that excluded the United States. Canada had stepped in because President Clinton had failed to get the special legislation he needed to make a deal with Chile when he wanted to. "Fast-track" legislation enables the president to negotiate a trade agreement and submit it as an all-or-nothing package to Congress for approval (as happened with NAFTA in 1993). Without fast-track, every member of Congress with constituents affected by the agreement would have a chance to amend the legislation, vastly increasing the complexity of negotiation while decreasing the chance of getting the trade agreement approved.[11]

Congress's rejection of the fast-track legislation was taken as an expression of American disinterest in Latin America, whereas Canada's action bolstered Canadian claims to a fuller leadership role in the hemisphere. Canada hosted the third summit of the Americas in 2001 and hoped to solidify its role as a hemispheric leader capable of acting with or without Washington. Still, many ways remained in which the Canadian government was forced, as Canadian editors often put it, to do America's dirty work.

Sometimes the task is a noble one, as it was in 1980 when Canadian diplomats cooperated with CIA directives to help get six American diplomats out of Iran. The diplomats, who were hiding in the Canadian embassy, were given Canadian passports and new aliases as members of a film production team. They left Tehran without detection, disguised as Canadians. In 1991, Canada sent 3 ships, 18 fighter aircraft, and 4,500 troops to participate in the Gulf War. In 1997, police in Ottawa arrested a Saudi dissident suspected by American authorities of having been involved in the deadly bombing of the Khobar Towers, an American military complex in Saudi Arabia. Canada agreed to deport the man, Hani Abd Rahim al-Sayegh, using a fine point in the law to send him back to his last destination before entering Canada, which was Boston. American officials grabbed him there and held him for several years as they investigated the bombing that took the lives of nineteen Americans. Finally, they sent him back to Riyadh for trial and, if found guilty, execution, despite Canada's opposition to the death penalty.[12]

Canada's willingness to help has sometimes left the country acting as junior partner for the United States, a frustrating role that stokes resentment throughout the country. In 1997, Mounties in Ontario provided backup to U.S. Treasury Department agents who came to Belleville, Ontario, to set a sting that netted several Canadians involved in selling U.S.-made Bell helicopters to undercover agents posing as Iraqi dealers. On the day of the arrests, the Mounties were operating mostly in the dark and did little but watch, having been briefed on the operation in their own backyard only the day before.

✳

It is a North American truism that whereas Americans know little about Canada (or Mexico), our neighbors know a lot about us. I saw this throughout my stay in the way Canadian newscasts identified the prime minister of Britain and the president of France by their full names and titles while referring to the U.S. president familiarly as President Clinton, as though the news were being broadcast from Indiana. American states also were mentioned casually, without the newscaster indicating that Kentucky or Arizona was in the United States. It might have made sense as a way to keep TV scripts tight, but it seemed a self-defeating habit in a country so sensitive about preserving distinctions between itself and its big sidekick across the border.

In practical terms, of course, it was logical just to say President Clinton. It would be almost as difficult to find a Canadian who did not know the name of the president of the United States as it would be to find an American who *did* know the prime minister of Canada. Canadian satires routinely make fun of American ignorance of the north. One program regularly sent a camera crew to American cities to expose America's foggy notions about its neighbor. When the program asked Harvard University students how they felt about Canada restarting the seal hunt on the ice floes of prairie-bound Saskatchewan, they found plenty of bleeding hearts and outrage but no one who questioned the geography.

Without trying too hard, Rick Mercer, host of the program "This Hour Has 22 Minutes," once even got the governor of Arkansas to admit that he believed the Canadian Parliament was built in the shape of an igloo.

"It's like being the kid in the back of the classroom who makes fun of the teacher when her back is turned," Mercer told me. "If you're really going to make fun of someone, it's funnier when it's someone powerful and important." An American film crew would have to search a long time to find Canadians so ignorant of American geography or politics. "Most Canadians are very fond of Americans; we're like Americans in so many ways," Mercer said. "And that in itself is kind of a sad statement, because Americans never talk about what it means to be American, they just know. But we have wasted countless hours trying to define ourselves, and in the end we define ourselves as Canadian by the fact that we are not Americans."

In early spring 1997, Prime Minister Chrétien, not a Canadian television crew, went to Washington to test America's tolerance for Canada. It was Chrétien's first official visit to the United States, though it was not a state visit, since the prime minister is not Canada's head of state. The Queen of England, who is also the Queen of Canada, is head of state. She is represented in Canada by an appointed governor-general, whose face, name, and duties are unknown to every American but who would need to be present for a state visit. It doesn't happen.

Still, when Chrétien visited, he was treated with pageantry and pomp, which Canadian officials gladly interpreted as signs of Canada's importance. At the time, Chrétien was expected to call a spring election, and a successful Washington summit would make him look internationally important in a way the rough-edged Quebec politician had not yet managed to achieve on his own. But Canadian officials also were concerned that not too much be made of the visit or the prime minister's relationship with President Clinton. The Mulroney-Reagan karaoke in 1985 was still a painful memory that made Chrétien leery. As leader of the opposition, Chrétien had criticized Mulroney and his party for getting too close to the Americans. Yet his own relationship with Clinton was friendly, and the White House was eager to please. For Chrétien, it was important to be seen with Clinton, but not to be seen too close to him or for too long. One of his aides complained during the Washington summit that the Americans were overdoing the hospitality: "They're loving us to death."

Chrétien had his hands full in that election because Canadian voters had gone hunting for bear in 1997. It was a time of intense cynicism about government, led in part by the way the Chrétien government had cavalierly reneged on promises it made in the 1993 campaign. At first the Liberals had opposed free trade but then they sang its praises. They also had promised to reduce the deficit and support Canada's extensive social safety net. They did shrink the deficit and balance the budget, but these moves required slashing provincial transfer payments for health, education, and welfare. And many voters believed the Liberals had promised to do away with Mulroney's goods and services tax. During the 1997 campaign, Chrétien enraged many with the patronizing tone he used to tell a waitress who asked him a question during a televised town meeting that if she had read his campaign material carefully, she would have understood that he had promised to replace the hated tax if—*if*—a better alternative could be found. No one had come up with an alternative.

As the 1997 campaign was getting under way, geography and nature conspired to test the resolve of Chrétien and of Canada. The gently raging Red River of the North, shallow as a wading pool but magnified by spring floods to an inland sea, was threatening the city of Winnipeg. It was considered the flood of the century. The Red River originates in the United States and flows northward into Canada. When I first called New York to discuss our coverage of the flood, a puzzled editor asked why. "It's already struck Grand Forks," he said, referring to the North Dakota city that had been devastated a few days before. I had to convince him, and other editors, that not only the Red but other North American rivers do indeed flow north.

I flew over the area in a Transport Canada plane and was taken aback by what the flood had done in just a few days. This was no rampaging torrent. The floodwaters had carved out no rough canyon. Instead, I saw stretching to the horizon a placid tide that was rising inch by inch, a sky-reflecting mirror that was ruining fields, farms, and machinery. And it was heading toward Winnipeg. Chrétien called out the army and then flew to the besieged city. Although he is a shrewd and experienced politician, he allowed himself to be rushed to the riverside by handlers who put a sandbag into his hands and had him toss it onto a flood dike. He then hurried off to his helicopter. The CBC aired Chrétien's brief stop, which made him look like a campaign huckster with little sympathy for the flood victims. He lost more support when he later rejected petitions from local officials to postpone the June 2 election in Manitoba because of the flood.

From election call to election day, the campaign lasted thirty-six days, but even that was too long for fed-up Canadian voters who did not believe they had much control over their government. "Finally This Is Election Day," was the front-page headline of the tabloid-sized *Toronto Sun* that day. In the end, voters stuck with Chrétien and his party. The election results reaffirmed the new political geography of Canada. The country had split into five regions—the Atlantic provinces, Quebec, Ontario, the prairies, and British Columbia. Railroads and phone lines might connect them, but very few themes were being sounded consistently across those regions. On the contrary, they were increasingly at odds with each other. The success of the right-wing Reform Party in picking up enough seats in Parliament to become the official opposition came in part from a series of ads in which it broke a cardinal rule of politics in Canada: Don't antagonize Quebec. In one such ad, Reform dared to point out that French Canadians from Quebec had served as prime minister for all but a few months over the previous decade.

The electoral victory gave Chrétien another opportunity to taunt his political opponents, who were mystified by his popularity. Chrétien eagerly began planning for the millennium transition, and laying the groundwork for a proper defense against the Quebec separatists who saw his new government as yet another snub to their plans for self-determination. He talked openly about running for a third term to repay all those who had placed their faith in his leadership. And he was less nervous about being seen close to Clinton. On the president's next visit to Canada, he and Chrétien were photographed playing golf together in Quebec.

✳

Chrétien's relationship with Clinton was typical of Canada's emotional relationship with the United States. He enjoyed the social contact with the younger American president, but he didn't want to appear less than completely independent, even though both he and the Canadian people understood the reality of living next to the world's only remaining superpower. In exchange for that coordination, Canada enjoyed a special relationship with the United States that had boosted its economy, defended its borders, and helped Canada gain a far more important place on the world stage than would have been possible without that relationship. Canadians didn't want to be seen as being indistinguishable from Americans. They insisted that they were different, in important and fundamental ways. I discovered some surprising aspects in which they were not only different from Americans but similar to Mexicans. Mexicans with sweaters, is how some Mexican friends had described Canadians. As I found out, there was more than a little truth in the analogy.

CHAPTER ELEVEN

God Save This Sweet Land of Liberty

✳

Canada and Mexico, as the saying goes,
have only one common problem between them.
This problem, of course, is their relationship with
the United States.

J.C.M. Ogelsby
Gringos from the Far North

T he woman got off the plane, took one or two steps, and stopped. She had never been in a place where the air was so cold that her breath froze into tiny daggers of ice and then fell to the ground. As Mexico's ambassador to Canada, Sandra Fuentes believed that to truly understand the vast, reticent country that was her charge, she had to touch Canada's frozen heart for herself. She was eager to learn the mysteries of a land so different from her own—where bitter cold replaced Mexico's scorching heat, where there was unrelenting flatness instead of towering volcanic peaks, where only a sprinkling of souls lived compared with the crowding that had turned Mexico City into one of the most monstrous places in the world. She had come on a trip organized by the Canadian government to live briefly with an Eskimo family. Although new to Canada, she already was aware that the family members would be insulted if she called them Eskimos. "Inuit" was the word she had been told to use, Inuit, meaning "the people" in the language of the Arctic.

Before Fuentes could offer any greeting to the Inuit who were waiting for her at the frozen airfield, one of them rushed forward. She was a teenage girl, a youngster who had never left the north or seen a city, a girl who had never tasted a corn tortilla or heard Spanish spoken except on television. The girl walked up to Fuentes with her fist squeezed into the shape of a pistol, smiled at the petite ambassador who was still catching her breath in the frigid air, and said one word: "Banditos."

Years later, when Fuentes told me about that unexpected welcoming, she was still infuriated. "Even up there," she fumed, "even there they had this image of Mexico."

Values and perceptions tend to get distorted when they cross borders, even borders as porous as those in North America have become. During her six years in Canada, Fuentes made it her duty to challenge every misperception of Mexico, which all too often was reduced in the minds of Canadians to a land of banditos and mariachi bands. She let no slight go uncorrected, no stereotype unquestioned. She was a tireless writer of letters to the editors of newspapers and a valiant spokeswoman for Mexican values. She was particularly sensitive about the image of Mexico in the business community since NAFTA had taken effect, because Mexico believed that Canada represented a magnificent opportunity for economic growth, if only Canadians could be convinced that it was safe to invest there. That meant that Fuentes sometimes was forced to abandon diplomatic courtesy to defend her homeland. Once, on a visit to an auto plant in a Canadian city, she arrived to find a table covered in big sombreros, colorful ribbons, and bottles of tequila. The local politicians who organized the visit told her the display demonstrated their appreciation of Mexico's contributions to North American life. "How do you like it?" they asked her. They were taken aback when the ambassador frowned and told them that instead of hats and liquor, she would have preferred to see a Chevrolet that had been assembled in Mexico, by Mexicans, out of parts that had been manufactured primarily in Mexico.

Even among neighbors living side by side along thousands of miles of shared border, unwelcome perceptions surface, and once they do, they are not easily reburied. Certain images are so readily accepted that they become cultural icons, used in books, films, and many other outlets. They are instantly recognized by all of us. Canadians and Americans generalize about their Mexican neighbors and see them as corrupt or lazy. Even if they don't always say so, Mexicans and Canadians see nearly all Americans as pushy and greedy and wrapped up in their flag and themselves. And the stereotype of overly polite and earnestly boring Canadians is fodder for stand-up comedians in the United States and Mexico. North America is littered with such fractured characterizations, and each nation responds to them in its own way. Americans tend to slough off the implied criticism from their neighbors. Mexicans, as Fuentes proved, resent it, and Canadians, ever analyzing themselves, mostly take it to heart.

Surveys have shown that Canadians tend to think highly of their country, but they rarely expect others to feel the same way, and they are surprised to learn that the image of Canada and Canadians that prevails outside North America is complex and substantially more positive than the one-dimensional branding that exists on the American continent. For many people in Europe, Asia, and Latin America, Canada represents a notable exception in today's world, a country that possesses the desirable aspects of American society—a high standard of living, a dynamic economy, widespread concern for social conditions—but without America's baggage of racism, excess, and violence. The citizens of most nations contacted by what then was the Angus Reid Group of Vancouver and Toronto ranked Canada among the ten most admired countries in the world.[1] Year after year it leads the U.N.'s quality-of-life rankings. When the U.N.'s 2000 list—called the Human Development Index—was released, Canada was again number one, with superlative statistics to boast about: Canadians had a life expectancy of 79.1 years, an adult literacy rate of 99 percent, and a real gross domestic product per capita of $23,582 (all categories based on 1998 data). The U.S. figures for that same year were 76.8 years, 99 percent literacy, and a per capita GDP of $29,605; in the U.N.'s methodology, that was sufficient for a third-place finish. Mexico meanwhile came in at number 55 of the 174 countries included in the index. (Mexico's profile included a life expectancy of 72.3 years, literacy rate of persons over 15 of 90.8 percent, and a GDP per capita of only $7,704.) Americans paid little attention to the rankings, and in Mexico the list was almost never mentioned, for obvious reasons. But Jean Chrétien and other Canadian leaders regularly waved the U.N. rankings to give legitimacy to their boast that Canada was the best place in the world to live.

Despite the sometimes negative generalizations about Canada within North America, the country's closest neighbors are among its biggest boosters. When they are asked where they might want to live besides the United States, Americans overwhelmingly select Canada.[2] Mexicans in the Angus Reid survey rated Canada the second most desirable place to live, after only the United States. However, in most other categories intended to measure respect or admiration, Mexicans picked Canada over every other nation, including the United States. They see Canada as a haven of civility, justice, and order, and in Canadians they find a whole group of people who may not speak their language but who understand the great advantage and heavy burden of living alongside the United States. Because they relate this way across the continent, Mexicans have come to expect a greater degree of respect and sincerity from Canadians. Accustomed to being criticized by Americans, they genuinely are hurt when they perceive that they are being judged harshly by their more northerly neighbors. That is how Ambassador Fuentes felt when she found that Mexico's reputation had preceded her even to the high arctic. And that is what transpired in 1997 when Canada's ambassador to Mexico, Marc Perron, decided to speak out.

Perron was an experienced diplomat who had been through many international tight spots. But he had never served in Latin America before arriving in Mexico to replace David Winfield. A French Canadian who grew up in rural Quebec speaking only French, Perron told me soon after taking up his duties in Mexico City that he believed his experience in Africa and the Middle East had prepared him adequately for the rigors of life in Mexico. Over a bottle of wine at a chic restaurant in Mexico City's Polanco neighborhood, within walking distance of Canada's somber brown brick embassy, Perron said he was certain he would be quite comfortable in Mexico because French Quebecers and Mexicans shared many similarities—including, of course, their Catholicism but also a predilection toward culture, a joie de vivre, and a volatile temperament—that made them particularly well suited to each other.

Perron presumed he would be able to talk to Mexicans in a more understanding way because of these shared Latin roots, and that he would warm to the language almost as quickly as his cheeks were warming to the wine. He was in for a surprise. I had found that in many important ways, Quebecers as a group do not align themselves particularly closely with Mexicans despite all that was said about their shared Latin roots. Quebecers have taken their language from Europe, but they derive their way of life from North America, in large measure the United States. Certainly Quebecers watch French films and read French magazines, but the streets of Quebec's cities are essentially American urban landscapes, lined with Chevrolets and McDonald's restaurants. Banks and businesses are run on a North American corporate model, not a French or European one. And even the daily schedules of work, meals, and recreation follow a North American pattern. Mexicans haven't adopted the same model quite so thoroughly, not yet anyway, and in some ways Mexico follows its own schedule, as any American who has struggled back to work in Mexico after a two-and-a-half-hour lunch that started at 3 P.M. can attest. Mexicans also have a quite different set of expectations when it comes to personal relations, corporate interaction, and diplomacy—where avoiding insult is, as Ambassador Fuentes knew and Ambassador Perron would find out, of the utmost importance.

Several months after I had lunch with him, Perron agreed to do an interview with *Milenio*, a Spanish-language magazine then as new to Mexico City as Perron was to Mexico. During the talk, the ambassador touched on the issue of corruption in Mexico and discussed the problems that Bombardier, the large Montreal company known best for making snowmobiles but increasingly active in mass transportation and railroads, had had with a government contract to build cars for the Mexico City subway. Bombardier thought it had secured the contract but then suddenly found that it had been awarded to another company. "When I arrived here I thought I knew all there was to know about corruption, but I was wrong," Perron said in the interview. He further intimated that the Bombardier contract had gone to another company with closer ties to the government. His remarks were quite candid and very negative, although delivered in an off-the-cuff way that did not indicate he was using the interview to convey a message from Ottawa. The article caused a diplomatic dustup. Perron claimed he had made the comments off the record, but the reporter insisted that the ambassador had to be aware the entire interview would be published because he had permitted photographs to be taken to accompany it. Mexican officials, including Ambassador Fuentes in Ottawa, protested that Perron had slandered Mexico's honor. Inside the Lester B. Pearson building in Ottawa, home of Canada's foreign service, diplomats secretly sneered that Perron had only had the bad judgment to express publicly what most Canadians knew intuitively but kept to themselves. Still, following the Mexicans' protest, Foreign Minister Axworthy made it clear to Perron that his resignation was expected, and Perron dutifully submitted the letter. He was swiftly removed from the embassy in Mexico and brought back to Ottawa, but he was not punished for the incident or forced to leave the ministry. And Bombardier eventually got a chance to submit a new bid for the contract.

✳

It was around this time in 1997 that my family and I had our own introduction to the ways our North American neighbors thought of us and each other. We had enrolled the children in two different Toronto schools. The boys went across town to a small school with a grand name, Royal St. George's College, "made royal by special charter from the Queen" as school publicity always made clear. Located in the same modestly offbeat Toronto neighborhood as Honest Ed's discount department store and the Albany Street home of urban critic and ex–New Yorker Jane Jacobs, St. George's was a compact example of the kind of creative adaptation that Jacobs so highly praised in her landmark urban study *The Death and Life of Great American Cities,* which she wrote before leaving the United States and moving permanently to Canada in the 1960s. St. George's utilized the foundation of an unfinished Anglican cathedral as the form on which the school was built. Together with an eclectic collection of older buildings and an asphalt schoolyard, St. George's made for a gutsy school that excelled at instilling spirit and building the confidence of the 800 boys who were there. It also was always short of cash, and always involved in raising funds.

Our daughter, Laura Felice, studied at the elegant stone castle of the Bishop Strachan School, a private school for girls in Toronto where she learned Anglican hymns and developed an abiding Canadian-style devotion to hockey. Not at all financially strapped like St. George's, Bishop Strachan nonetheless devoted much energy to raising funds for new equipment and scholarships for girls who needed them. Miriam helped out in the school shop, and at Christmastime she agreed to sell poinsettias with other mothers. At an organizing meeting one day, the women finalized their order with a local nursery for hundreds of holiday plants. They also planned to buy several live Christmas trees for the school. At one point in the meeting, Miriam suggested that since they were already buying so many plants, they should simply ask the nurseryman to throw in the trees for free. "The least he could do," she said. The Canadian women looked at her suspiciously until the leader of the group raised her voice. "Miriam," she said in an officious tone, "please stop being so American."

Canadians can be considered the original anti-Americans; their feelings of antipathy toward certain aspects of the United States date to the first days of the new republic. But those negative emotions have always been tempered by moderation, admiration, and necessity. "Even at its period of greatest intensity, anti-Americanism in Canada tended to be limited to plucking the occasional feather from the eagle's tail," Canadian historian Jack Granatstein wrote.[3] In election debates, candidates routinely criticized their opponents' "American-style" ideas or "American-style" campaign, which had included name calling and negative ads.

At this time, Canadian awareness about Mexico was just beginning to dawn. NAFTA was still fairly new, Mexico seemed far off, and although many Canadians vacationed in and traveled regularly to Mexico, few Mexicans made their way north. Those who did generally encountered curiosity but sometimes also suspicion or misunderstanding. After we were in Toronto for almost two years, Gabriel Guerra was named Mexico's consul general in Toronto. Guerra is one of a breed of young Mexicans coming into positions of power in Mexico. Like many others, he came from a background of privilege: the son of a diplomat and one of Mexico's first feminists, the celebrated writer Rosario Castellanos. As an adult, he lived in Russia and Germany, and he is fluent in English and German besides his native Spanish, which in Mexico has a melodious sing-song and a formality that, when compared with the Spanish spoken in other Latin American countries, is the equivalent of what British English sounds like on the streets of New York.

Guerra is equally comfortable advising international clients as head of the Mexico City office of an international public relations firm as he is giving a traditional Christmas *posada* festivity or a Day of the Dead repast. I had met him in Mexico in 1993 when he was President Carlos Salinas's head of communications for international media. He left Los Pinos in 1995 and entered the private sector, only to return to government in 1997 as consul in Toronto. He found a stately home in Toronto's Bridle Path section, a new neighborhood of sprawling, often gaudy homes occupied almost exclusively by wealthy Canadians. Soon after settling in, he and his wife Sabrina invited a neighbor over for drinks. The encounter was pleasant, but when the neighbor was about to leave, she leaned over to Sabrina and with a serious expression told her she was a little disappointed. "You don't look Mexican, you know, you don't have an accent, and, if I may say so, you're not very exotic." Ambassador Fuentes said her experience in Canada was similar. "People were always saying 'You don't look Mexican.' Some even added 'You don't have an accent in English or French,'" she said. "I enjoyed answering back 'But you don't look Canadian.' After all, what does a Mexican look like? Or for that matter what does a Canadian or an American look like?"

We expect Mexicans to be different from Americans and Canadians, just as we—and the Mexicans too—expect Canadians to be our nearly identical twins. During an interview with Prime Minister Chrétien in his office in the center block of Canada's Parliament building—a neat stone and copper testimonial to empire—I asked if Canadians weren't just like Americans. "No," Chrétien insisted, "we're very different." He listed some of the ways in which we are not alike, a favorite Canadian pastime: Canada has less violence and racial difficulty, better social systems, and fewer rich people proportionately and fewer poor people.

I could see, through the window behind him, the great lawn in front of Parliament and beyond, across Wellington Street, the squat limestone building that then was the U.S. embassy. The Stars and Stripes that flew outside the office of the U.S. ambassador waved in the breeze just over the prime minister's shoulder. I knew that Canadian officials had long lusted after the prized location and hoped that once the Americans moved to a newly built embassy (which they did in 1999), the wood-paneled office of the U.S. ambassador to Canada might be occupied by some high-ranking Canadian official, perhaps even the prime minister himself, although for more than a year and a half after the Americans vacated the building, the Canadians put no plans into motion.

"We have, in my judgment, a more balanced society here than you've got in the United States, without offending anybody," Chrétien continued. Canada is just better, I would have expected him to say, had my tape recorder not been turning. His was the kind of righteousness I heard expressed repeatedly as I traveled across Canada, whether the issue was about the United States overstepping international concepts of legality, such as the Helms-Burton act against Cuba or, more routinely, about the inequities of the American medical care system that many Canadians, including Chrétien, believe leaves all but the wealthiest Americans unprotected. Canadians also like to play a game of charades about the United States, a pastime at which Chrétien was well practiced. Knowing that most Americans never think about Canada except when television meteorologists mention cold fronts, Canadians say that being off American radar screens doesn't matter to them at all. And yet, when bilateral relations are discussed in a policy debate, Canadians are upset that Americans do not look at Canada the same way Canada looks at itself. "Nobody knows who is the prime minister of Canada in your country," Chrétien said in the interview, but he wanted me to know that it didn't bother him. "Nobody votes for me in the United States. I don't give a damn if they know me as long as the people are happy here. That's what counts."

As the U.N. quality-of-life rankings show, people have much to be happy about in Canada, even if they themselves are not always happy. Canadians enjoy all those qualities and advantages that are considered part of the good life everywhere else in the world. But that peaceable kingdom comes at a price, one that Chrétien recognized before he became prime minister but rarely mentioned afterward. His grandfather emigrated to New Hampshire along with many other Quebecers in the last century because Canada had stifled their dreams. Chrétien conceded in his memoirs that Canada wasn't designed to help everyone who wanted to get ahead, so "it compensates for having fewer opportunities by having cleaner cities, less violence and more social benefits, such as medicare."[4] The statement was characteristically Canadian and, although Chrétien may not have intended it to be taken this way, a clear declaration of the fundamental difference between Canadians and Americans. Chrétien, like most Canadians, always seemed to be at his ledger book, tallying up accounts and making sure that everybody had the same amount, and no one had too much or too little.

We may not eat the same foods, read the same books, or pray in the same houses of worship, but Americans, Canadians, and Mexicans share more with each other than they do with the European nations from which they sprang. Even Quebec, for all the distinctiveness of its language and culture, has far more in common with other North Americans than with the French across the ocean. During his 1997 trip to Washington, Chrétien pointed out that Canada does more trade in a year with the state of Arkansas than it does with all of France. The best measurement of the strength—or weakness—of a North American identity may be found in a survey of values that was compiled by three scholars—one an American, one a Canadian, and one a Mexican. Ronald Inglehart is a professor of political science at the University of Michigan; Neil Nevitte also is a political scientist, from the University of Toronto; and Miguel

Basáñez, one of Mexico's first independent pollsters, taught and collected data at the Autonomous Technological Institute of Mexico and the University of Michigan before founding his own international polling and research firm in New Jersey.

The trio based their study of North America on information taken from surveys done from 1990 to 1993 in over forty-three countries to compare the most fundamental values of a society.[5] They also used a similar survey from a decade earlier to gauge the degree to which those attitudes had shifted. Inglehart, Basáñez, and Nevitte focused on the three nations under North America's big top and came to a fundamental conclusion about the North American identity: Although each country maintains its own culture, the basic values of all three North American societies are converging and becoming more alike than different as time goes by. They noted that in the United States, Canada, and Mexico, people generally had less confidence in government institutions, the armed forces, and the police than before. People in all three countries expressed the feeling that they had less confidence than before in churches, schools, the legal system, and media. Although there still are significant differences in the degree to which Americans, Canadians, and Mexicans defer to authority, people in all three societies expressed less willingness than before to obey instructions blindly.

"What is happening is not an Americanization of North America but a common response to global forces," the trio wrote. They found that although all three societies appear to be changing and transforming themselves simultaneously into something that none has yet achieved, the direction in which they are heading is clear. And Mexico is traveling furthest and fastest. Mexico has joined the cohort of countries that once expended most of their energy on meeting the basic necessities of life, like finding food and shelter, and now are looking for those factors that make life better and constitute what the trio called postmaterialist society. "North Americans with ever greater frequency want the same things for themselves and for their children," they wrote, "and if the types of public options they select are more and more similar, the fundamental question arises: what purpose do contemporary North American borders serve?"

Inglehart, Basáñez, and Nevitte then went a step further and asked what only a few years back would have been an unbroachable question: What if borders didn't exist? They found that 46 percent of Americans favored abandoning the border with Canada, not surprising perhaps since the United States had coveted the northern territory for almost two centuries and Americans do not fear Canada at all. But an unexpected response came from both side arenas of North America's three-ring circus. Some 24 percent of Canadians thought it would be a good idea to erase the border along the forty-ninth parallel, and a quarter of the Mexicans surveyed said they would support a proposal to dissolve the border and live under one big top with the United States.

These findings did not suggest that all differences across the continent had been leveled because NAFTA lowered tariffs and Hollywood inculcated the same worldview in everyone. The world values survey showed that Mexicans by a wide margin still were far less likely than Americans and Canadians to see anything wrong with hopping on a bus without buying a ticket, buying stolen televisions, having an extramarital affair, accepting a bribe, hitting a parked car and leaving without filing a report, and committing a whole host of other moral infractions, up to and including drinking and driving, and assassinating a political leader. In general, the differences between Canadians and Americans remained a matter of degree rather than perspective. Compared with Canadians, Americans were more religious and more interested in politics, they took more pride in their work, and they were more willing to fight for their country. A few more Canadians than Americans thought that government ownership of business should be increased, and that their country was being run by greedy capitalists only out for themselves. Canadians trusted each other slightly more than Americans did (and much more than did Mexicans), and they tended to have more confidence in Americans than Americans had in their northern neighbors.

Information like this opens a wide window on a society, but it is never as convincing as tripping over such differences in the ordinary course of life. One such moment when I most clearly felt the difference between Canadian and American societies was when our two youngest children were twelve and fourteen years old and ready to receive confirmation, the sacrament that brings the children fully into the Catholic church. When our oldest son Aahren had received confirmation, we lived in Mexico, and we enrolled him in the religious instruction classes at the Mexico City church where we regularly attended mass. A few years later in Toronto, I tried the same approach. I went to the church we attended and talked to the forgetful pastor about enrolling Andrés and Laura Felice in confirmation classes. The priest said he would have been delighted to sign them up, except that there were no such classes. He explained that since the parish runs its own Catholic school, and because of Canada's historical French-English/Catholic-Protestant split, parochial schools in Ontario are supported with public funds. Thus, with the burden of paying a heavy tuition removed, Catholic parents overwhelmingly choose the Catholic schools. In short, almost every child in the parish who was old enough to receive confirmation was enrolled in the parish school, which provided religious instruction and preparation for confirmation and the other sacraments in the everyday curriculum.

The incident revealed the kind of misperceptions and broad assumptions that Americans bring to Canada. Protestantism was officially sanctioned long ago in English-speaking Canada, and eventually Methodists, Congregationalists, and most Presbyterians were brought together in the United Church of Canada in 1925. In Quebec, the victorious British had allowed the French Canadians to keep their Catholic religion, and the church defined Quebec's character and shaped its outlook well into the 1960s. But the bonds of compromise holding Canada together required that both religions be publicly supported in such areas as education. Other religions were tolerated but not supported. In Mexico, despite the heavy influence of the Catholic church, nuns and priests were forced out of the schools during the anti-Church movements of the late nineteenth and early twentieth centuries. Other religions have been permitted to operate, but in Chiapas and other parts of the country the competition between Catholic and Protestant evangelicals has led to direct conflict and, occasionally, violence.

The United States became the first country on the continent where religious participation was as voluntary as belief itself. All faiths were eventually allowed to flourish. This religious free-market generated competition that made the denominations more strident and filled their followers with more fervent conviction than elsewhere. Belief in God and adherence to a strict moral code remain areas in which Canadians and Americans are most unlike each other. No religious right has risen to any level of influence in Canadian politics despite the openly religious stands of some politicians, particularly those from western Canada. Surveys show that Canadians are less likely than Americans to believe in God, to go to church, or to get upset over public morality issues such as President Clinton's relationships with women. The differences are clear even in foreign relations. The United States has followed a foreign policy that often seems delivered from the pulpit: It opposed communism with religious zeal and not only refused to trade with countries like Cuba, Libya, or Iran but expected other countries to refrain from trading with them as well. Canada has often taken a morally superior position before the United Nations, yet it has done business with embargoed countries. When the United States refused to sell nuclear power plants or nuclear technology to China, Prime Minister Chrétien himself went to Beijing in 1996 to close a $3 billion deal for two Canadian-designed nuclear reactors. (A few years later, in 2000, the United States signed a trade deal with China.) Of course, Canada has never closed the till on Cuba, and trade with Iran flourished during the long standoff between that country and the United States.

Canadian nationalists might use anything that highlights differences across the northern border to defend Canada's right to exist, as though Canada were the sovereign equivalent of nonfiction literature or nonflammable materials, defined by what it is not rather than what it is. The exercise of gathering up and highlighting such differences has become a regular habit of Canadian life. Academics and government officials are particularly addicted to the game and frequently would lasso me or some other resident American to participate in that dreaded ritual, the academic conference on Canadian identity. One at the University of Toronto in 1998 also included former prime minister Kim Campbell, who performed the typical Canadian two-step: First build up Canada over the United States, then show how inferior Canada is. She started by saying that Canada had a more coherent social and political philosophy than the United States. But, she said, Canada was constantly weakened because it had nothing like America's mythology to give shape and substance to national character. In effect, Campbell—prime minister for a few months in 1993 after Mulroney resigned and later Canada's consul general in Los Angeles—was suggesting that the answer to the country's fundamental dilemma might be a dynamic Hollywood script writer. Her presentation convinced me that self-doubting was not limited to bureaucrats but was a phobia that extended to the highest offices in Canada.

Another member of the panel, Gregory Johnson, suggested that Canadians may be so overly sensitive that they perceive slights even where none are intended. He told the story of his arrival in 1996 as the new U.S. consul general in Toronto after many years of diplomatic service around the world. "There was a group of people at the airport to greet me," Johnson recalled. "I had just gotten off the plane, and I told them how glad I was to be in Canada and how much I looked forward to working in a country that was so much like America. Later my staff told me that I may have stepped on a few toes by saying that, but at the time I wasn't even sure what I'd done." Even before he got to his limousine, America's new representative in Canada had unwittingly reopened the oldest and deepest of wounds in Canada's national psyche.

The problem at the heart of this national identity crisis is by no means unique to Canada, although the response may be Canada's alone. The taproot of Canada's neurosis is the long, undefended border it shares with a country that has similar roots, essentially the same language, and by and large the same values. The characteristics are not much different from those in Austria, a small state next to much larger Germany, or Guatemala, almost indistinguishable from Mexico (and for centuries a part of the vice royalty of New Spain along with Mexico and what became the nations of Central America). But Austria is not racked by endless debate over what it means to be Austrian. Guatemalans have many problems to worry about, but whether they are too much like Mexicans is not one of them. Canadians have so perfected the doubting of their identity—and by degree their country's right to exist—that they have helped create a self-fulfilling prophecy, and a debilitating and wasteful one at that.

The roots of Canada's discontent have been well documented, and little can be gained by rehashing them. But if Canada is ever to get over this self-doubt and to stand comfortably on its own, it will have to stop picking at its sores—in essence, it must stop being ruled by its history, a history that even within Canada is far too little known or appreciated. Perhaps Kim Campbell was right—Canada could use a good script writer, or a director like Steven Spielberg who could take the story of David Thompson, Canada's Meriwether Lewis, and create an epic tale of his exploration by canoe and on foot of some 80,000 miles of western territory never before seen by European man. Without apologies, some Canadian writer could capture the mystery and exploits of a seventeenth-century governor of New France, Louis de Buade, Comte de Frontenac, who was known to the Iroquois as Onontio—Great Mountain. Frontenac thought himself the personification of the sun king of the wilderness, and even in the wilds of New France, he dressed in full Parisian finery, floating down the mysterious rivers in birchbark canoes to the shores of Lake Ontario. He talked to the Indians there about peace and understanding, but he ordered the construction of a mighty fortress from which to fight them. Years later, in 1690, when American colonists tried to take Quebec, the invading commander sent a messenger to Frontenac demanding his written surrender within an hour. His "High and Mighty Lord" summoned all his arrogant rage and told the messenger, "I have no reply to make to your general other than from the mouths of my cannon and muskets."6

Canada has its heroes, but it also has turned self-flagellation into a national pastime. There are few airports like Toronto's where the bookstore shelves seem to carry as many nonfiction books about what's wrong with Canada as they do quick-read novels or books of crossword puzzles. This mass of literature is the result of a peculiar cycle in which the government's response to doubts about national identity is an elaborate system of subsidies and quotas that promote the production of material about the search for national identity. For a time it seemed nonfiction publishing had become an industry of humiliation. "We are that strangely distracted people who cannot quite listen to our singers, remember our history, or find our voice when a beloved leader dies," wrote Ray Conlogue in *Impossible Nation*, part of the 1996 crop of national introspection. The following year Kenneth McRoberts published *Misconceiving Canada*, in which he blamed much of Canada's dilemma on Pierre Trudeau. Many Canadians believed Trudeau had saved Canada from the separatists and had bequeathed the nation a new soul, but McRoberts said Trudeau's efforts had backfired: "Rather than undermining the forces of Quebec separation, the strategy strengthened them, bringing Canada to the brink of collapse," he concluded. He ended the book in typical Canadian fashion by adding a final vacillation: "We would have been better served by being more modest in our ambition and more patient with Canada's inherent complexities." More patience, after almost 200 years of dithering. Bob Lewis, the former editor of *Maclean's*, Canada's national newsweekly magazine, once pointed out to me that a Canadian invented the painted stripe in the middle of the road. It was his way of explaining how difficult it can be for Canadians to come to conclusions.

Now and then there have been attempts to buff Canada's image, to focus more positively on the richness of its past and to strike boldly into the future. Canadian heroes tend to be collective types rather than individuals, as though the country were reluctant to lavish too much praise on a sole individual. Canadians honor the Mounties but usually not any single Mountie. Peacekeepers are honored lavishly but not any single member of a peacekeeping force. Bob Lewis of *Maclean's* attempted to force Canadians to break old habits and focus on individual faces by voting to help the magazine select the 100 most important Canadians of all time. But how to do that—to pick one person to top the list, the single most important person in the country's history, without alienating either the French if the choice was an English speaker (like Sir John A. Macdonald, Canada's first prime minister and an architect of confederation) or the English if the choice was a Francophone (like Samuel de Champlain, the intrepid conceptualizer of New France)? The middle of the road can be a comfortable spot if the traffic is light, and in the end *Maclean's* appeared to split the difference between French and English by selecting bilingual Georges Vanier as the most important Canadian of all time. Vanier was a much admired hero of World War I and later was appointed governor-general of Canada, the Queen's representative. People liked him, but even *Maclean's* acknowledged that his most tangible accomplishments as governor-general were limited largely to his abilities as a captivating speaker in both French and English, no small feat in a divided nation.

Canadians devoted enormous energy to debating the legitimacy of their national identity and the merit of their culture. They were at it constantly—in debates at our children's schools, in beer commercials on television, and even at the end of hockey games as they bemoaned the decline of Canadian influence in the national pastime. The topic was an infinitely renewable source of energy that fueled countless debates and dinner discussions that invariably were dragged like a branch caught under a car to the pinnacle of national humiliation: the list. The list was the compendium of all those famous people who were Canadian but who found their fame and fortune elsewhere, namely the United States. This always struck me as self-defeating, a public admission of the very things Canadians were most worried about—that is, that Canadians and Americans could be distinguished by little more than the way Peter Jennings, a Canadian, pronounced "about." From Superman (Joseph Shuster, the artist who drew the original Man of Steel, had been born in Toronto and moved to Cleveland with his family when he was a child) to the late John Candy (the he-man-sized comic who began his career on Canada's Second City TV troupe and who died while filming in Mexico), the list that was intended to inflate Canadian pride always seemed to me to do the opposite. More than anything else, it supported the premise that Canada's most natural role was to prepare talented prospects for the big leagues south of the border. "Taking sports as a metaphor for the country, our predicament was best illustrated by the plight of the Montreal Royals, a Triple A ball club," wrote Mordecai Richler, the Canadian novelist and commentator. "Come the crunch, the ball club, like our country, was no more than a number one farm club."[7] The arrival of the woeful Montreal Expos and the Olympic Stadium they cannot fill did not seem to do much to change Canada's minor-league image.

Identifying Canadian stars in the American firmament can be a fool's game, but searching for genuine ways in which Canada is different from the United States has always intrigued serious observers of North America. Charles Dickens contrasted the two cultures sharply, especially after he began a celebrated feud with the American press, which turned against him in the middle of a grand North American tour in 1842 because of comments he made about the United States and its copyright laws. He extolled young Canada as "full of hope and promise" and, not surprisingly perhaps, given the rough treatment he received on some of his speaking engagements in America, found English-speaking Canadians to be well mannered and infinitely better behaved than Americans. He even expressed the feeling that the part of North America still loyal to and under command of Britain and the Queen was a finer land: "advancing quietly, old differences settling down, and being fast forgotten; public feeling and private enterprise alike in a sound and wholesome state; nothing of flesh or fever in its system." Compare that tribute with his description of a settlement in the Catskill Mountains of New York State: "Hideously ugly old women and very buxom young ones, pigs, dogs, men, children, babes, pots, kettles, dunghills, vile refuse, rank straw, and standing water, all wallowing together in an inescapable heap, composed the furniture of every dark and dirty hut."[8]

Even today, Canadians and Americans find that crossing the border takes them into a land that is comfortably familiar yet slightly out of sync, a parallel universe that despite outward similarities feels undeniably different and functions in a distinct fashion. The broadest dividing line between the two nations has always been the monarchy and the parliamentary system of government that goes with it. The United States rejected it, Canada accepted it, and that made all the difference. The monarchy no longer is a substantive presence in Canadian life, but it is the link that connects Canada to Britain. Every new citizen of Canada pledges allegiance to a foreign monarch, the Queen of England, whose throne is across the ocean. Every Canadian carries coins that bear the likeness of the Queen—the only way to distinguish a Canadian penny from an American one that is the same size, color, and material. Every post office and government building, every school, and many churches in Canada all are adorned with a portrait of Queen Elizabeth and Prince Philip. When Aahren wanted to continue with scouting in Canada, he was directed by Royal St. George's College to the Duke of Edinburgh program, where the highest honor is to receive your award directly from Prince Philip himself.

Aahren wasn't in Canada long enough to get to meet the duke, but one June we got a special insight into how the monarchy separates Canadians from Americans. It came during the graduation ceremonies at Aahren's high school, St. George's College, which were held at St. James Cathedral in downtown Toronto. The school's choir performed several traditional hymns that everyone else seemed to know but we didn't. Then some familiar notes sprang from the organ. In a moment we found ourselves on the threshold of two worlds, feeling the same emotions that come with crossing a border. The Canadian families surrounding us, including those who had originally come from Scotland or Greece or Hong Kong, began to sing out "God save our gracious Queen, Long live our noble Queen, God save the Queen!" As we stood beside the graying banners of past British patriots and the brass plaques honoring heroes of imperial campaigns in the untamed Canadian west as well as the Horn of Africa, we found ourselves unable to resist reciting "My country 'tis of thee, Sweet land of liberty, Of thee I sing." This wasn't only homesickness at work. The two anthems sound similar because the Rev. Samuel Francis Smith, a Baptist clergyman in Boston, wrote the words to the American paean in the early nineteenth century and lifted the melody—he unconvincingly claimed it was unintentional—from "God Save the King." "America," the formal title of his song, was first heard at an Independence Day ceremony in 1831, when many Americans would have found themselves in much the same situation as we were—trying to fit new words to an old and familiar tune. After attending that recital at St. James Cathedral, I came to think of these kindred songs as symbols of the parallel lives of Canada and the United States. Reciting "Let freedom ring!" while everyone else in the cathedral sang "God save the Queen!" encapsulated the difference between the Canadians and us in a compact, elemental way. We laud the freedom that we as Americans have a right to expect. For the northern side of our border, allegiance to the Queen—not democratic rule—provides Canadians their most prized freedoms. Every time I heard this song played, I was reminded of the way in which the sweet land of this continent has evolved. We are that close, and that very far apart.

When I took over *The Times*'s office in Toronto, I found an old, badly bent metal letter opener in a desk drawer. The red paint on the handle was scratched, and it was stamped "Made in England." I could only guess its age. The presence of such a simple item made me realize that it once had been as common for an office in Toronto to have a letter opener made in England as it would be today for that office to have an IBM computer. Britain had been Canada's touchstone and major cultural influence for a long time. "A British subject I was born—a British subject I will die," said Sir John A. Macdonald, who was born in Scotland and became Canada's first prime minister. Britain was Canada's largest trading partner through World War II. Canada remained a British colony in the strictest sense until the Statute of Westminster was passed in London in 1931. Canadians carried British passports until 1947, and British citizens in Canada were allowed to vote in local elections until 1975 even if they had never become Canadian citizens. The British Union Jack was still raised over Parliament on Victoria Day during the years I lived in Canada.

But Canada's ties to the United Kingdom had loosened considerably. American public television presented more hours of British programming than all of Canada's television stations. Every so often, as the news cycle slowed, an official in Ottawa would float the idea of abolishing Canada's ties to the monarchy, arguing that the throne already was irrelevant. Comparisons then inevitably would be made with Australia, another stable, English-speaking, former British colony seeking to change its image to that of a more mature and independent democracy, which for many Australians meant ending formal ties to the British throne. But before anyone in Canada could question the money and energy entailed in maintaining ties to the monarchy—the governor-general and the system of lieutenant governors in each province and territory—or the contradiction of citizens of a democracy pledging loyalty to a foreign queen, Canada's monarchists would launch a spirited counterattack based on tradition, and the motion would be quietly withdrawn. The association with Britain maintains a powerful, though increasingly subconscious, hold on Canadian culture. Without the Queen, diplomat Alan Sullivan once told me, Canadians would simply be "Americans with a health plan and without a handgun."

Defining Canada by its medical program risks reducing the nation to an employee benefits package and stranding its people without identity or will. Andrew Coyne, a conservative columnist in Toronto, once wondered in print what would happen if Washington ever enacted a universal health care program. "I would hope that would not be an argument that Canada should get rid of it," he wrote. The universal health care system on which Canada hangs so much of its national identity dates only to the mid-1960s, a time when ties to Britain were almost severed and the nation was desperately trying to understand what it was. That era also saw the first stirrings of the separatist movement in Quebec, which exacerbated Canada's mounting identity crisis. Clutching at ways to counter these powerful forces, Canadians came up with a patchwork quilt in which to wrap themselves when their national identity was threatened. They adopted a new flag but retained their allegiance to a foreign monarch, believing that their freedom—and their distinctiveness—would best be assured by the crown. It made for a strange mix. "A socialist monarchy" is what Canadian author Robertson Davies called the contemporary Canada of crown corporations and state-controlled medicine.

Compared with the United States and Mexico, Canada is a young nation. Not even 150 years have passed since its disparate parts were stitched together, and not until 1949 did the last remaining British colony—Newfoundland—join with the other provinces. To this day, not all Canadians seem to have quite accepted the idea of belonging to a single state, although it is clear that they all have long since decided to live by a common code—even in Quebec—under which decency and civility count and limits on individual behavior are not only recognized but accepted. In the years I lived in Canada, I met only a handful of Canadians I thought would have been willing to fight for their country. But I never found a public telephone that didn't work when I needed to use it, or a parking meter that wasn't functioning when I put in a quarter. A society in which every public service always functions is a society in which concern for the public good is paramount. That premise can take some getting used to for an American, even on the simplest level. For instance, some parking lots in Toronto have neither meters nor attendants. Instead they have machines that automatically print receipts for time paid, with the receipt then placed in the windshield. This kind of system is used all over the city, even on the old waterfront in isolated lots near the ferries to the harbor islands. I never saw the lots being patrolled by police or by parking attendants. The honor system reigned. And the machines always worked. My experience in the United States and especially Mexico—where the only public phones that weren't vandalized were those that had been rigged to operate without coins— warned me that the Canadian machines would swallow my credit card or take my money without spitting out a receipt. It never happened.

Canada remains an experiment, an inchoate collection of people and promises that did not coalesce with a single national purpose and thus had to find its own way to develop a more diffuse national culture. Two distinct societies grew up alongside the broad St. Lawrence, one predominately statist and French speaking, the other steeped in British notions of commerce and risk taking. Contact between French and English was almost nonexistent except for the necessary exchanges between businesses in Montreal and the fortress stronghold of Quebec City. In 1837, the year Queen Victoria ascended to the throne, rebels in both Toronto and Montreal took up arms against the British, although for different reasons. The revolts were quickly put down, but the sentiments that fed them—and the quick support the rebels received from sympathetic forces in the United States—led the British to rethink its North America policy or risk losing everything to the United States in the way Mexico had lost Texas.

"The danger, however, which may be apprehended from the mere desire to repeat the scenes of Texas in the Canadas, is a danger from which we cannot be secure while the disaffection of any considerable portion of the population continues to give an appearance of weakness to our Government," wrote Lord Durham, a prominent Victorian who had been sent by the Queen and the colonial office to restore peace in British North America in the wake of the 1837 uprisings.[9] After spending five months investigating the precarious state of Britain's new-world empire, Durham issued a report that was sharply critical of the way the colonial office had bungled things in North America. In his view, the British government, following the American Revolution, had tried to retain possession of its holdings in North America by deliberately keeping the parts divided. Squabbling between French and English had been tolerated because it prevented the two sides from joining together to resist British forces, as the rebellious Americans had at last managed to do in the late eighteenth century once they set aside their differences. Lord Durham

also found that the same policy had reduced Britain's remaining possessions in the new world to rough, angry settlements that lacked direction,
a viable sense of the future, or a national soul—a criticism that could be
made of Canada today.

I found that Canadians often were too hard on themselves, too critical
of their perceived faults when they should have been more focused on
celebrating what they had already accomplished. Though it lacks the
historical power of the Stars and Stripes or the mythical resonance of
the snake-eating eagle on the Mexican tricolor, the Canadian flag has
succeeded in projecting a fresh image of Canada around the world. Perhaps it is because the maple leaf has no connotation of conquest and has
never stood for military might that it is welcomed in so many lands. People relate to Canada with the same class of emotions they feel toward
places like Yellowstone National Park or some other natural wonders, a
comfortable mixture of admiration and awe for surroundings at once so
magnificent and so distant. Japanese families save money for as long as a
decade just to visit the Canadian arctic and see the northern lights, a
majestic phenomenon that epitomizes Canada's most universally recognizable landscape, its pristine, unlimited wilderness.

✳

John Jennings, a professor of history at Trent University in Ontario, is a
trim man with a voice as wispy and evocative as hickory smoke. He is
also a canoeist, which he believes gives him insights into one of
Canada's most enduring images, the frontier *voyageur* who pushed into
the uncharted wilds of North America to trap beaver and hunt moose.
For years Jennings was convinced that the humble canoe should become Canada's national symbol, something that would stand for
Canada's character the way the Conestoga wagon stands for the American west or an Aztec pyramid for Mexico. In a museum he helped create
in Peterborough, Ontario, Jennings used an impressive collection of canoes ancient and modern to retell the story of Canada. Early settlers
marveled at how light and swift the native birchbark canoes were. When
they tried to enlarge them to carry pelts from the interior, they found
the canoe easily took on the extra weight. The Europeans continued enlarging them until one canoe could transport eight men and over a thousand pounds of equipment and yet be light enough to be carried over
portages. "That's the symbol of why Canada's here today," Jennings told

me. Canada's most well known artists, the Group of Seven, used canoes to convey a dual sense of tranquillity and pristine wilderness—both present at Canada's core. Former prime minister Trudeau, a dedicated canoeist, wrote in his *Memoirs* that canoeing distinguishes between needs and mere wants; it is a skill required for people of a land with as much geography as Canada. "When you are canoeing," he posited, "you have to deal with your needs: survival, food, sleep, protection from the weather," which have always been recognized as the essentials from which the Canadian character developed. In Trudeau's mind, to canoe was to be Canadian.[10]

With jet flights, heated socks, and remote starters drivers can use to warm up a car without leaving the house, the image of Canadians being consumed by their daily battle with nature has grown a bit threadbare. I've seen post stores in remote arctic villages selling bananas and telephones in the shape of Elvis. But the essence of a place where climate and topography determine fate still applies in an elemental way to Canada, even in its largest city. Toronto certainly has lost much of the Protestant grimness that once determined its character (although a small downtown street is still called Temperance), and it has built an underground walkway system that makes the climate irrelevant. The contemporary city has taken on a new Canadian character. It resembles a gigantic international airport terminal, crisscrossed by people from 169 countries who speak 100 different languages. The city has three Chinatowns and countless neighborhoods where individual ethnic groups—from Albania, Guyana, Morocco, and many other nations—have quickly left their mark. Toronto hosts international film festivals and the biggest rock concerts and often is used by television and film production companies to stand in for New York City. Yellow cabs and bags of garbage once were added to the streetscapes to make them look more like the Big Apple's. Now only the cabs are brought in.

What the filmmakers never show, however, are the many Toronto streets lined with tight, unwelcoming brick half-houses—they're called duplexes, with a shared wall between them. Even on the brightest summer days, they convey an aura of coldness, of huddling together for warmth against a chilling wind. Moving to Toronto from Mexico City at first caused us consternation, as we sought a house that provided even a small amount of the airiness and light we had grown used to in Mexico. Many of the houses we considered renting were drowned in darkness throughout the day, and the front sidewalks seemed to harbor a vengeful cold just below the surface. As we continued house hunting, the availability of light became increasingly important. In the end we selected a house that had almost no outside space, no yard for the kids to play in. The house was long and narrow and built of stone that we feared would always radiate cold. But it sat on a sunny southwest corner lot. In the fall, a giant copper beech tree with its halo of leaves turned sunshine yellow painted the interior of the house with splendid light. And even during the shortest winter days, it was briefly bathed by the weak Canadian sunshine.

When most Americans think about Canada, they feel warm and generous toward the country. They don't like the north's high taxes, and they find the country's politics insufferably boring, but they admire its immense landscape and its trophy wildlife, and they find Canada's livable cities a wondrous contrast to their own. Mexicans are attracted by Canada's environment too, but they routinely tell survey takers that they like Canada's fairness and open society best—sentiments I heard repeated by the migrant farmworkers in Ontario who returned to Canada each year to work in the fields. During our three years in Canada, there were times I felt a connection to the days when the continent was all mystery and power, barely explored and almost totally unknown.

Even in the parts of Canada most marked by human history, like Newfoundland, where the Vikings landed 1,000 years ago and the crew of the *Mayflower* stopped to pick up fresh water on the way to Plymouth Rock, it wasn't hard to find places where the veneer of civilization was very thin indeed. One summer we traveled to Cape St. Mary's on the southern tip of Newfoundland. Setting out from old St. John's, we drove a few hours along the main highway, then caught a secondary road. Even after detouring for a few hours to talk to Stan Tobin, a local Newfoundlander whose family has been smitten by the landscape for centuries, we were at the St. Mary's wildlife sanctuary by early afternoon. Long-tailed sheep ranged freely over the meadow, and an entire cliff, just an arm's length removed from the mainland, was alive with a colony of uncountable gannets, a large seabird with white feathers. We saw nothing made by man and only two or three other people in the distance, even though it was a Saturday in summer. The gannets were close enough to touch, hundreds of them soaring the wild winds near us, thousands and thousands chattering in their nests attached to the cliffs below. The crashing North Atlantic sent up saltwater rainbows, and the air was redolent of fish and seaweed and the raw fecundity of life. The sleek bodies of the gannets hung still in the wind, only a small feather at the side of their heads or the tip of their wings making the slightest motion. They filled the air in such multitudes and were so blind to us, so unconcerned about our presence, that I imagined this must have been the scene greeting the earliest settlers who came to that same place and thought they had stumbled upon a truly new world inhabited by such numbers of animals that the seas would always jump with fish and the air beat with feathers and soaring bodies. I saw the same.

Stan Tobin had told me he felt that strong connection to the past whenever he went to be near the birds at Cape St. Mary's, which he did often. Stan admitted that he had long ago accepted the irrationality of living in a place of such hardship and scarcity as he does, but he could never leave without losing a part of his heart. A few other Canadians I spoke to expressed a similarly strong link to their country's essence and seemed enriched by all that had so captivated people from around the world. Far more often, however, I found that Canadians would rather talk about the border than the wilderness, and in one way or another compare their country with the United States. They might occasionally concede that the close relationship with America had been economically beneficial for a country endowed with abundant natural resources but small markets and only a few great cities. Then they would insert a caveat, arguing that these undeniable economic benefits had been offset by the great damage done to Canada's culture and self-esteem by the encroachment of American culture. I soon realized that the debate about culture was as common an aspect of Canada's character as were maple trees and the cries of loons.

CHAPTER TWELVE

Ant Eggs, Cod Tongues, and the Essence of Culture

✳

American woman stay away from me /
American woman mama let me be

The Guess Who
Canadian band, 1970

T he common Canadian position on culture was never displayed
more clearly than during an international conference Canadian
officials held on a muggy summer day in Ottawa in late June
1998. Canada had brought together the culture ministers of nineteen
different nations from around the world to plot a strategy for keeping
their television, motion picture, and magazine industries safe from
American cultural predators. With global trade advancing quickly and
technological innovations like the Internet and satellite television signals
making it impossible to halt cultural products at borders, Canada and its
allies argued that global trade agreements should not treat culture like
asparagus or bicycle tires or any other consumer products that cross
borders free of tariffs and customs. Because of the special nature of cultural goods, and their intrinsic importance to the identity of a nation, exceptions should be made. Sheila Copps, the head of Heritage Canada,
the ministry that acts as the nation's cultural guardian angel, declared at
a news conference: "As we move into the next phase of globalization, we
need to have trade accords that respect cultural diversity." What Canada

had attempted to do during the meeting, she said, was "ensure that culture is not relegated to the sidelines."

It was a battle Canada knew well. Its trade negotiators had fought hard for cultural exemptions to be written into NAFTA to protect all aspects of what could be considered Canadian culture and art. But Canada and Copps were growing increasingly dissatisfied with the limited protection the exemptions offered. NAFTA allowed Canada to rope off certain areas of culture from the regime of zero tariffs and free trade, but if the United States disagreed with Canada's actions, it could retaliate with tariffs of its own or challenges before a trade arbitration panel. Copps was not a happy woman.

The villain of the day in Ottawa was clearly the United States, which had deliberately been excluded from the international conference. Copps said no invitation had been sent to Washington because the United States had no counterpart to her ministry, no cabinet-level department devoted entirely to culture. Britain, Italy, and the other nations in attendance were represented by ministers, but who, she asked, would represent the United States? The explanation enabled Copps to deflect only some of the criticism aimed her way because it was transparently false. The representative of at least one other participating country did not hold a cabinet position. Rafael Tovar y de Teresa of Mexico was president of the National Council for Culture and Arts, an organization that played a similar role in Mexico to the one played by the National Endowment for the Arts in the United States. Copps couldn't say so publicly, but the real reason for excluding the Americans was to give all the ministers the chance to express themselves freely about the threat of cultural imperialism without fear of directly offending the one nation considered to be at the heart of the problem—the United States.

In the development of a new North America, the meeting was a landmark because for the first time both Canada and Mexico had come together to discuss a common cultural problem. There was ample symmetry between the two countries and their commercial dealing with the United States. But culture was different. This was a far more serious issue in Canada than in Mexico, which believed it was protected from wholesale American cultural invasion by the Spanish language. But Mexico had already lost many minor skirmishes in its own culture wars.

American sitcoms dubbed into Spanish already had slipped into the prime-time television lineup. The Mexican movie studios that churned out hundreds of films in the 1940s and 1950s had gone into steep decline, and the majority of feature films shown at Mexican cinemas came out of Hollywood. The extent of Hollywood's domination was surprising and unmistakable. The new movie theater at the Santa Fe Mall that Mexico City officials had been so eager to show me in 1993 was one of the largest in the city with fourteen screens. Popcorn could be ordered with salsa, and taco chips came with real jalapeño slices. But usually when we went to see a movie there, thirteen of the fourteen screens showed Hollywood releases. A film from Spain or South America was rare; from Mexico rarer still.

As an experiment, Disney once released the dubbed version of *The Lion King* during its first North American run. Normally several months are needed for the dubbed version to arrive in Mexico City, but this time the studio hoped to cash in on the tremendous hype surrounding the English version of the movie, which was also being shown with subtitles. The Spanish-language film proved to be a dud, and many Mexicans preferred going to see the other. Even though the dialogue and songs were in English, it featured the voices of Elton John and other original performers that Mexicans wanted to hear. English lyrics were common all over Mexico, and it was not at all unusual for the deejay of a Mexico City radio station to speak Spanish but play American music. "When they ask Mexican children who is the father of their country, it is possible that many don't know," Fidel Castro once said in an attack on American cultural imperialism that ended up being a broadside against Mexico. "But they sure know who Mickey Mouse is."[1]

Tovar y de Teresa did not publicly endorse the blackballing of the United States from the Ottawa meeting, but he was otherwise well in sync with the group's agenda, so much so that he announced that Mexico would host the group's next meeting in a year, but this time the United States would be invited. "Culture is open to everyone, and we are for diversity," the long-haired aristocrat told me. He said he understood Canada's concerns but felt Copps and the others should have had more confidence about the strength of their own culture and a little less fear about the corrosive effect of living alongside the United States. "What we're hoping to achieve in these meetings," he said, "is a common point of reference."

The fear Tovar y de Teresa had remarked on was the reason I was forced to interview him in the hallway during a break in the meeting. I had flown to Ottawa to cover the culture strategy sessions, only to find that although Heritage Canada had issued press credentials, the meetings were closed to the press. Gag orders are common in Canadian court cases—one more indication of Canadians' greater willingness to surrender liberties—and I knew that Canadian reporters regularly agreed to give up their cellphones and be locked up for hours reviewing a budget document or a commission report until government officials gave permission for the news to be released. But no one had warned me that the Canadian government would try to keep a culture meeting secret after inviting reporters to cover it. Only one other reporter, Craig Turner, an American colleague from the *Los Angeles Times*, had assumed, as I did, that if the culture ministers' program did not specify that the meetings were closed to reporters, they were open. When I tried to argue this point, conference organizers pointed out that all the Canadian reporters present had understood that the only open sessions were the photo opportunities between meetings. They were right about that being the understanding of the Canadian press, but I felt it was an insufficient response in a country that prides itself on its openness. At least if organizers tried the same tack at the following year's meeting in Mexico, I thought, no one would expect anything different because government meetings there were routinely closed.

We were limited to talking to the participants in the hallways between sessions and at the press briefing after the conference ended. During the briefing, the Italians proposed establishing a television news consortium in Europe to rival CNN. The Brits were defensive about the cultural treasures in their museums, particularly the Elgin marbles of ancient Greece that had long been a sore point with the Greeks. Copps and Lloyd Axworthy were the most vigorous in waving the culture-not-trade banner, demanding cultural exemptions in any future free trade pact or multilateral agreement on investment. "What we've taken today are only small steps in a very large process," Copps concluded. Tovar y de Teresa called the proceedings historic, and after the other ministers made a few self-serving comments and not-so-oblique digs at U.S. policy, the conference ended.

The cultural paranoia on display in Ottawa was partly an expression of self-preservation. Although Canadians like Sheila Copps derided Americans for treating culture as just another commodity, the alarms I heard about the grave threat to Canadian culture came most often from those who made their living in culture and the arts. They were the ones who most felt threatened by American success because they often were not sure they could compete commercially in an open market. The Canadians who were confident about their competitiveness wanted little to do with Canada's system of force-feeding Canadian culture to the marketplace. For example, Canada's cultural elite objected to Hollywood's dominance, but the Cineplex Odeon theater chain, owned primarily by Canadians, devoted 90 percent of its screen time to Hollywood productions. The government guarantees screen time for Canadian films, radio play time for Canadian recordings, and television time for locally produced shows, all determined by a complicated system assigning points according to the degree of Canadian input. "American Woman" was a triple winner because it was written and performed by the Guess Who, a Canadian band, and was produced in Canada; its anti-American message only made it more popular, and it was played incessantly on Canadian radio. Many of Celine Dion's recordings, however, did not qualify because they were written by Americans and produced in the United States, but they too were played continually because they were popular.

The points system gave many bands and film producers their start. But whenever Canadian regulators proposed increasing the requirements for Canadian content on radio or television, invariably it was the radio and television station owners who complained most loudly that they would lose money if they were forced to drop an American sitcom to make room for one more subsidized Canadian drama or top-40 substitute.

Some government attempts to interfere with the free flow of cultural goods backfired completely, as happened in 1996 and 1997 when Canada refused to formally recognize the satellite services that were beamed across North America by direct-to-home television companies in the United States. The problems started because satellites are indiscriminate about national identity and can't be focused so precisely that their signals stop at the border. So for many Canadians, the American satellite signals were beaming all around them while a series of embarrassing technical problems kept Canadian satellite services unavailable. The Canadian satellite companies convinced regulators that banning the American services would protect the domestic programming they claimed Canadian consumers wanted. Regulations required that at least half the programming on a satellite service be Canadian. The Canadian companies had no choice but to meet that standard; American companies ignored it. Buying the dishes was not illegal, but Canadians who paid to have a false billing address in the United States just for the satellite contract were technically breaking the law. Despite the ban, more than 200,000 Canadian households bought gray-market satellite dishes to pick up the U.S. signals. For a time the Mounties raided a few electrical appliance stores that kept gray-market dishes on their shelves, assuming they were connected to illegal addresses south of the border. In late 1997, two Canadian satellite services finally began operating, but many Canadian households resisted bargain offers to become totally legal and chose to keep their American television signals.

Even with the content requirements, Canadians and Americans see many of the same television programs. They rent the same movies and hear the same music on the radio or over the Internet. The same sexual and violent content that concerns American parents and is blamed for the deadly shootings in American schools is widely available and broadly seen in Canada. But Canada's rate of violent crime remains a tenth that of the United States. Canadian sociologist Michael Adams set out reasons for the disparity that stem from fundamental differences in our societies: Although there are just as many guns in the Canadian west as in any part of the United States, Canada's gun controls laws are stricter, especially for pistols. Canadian cities have not been stung by the racial polarization that exists in America. And except in aboriginal communities, Canada suffers less from the generation-to-generation poverty that has handicapped so many Americans who eventually turn to violence and crime.[2]

Most of Canada's writers and artists belong to the same club of cultural nationalists as Copps, but a few take a radically different view of the border. Film director David Cronenberg chooses to work in Canada instead of Hollywood. He believes that Canadians and Americans share a culture based broadly on Western ideals, with minor differences dictated by the side of the border where films are made or seen. "Our countries are innately different, although joined at the hip," he told me one afternoon as we drove in his black Land Rover along the Don Valley Parkway in Toronto. This is the same strip of highway where he filmed part of his controversial movie *Crash*, about social misfits who become sexually aroused by automobile accidents. Cronenberg rejected the notion of a purely Canadian culture. "To be Canadian is partly to be American, there's no question about it. It would be foolish to deny it. That's why this desire to find that thing which is uniquely Canadian is a chimera. It's a fantasy, it doesn't exist. There is no culture anywhere in the world that exists in a vacuum.

"I've never worried about how Canadian my films are," Cronenberg went on, sometimes veering wildly to avoid the traffic around him, yet always careful to use his directional signals, a typical Canadian contra-diction. "I'm writing productions, directing my own films. They're fil-tered completely through my nervous system. I'm working with Canadians on the films, primarily, and I'm assuming that that will take care of itself."

Cronenberg stands out among Canadian artists, not only because of the strangeness of his movies but in the nondiscriminating way he treats the border. I found his comfortable conception of Canada much more in line with that of younger people in Canada than were the rigid positions of people like Copps. Canadians just graduating from college now take American cultural dominance for granted, and even those in arts and culture are not any more threatened by it than by British success in pop music or musical theater. Even in Quebec, young Canadians accept the fact that American cultural influence is deep and abiding. Generally, the English language is stopped at the province's border, but American pop culture slides across effortlessly, and McDonald's and Dunkin' Donuts have a visible presence. The most popular television program in Quebec is *La Petite Vie,* a half-hour sitcom that leaves the streets of rural Quebec deserted during its Monday evening time slot. In its market, *La Petite Vie* is unbeatable, often drawing higher than a 70 share. On American televi-sion, the ratings of even once-a-year spectaculars like the Super Bowl are modest by comparison. The comedy of *La Petite Vie* is uniquely Que-becois, laced with inside jokes and slapstick put-downs that would be intolerable insults if performed by anyone other than Quebec comedian Claude Meunier. During an interview at a Montreal restaurant, Meunier told me that for all its local flavor, the program is actually very American and was inspired by *Saturday Night Live* and the skits of John Belushi. Comfortably bilingual, Meunier is one of Quebec's most beloved per-formers and has become a symbol of French culture in Canada. But he owns a vacation home in Maine and says he usually listens to music with English lyrics. Even Celine Dion, who did not speak English when she began her recording career, told me she did not become a superstar un-til she started singing songs in English like the ones she used to listen to when she had no idea what the lyrics meant. "The truth is," wrote Que-bec author Jacques Godbout, "our ideas come from France, but our myths, fictions, credit cards, and comfort come from the United States."[3]

Perhaps viewing culture as something thin and weak and in need of protection is simply the wrong approach in the context of the new North America. Maybe culture needs to be understood as having several layers. On one level, the films of Arnold Schwarzenegger exceed individual cultures and can appeal broadly across many languages and boundaries. A Stephen King horror story may be filled with American consumer products and American settings, but the peculiar satisfaction of seeking to be frightened is universal. McDonald's may be picketed as a symbol of American cultural imperialism in a dozen countries, but its bland taste disproves links to any ethnic group or culture. The consumer culture represented by American consumer products may be prevalent, but to see that as the culture of North America would be wrong. To find the roots of the continent's cultures, it is necessary to explore the foundations of its nations.

I was able to do so in Mexico with the help of people like Gabriel and Sabrina Guerra, who taught me that a pair of crossed long knives stuck into the ground can keep away the rain on the day of an outdoor fiesta; that one never eats the top tortilla in a proffered stack because it is stone cold; that being invited to have a *cafecito*, a tiny cup of very strong coffee, and a brief chat was the Mexican government's way of making known its displeasure with an article I had written (there were other, less gentle ways too); and that in season, few things are more exquisite than *escamoles*—sautéed ant eggs spread over a fresh, warm, hand-patted corn tortilla.

Guerra showed me which Mexico City restaurants could be trusted to prepare the *escamoles*, and he instructed me in the proper way to scoop out a small portion of the eggs—which look like nothing more than tiny bits of cooked pasta. The thought of them was revolting at first. But once I watched him put the eggs on a warm tortilla, then spoon on guacamole and salsa, I felt I could do the same. The taste was subtle, and the revulsion wore off unexpectedly fast, especially since the *escamoles* were accompanied by the aged tequila that Mexicans drink but that until recently never made its way north of the border. The *escamoles* were only part of my initiation in the essence of Mexican culture and a warm-up for the *gusanos de maguey*, segmented worms from the maguey cactus plant. They are distant cousins to the unpleasant little surprises found at the bottom of a bottle of mescal, only these are about as long as a McDonald's french fry. Before I left Mexico, Guerra provided both the challenge and the moral support I needed to try my first plate of fried worms (eaten on tortillas, with a sauce laced with *pulque*, a powerful, syrupy liquor made from cactus and passed down from the Aztecs). Years later, in the comfort and safety of Toronto, far from the stern murals of Diego Rivera and the heroic statue of Cuauhtémoc, I found out Guerra had only pretended that eating *gusanos* was routine for him. He had been hiding behind a mask at the restaurant when he filled the first tortilla with four or five worms and then ate it as if it had come from Taco Bell. In fact, he had never eaten one before, and our meal had been an initiation for him as well as for me. But he could never have admitted that while he was there in Mexico, and certainly not to an American, which was an essential lesson about Mexican culture.

In a similar experience far north of Mexico, on a blustery day in June that felt more like December, I watched Queen Elizabeth and Prince Philip sit stiffly through a ceremony marking the arrival of John Cabot in North America 500 years before. The fact that historians were sharply divided over whether he had landed in Newfoundland or Cape Breton Island did nothing to dampen the spirits of the local Newfoundlanders who had claimed the port town of Bonavista to be the one true spot, just as England itself, 500 years earlier, had bullied its way past Portuguese and French claims to the island in order to establish the legitimacy of its own claims—based on Cabot's voyage—to the whole of North America. When the ceremony ended, I returned to St. John's, and filled with the spirit of this unusual and historical corner of the continent, I was eager to experience the authentic Newfoundland. I went to the Cape Spear lighthouse, the easternmost point of North America, and watched humpback whales playing near sherbet-green icebergs. I paced uneasily through the dank corridors of the World War II gun emplacement at Cape Spear, where soldiers of what then was still a British colony braced for an invasion that they feared would come, holding onto orders, only recently revealed, to torch the entire city of St. John's rather than let it fall into Nazi hands.

By late afternoon, Newfoundland had seeped into me as surely as had the returning cold and mist. Here finally I had found a part of Canada far enough from the border to be above the high-water mark of American influence. Local fisherman had told me that to truly know Newfoundland, to be initiated into the community of "The Rock," as the island is known, I had to partake in a ceremony that locals prize above almost everything else—eating fried cod tongues. These are so much a part of Newfoundland that they had been served to the Queen and Prince Philip. I had stayed at the same hotel as the royal couple, so I decided that there was as good a place as any for my initiation into Newfoundland society. When the plate of fried tongues arrived, they were not the lavender petal-size delicacies I had imagined. They were the rough dimensions of a human tongue—fried firm and fanned out on a small plate in front of me. "Everyone has them," the waiter at the Hotel Newfoundland assured me in the Irish brogue that identified him as clearly as did his name tag. "Cod tongues are a part of Newfoundland." They looked like miniature fillets of white fish, not much different from a McDonald's filet-o-fish. Slightly slimy, salty like a raw clam, they evoked the dark sea around this ancient island.

The restaurant's windows looked out over St. John's harbor and beyond that to the stormy waters of the Atlantic Ocean. That day, with the sea in front of me, it seemed to be the most natural thing in the world for the British to have sent fishing fleets to this far-off place to pick up the cod and carry them back across the ocean. They kept returning, and eventually the attraction became the new world itself and all the opportunity it offered for starting over. I thought of all the North Americans, including my grandfather, who had traveled across the same waters to begin life again on this continent of ambition and dreams, a place that I was only then coming to feel part of.

Even when we stumble across aspects of culture as distinct as ant eggs or cod tongues, it isn't immediately apparent that they represent anything more than a local oddity. We know far less about any other nation's history than the fractured bits that surveys show we know about our own past. But history is what shapes a country's character, and with understanding a whole world can be revealed in a culture's simplest artifact. I did not realize it at first, but the *escamoles* of Mexico tell a tale spanning half a millennium. They were a food of the Aztecs, almost certainly sold at the teeming market of Montezuma's capital city, Tenochtitlán, which lies in ruins beneath the streets of Mexico City. *Escamoles* now represent that Indian part of Mexico's culture, which every Mexican claims to be proud of. They advertise the availability of the eccentric food the way the French in Quebec extol the arrival of that season's first Beaujolais. Yet as I learned while I lived in Mexico, the best restaurants that charge the most for the humble dish of the Aztecs outright refuse to serve Indians.

In a similar fashion, the cod tongues of Newfoundland serve to narrate a chapter of the history of Canada. The cod in the cold, clear waters of the Grand Banks lured Europeans when the first explorers failed to find either gold or an easy passage to the Orient. French fishermen could fill their holds with cod and preserve it on board using the abundant salt produced on the coast of France. The cod was sent to the fish stalls in Paris and satisfied the huge demand for fish during days of fasting and abstinence in the Catholic church calendar. British fishermen also mined Newfoundland's waters for food, but they had to find a different way to treat the cod because the British Isles produced little salt. They devised a method of drying the fish on land, a process that used less salt but that required more time spent anchored on the coast, coincidentally providing them a foothold in North America. Newfoundland stayed in British hands until 1949, when the colony voted to join Canada and officially sever its 500-year-long official connection to England, though it remains the most British part of Canada. While it lasted, the cod fishery was the dominant force for economic development and culture on the island. The fishing life was celebrated in song, and the cod was treated with a rough respect. No part was wasted, not if it could be sold, and that included the tongue.

In time, as I lived and worked beyond the ends of America, feeling slight vertigo each time I had to refer to the United States as being either north or south, up or down, the richer dimensions of our foreignness began to seep through, as did the interconnectedness that characterizes life here on the American continent. I found not differences so much as variants, the same basic form with some details changed. Canadians buy milk in large containers the way we do, but theirs comes in plastic bags, not gallon jugs. Mexican restaurants have early-bird specials, but they begin at eight o'clock. Policemen are rare in Canada's orderly and civil cities; Mexican police see traffic violations as a way to get their lunch for free. When our children attended school in Mexico, they began each day reciting the Mexican pledge of allegiance with their right arms outstretched stiffly in a pose uncomfortably close to a Nazi salute. In their Canadian school, they were taught to sing the anthem "O Canada" without putting their hands over their hearts. The handful of Canadians who play major-league baseball throw with their right hands and bat from the left side, a habit picked up from their early days holding hockey sticks. Basketball is popular in rural Mexico but only because the concrete courts are used for drying coffee beans. And every television in every city carried commercials for Pepsi-Cola, some in English, some in Spanish, and some in French.

And yet, by living there, by walking and talking and watching and waiting, I was able to see Mexico and Canada emerge from the blank places on the weather map where I had first known them and become authentic places with their own character and their own soul. I found it easier to look for the personality of the country in a particular place, and sometimes it was a place most unexpected. One day I was walking up Yonge Street, the main commercial thoroughfare of Toronto, when I came upon something that seemed to embody the essence of Canada. Tucked away behind a small parking space between Aida's Falafel and a local hardware store was a chain-link fence and an open door I hadn't noticed before. Yonge Street in this area of Toronto is a uniform strip of storefronts, but this gate led to, of all things, a cemetery. I had lived in Toronto two years without ever guessing it was there. The tombstones were all from the nineteenth century, and most bore the names of Irish and Scottish families who came to Canada in those years. We were not far from the heart of downtown Toronto, yet only 100 years before, this had been the far fringe of the town, a final outpost of British North America before one headed into the numbing expanse of the northern country. At the center of the burying ground was a strange, squat building made of yellow brick. A plaque on the side identified it as the winter vault. It was used to hold the coffins of those who died during the long hard Canadian winter, when Toronto's frozen ground was impenetrable. Through the winter the deceased were stacked up in the winter vault like cordwood. Then, when the gray clouds evaporated and spring skies allowed the sun to warm the earth, the ground yielded to pick and shovel, and the community took care of its history.

The vault gave shape to winter as an inescapable force of Canadian life, and death. Canada belongs to winter, and I never felt the nation's character around me more strongly than when the winds howled and the cold snapped off my breath as soon as I faced north no matter where in the country I might be. What defined Canada was the way the hardship of winter had somehow been tamed, or at least tolerated, so that people of a special breed could continue searching for opportunity. Accompanying a Canadian driver across hundreds of miles of frozen lakes in his eighteen-wheeler hauling fuel or heavy equipment that could crash through the ice at any moment gave me a sense not only of the Canada found in the days of exploration but of all the American continent then. Here was a vast and hearty land with the spirit of a Sable Island stallion still to be tamed. As the winter vault made clear, nature here made even death difficult.

Yet somehow the people of the north not only survived in the unforgiving climate, but they even thrived, spectacularly, building up from the wilderness a nation known everywhere for its civility. Duality is a notable characteristic of Canada's culture—both French and English, both geographically large and yet small by the number of its people. At one and the same time, it is most civilized and most untamed. I thought of this aspect of Canada's nature often, but never more so than on a sunwashed June day when the cellist Yo-Yo Ma sat on a boulder at the water's edge in Toronto, only a few miles from the winter vault, and filled the air with the moving notes of the six Bach unaccompanied cello suites. Ma had dreamed for years of putting musical inspiration into physical form, a way of blending the duality of both worlds. He initially approached Boston with his idea of building a park based on an interpretation of the Bach suites, but that most civilized of American cities believed the project would cost too much and turned him down. Then he tried Toronto, where he had studied as a young man. City officials willingly surrendered valuable waterfront land for the music park and then helped build it. The result is an expression of both one man's spirit and the character of a country, accustomed to hardships, that has learned to celebrate beauty wherever it can be found, or planted. The collaboration between Ma and local landscape architects transformed a few acres of derelict waterfront on Lake Ontario into a rare space where form follows emotion, not function. Thus, a winding path takes visitors through six segments, each a reflection of Ma's interpretation of Bach's music. A childlike section inspired a maypole on a hill, and the final gigue of the Bach suite gave shape to a stunning outdoor dance stage.

To extract such civility as the music garden from a land of such hardship as Canada required a degree of consensus and cooperation that might have been impossible to achieve in a society more dedicated to individual rights and freedoms, like the United States. It required a conscious decision of a society to build a winter vault and a broad commitment from many people to see that it continued to operate, and that kind of cohesiveness developed into Canada's cooperative and sometimes smothering character. Almost every Canadian I met, including Prime Minister Jean Chrétien, had tacitly agreed to the basic pact that exchanged a blanket of social comfort for the limited set of opportunities Canada's system allows. The impact of that agreement is unmistakable. Canada has no large private university, and only a select few of the publicly supported ones can innovate and lead the way a Stanford or a Harvard can. Support for research is miserly by international standards, and universities have limited ability to transform students. Still, few

Canadians complain, because public support keeps tuition comfortably low, along with expectations. "In Canada, the expectation is that students will basically remain, ethnically and geographically, 'who they are' and 'where they come from,' and become merely better educated versions of their parents," wrote Henry Srebrnik, a political scientist who taught at both Gettysburg College in Pennsylvania and the University of Alberta in Edmonton.[4]

Across the breadth of Canada, there are only five domestic banks to handle nearly every banking transaction; the result is conservative practices that make small business loans difficult to obtain. Foreign banks are effectively kept out, but the quid pro quo for such limited competition is a uniformity that makes it possible for all checks from coast to coast to be cleared in a single day. I heard Canadians regularly boast that their medical care was universal and free, unlike ours, though they also complained freely about the system's defects. Waiting times for cancer treatment were too long, they said; some hypochondriacs clogged up the system by visiting several doctors for the same minor malady; nonemergency heart-bypass operations had to be put off for months until hospital space became available. And yet any suggestion of opening clinics for those who wanted to pay extra for services was immediately attacked as encroaching Americanization. That is a reflection of the Canadian value of civility, but sometimes it can be disquieting for Americans because it comes across as complacency. For instance, when a Toronto men's clothing store—one of the country's oldest—closed in 1997, its owner, the forty-nine-year-old grandson of the founder, said he was giving up because he couldn't tolerate change. "To survive I would have to get modern," he told a local reporter in Toronto where the store had operated since 1902, "and that's not my flavor."[5] Canada has no mail delivery on Saturday, the most important newspapers in the country do not publish on Sunday, and the sharpest criticism of the Canadian economy made by the Organization for Economic Cooperation and Development was that it lacked innovation, research, and competitiveness. Being second best is widely accepted in Canada as being good enough.

✳

If Canada is winter's country, Mexico belongs to summer. I found that notion captured perfectly by a muddy hillside above Mexico City, in the outer fringe of Cuajimalpa. There, poor families laid claim to land simply by occupying it. Their first task usually was to cut branches from a nearby tree and build a fence around their property, to keep animals and children in and other squatters out. After a few days, the fence itself would start to sprout, sending out buds and green runners that made the fence seem alive.

Those living fences captured the promise of the country, and also the curse, because without water the fence posts eventually shriveled and died. Mexico has no winter to speak of, no killing frost or winter vault. But living things die for lack of nourishment, and death becomes so common that Mexicans long ago learned to tolerate it. *Reforma*, a major newspaper in Mexico City, once casually ran a column giving helpful hints on what people should do if they happened across a dead body in the street.[6] We once saw highway workmen repaint a yellow traffic stripe right over the carcass of a dead dog. It stayed that way for months.

Eventually the families on the hillside in Cuajimalpa replaced the tar-paper shacks with one- or two-room houses made from cinder blocks, steel reinforcing bars, and concrete they carried in old five-gallon tins. The corner posts of these houses were often left so that the reinforcing rods jutted up past the roof line. The free ends, reaching like upraised arms to the sky, were called *castillos* because they were like the turrets of a castle. For me, they were confirmation that Mexicans believed tomorrow could be better, that eventually there would be enough money to build a second floor onto the house. This fundamental optimism sometimes bordered on fantasy, given the desperate conditions of so many of the families there. But that kind of blind belief in a better tomorrow was a basic part of Mexican culture, as was the altered concept of what "tomorrow" meant. The common term *ahorita* infuriates Americans, whether they are corporate executives relocated in Mexico or homeowners dealing with their landscapers in Texas. Americans think *ahorita* means "just a minute." To Mexicans, it is license to "get to it when I get to it," which often means tomorrow or later.

✳

Sheila Copps's culture conference in Ottawa produced nothing concrete but the agreement to meet again. Besides the alignment of Canada and Mexico in a public stance against American cultural imperialism, the most significant aspect of the conference lay in Canada's apparent need to keep the sessions themselves under wraps. That attitude represented a defensiveness about culture and sovereignty that is an unmistakable facet of Canada's character. Few nations so free from the threat of military invasion have ever obsessed so much about protecting their culture and sovereignty as Canada, with contemporary Mexico not far behind. The U.S.-Canada frontier may be the longest undefended border in the world, but that refers only to the absence of tanks and barbed wire. The cultural front has been mined at one time or another with protections, subsidies, tax shelters, and nontariff barriers. A constant of North American life is that Canada and Mexico sometimes openly, usually subconsciously, fear an American *Anschluss,* a cultural and economic expansion of America's dominance that would swallow them whole and make them little more than administrative divisions of the world's most powerful nation-marketer. Naturally, they try to protect themselves.

The belief of Canada and Mexico that their cultures needed to be shielded from the United States permeated other aspects of their relationship with America. On one level their fears were understandable. If Coca-Cola could penetrate China and Disney make Mickey Mouse a star in Paris, how could the two countries that share borders with the immense power of America's culture machine reserve some space for themselves? France, Italy, and other nations separated from the United States by language and many more miles than is either Canada or Mexico worry about their cultures withstanding the American onslaught, so it was natural for two nations that are Hollywood's neighbors to be anxious about theirs. And culture was only one level of concern. Since the shadow of the United States also falls on their economy, on their history, and ultimately on their sovereignty, where, they asked, would it stop?

Such foreboding was common in Canada. And yet, despite all the hand-wringing at the culture conference in Ottawa, both Canada and Mexico well understood that the increasing closeness of the American continent had already brought them unprecedented well-being. With NAFTA, trade was booming in 1998, and without spending a significant portion of their national wealth, both Mexico and Canada had access to the most advanced technology, health care, and national defense systems in the world, courtesy of their special relationship with America. Their dilemma was figuring out how to exploit the American continent without being exploited by America. Mexico had been doing so in an elemental way for years, but the country's leaders realized they needed to move beyond that. It was not sufficient for officials to relieve some of the social pressures building up in Mexico by turning a blind eye to the vast stream of illegal immigrants crossing the border in search of more than mere survival. The migrant workers send millions of dollars back to Mexico to support their families, but each Western Union money transfer, and each CD player carried back by a returning worker at Christmastime, amplified a craving for a Mexico that did not exist, and a further acceptance of a United States in tantalizing proximity. Over time, such forces can erode a nation's identity and expose the weakness, or strength, of its character.

Each nation has its own character, and conceiving of this complex continent this way makes it easier to understand what North America is. In literary terms, the archetype of the United States and its literature might well be Adam, with both the nation and its art beginning innocent and without tradition. Canada, based on the ancient kingdom founded by the French, and later conquered by the English, fits the character of Noah, starting fresh but having to carry along a substantial, failed history.[7] Finally, because of its enigmatic history and its dual identity as the most Spanish nation of Latin America and at the same time the most Indian, Mexico resembles Cain, forever bearing the mark of an unpardonable sin—the sin, in the sad history of ancient Mexico, of having welcomed its own destroyer.

Often in talking about these three countries, we are left with nothing but symbols. Margaret Atwood saw the frontier as the ultimate symbol of the United States, a territory that was new, unchallenged, and open for settlement.[8] When the United States ran out of frontier, the lone cowboy became a heroic symbol of the American spirit. In Canada, the wilderness had an equally powerful hold on the imagination, but for much of the nation's history, mere survival—overcoming the harshness of the climate and the grudging nature of the land—most closely identified the Canadian character and the nation's abiding view of itself.

The far older culture of Mexico, with its roots deep in Mesoamerican prehistory, was not marked by that same sense of venturing into the wild, which had long before been explored and understood, if not necessarily tamed. Rather, Mexico seems to be forever awaiting the return of its savior. In 1519, the Aztecs believed that Hernán Cortés was the plumed serpent god Quetzalcóatl, who had long before departed in a boat vowing to one day return in power to lead his people. As contemporary Mexicans experimented with democracy, they seemed not to realize that democracy arises from the acts of individual members of a society, and instead they awaited the arrival of another powerful being to rescue them. For Mexicans, the most important frontier has always been the space within themselves. It is the line between European and Indian, between openness and wearing a mask. And as has occurred so often in their past, there is a sense that it will be some force from outside, someone from another time or place, who will put things in order. From this cultural perspective, Mexico's long romance with caudillos becomes more understandable.

History, culture, and language provide many paths of understanding. Yet most Americans are almost clueless about their neighbors, both those to the south as well as the north. Americans tend to have a myopic view of their borders. They see the one with Mexico looming larger than it is, the final barrier between them and a strange, violent, and infinitely wilder society than their own. There they want to have steel walls and infrared scopes to patrol night spaces and keep out dark little men they don't necessarily like. But then Americans tend not to recognize the border with Canada at all. We found this singular trait perfectly captured in the Barron's *Profiles of American Colleges* book we used to help our oldest son through the college application process. "Students come from 50 states," Barron's wrote of the University of Notre Dame, a school of interest to Aahren, "40 foreign countries, and Canada," leaving Canada in the penalty box of nationhood, neither American state nor foreign country, once more defined by what it is not, rather than what it is.

"If the national mental illness of the United States is megalomania," Margaret Atwood wrote in the *Journals of Suzanna Moodie* in 1970, "that of Canada is paranoid schizophrenia." No wonder. English. French. Not American. Not foreign. There is not a single solution in which it can't find a problem. Mexico, the land that wears Indian masks, European masks, ancient masks, and modern masks, suffers from self-delusion. "We tell lies for the mere pleasure of it, like all imaginative people, but we also tell lies to hide ourselves," wrote Octavio Paz, referring to himself and other Mexicans. "Lying plays a decisive role in our daily lives, our politics, our love affairs and our friendships, and since we attempt to deceive ourselves as well as others, our lies are brilliant and fertile."9 Even in their perceptions of themselves and each other, Mexicans and Canadians reflect inward, while they see the United States as projecting outward, and most often that implies a large shadow moving north and south across their borders.

Mexicans use the word *norteamericanos* when they refer to the United States, since they consider themselves rightly to be Americans too. But they also use that same word for Canadians, because in their minds Canadians are Americans in sneakers instead of cowboy boots. "The hardware is the same, it's the software that's different," Antonio Oca-ranza, a Mexican official, once told me as he tried to explain how the rest of the continent appears to him and other Mexicans. To Octavio Paz, the two northern countries spoke with one voice and saw the world with one pair of eyes. "North Americans consider the world to be something that can be perfected," he wrote in *Labyrinth of Solitude*. Mexicans, how-ever, consider this world to be "something that can be redeemed."

Our shared past in North America has been marked with suspicion and mistrust, and for a long time that shaped the three nations' charac-ter as well. If Americans don't trust government, if Canadians don't trust democracy, and if Mexicans don't trust anyone, not even themselves, how could the three nations possibly have had anything in common? The events of the past few years have forced the American continent to see itself differently. In so many ways, only minor differences now sepa-rate us, which clearly was the concern of Sheila Copps, Rafael Tovar y de Teresa, and the other ministers who circled the cultural wagons in Ot-tawa in 1998. With global trade and borderless technology, we may be too close now to be separate even if we wanted to be. There may be times when the three North American nations disagree over policy ques-tions such as those on the table in Ottawa. And there certainly may be times when the American view of labor rights or environmental protec-tion clashes forcibly with Mexican and Canadian views. But it has be-come increasingly clear that just as the three nations were conceived at the same time, under similar circumstances, by similar people, we re-main united by our common history and our shared future. Canada, Mexico, and the United States are an American trinity, albeit at times a reluctant trinity. "The Americans are our best friends, whether we like it or not," Robert Thompson, leader of Canada's Social Credit Party, once proclaimed. Jealousy, resentment, and mistrust have been the marks of division, but they could never supersede geography and common pur-pose. "Poor Mexico, so far from God, so close to the United States," the Mexican dictator Porfirio Díaz lamented before being deposed. More than eighty-five years later, General Barry R. McCaffrey, commanding the American war against drugs, showed that the same sentiments of disdain remain with us, but coated with the veneer of a new reality. "We are stuck with them," he said of Mexicans, "culturally, politically, eco-nomically." Henry Kissinger best expressed the inevitability of the close bonds between the United States and Canada. Increasingly it can be applied to Mexico as well. The nations of North America, as he said, "are doomed by geography and history to friendship."[10]

✳

After living at both ends of America, I arrived at the conviction that the continental culture the doomsayers fear is the consumer culture of Sears and McDonald's and other widespread commercial enterprises. That culture lies over the continent like a glacier, but it has not ground down the deeper cultures that continue to make the three nations distinct. There is not a sole North American way of living. The land is too vast, the people too different, to support that. And who would want it? Who would want the old English shore of Newfoundland, where the hearty souls of clingy villages like Petty Harbor sound as if they had just come from Ireland's green mesas, to feel like Baltimore or Miami or the steamy pits of Coatzacoalcos? What would we gain if the giant radishes that the Indians of Oaxaca elaborately carve at Christmastime were sold as Christmas ornaments in Wal-Mart or Canadian Tire?

What I did find from one end of America to the other was an emerging continental character. It recognizes borders but easily transcends them. Celine Dion records albums in both French and English and has achieved success across all borders. Mexico's Luis Miguel and the Tex-Mex star Selena, before her death, moved effortlessly across the border and performed comfortably before adoring fans in both countries. Satellite television not only can blanket the entire continent but also can increase the availability of programs almost without limit. This is a metaphor for the developing continental character, for while everyone from Resolute in the Canadian arctic to Tapachula in Chiapas could watch *The Simpsons* by satellite, they could also receive a program on Inuit throat singing or Tzeltal tribal dress. Increasingly, the three nations of North America are becoming aware of these parallel options, and that in itself is becoming a part of the emerging character. With only three nations within the American continent, efforts at a European-style balance of power were abandoned in the nineteenth century, which left the United States to expand its influence. No border is strong enough to stop that advance, but as the economies and societies become more entangled, linkages multiply, and are not always met with resistance. The flags of all three nations are increasingly appearing side by side, on everything from the labels in T-shirts to tour buses and freight delivery trucks that wander across the continent. Soon there could be a professional basketball or baseball franchise in Mexico City or Monterrey to compete with teams in the United States and Canada.

As the foundation of a continental character continues to form, counterpressure is inevitably being felt within the three nations of North America. The most powerful and centrifugal forces are self-government and tribalism, which seek to empower individual groups within the larger society until they eventually spin off into nation-states of their own. As the identity of the continent became more distinct in the years 1998–1999, the fundamental characteristics of a nation became less so, and nowhere were these conflicts exhibited more clearly than on both ends of Canada, in the tribes of Pacific coast Indians and in the ever-restless Quebecois.

CHAPTER THIRTEEN

Nations of Nations

✳

[M]ore than language and culture,
more than history and geography,
even more than force and power,
the foundation of the nation is will.

Pierre Elliott Trudeau
Federalism and the French Canadians

During the summer of 1998, a seismic shift hit continental America, and its epicenter was a remote piece of paradise. The native people of the Nass River Valley of northwest British Columbia near the Alaska border claimed to be the rightful owners of a tract of land about the size of Guadeloupe, the Caribbean island for which France had once been willing to trade all of Canada. More than just gaining title to the property where they and their ancestors had lived since the last ice age, the Indians demanded that the government of Canada officially recognize the existence of their ancient nation. To do this, they used all the modern methods of communications, including the Internet. "We are Nisga'a," they posted on their tribal website. "We intend to live here forever."

Their "here" is the coast of an American Eden, portal to a kingdom of ancient tree giants with mossy beards, of crystal waters exploding with swarms of exquisite fish so bountiful the streams glitter like silver, a place where mountain peaks are crowned with snow all year yet warming breezes drift ashore from the sea and keep the land green and fertile despite its northerliness. For eons the Nisga'a, like the many other Indian tribes who lived along the American continent's northwest Pacific coast, did not know want or recognize fear. Then came the nights more than two centuries ago when strange men appeared to come from far out at sea traveling on paths of light laid down by the moon. Later, more men came. The ships all bore different markings, and the men in them uttered strange sounds the natives did not understand. Their intent, however, was always clear: Each group of newcomers claimed ownership of the Indians' land.

Using oral histories like these, British Columbia's Indians had tried to prove to Canadian courts that they were not only tribes but nations— nations within the nation of Canada. In 1998, I traveled to the Pacific Northwest several times because it seemed clear that the way these cases were being decided could influence the shape of North America and change the way we define a nation, with ramifications not only across Canada but throughout the continent. With stakes that high, the battle over the land was fierce, but then this enchanted territory has long been coveted by many.

At the end of the eighteenth century, bits of the northwest coast were claimed by Russia, Spain, Britain, and the young American republic. Simply planting a flag was not sufficient; possession of paradise was determined by the will of those who settled the land, and the force they brought with them. As the nineteenth century dawned, Britain and the United States had the strongest claims. They tried to settle conflicting territorial questions peaceably, but all attempts failed, including the joint occupation that both countries agreed to in 1818. Much of the rest of the border between British North America and the United States would be fixed by the 1840s, with the exception of a remote forested tip of Maine. It seemed the contestants had only one option left: war. The British were well aware that American settlers had aggressively seized Texas from Mexico, and they feared something similar in the northwest, especially when they heard American expansionists shout "Fifty-four forty or fight!" The words were not merely a political slogan. They represented a vision of an American republic that spread from the straits of Florida to the border of Russian territory in Alaska at just above the fifty-fourth parallel. The British worried that the United States also had designs on Alaska, and if the Americans struck a deal with the Russians, they would end up controlling all the fishing stocks and protected harbors along almost the entire western shore of North America.

Despite efforts by the Hudson Bay Company to establish and maintain British control, by 1846, ever greater numbers of American settlers had poured into the disputed territory. London was so sure of being drawn into an unwanted confrontation with the Americans that it sent a detachment of army regulars to the Red River colony, then the westernmost outpost of British North America, to protect the established border at the forty-ninth parallel. Realizing the Americans were itching for a fight, Britain offered a settlement extending the forty-ninth parallel west through the Strait of Juan de Fuca, while maintaining control of Vancouver Island. This established a quid pro quo for the future of North America. Both Britain and the United States agreed to respect each other's power and right to be on the continent, which freed Britain from the obligation of defending Canada and enabled London to focus instead on Europe and colonial India. And the agreement permitted President James K. Polk to train America's expansionist attention on Mexico.

We Americans tend to wrap the settlement of our part of the continent in patriotic glory. Living on the ends of America forced me to see our history from different perspectives, which suggested an analogy about the formation of the United States that could be seen as a monumental game of Monopoly: Mexico was a player who ran out of cash, and luck, and ended up losing almost half its holdings to another player. The British province of Canada was so distracted by deciding whether to be the racing car or the top hat—or both—that it fell far behind. Another player, France, simply lost interest, sold whatever property it still had, and got out of the game. And an upstart player, the United States, bought everything in sight. When Napoleon decided in 1803 to unload the vast Louisiana territory for $15 million because he could not afford to defend it, the United States did not hesitate to buy. After forcing Mexico to surrender its territory in the west, it pushed Santa Anna into selling another slice of the Arizona desert in 1853, which gave an American railroad access to the Pacific. And in 1867, William H. Seward, President Andrew Johnson's secretary of state, successfully negotiated the purchase of the magnificent wilderness of Alaska for less than two cents an acre. America's Manifest Destiny was being fulfilled, piece by bargained, bartered, or bullied piece, and only the colony of British Columbia stood in the way of America's dream of dominating the entire Pacific seaboard.

Even though a border settlement had been reached, that precarious position helped push a reluctant British Columbia to join the Canadian confederation in 1871. At the time, Indian inhabitants of the province far outnumbered white settlers, but the natives were overlooked and their claims to the land ignored. No treaties were signed, and the Indians were restricted to reserves that covered only a fraction of their original lands. That situation continued for more than a century, but then the native groups of British Columbia pressed their claims for the land. Because treaties are legal contracts, they went to court. By 1998, Indian claims against the government of British Columbia for control of ancient lands were so numerous and so encompassing that in total they accounted for every mile of the province's territory, including not only the forests and mountains but Vancouver and the other major cities as well.

For many years, the provincial government stubbornly refused to recognize any claim or to cede control of any land to the Indians. But that firm position began to waver in 1998 after the Supreme Court of Canada reached a landmark decision. Based in large part on an interpretation of the constitution's charter of rights and freedoms, the court recognized that certain Indians in British Columbia had never fully surrendered their claims to traditional lands, even if they had complied with government demands to move onto reservations. Non-Indians in the province were infuriated by the court's action. They were especially galled by the court's determination that the legends and oral histories of native tribes like the Gitxsan—who claimed 22,000 square miles of British Columbia mountains and forest not far from the Nisga'a—were legally binding evidence in the proceedings used to establish Indian territorial rights. Despite fierce opposition to the justices' interpretation of law, however, the provincial government had no choice but to negotiate with the tribes. The Nisga'a land claim, which had been filed more than a century earlier, was the first to be recognized, along with the tribe's demand to be treated as a nation.

In August 1998, the government was ready to sign a treaty recognizing the Nisga'a as a virtual nation within a nation. I flew as far north into British Columbia as I could and then drove the rest of the way up to Nisga'a territory. The narrow road skirted the mighty Nass River and passed through forested valleys of giant hemlock and Sitka spruce. Finally, after crossing the crumbled black remains of an ancient lava bed, I arrived at Gitlaxt'aamiks, the ancestral home of the Nisga'a. The settlement, which on contemporary maps of the province is called New Aiyansh, was as dirt poor as the surrounding landscape was rich and lush. The streets were unpaved, sewage ditches were filled with rubbish, and it seemed in front of every house was a junkyard of rusting equipment. The houses themselves—modern buildings with the pitched roofs and pastel siding that clearly identified them as government-sponsored construction—were scattered haphazardly along the rutted streets. Some were only half completed; some had little more than foundations and walls, waiting, I was told, for their owners to save enough money to be able to finish them.

I had walked the paths of other reserves in Canada and seen similar disarray. Each native community was a disappointment that seemed to put the lie to notions about the nobility of Indian life. After I spent time in each place, those initial impressions did not fade. But I was eventually struck by the overpowering sense of community in those places—not readily apparent in many of America's cities and towns—that was rooted in the totem of ancient traditions and endless struggles by which the people have somehow managed to maintain dignity. In New Aiyansh, I stayed with a Nisga'a family, and the first morning they invited me to breakfast. Lorene Plante, the owner of the house, served bacon and eggs, and in a voice as pliant as a pine bough bending in the wind, she told me she had worked hard to put her house in order. Her dining room was neat and orderly, the windows covered with shades, the walls lined with store-bought knickknacks that would not have been out of place in Vancouver or Toronto. She served milk for coffee in a small pitcher. Lorene turned on the television news to hear the weather forecast.

Despite the appearance of conformity and contemporary Canadian bliss, the daily life of the Nisga'a at the dawn of the twenty-first century was substantially different from that of most other North Americans. The apparent disarray on the streets of New Aiyansh was not wholly un-planned. The community had a natural pattern, a vestige of ancient ways, and was dominated by a single central structure. That ceremonial lodge was a large wood-paneled hall, with a floor like that in a high school gym and a stage befitting a community playhouse. The 5,000 Nis-ga'a still divide themselves into four matriarchal clans—named orca whale, wolf, raven, and eagle—that determine patterns of marriage and leadership. They still practice the potlatch ceremony, which had been outlawed for generations by white officials who mistrusted large gatherings of Indians. Each clan takes a turn organizing and running a party that lasts an entire day (sometimes several days) and is filled with story telling, dance rituals, and feasts modest by all standards but those of the reserve. The Nisga'a still fish and hunt, but, as they declared on their website, they also are lawyers, teachers, administrators, and businesspeople, and it seemed as I searched for a space in the crowded parking lot by the lodge that every one of them drives a hefty pickup truck.

Lorene Plante runs a small business out of her house, and her fax machine is kept busy most of the time with orders for the art pieces that she sells on commission. It is quite a modern enterprise, but she has made sure her children all know the Nisga'a legends and the Nisga'a ceremonial dances. She told me she would never leave New Aiyansh or even think of living farther away from the lodge than a five-minute walk. The Nisga'a have round faces etched with lines and furrows that themselves tell stories as the people narrate tales or perform elaborately choreographed blanket dances. But with outsiders, the Nisga'a usually raise a veil that leaves them stone-faced. The morning I was in New Aiyansh was an exception, and Lorene smiled with the freshness of a spring flower poking through the snow. She said she couldn't really express in English what she felt, but she was excited because the treaty finally meant the Nisga'a would become a self-sufficient nation, as they had been when they lived off the land before the arrival of white men.

The Nisga'a, like the Tarahumara of Mexico's northern mountains, had never been conquered—except by poverty, sickness, and despair. Both groups cling to the land and replenish their souls even when the land does not provide enough nourishment. But in 1998 the Nisga'a were given something few of North America's first nations ever received—the right to govern themselves in almost every respect across almost 800 square miles of their own territory. They remained a part of Canada and agreed for the first time to pay federal taxes. But under the terms of the negotiated settlement, they won the right to levy additional taxes in their territory, and decide how those local revenues are spent. They received federal and provincial aid as did any other local community, but they controlled the timber and minerals and all the other resources of the land, a right other communities do not have. In effect, they constituted their own government, but in a way that angered other British Columbians. Representation in the Nisga'a government was limited exclusively to Nisga'a, despite the presence of more than 100 non-Indians in the Nisga'a territory.

During the signing ceremony, Chief Joe Gosnell, wearing a traditional headdress of snow-white ermine fur and spikes of seal whiskers, declared the treaty a momentous achievement that the Nisga'a had been waiting for since the last century ended. Like Lorene Plante, he was unable to give full expression to his feelings in English, but he said it was a time for celebration. Few people outside the Nass Valley felt the same way then, and throughout British Columbia the agreement triggered angry reactions. Some worried that by trying to solve one problem, the treaty violated individual rights outlined in Canada's constitution. Some argued that heritage restrictions limiting elected government positions in the new territory to Nisga'a candidates were discriminatory. A few even called them racist. Most opponents of the treaty felt the agreement set a dangerous precedent that would damage the advances made in relations between Indians and whites in British Columbia and possibly throughout Canada, forcing the federal government to reopen existing treaties and land claims in every province and territory. Indians saw that prospect as a fortunate one; other Canadians were frightened. For native groups from Alaska to Chiapas the Nisga'a treaty was the kind of action that would usher in a fresh era for the original settlers of the new world. With free trade and instant communications, Indian groups in all three countries were beginning to form alliances—including the initial parts of their own free trade network—and were emboldened to press even harder for self-government.

The Nisga'a felt their opponents were deliberately misinforming Canadians about the treaty: It was not discriminatory, they said because the Nisga'a were willing to offer Nisga'a citizenship to the whites in the territory. They said it would not create a haven where Canadian laws did not apply; in other words, it would not create a nation within a nation. But those on the other side of the debate feared that self-government could undermine national sovereignty. They pointed to the tribes in the United States that were using their independence to make controversial decisions, including the establishment of gambling casinos on their reservations and the creation of toxic waste dumps, and asked who was protecting the rights of the surrounding communities. In Mexico too, the Maya of Chiapas were demanding that the government create zones in which Indian customs could be used, and opponents raised concerns that some Indian tribes do not allow women to participate, which would be unconstitutional. But the greatest objection to Indian sovereignty was in Canada itself, where opponents of the Nisga'a treaty argued that its provisions threatened the legal framework of confederation. They feared that self-rule would become one more corrosive element that would make Canada—despite all its resources and obvious good fortune—a failed experiment, a noble trial that had been blocked by the most basic questions about what makes a nation.

✳

Such existential challenges as debating what makes a nation are like beer nuts for Canadians. They seem to never have enough, even after decades—some would argue centuries—of conflict over whether Canada is a country. The question became especially pertinent as the twentieth century ended and the national borders of North America began to blur. Concern about national identity surged, just as it had in 1867 when confederation kept Canada out of American hands. But important though that historical process had been to Canada, it had not resolved the touchstone issue—is Canada one nation, or two, or many? When the decision was made to form a confederation, no referendum was held. The province of Quebec, where the issue of confederation carried the most resonance, had agreed to join the other provinces without asking inhabitants what they wanted, fearing the answer to such a question would surely be no. Modern leaders of Quebec have shown little reluctance to ask Quebecers about their future in Canada, and in the process, they have created conflicts that have consumed the country. Both times Quebecers were asked in public referenda if they wanted to change the status quo—in 1980 and 1995—a majority of voters said no. But separatist leaders vowed to keep trying until they were successful.

In the summer of 1998, it seemed the Nisga'a treaty would inflame separatist sentiment again because the Pacific coast Indians had received some of the same powers Quebec had been demanding—self-rule, cultural recognition, and the right to control their own destiny. Then a few weeks after the government signed the treaty, the Supreme Court of Canada issued an opinion regarding Quebec's anticipated next referendum on independence that again raised doubts about the future of the Canadian nation.

I had returned to Mexico by then and was working there temporarily when Canada's high court tried to apply some basic common sense to the Quebec situation. The justices determined that a simple majority vote by Quebecers was insufficient to extricate the province from Canada. The constitution contains no outright ban on separation, nor does it recognize an automatic right for a province to secede. But the court found that if a sufficient (though unspecified) majority accepted a clearly worded question about separation, the federal government would be obligated to negotiate in good faith the breakup of the nation.

Watching from across the continent, far from the frantic attempts of both federalists and separatists to spin public opinion, I could see the court's words for what they really were: not the final directives both sides wanted but merely traffic signals warning that the next blind curve in Canada's unending constitutional crisis was up ahead.

What the court issued that summer was one of Canada's legal anomalies. Canada's constitution allows the government to ask the Supreme Court to take up issues of law and give opinions on purely hypothetical legal questions, something American courts cannot do. These opinions, called references, are requested sparingly by the Canadian government. There had been seventy-four others before Jean Chrétien, truly frightened by the near loss to separatists in the 1995 referendum, asked the court to help resolve two prickly points from the previous referendum. The first was whether action as momentous as the breakup of a nation could be triggered by a simple majority vote in a single province, leaving the fate of a nation of 30 million people, in theory, up to just one Quebecer. Second, Chrétien wanted to know if the separatists could be forced to ask a clear and unambiguous question. He had been incensed by the deliberately confusing form of the referendum question in 1995: "Do you agree that Quebec should become sovereign, after having made a formal offer to Canada for a new economic and political partnership, within the scope of the bill respecting the future of Quebec and of the agreement signed on June 12, 1995?" The only possible answers were yes or no, but surveys showed that most voters were confused. Since it would be simple to phrase the question as clearly and directly as "Do you want Quebec to separate from Canada?" Chrétien and other federalists charged that the separatists intended to found their new nation not on the piers of law but behind the curtains of obfuscation.

The Supreme Court decided both points in Chrétien's favor. A simple majority, while sufficient for selecting a prime minister, did not adequately reflect the gravity of a decision so permanent as ripping apart a country, which obviously could not be undone by the next election. If not a majority of 50 percent plus one, then what? The court saw this as a political question best settled by the government. Chrétien's point man on national unity, Stéphane Dion, found that in the fourteen instances around the world since World War II where separation had been decided by the ballot, the average winning total was over 90 percent. Chrétien seemed to settle on 60 percent, though he lacked the support in

Parliament to get a measure approved the first time he presented it. Likewise, the court agreed with Chrétien that asking a fuzzy question was a shaky start for a new nation, or for the unjust end of an existing democracy. Here too the court left it to Parliament to decide the fairest solution.[1]

Separatist leaders tried mightily to spin the court's opinion in their favor. They claimed the court had ratified their position by declaring that the rest of Canada must negotiate separation with Quebec after a winning referendum. But then the separatists dismissed the court's lack of detail on the wording of the question and the exact winning percentage as being of no account, since the justices were appointed by the prime minister and therefore, they claimed, in no way representative of the people of Quebec.

Such rhetorical somersaults are not uncommon in Quebec, and it has been that way since the modern separatist movement began in the 1960s. The roots of the movement are buried deep in the discontent of the province's history and the failure of New France—which is why the province's license plates say *"Je Me Souviens,"* I Remember. But the reasons for its emergence in the 1960s are more subtle. A complex combination of religious, societal, economic, and political forces converged just when Canada's own identify was undergoing a transformation. Quebec's "Quiet Revolution" coincided with the 1967 centennial celebration of Canadian confederation, which marked Canada's emergence from the shadow of Britain. Universal health care system became a national symbol during this time. The rest of the nation's transformation was overseen by Pierre Trudeau, who applied his strong personal convictions and a global perspective to create an ideal Canadian—a peace-loving, bilingual, compassionate, and independent member of the world community. As the 1960s had begun, Quebec was in upheaval. The province had finally thrown off the heavy robes of an extremely conservative Catholic hierarchy that had preached the values of rural life and the dangers of self-absorption. This had shaped Quebec in myriad ways, from its high birthrate to its ugly strain of anti-Semitism. Almost immediately upon containing the church, however, Quebec began to worship at the altar of a nationalism that was just as domineering. No one suffered the frustration of switching masters more than Trudeau. "Were we to leave the abusive tutelage of our Holy Mother church and free ourselves from an atavistic vision, only to throw ourselves now under the shadow of our

Holy Mother Nation?" he wrote. "Instead of remaining committed to politics based on realism and common sense, we were plunged into the 'politics of grandeur' whose main preoccupation all too often was rolling out red carpets."[2]

Even a leader as headstrong as Trudeau could not handle all the conflicts bubbling up inside Quebec. The initially petty violence of a small independence group, the Front for the Liberation of Quebec, escalated, and in 1970, Canada was stunned to learn that the FLQ had kidnapped James Cross, a British trade official in Montreal, and was demanding $500,000 in gold for his release. A week later, Pierre Laporte, the provincial labor minister, was also kidnapped. Panic spread throughout Montreal and the rest of the province. Nothing like this had ever happened in Canada. Trudeau said he was responding to demands from Quebec officials when he invoked the War Measures Act, suspending constitutional guarantees in the province and ordering the army into the streets of Montreal. Within hours, more than 400 people were arrested. Most were never formally charged, but they were held for more than forty-eight hours on nothing more than suspicion of fomenting revolution. Authorities uncovered plots for the kidnappings of other officials, including the American and Israeli consuls in Montreal. While Parliament was still in emergency debate over imposition of the War Measures Act, Laporte was found dead in the trunk of a car at the airport. Trudeau was accused of attempting to use the extraordinary powers of the War Measures Act to destroy the separatist movement. He denied that was his intent. But he was convinced that the violence would be the end of the Quebec separatists, only to have to watch René Lévesque elected premier of Quebec six years later.

Lévesque was a chain-smoking former journalist with a poet's sense of imagery, which he employed to shape the separatist movement. At the very beginning of his manifesto on Quebec independence, Lévesque declared "We are Québécois," and within a few paragraphs laid out the central position of the separatists.[3] This battle for Quebec—unlike the one on the Plains of Abraham 200 years earlier—would not shed blood, necessarily, but would be based on blood, the pure blood of those French-speaking people who believed in a French-speaking nation in North America. In Lévesque's vision of nationhood, the lines were clearly drawn: Anyone not loyal to Quebec, to the history of the French people in North America, to the idea that Quebec is the soul of the

French-speaking people in the new world and the only place they are at home, "anyone who does not feel it, at least occasionally, is not—no longer—one of us."

Lévesque and his colleagues were convinced that negotiating a better deal within the existing structure of Canada was folly. "At the most optimistic estimate, Quebec would need 25 years of negotiations to obtain an ersatz special status (and by that time, in the year 2000, the probably English-speaking majority in Quebec, made up of Britons and anglicized New-Quebeckers, would not even want such a special status)," Jean Marc Leger wrote in *Le Devoir* in the late 1960s. He correctly anticipated the drawn-out process of constitutional wrangling that consumed Canada for a quarter century, but he missed by a wide margin what the negotiations would accomplish. As the new millennium arrived, Quebec was more French than ever before, the result of an exodus of English-speaking Quebecers alarmed by Lévesque and the fiery rhetoric of his followers. Canada too was nominally more French after Trudeau's bilingual policy, but what that in fact meant was sometimes mystifying.

Whenever we visited home, colleagues and friends assumed we spoke French most of the time in Toronto, another sign of how little Americans knew of Canada. The truth was that we heard Spanish on the city's streets and in its stores far more often than French. Even a generation after Canada officially declared itself a bilingual nation, there was no guarantee that French-speaking Quebecers could order a meal in Whitehorse or Calgary in their own language. Bilingualism was imperfectly applied and irrationally resisted before Trudeau's vision of a bilingual Canada had a firm chance to develop. After our boys enrolled at Royal St. George's College, they quickly caught up with their classmates in French class and soon leaped ahead, aided by their fluency in Spanish. Their French teachers told us the difference was that the other boys received no encouragement at home because their parents felt French was being rammed down their throats. My research assistant Kalyani was born in England of Indian parents. When they told her the family would be moving to Saskatchewan, Kaly was worried that her French would not be good enough for living in a bilingual country like Canada. But out on the prairie, she never used French. That did not mean the essential elements of democracy were not available to French speakers, no matter where in Canada they lived: Voting information, parliamentary proceedings, and activities of the court were given in English or French. Beyond that, Canada offered a degree of access for French speakers that

Mexican Americans could only hope to find across the United States. Even in as remote a place as Yellowknife, in the Northwest Territories, telephone directory assistance, Rice Krispies boxes, and the safety instructions on any commercial flight arriving or departing the local airport, along with many other products and services, were available in French, just as they were throughout the country.

Although Trudeau's language measures were intended to help forge national unity, they triggered extreme countermeasures in his native Quebec. There would be no bilingualism in Quebec—French was the only official language. Tough language laws prohibited the use of English either on public signs or in the workplace. This created endless conflict and many bizarre situations. Jan Wong, a friend who was born in Montreal, once told me about her father, who owned a well-known Chinese restaurant in Montreal near the Olympic Stadium. Language laws forced him to drop the apostrophe from the restaurant's name—there is no apostrophe in French. So his restaurant was simply called Wong. And because the restaurant had more than fifteen employees, all of them Chinese, the law required business to be conducted in French. That meant signs telling staff to wash their hands before leaving the rest rooms had to be in French, even though most of the waiters and waitresses read only Chinese. The province employs inspectors to monitor the size of French and English on public signs, and has been known to confiscate products from matzos to Dunkin' Donuts bags because they violated the language laws. One spring, I heard a local English radio station broadcast a news report announcing that the government had passed a new law requiring all English gravestones in Montreal's cemetery to be recarved in French. Calls from incensed listeners flooded the station, even though it was April Fools' Day.

✳

Like those who opposed the Nisga'a treaty in British Columbia, many Canadians who were against the separatists just didn't grasp what was bothering Quebecers. Since Lévesque's time, the French majority in the province had won substantial economic and political powers only dreamed of before. With these gains, much of the bigotry and discrimination that had once poisoned relations between the English and French in the province had ended. The federal government handed over to the province the control of immigration, job training, and culture—

powers that Lévesque and others had said Ottawa would never surrender. Quebecois arts and culture were thriving, and Quebecers' domination of the province's media was almost absolute. One of the province's largest newspapers, *La Presse*, treated the release of the season's new Beaujolais as front-page news. And the civil service had become so overwhelmingly French that English speakers in Montreal complained they were being discriminated against because they did not speak French.

By the end of the twentieth century, voters in Quebec overwhelmingly felt the problem was not, as Leger had predicted decades before, that negotiations had gotten them nowhere, but rather that the constant threat of separation had damaged Quebec and substantially reduced the quality of Quebecers' lives. Weary of the never-ending squabble, many Quebecers made it clear in 1998 that they wanted nothing more to do with separation, at least for the moment. The Quebec government tried to use the Supreme Court's summertime opinion on separation to whip voters into an anti-Ottawa mood. Canadian law allows only one referendum vote per term of the provincial Parliament, which Quebec had haughtily named the National Assembly in 1968. The separatist government needed to win another provincial election to set the clock ticking for a third referendum on independence.

The Liberal opposition in Quebec had it no easier that year. Jean Charest, a popular federal leader from Quebec, was talked into quitting the federal Conservative Party he led and running for leadership of the provincial Liberals. Party officials believed only he could rescue the province from the separatists. Charest knew that Quebecers did not want another referendum, but neither did they want to completely rule out the possibility of having one. Surveys showed that Quebecers believed threatening Ottawa with separation was a good approach. Their favorite analogy likened the menace of separation to holding a knife to the throat of the rest of Canada, which they believed made Ottawa much more willing to meet Quebec's demands. The strategy had been effective for over thirty years, and they saw no reason to drop the knife, even if they had no desire to consummate separation.

Backed into a corner, the separatists responded cleverly. Premier Lucien Bouchard promised that if he was reelected, there would be another referendum on independence, but only when conditions guaranteed it would be successful. Until then, the separatists would work to create those winning conditions, which meant improving the economy, strengthening social services, and getting the province's lopsided finances in order. But while Bouchard preached patience, others in the separatist movement saw a window of opportunity closing in Quebec because of the province's changing demographics.

Quebec once boasted a birthrate of 3.9 per woman of childbearing age, the highest in North America. This was considered *"le revanche des berceaux,"* the revenge of the cradle that would compensate for the British defeat by producing enough French-speaking children to keep the dream of New France alive. But all that suddenly changed in the 1960s when Quebecers turned their backs on the Catholic church. Once Quebecers rejected the rigid rule of the clerics, marriage rates plummeted, divorce skyrocketed, and birth control became widely available. As a result, Quebec's birthrate declined to 1.5, below the rest of Canada and most other parts of the world. This brought new challenges to the search for equilibrium between the French and English populations, a struggle that dates to the conquest.

In the eighteenth century, Britain had planned to assimilate the French into British North America, but even British pluck was not up to the challenge. There were 60,000 French settlers, and they constituted more than 95 percent of the population of New France. Immigration from the British Isles steadily increased the English population, and along with it the strife between English and French. When Lord Durham sailed from England in 1838 to investigate the cause of several uprisings in British North America, he found that the French and English hated not the government but each other. "I found two nations warring in the bosom of a single state. I found a struggle, not of principles, but of races," he wrote.[4] In part, Lord Durham encountered the handiwork of British colonial policies that deliberately sought to keep French and English divided and therefore more easily controlled. Durham blamed the forces of separation for Canada's failure to match the success of America, a criticism still heard today. He toyed with the idea of forming three separate provinces—what are now Quebec and Ontario as well as a third formed of Montreal, surrounding parts of English Ontario, and the Eastern Townships of Quebec that were settled by Loyalists under the system of English law. Under such a structure, the rural French who in his view were hopelessly rooted in the prerevolutionary conservatism of French society would have remained isolated, while the most dynamic part of Quebec, where British merchants had already established a commercial hierarchy, could grow unmolested until the English outnumbered the French.

"The institutions of France, during the period of the colonization of Canada, were, perhaps, more than those of any other European nation, calculated to repress the intelligence and freedom of the great mass of the people," Durham reported. In the end he rejected the idea, but his disdain for what the French had created in North America was obvious. "Along the alluvial banks of the St. Lawrence and its tributaries, they have cleared two or three strips of land, cultivated them in the worst method of small farming and established series of continuous villages, which give the country of the *seignories* the appearance of a never ending street."[5]

That is the essence of what I saw as an Air Canada jet approached the Quebec City airport late on a Sunday night just before the 1998 Quebec elections. A dusting of snow revealed the outline of the distant past that had left such an imprint on Quebec, and on Canada. Their fields were not abundant rectangles as in the United States. Instead, the bank of the St. Lawrence looked like a swatch of corduroy. The outlines of the old fields were long and narrow, and they led directly to the black river. All the land would have belonged to a single French lord, a seigneur, who received title for the land from the crown as a reward for coming to the new world. Farmers themselves were tenants who paid the seigneur rent and duties each year. Without the capacity to accumulate wealth easily as the colonists in New England did, the French settlers tended to stay put. They did not set out for the west when their children grew up or the land became crowded. Instead, they divided the land into narrower and smaller parcels, similar to the pattern followed by *ejidatarios* in Mexico. Neither did these settlers have the money to start a business, since the feudal system kept them indebted to the lord, whose primary goal was accumulating wealth and returning to Paris high society.

Today, Quebec's population accounts for less than a quarter of Canada's 30 million residents. Demographers predict that in another century that figure could drop to 16 percent. The few remaining French-speaking enclaves outside Quebec continue to wither. The major exception is the province of New Brunswick, which happily contains large numbers of French-speakers, English-speakers, and people who are comfortable in both idioms—without ever talking of separation or independence. An island of French in an English-speaking sea, Quebec was left with little choice but to admit more immigrants, although some rued the day that happened.

More than 225,000 immigrants arrive in Canada every year, but because of limitations on language and economic opportunity, only about 15 percent of them go to Quebec. In their zeal to promote the French language, officials there recruit French speakers from many parts of the world and give them preferential treatment. Most newcomers must send their children to French schools. This is a way for Quebec to ensure the continuity of French in North America, but there is no way to force the new Quebecers to accept the concept of a Quebec nation. Immigrants tend overwhelmingly to vote against independence, which had provoked an angry Jacques Parizeau to make his referendum-night attack on "the ethnic vote" in 1995.

Separatists argued that such demographic trends were more than offset by the declining population of English-speaking Quebecers in Montreal and the Eastern Townships along the south shore of the St. Lawrence River. Since the 1960s, more than 200,000 English speakers had left Quebec, so many that the French became a majority of over 82 percent in the province. Even so, some of the fire seemed to have dampened in the independence movement. Dinosaurs like Parizeau belonged to an entirely different generation, one that had first grasped the idea that Quebecers needed to be masters of their own house back in the 1960s. Young people who lived their entire lives under the referendum sword now talk about separation only when provoked. They might attend a separatist rally or the nationalist parade on St. John the Baptist Day, but their concept of an independent Quebec often does not rise from a deep emotional well. They might occasionally lean toward separation, but it is not at all certain they would vote for it.

"If you hear somebody talking about separation, they are probably not from Quebec," a Quebecer, Francois Taschereau, told me one evening in Montreal's old town, where cobblestone streets pulsed with music and performers and the idea of a political fight for separation seemed distant. A former member of the foreign service who became a public relations consultant, Taschereau has lived the independence debates his entire life. His great-granduncle had once been premier of Quebec, but he made it clear that for him, his young family, and their circle of young friends, separation was an old, tired, and insufferably tedious subject.

Bouchard and the Quebecois Party went on to win the 1998 election, but they lost the popular vote to Charest and the Liberals. These results chastened the party, and especially Bouchard, whose separatist credentials already were being questioned. Bouchard had once been part of Mulroney's cabinet, and had married an American from California known to have insisted that their children speak both English and French. As the final tallies came in on election night, I watched Bouchard enter party headquarters in Quebec City looking like a shell-shocked soldier climbing out of a foxhole. In his subdued victory speech, he conceded that voters had made clear that this was not the time for another referendum. Quebec's rendezvous with destiny was delayed, he said, but not abandoned.

The rest of Canada breathed a collective sigh of relief. Still, despite the separatists' sobering election results, the demographic time bomb, and the ennui of Quebec voters, the threat of a breakup remains. Canada is still included in some lists of unstable countries, as was the case in a conference on democracy I participated in at Tufts University in Boston at this time. Canada was paired with countries like Northern Ireland, Pakistan, and East Timor in panels on ethnic conflicts and racial strife. Peace in the province rested on a very thin layer of ice. A provincial premier's ability to call a referendum election at any time and with little more than a month's notice meant that Bouchard, or a more aggressively separatist leader, could capitalize on some slight from Ottawa—real or perceived—to convince voters that the only way to keep Quebec from suffering such humiliations again was to become its own nation. It is not difficult to imagine public opinion in a media-drenched place like Quebec being manipulated for the five weeks that would elapse from the moment the Quebec premier called for a referendum and the vote. In addition, sentiment in the rest of the country seems to have undergone a transformation. The last referendum unmasked Quebec to such an extent that people in the rest of Canada lost some of their fear of the separatists. More now said "Let them go," when asked about the separatists, either because they believed Quebecers would never really vote to leave Canada or because after so many years of threats they did not care whether Quebec did go.

In his later years, long after leaving office, Trudeau still could gather a crowd of admirers wherever he went. But he also was reviled throughout Canada by those who rejected his vision of a bilingual country not chained to its divided and suspicious past. Quebec remained part of Canada, but it was no happier than before. The rest of Canada was unable to fully develop an identity of its own without worrying that it would distance itself from the historical notion of two founding nations and further estrange Quebec. Through it all, Canada was able to reach a deeper understanding of its flaws, but sadly no more acceptable a concept of what kind of nation it wanted to be, with or without Trudeau, with or without Quebec. "My Canada Includes Quebec" was a bumper sticker I saw on hundreds of cars in Canada, a fading, peeling sentiment left over from the referendum battle. But the sticker seemed to convey a melancholy message that was contrary to the clarion call to unity it was intended to be. "My Canada" reinforced the schizophrenia of Canada, a land where everybody had an individual concept of the country, whatever that might include or be, a land of multiple personalities that was never quite sure which one was dominant at the moment. "My Canada" may not be "Your Canada," the bumper sticker said, and the implied message it gave was "I don't care."

I rarely heard Canadians talk of themselves without letting their history get in the way. They almost always chose to limit their reach and narrow their focus to the fact that there were two points from which Canada began, rather than that French and English have lived together and accommodated each other—not always perfectly but mostly without violence—for almost 250 years. Quebec should not stay part of Canada only to preserve the status quo and provide a reasonable model for other would-be nations around the world. But at the very least, Quebec—and Canada—should not be tricked into breaking apart, with misleading questions, slim majorities, and the manipulation of public opinion by a small group of extremists. A people should be carried to independence by a groundswell, not a slight tremor. And the nation they are seeking might already exist.

※

One unifying feature of Canada's psyche is the Arctic, a brooding, white, inescapable presence. It may be the most powerful element connecting places as disparate as Newfoundland and Alberta, a common factor whose destructive force and creative power leave their mark on every Canadian's soul. The Arctic may be capable of uniting a nation, and of creating a nation within a nation.

Few Canadians have ever visited the high Arctic, let alone live there, and only a handful know the secrets of the northern lands the intimate way John MacDonald knows them. Over the course of a few days that I spent with this hearty northerner, I got to peer into the most universal part of Canada's past. One cloudless night in the Arctic outpost of Igloolik, over a meal that included graciously offered squares of narwhal skin, called *muktuk*, I listened to MacDonald recount how he had come to the north forty years before to work with the Hudson Bay Company. He had sought adventure and fell utterly under the spell of the arctic sky.

MacDonald was born a Scotsman, from the Isle of Skye, but he was raised in Britain's African colony of Nyasaland (now Malawi) with his intrepid family. His was the kind of international upbringing that marked the British empire for the first half of the twentieth century, when adventurous souls left Britain and flung themselves to distant lands wherever the Union Jack flew. He attended a boarding school in Scotland, and then decided to pursue a boyhood dream by joining the Hudson Bay Company, the legendary enterprise founded in 1670 that for 200 years owned the charter to the greater portion of what now is the Canadian north. Here, finally, MacDonald felt at home.

He encountered in the north not an uninhabited wasteland or a frozen desert but a place of unimagined variety and uncompromising life. He was quickly drawn into the culture of the Inuit people who lived in the region, and eventually made the study of their traditions and customs his life's work. He was especially drawn to Igloolik, a small island 1,000 miles from the North Pole where Inuit had lived for 4,000 years. The outlines of prehistoric stone houses are still easily visible on the cliff above Turton Bay. MacDonald's own Igloolik Research Center is housed in an exotic fiberglass structure shaped like a mushroom. The federal government once considered this a viable experiment in arctic living. The main circular floor is perched atop a narrow stem some twenty feet off the ground to prevent the permafrost beneath from melting. Inside are offices, labs, and a library that now has one of the most extensive collections of Inuit folklore and oral histories in the world.

"The elders are going fast, and the last real details of an entirely unique society are being lost," MacDonald explained. He and his staff have conducted hundreds of interviews with surviving elders like Noah Piugaattuk, who recalled that he saw his first white man "around the time hairs started growing on my chin." Others remembered life before regular contact with white men, before snowmobiles and television sets and home-brew alcohol. The research helped Igloolik, one of the most traditional Inuit communities, revive the traditional midwinter ceremony welcoming back the sun after weeks of arctic darkness. That long winter night is not as profound as most people believe. "I've been in darkness in Africa where you just do not know what is in front of you, but this never happens in the Arctic," MacDonald said. For six weeks, the sun never appears. But the sky lightens to a pale evanescence for at least a few hours at midday. When the sun finally pops up again over the horizon, no matter how briefly, it traditionally was reason for the Inuit to celebrate.

That was the ceremony I had gone to Igloolik to see in January 1999, the reason I was willing to spend more than $100 a night to sleep inside Igloolik's newest (and only) hotel, a series of bouncy modular boxes bolted together and called the Co-Op Inn. Everything from toothpaste to apples is expensive in Igloolik, where nothing but ice grows for at least nine months of the year. Being that far north was disorienting, but only if you thought about being thousands of miles above the place on the map considered home. I found myself more than once tracing the distance between New York and Igloolik on the globe in John MacDonald's office. He must have done something similar too, because the place on the globe marked Igloolik was almost worn away.

Once I overcame that perceptual vertigo, being in Igloolik seemed remarkably ordinary. The rough houses of imported wood built over the previous twenty years were not much different from those anywhere else in rural North America. They were arrayed along more or less regular streets packed hard and deep with snow. There were two supermarkets, two schools, one restaurant that was part of the hotel, and two churches, one Catholic, the other Anglican. The cold was fearsome, with temperatures normally hovering around –70 degrees (and sometimes much colder), but since it is inescapable, there was no choice but to prepare for it with the heaviest of clothing and the most ample of precautions.

The flight that brought me to Igloolik left from the same airport in Ottawa where I had departed for Cuba several times. After only fifteen minutes in the air, as the plane headed straight north, all sign of civilization disappeared. From the frost-edged windows of the plane, all that was visible below was a frozen sea of white. It was the same sensation as being in a jet that climbs above the clouds on an overcast day. From that vista, there are no roads, no mountains, no church steeples or football stadiums. Just a wrinkled white bedsheet, as far off as you can see. The same vista continued for more than five hours before the plane landed at Iqaluit, on the southern tip of Baffin Island, just below the Arctic Circle. There we changed from the commercial jetliner to a compact Hawker Siddley 750 propeller plane. The movable bulkhead was squeezed toward the back of the plane, and in what would have been the first seven rows of passenger seats were boxes of pork chops and other frozen foods to be delivered in Igloolik. The air in the cabin was cold enough to keep the supplies well preserved and to force every passenger to remain huddled inside a heavy parka during the flight. Again the plane crossed over a land totally without features before finally skidding in on the icy runway at Igloolik.

The only moment I ever felt more isolated than that flight came when a fellow reporter, Chris Wilson—who like John MacDonald is an intrepid commonwealth traveler who came from South Africa—and I took out a dogsled team in Igloolik. A young Inuk with a dozen wild dogs brought us across the undulating ice of Turton Bay to the gravesite of Alexander Elder, a mate aboard H.B.M. *Hecla* who died on a voyage of discovery in 1823. We arrived there just after noon. The sun did not appear that day, but the sky had lightened to a pinkish orange the color of a tropical drink at a Cancún hotel. The ice across the bay was not flat. It rippled, in some spots gently, like a pond in a spring rain, in others quite violently where planks of ice had collided against each other and formed jagged peaks that the dogs ran around.

The sky and the snow faded to the same gauzy color, roughly the tone of wood smoke. Had it not been for the way the sky seemed to fray into lighter shades directly overhead, it would have been impossible to locate the horizon. Elder's limestone grave, no more than two feet high, was the only imprint of man's hand other than us at that moment. Elder had come with Sir William Edward Parry in search of the fabled Northwest Passage. The entire crew of Parry's ships *Hecla* and *Fury* wintered over on Igloolik, but when the waters opened with the summer thaw, Elder was left behind. The cold of his grave, the absolute loneliness of the spot where he had been laid to rest by his shipmates, tried to creep into the heavy layers of clothing I wore. The sight of the grave must have been enough to make any British sailor shiver for decades afterward, and it was Elder's fate, not the −70 degree temperature and howling wind out on the ice, that left me feeling more alone than I'd ever felt before, or have since.

John MacDonald later pointed out that the English sailors and Scottish whalers who came to the Arctic had left behind far more than poor Elder's grave. They brought their culture with them, and shared it freely with the Inuit. There's no point judging their motives, or trying to assess the damage they did to the native people. Rather, when I watched the Inuit of Igloolik ceremoniously extinguish their seal-blubber lanterns to welcome back the sun, and then cap off the celebration with a rousing square dance to a Scottish tune from 150 years earlier, I realized that cultures should not be judged on the basis of their purity. Rather, success should depend on the degree to which they adapt to influences outside their own. That applied equally to the Inuit and to the Nisga'a and even to the French of Quebec. The Inuit danced to the simple square-dance tunes for hours. Some adults had learned the old Scottish melodies long ago, and dancing to them was as natural as performing the traditional drum dance, and more fun. For someone like Nathan Qamaniq, a walrus of a man with a drooping mustache and almond eyes, the square dance was part of his culture, just as the large igloo of blue ice blocks he had helped build to teach the youngsters about traditional ways was a precious cultural artifact.

The morning after the dance, a Sunday, I saw Nathan among the dozens of Inuit who attended mass at the Catholic church in a ceremony celebrated in the Inuktitut language. The service was another example of how cultures, and nations, are built. Instead of candlesticks, the altar was adorned with a crossed pair of walrus tusks. The pulpit was covered not with carved oak wood but the beautiful skin of a ringed seal. And when the mass ended, the faithful sang about the bonds of community to music that sounded unexpectedly familiar. I listened with surprise as the first notes came from the old piano, but soon it was evident that the Inuit were singing to the melody of "Auld Lange Syne," another inheritance of those outsiders who, like Elder, had set foot here long ago.

Perhaps more than any other people in North America today, the Inuit have been forced to adapt rapidly to a changing world. What transpired in the Arctic over the past fifty years repeated the encounters that have taken place all over the continent since Cortés challenged the Aztecs in 1519. Had Elder met his unfortunate fate today instead of in the nineteenth century, he would have been portrayed as an agent of globalization, a dangerous infiltrator whose presence posed a threat to an endangered culture. Parry might never have been allowed to drop anchor, nor would the Inuit have offered to help him through the arctic winter. But instead of shutting themselves off, the Inuit have used their superb skills of adaptation to survive, as they always have. They see nothing wrong with riding snowmobiles while dressed in their traditional caribou britches. They continue to rely on the long sleds of their ancestors. Once the sleds were made of whale bone and caribou hide. Now they are made entirely of wood, nails, and plastic that come from the south. The Inuit can walk to the co-op store to buy a package of cake mix, but they also will slaughter a caribou on the floor of their kitchen and slice off a beet-red chunk of leg meat to chew on while watching television. Of course, there are conflicts: They have been devastated by gambling, alcohol, and gas sniffing, and now that they no longer follow the caribou herd, their lives in the settled communities can be empty and dark. Most standard measures of quality of life for which Canadians are so proud are abysmal in the north: Unemployment, suicide, and alcoholism plague Igloolik and other Arctic communities.

Inuit leaders are worried about such things, but they also realize that change has come to Igloolik quickly, and adjusting will take time. Just one lifetime has been enough for someone like Rosie Iqalliyuq to evolve from a nomadic, stone-age life to the domestic comfort I saw the day I met her. Even at ninety-six, Rosie still expertly wielded her moon-shaped *ulu* knife to slice open a frozen arctic char while watching *The Simpsons* on television inside her subsidized house. On her arm, faint as small veins under the wrinkles and folds of her skin, she still bore the tattoos she had received as a teenage girl. Inch-long slashes were laid out in two rows along her forearm, one with thirteen lines side by side, the other a parallel row of eight lines. She said they were just designs, not symbolic of anything, and her only regret was that she had not been allowed to have her face tattooed as the other young girls did back then. Her father said she was too much the Inuit equivalent of a tomboy, and he thought girls' tattoos would look strange on her. As I talked to Rosie, the markings seemed like pentimento of that other age, an ancient world that had practically disappeared. The changes had bewildered her. She struggled to understand what had happened to the ancient patterns of her life, and she could not even conceive of the issues that affected the nation in which she lived. She knew nothing of Canada's struggle for identity or of the festering sore of ethnic tribalism that was eating away at the country. In fact, until just recently, she admitted, she hadn't even been aware that she lived in a country called Canada.

Most Inuit do have a conception of Canada, and of their own culture, which they are desperate to save. "We have never spilled a single ounce of blood over the land to preserve our identity as Inuit," George Kuptianuk, an Igloolik official, told me. His words echoed those expressed by René Lévesque at the start of the separatist movement—the oath of blood, the yearning for identity. "We always accepted new changes and worked around them," Kuptianuk said. "Inuit have lived here for 4,000 years, and hardly anything changed until the government and the missions came." He was six years old before he lived in a wooden house, and although he was in his forties when I met him in Igloolik, his voice still had a trace of awe when he recalled how he once gave a discarded candy wrapper to a friend as a Christmas gift. There was no candy inside, but the wrapper shone like nothing he'd ever seen before. "Ottawa has already imposed a lot on us," he said, "but we have been strong enough to say no when it became too much and gentle enough to work our way through those things we could not prevent."

That gentle persistence accompanies Inuit culture, a doggedness that only a people capable of standing at an ice hole for an entire day waiting for a seal to surface could ever harness productively. Like the Nisga'a, the Inuit have longed to return to the time when they controlled their own lives and their own land. They first raised the demand, gently, in 1976 and were willing to wait for the government to approve the daring proposal that they be given control over half the Arctic where they lived. Finally, in the early 1980s, the Mulroney government agreed to split the Northwest Territories in two in order to create a place where the Inuit would be the majority and thus be in a position to govern themselves. Nunavut, which means "our land" in Inuktitut, would be roughly the size of western Europe. It would have twenty-eight times more caribou than people, ten times more trucks and snowmobiles than there are miles of road, and only 27,000 people in twenty-eight far-flung communities, including Grise Fiord, the northernmost settlement in the world, which the Canadian government created in the 1950s to fortify Canadian sovereignty over the region.

In late March 1999, I made the long trip north to the Arctic again, this time stopping in Iqaluit, which once went by the English name Frobisher Bay. The Inuit had selected the tiny community to become the new capital of Nunavut. All hotel rooms had been booked by officials coming to the ceremonies marking the first official change in the map of North America in fifty years, so I stayed with a friend. Kenn Harper is a Canadian from Ontario who, like John MacDonald, had long ago succumbed to the spell of the north. Harper found opportunity in Iqaluit, the raw kind of commercial possibility that had turned Dawson into a Yukon boomtown a century before. Harper owned the biggest independent store in Iqaluit, along with several of the largest commercial and residential buildings. The decision to make Iqaluit the capital spurred him to get busy building housing for the new territorial government workers. He even owned the local Radio Shack store, and when Iqaluit got cellular telephone service just before the Nunavut celebration, Harper sold out his stock of cellphones in a few days.

Harper is the kind of swaggering, self-confident character that the north seems to attract but the rest of Canada finds difficult to tolerate, in part because they are so American. He learned Inuktitut and steeped himself in Inuit lore. He was outspokenly critical of the way the Inuit were sometimes coddled by the government and treated like children. He ranted against racial quotas and Canadian officials so concerned with being politically correct that they gave Inuit key positions not because they had the necessary skills but because they were Inuit. "I may be a voice crying in the wilderness, but I tell you there simply aren't enough adequately trained or educated Inuit to go around," Harper told me in the overheated office above his Arctic Ventures store in Iqaluit. He agreed with a prominent local Inuit leader who once said that he'd rather have a capable white man fill a position than an inept Inuk, the word for a single Inuit person. "There's nothing magical about being an Inuk that allows you to do what no other people on earth can do," he said. "You can train someone to shovel snow, and you can train someone to run a snowplow. I don't think you can train someone to become a deputy minister, but this government believes you can."

Finding enough trained professionals to take over several hundred government positions was only one problem facing Nunavut. In the end, many non-Inuit from the government of the Northwest Territories were given new contracts to stay on until they could be replaced. But the most pressing issues, such as Nunavut's lack of a viable economy, were either ignored or papered over with the best of intentions. As one of its first acts, the new Nunavut territorial legislature picked Paul Okalik to be premier. The earnest thirty-four-year-old Inuk with a slender back and a voice soft as falling snow had only a few months earlier become the first aboriginal man admitted to the bar in the Arctic. At a press conference, he was asked about Nunavut's chances of ever getting off the government dole. He talked vaguely about the recent discovery of diamonds north of Yellowknife and said such activities could support Nunavut for decades. But he admitted that exploratory drilling was far off. The only substantial idea he offered for opening Nunavut's economy and providing jobs was to use NAFTA to challenge the Marine Mammal Protection Act's ban on importing seal skins to the United States. Okalik wore a vest made from the skin of a ringed seal, the kind of skin that used to generate cash for many Inuit hunters. "There's no need to protect these sea mammals," he said, showing off the vest but not much awareness of political reality in North America. He promised that his government, though dominated by Inuit, would be open and responsive to all. But he said it would find an Inuit way of doing things.

A day later I stood beside Okalik on the shore of frozen Iqaluit Bay the moment Nunavut came into being. It was midnight, March 31, 1999. The temperature was about –45 degrees, and the frozen bay was filled with people. As the first fireworks went off, two dogs from a sled team broke loose from their harnesses. They howled at the sky and dashed across the bay, long leather straps trailing behind them. "You never know what to expect," Okalik said, his words especially apt in the Arctic. But there was little uncertainty about the importance of this event, a historic moment for the Inuit and the beginning of a new era for not only Canada but continental America.

The sun rose later that day on a celebration still under way. The local community had been invited to the Canadian Air Force base, where U.S. bombers once were refueled, for a formal ceremony and a meal of traditional northern foods. I took a cab from Kenn Harper's house. The driver, like many others in Iqaluit, was a Quebecer who had been drawn by the strange elixir of freedom and opportunity the north held. He did not want to talk much, but then he didn't have to. He told much about himself by the way he held the steering wheel. He hooked his right thumb under the spoke when he turned the wheel. The fingers on his right hand were missing. When a call came in on the cab's two-way radio, he steadied the wheel with the stump that remained on his left hand—the fingers and thumb were gone—and managed to pick up the handset by pushing his thumb against the palm of his right hand. It was the cold that had got him, and the booze, a tragedy that everybody in Iqaluit knew. The driver got so drunk one night that he passed out against the side of a building. By the time he was revived, frostbite had him. I had already experienced how fierce the cold could be. I had stopped one morning to take a photograph in a –90 degree wind chill, and the wind literally blew the skin off my ears in just a few minutes. During an interview later, the Inuit official I was talking to saw my blistered ears and asked what had happened. "Blistering's good," she said in the casual deadpan common in the north. If skin blisters, she said, "at least your ears won't fall off."

Because Iqaluit has no buses, cabs usually pick up several passengers on every trip. We stopped in front of a small brown house and a local woman got in. She wore a light blue parka with the fur-lined hood pulled down, so I caught only a glimpse of her face as she slipped into the front seat. We started to talk. I asked if she was proud of what was happening to her land. "I am proud," she told me, "but I am not from here. I'm Mexican." María Teresa Moctezuma, a teacher, said she had taken a trip to Montreal from Mexico in 1982 and liked the feeling of Canada so much she decided to relocate. One year she participated in an educational program in Iqaluit and again was so captivated by the surroundings that she stayed. She felt an affinity with the Inuit, despite their obvious differences. "All indigenous people have the same problems stemming from the fact that originally we all were conquered by someone else," she said. In one sentence she had captured the essence of both Canada and Mexico. The cab went as close to the air base as the Mounties would permit and let us off.

A mean arctic wind whipped the maple-leaf flags that had been strung on a row of poles leading to the air base, but Moctezuma seemed oblivious to the cold. "Our religion, our language, even the way we are able to teach our children all have been affected by the relationship to the conquering race," she said. She was encouraged by the way Canada had decided to recognize Nunavut even though the Inuit had no real power and had not tried to use violence, pressure, or any tactic but moral suasion to change the mind of a nation that had once ignored their plight. "When I first came here, these children were forced to learn about how a tree grows and what a tree is made of, but none of them had ever seen a tree because none grows here," she said. Now she hoped that with Inuit in charge they would regain some of the power they had lost through their contact with white society. "This will have repercussions around the whole world," she said, "and I hope in Mexico too."

✳

The scope of what Canada had attempted in the far north began to sink in no more than a week later when I was in Europe, where the NATO bombing campaign against Yugoslavia had begun. On big stories, it is not unusual for *The Times* to send reinforcements from other bureaus to supplement the work of local correspondents. Other newspapers also brought in reinforcements, but I had the advantage of seeing firsthand the contrast between how the dreams of two groups of people—the Inuit and the Kosovar Albanians—had been addressed. Both were minorities within their countries, people with ancient traditions and a connection to the land predating the creation of the nations to which they belonged legally, if not emotionally. But for the Albanians in Kosovo, the quest for self-government and the right to lead their own lives had been blocked by repression and hate. Belgrade had no intention of recognizing the Albanians' rights, and NATO had launched its imperfect bombing campaign to put an end to the terror that had displaced hundreds of thousands of Kosovars. But it too opposed giving the Kosovars their own nation.

The comparison with Nunavut was unavoidable. There, without the spilling of blood or even the threat of violence, the rights of the minority had been recognized and respected. Just as important, the rights of the minority within the minority—the non-Inuit like Kenn Harper—had also been preserved. Unlike the race-based provisions in the Nisga'a treaty, the government established in Nunavut was a public government, open to Inuit and non-Inuit alike, even though the Inuit will control the government for the foreseeable future. Diversity and adaptation, the two principal characteristics of Nunavut, were designed into the new territorial Parliament in Iqaluit. It was built in the shape of an igloo, and in a resounding affirmation of tolerance, translation booths were installed for three official languages—English, French, and Inuktitut.

Certainly many different factors were at play in Nunavut and Kosovo, not the least being that the land in the eastern Arctic had little commercial value, and the harsh conditions scared away all but the most hearty souls. But the same could be said of North America two centuries earlier when France and England fought for control of a hostile wasteland that Voltaire had dismissed as "a few acres of ice and snow" not worth fighting for. By establishing Nunavut, Canada had not given away title to worthless land. Instead it had realized the frozen land's potential as an experiment in nationhood, and as a notable model for cooperation and coexistence in a world increasingly spinning in a centrifuge of tribalism and ethnic hatred. Laurier LaPierre, a Canadian historian and author, once said that as the new millennium began, Canada may have been one of the most important nations because it was able to show how cultural diversity could be protected without surrendering the viability of nations. "Our destiny," he wrote, "is to be an example to other nations."6

While I was in the Balkans, Václav Havel visited Canada and addressed Parliament on April 29, 1999. The poet-president of the Czech Republic, which had peacefully separated from Slovakia only six years earlier, claimed that the nation-state as the highest earthly value of a national community had already passed its peak. He predicted that traditional concepts of borders would be replaced by a recognition that "human beings are more important than the state." Touching on what was happening then in Kosovo, but also by allusion to his own country, to Nunavut, and to the separatist movement that had caused such strain in Quebec, Havel told the members of Parliament: "In the next century, I believe that most states will begin to change from cultlike entities charged with emotion into far simpler and more civilized entities, into less powerful and more rational administrative units that will represent only one of the many complex and multilevel ways in which our planetary society is organized." He foresaw a world in which traditional states ceded power to nongovernmental organizations on the one hand and international and global agencies on the other.[7]

"There exists something of higher value than the state. That value is humanity," Havel said. His clearly was not the message that Parizeau and the separatists had been sending from Quebec City for thirty years, which said the state was the most valid expression of a people. One time I asked an avowed separatist in the Quebec government how independence for Quebec would improve the lives of the men in overalls who were digging up the cobblestone street near the government offices on the Grand Allée in Quebec City. Or, for that matter, how would independence make it easier for any of the province's 7 million people to get a job, send their children to school, help them take care of their elderly parents, or feel more secure? He stammered and hedged in the way I saw repeated over and over by every separatist I ever spoke to. They all protested that it was not that simple, but eventually they conceded that the day Quebec's independence would be declared, the ditch digger and his family would probably not notice any difference at all. But nationhood is the destiny of the French-speaking people in North America, the official said, and that destiny must be fulfilled. In contrast, Havel said that "our destinies are now merging into a single destiny," a time as never before when "human freedoms represent a higher value than state sovereignty."

Nations used to be defined by geography and language, but for what do such measures count when distance itself has lost meaning? Telephone companies charge the same rate for a call next door as for a call to the other end of the continent. Computers translate documents, the Internet publishes novels, and satellites spill television signals indiscriminately across any border. A more contemporary definition of a nation might be that proposed by the French historian Ernest Rennan who believed that nations are formed by people doing great things together.

The aspiration to do great things, or the exigencies of calamity or hardship that make it essential to accomplish them, sustain the concept of nations even as ethnic, racial, and tribal demands for self-government threaten to pull nations apart. But the global dimensions of the economic and political world that is forming leave small nations increasingly vulnerable. To some thinkers, the new North America that began to take shape after 1993 may offer an alternative. That continental community could "preserve the existence of the nation-state and that of small nations at an equal distance from old-style imperialism and international anarchy," Octavio Paz wrote in 1993. "That community would be the beginning of the international order that politicians have promised for so long."[8]

It isn't clear whether Paz would have considered an independent Quebec the kind of small nation that could be sustained by a continental community, or if he was referring to Canada itself, which is diminutive in almost every measure but geography. Would a Maya nation in southern Mexico be able to survive? Would the Nisga'a? Ultimately, will it become necessary for North America to follow a path similar to the one taken by Europe, using NAFTA as a foundation on which to erect a common market and continental union? No answers to these questions were available by the time officials from Canada, Mexico, and the United States gathered in Montreal to celebrate the fifth anniversary of the trade pact, but it became clear at that session that a new North America was rapidly taking shape.

CHAPTER FOURTEEN

Sons of the Middle Border

*

For a transitory enchanted moment man must have held his breath
in the presence of this continent, compelled into an aesthetic
contemplation he neither understood nor desired, face to face
for the last time in history with something commensurate
to his capacity for wonder.

F. Scott Fitzgerald
The Great Gatsby

Brian Mulroney strode to the dais with all the burly confidence
that comes from thinking history had proved him right. The en-
thusiastic applause from the audience of several hundred free
traders, continental corporate executives, and officials past and present
from the United States, Mexico, and Mulroney's own beloved Canada
who had gathered in Montreal was a rare display of affection for a man
who had become a lightning rod for criticism almost anywhere he had
gone in recent years. "God, how I miss the adulation," Mulroney blurted
out as he took the microphone.

The Renaissance Hôtel du Parc in downtown Montreal had been
taken over by the front ranks of Mulroney's supporters that crystalline
spring day in 1999. They had brought together many of free trade's original players, joined by a smattering of critics and doomsayers, to recognize publicly the former prime minister's vision for Canada and for
North America. Their goal was to assess the triumphs and failures of
NAFTA's first five years, as well as take the measure of the entire decade
that had passed since Mulroney rammed through the original free trade
pact between Canada and the United States. In so doing, they hoped to

initiate the formal rehabilitation of Mulroney's reputation and establish his place as an architect of North American history. In fact, the gathering itself was substantiation of the process that was repositioning Canada and Mexico from the ends of America to the beginnings of a new American continent.

Still, much of the two-day conference appeared to revolve around Mulroney, recently gone sixty, silver-haired and silver-tongued. He was quite a bit beefier than during his nine years as prime minister, a period during which he and his Conservative Party recorded Canada's greatest electoral victory and most devastating political defeat. His fall from grace was widely believed to have commenced with his decision to reverse a century of commercial protectionism and set Canada on a course of free trade and open borders. Mulroney had become the man who sold out Canada.

If it wasn't exactly a neutral forum for evaluating NAFTA, it at least was one in which many of the original participants were willing to relive their glory days. Former President Bush was there to declare that the trade agreements "reflected a mutual commitment by the respective countries to build a common future based on shared values rather than on past differences." James A. Baker, Mr. Bush's secretary of state and President Reagan's secretary of the treasury, described his eleventh-hour decision in October 1987 to save the original free trade agreement with Canada by forgoing every last commercial advantage and focusing instead on what would sell politically in Congress. Canadian Simon Reisman recounted in his bulldog style how he had gained some bargaining room that helped an outmatched Canada stand its ground in tough negotiations with the United States. Mexico's Jaime Serra Puche could not disguise his lingering dismay at the intransigence of the U.S. Congress and the horse-trading that President Clinton had resorted to—including a promise to go fishing with one fence-sitting congressman—in order to get the trade agreement approved. Dozens of North American trade warriors at the head table recounted their exploits as if they were the star players of a winning NFL championship team. And like gridiron stars, they paid tribute to their coaches.

"As important as the work of negotiators was," Baker said solemnly, "the FTA, my friends, was ultimately the creation of two men: Ronald Reagan and Brian Mulroney." Baker also extolled the "imperative of political will" that had led to the signing of NAFTA despite a storm of protest from labor unions and environmentalists, among others. Partisanship apparently prevented him from mentioning President Clinton's late efforts to rescue NAFTA, but he gave credit to President Bush and to President Salinas who, he said, along with Mulroney "had the conviction and courage to make the dream of free trade a reality." A dreamlike aura hung over the Montreal conference that day, what with all the security precautions, several television new crews, and the tingle of celebrity surrounding the attractive women who escorted Canadian designer Peter Nygard, who knew Mulroney and had an obvious personal interest in matters of trade. During the breaks between sessions, Nygard and company attracted far more attention than the graying statesmen and the weighty books on trade and diplomacy that they tried to hawk.

Those books and many others have laid out the material impact that free trade has had on North America. The consensus was that unshackling the continental markets had produced more trade, more commerce, and more jobs. In fact, the agreements helped put the United States, Canada, and Mexico in the position of conducting more trade with each other than any three nations in the world. If all the goods and services crossing the borders of North America were added up, the total would have come to more than $570 billion a year, an amount greater than the entire gross domestic product of Spain, one of North America's founding nations. Each leg of the American trinity had clearly been strengthened by free trade: Canada-U.S. commerce had grown by about 20 percent in the first five years of the original trade agreement and then had exploded under NAFTA, jumping 80 percent since 1994. Canada-Mexico trade had doubled in that time. And cross-border commerce between the United States and Mexico, despite the peso crisis of 1995, had been boosted an exceptional 17 percent a year since the first day in 1994 when the Zapatistas had labeled the agreement a death sentence. The flow of goods across both borders had grown from a steady stream to a mighty river that totaled from $1.5 billion to $2 billion a day, double the daily trade with all of Europe and more than five times as much as U.S. trade with China.

That powerful commercial current had dug its own course through the continent and was changing the economic and social landscape at every turn. The United States traded more with Mexico than with Japan, and more Canada-made products were sold in America than in Canada itself. Even critics had to concede they had trouble hearing Ross Perot's "giant sucking sound" of jobs being dragged across the border. Rather, more than 16 million new jobs had been created, and though all certainly were not due directly to free trade, the market for exports was a powerful booster of each nation's economy. More than goods and services were moving over the borders. In 1999, U.S. Customs agents handled more than a half billion individual crossings over the borders with Canada and Mexico, the equivalent of the entire continent rearranging itself in a vast game of musical chairs over the course of the year. All three countries invested more in each other, provided more services to each other, and generally were more aware of what was happening on each other's streets and highways than ever before.

The participants in the Montreal conference portrayed NAFTA as an instrument of unusual vision that had turned centuries of continental antagonism on its head. And they resoundingly made the point that geography, history, and even sovereignty—the triggers of countless conflicts in the past—had become less important than the lives of the 400 million people on the American continent. Baker told the conference that the agreements had "committed our countries to looking outward rather than inward, to fostering a desire to excel instead of a fear of competition, to encouraging productive cooperation and not destructive resentment." NAFTA, he declared, "marked a true revolution in relations among Canada, the United States, and Mexico—a revolution that allows all of us to look forward with confidence to the next century and indeed the next millennium."

Even that revival-meeting spirit, however, wasn't enough to dim the ardor of some opponents, or to obscure the toughest questions about the changing nature of North America. Thousands of workers had been displaced when big corporations slashed waste and redundancy from their operations across the continent and turned all of North America into one huge corporate division. The United States was importing far more than it was exporting, which made the trade deficit worse than ever. Almost everyone but the bureaucrats in charge of implementing the side agreements on environment and labor (the kind of protective shields that demonstrators would demand from the World Trade Organization in Seattle a few months after the conference) considered them ineffective protection against the excesses of continental trade. Even the positive figures on trade growth were challenged. Critics charged that the recent economic recoveries in Canada and Mexico had actually been spurred by the hot U.S. economy and weak currencies in both countries, and had little to do with free trade.

They were at least partly right. The Canadian dollar had been in a long, steady decline throughout the 1980s and 1990s. By June 1999, the Canadian dollar was worth only about U.S. $0.65, a near-record low. That meant everything Canada manufactured cost less in the United States, an obvious plus for Canadian exports, just as the peso crisis had made Mexican exports to the United States cheaper by a wide margin. The currency imbalance across both borders also meant that it would cost American manufacturers less to run their factories in Canada and Mexico. Because relocations are complicated decisions, nobody knew exactly how many American manufacturing jobs had been lost to Mexico with its lower wages and to Canada with its personnel costs made cheaper by the universal health care provided by the government. However, it was clear that many of the factories that relocated from America's industrial heartland and to foreign soil exploited those relative advantages.

In the first five years that NAFTA was in full operation, some 260,000 workers in the United States qualified to receive special unemployment benefits under an American program to compensate those who lost jobs because of free trade. In an economy the size of the United States, that was not considered a statistically significant loss, and the dislocation was eased by the new jobs that helped push down the unemployment rate to its lowest level in thirty years.[1] But for every person thrown out of work because of free trade, there were ten or a hundred or a thousand who feared losing their job to a low-paid Mexican or a Canadian with a national medical plan. Being unemployed in America could mean joining the 40 million Americans without medical insurance. In Canada, health care is not linked to employment, and people there were far more willing to tolerate higher unemployment rates without panicking. Canadian joblessness is perpetually twice as high as in the United States, yet the discourse over jobs rarely reached even half the decibel level as on the American side of the border. Mexico's peculiar method of calculating unemployment made the issue moot even if people there had felt complaining would do any good, which they didn't. Anyone in Mexico who had any income at all during the course of a week was considered employed. That included the adults who sold chewing gum at traffic lights and the ones who hawked rubber masks of President Salinas near the American embassy in Mexico City.

Another group of critics was on the minds of the conference organizers even though this group had supported NAFTA. Quebec had energetically championed free trade from the very beginning for its own reasons, but English Canada had always suspected that Quebec separatists were less interested in Mulroney's vision of Canada's continental future than in their own dream of an independent Quebec nation that would be automatically entitled to the benefits of NAFTA. The same kind of deep-seated suspicions led English Canada to question the motives of Quebec officials who suggested that a common currency like the euro would further facilitate trade in North America. The separatists had dismissed as inconsequential the concerns of officials in Ottawa and Mexico City that a common currency could threaten national sovereignty. Of course, dollarizing the North American economy would have the practical effect of eliminating one of the separatists' thorniest problems: whether to keep the Canadian dollar after declaring independence or mint Quebec's own currency.

Trade. Tribalism. National unity. International policy had become so intertwined with domestic politics in North America's new age that it was impossible to discuss one without taking into account the others. The true reflection of what had happened on the continent over the previous few years lay not in the cold figures of commerce and industry but in the sweeping transformation of the ends of America. As James Baker had pointed out, the demand for transparency and the pressure of competition were freeing Mexico and Canada from the traps of their past. In Mexico in particular, the regular reporting of financial data forced government spending into the open. By the summer of 1999, reserves were being reported on the Internet, and there were few secrets left about Mexico's resources.

The bond rating agencies in New York constantly monitored these reports and used them to set Mexico's credit rating, which had a huge impact on how fast Mexico's economy could grow because those ratings determined how much it cost Mexico to borrow money. The transformation from clandestine ways to full transparency seeped into other areas of Mexican society as well. Preventing foreign investors from becoming too jumpy at election time had helped regularize the electoral process. Citizens were given seats on the federal electoral institute, which oversees elections. As polling became more widely used for market studies, public opinion surveys became more accepted during campaigns, which also limited electoral shenanigans.

The trade-related changes in Canada were not quite as evident as in Mexico, but they were substantial nonetheless. With continental competition staring them in the face, Canadian corporations were forced to streamline. The federal and provincial governments had to do the same. That produced a wholesale reexamination of Canada's comprehensive social safety network, from universal health care to welfare and education. Prime Minister Chrétien oversaw some of the deepest and most painful spending cuts Canada had ever enacted, but he and finance minister Paul Martin managed to balance the budget in 1998—for the first time in nearly thirty years.

Another way to gauge the true impact of the continental conversion is to see North America not only in terms of trade but also in the extent to which the three nations intervened in each other's affairs. Some traditional restraints were relaxed in a remarkable way. The United States had a long history of interference in the affairs of Mexico. It began soon after Mexico won its independence, and occurred so regularly thereafter that in Mexico City's Museum of Interventions, the United States is featured in all the biggest and most prominent displays. But with the NAFTA vote in 1993, America for the first time became an overt and active participant—with Mexico's blessing—in the domestic economy and in Mexican society. Thus the rescue package of 1995, the cooperation on the interdiction of illegal drugs, the signing of NAFTA itself, and other incursions did not constitute another landing at Veracruz. Nor were they altruistic extensions of a helping hand. Washington realized these problems did not belong only to Mexico. However veiled, these actions of cooperation were recognition that despite all that had happened in the past, we Americans were not on this continent alone.

The past hovers over Mexico like the clouds on the Popocatepetl volcano, and it—like the clouds—never vanishes for long. At the NAFTA conference in Montreal, Jaime Serra Puche brought Mexico's past with him. Once considered a potential candidate for president, Serra had been forced to resign as Mexico's treasury secretary after the bungled peso devaluation. When it later became clear that the fault was not entirely his, Serra, like Mulroney, tried to rehabilitate his reputation. He shaved his bristle-brush mustache and returned to Mexico as a private consultant. When I talked to him at the Montreal conference, only a year remained of President Zedillo's administration. Serra Puche was not ready to believe that Mexico had yet matured all that much since 1994. For the previous three decades, the change of administration every six years had brought an economic crisis. The implosions came with such regularity that domestic and international investors would start worrying well before a new president was even sworn in. At the Hotel du Parc, Serra told me he expected the year 2000 to be at best a difficult year for Mexico, and at worst a repeat of the calamity of 1994. "Just thinking about it," he said, "makes my skin crawl."

Shortly after the Montreal conference, President Zedillo tried to respond to some of the uncertainty over Mexico's economic destiny. Mindful of the international market's persistent wariness about Mexico's ability to make the transition from one administration to another without stumbling, President Zedillo announced a contingency plan of some $23.7 billion from international financing sources to ensure that Mexico had sufficient reserves to pay all its debts.

Such lingering doubts about Mexico were widespread. The nation's painfully slow transition to full democracy kept the country vulnerable to economic and political shocks, the kind of temblors that rattle its stock market and dry up direct foreign investments. Many fundamental shortcomings also remained. Mexico had broadened the range of its exports, but it remained heavily dependent on oil to keep the economy greased and unemployment within manageable limits. An oil glut that would depress prices on the international market could severely strain Mexico's social safety net. Petróleos Mexicanos, Pemex, was still the most sacred cow in the Mexican economy, and attempts by President Zedillo to privatize small parts of it had been stopped cold by the unions and by Mexican nationalists who refused to allow the oil industry, which had been nationalized in 1938, to be touched. It was apparent, however, that Pemex was not as productive as it could be, and that it sorely needed investment and expertise from outside. This was a strategic worry in Mexico and also north of the border. Mexico's oil was expected to become increasingly important for the United States as Washington attempted to replace politically volatile sources of oil in the Persian Gulf with more reliable sources. Volatility in our own backyard would be especially unwelcome.

The broader consequences for Mexico of entering an agreement like NAFTA were apparent to some of the country's leading intellectuals. Octavio Paz had openly lobbied for NAFTA's passage even though he appeared slavish to the government by doing so. "The creation of a great continental market would be the first step toward the founding of a community of American nations," he wrote in an op-ed page article in *The New York Times* just before the U.S. Congress voted on the pact in 1993. "NAFTA looks like the first step in a grand design. Its goal, therefore, is historical, transcending economics and politics. It is a reply to the terrible challenge of our historical moment."[2] He was not suggesting that economic measures, no matter how sweeping, could in themselves transform Mexico. But before he died in 1998, he described NAFTA as the opening gambit in a complex game in which the past was pitted against the future. He believed, as did many others, that the transparency and openness the global market required would spill over into society and force the ruling party to respond to the Mexican people's intensifying demands for democracy.

Some of those responses were already on the horizon in 1999. That summer the PRI conducted its first-ever primary to select its candidate for the presidential elections in 2000. In theory, this ended the long tradition of one president personally naming his successor, as Zedillo, the accidental president, had promised after his own autocratic selection by Salinas. However, the results of the primary reflected what probably would have happened had Zedillo thrown reform promises to the wind and continued with the practice of the *dedazo*. Voters had no requirement to register with a party; the primary was open to any Mexican, a recognition of the PRI's almost universal hold on Mexico. The only requirement was imposed on candidates, who had to have previously held public office. That prerequisite was in response to a change the party itself had demanded after Zedillo—who had never run for office—replaced Luis Donaldo Colosio. No one doubted that Zedillo's preferred candidate was Francisco Labastida, a bland former governor of the state of Sinaloa named by Zedillo to the important post of minister of the government and of internal security, traditionally considered a PRI stepping-stone to the presidency.

The primary may not have marked the end of Mexico's "perfect dictatorship," but the rules had clearly changed. By exposing its selection process so completely, the PRI had risked internal division and a loss of control. Not everyone in the party was willing to follow the script, and one renegade PRI governor, Roberto Madrazo of Tabasco, spent so much money on American-style television advertising that he seriously jeopardized the party's carefully orchestrated demonstration of its willingness to reform itself. In the end, Labastida became the PRI's presidential candidate, just as he probably would have under the old system. After opposition parties failed to join forces against him, Labastida became the overwhelming favorite to continue the PRI's durable record of holding onto power longer than any other party in the world. Many death notices for the PRI had been printed in the past, but they all proved to be premature. The question was not "Will the PRI survive?" but "What will the PRI become?" Mexico was being catapulted toward real democracy by forces that in other countries had taken a century. The 1999 primary election signaled that Mexicans had acquired some of the mechanisms needed to dismantle the PRI, if that was what they truly desired. But this first primary suggested that Mexicans themselves were not certain what they wanted.

"We Mexicans have a history of looking for a big man, a domineering figure, to lead us. It's bred in the bones," a friend, Aida Lambuth, once told me while I was visiting Mexico. "It goes back to the Aztecs and their emperors, who had power over everything, to the *encomienda* system established by the conquistadores, to Porfirio Díaz, and now to the PRI. We've always had the thought that the big man is going to take care of us." She admitted that she came to see her society in a different light after she married an American—John—who is both enchanted with and repulsed by Mexico. Aida's love for her homeland had not diminished, but she saw its defects more clearly. "We don't have a habit of working together, not at all," Aida said. She was reminded of this every time she walked along the Paseo de la Reforma in downtown Mexico City. "Count the stands along the sidewalk and see what they're selling. If there are ten stands in one block, all ten are selling the same silly things—candy, gum, cheap magazines. All the people are trying to get their own little piece of the same market, without worrying about anyone else." Driving through the wealthy Mexico City of Techamachalco, she saw the same pattern. "The outsides of the buildings are covered with cables because every person has his own television antenna instead of joining up and getting one common unit. And nobody ever pays the condo maintenance fees, even though everyone is supposed to, because the people are afraid the money will only be stolen."

The kind of thinking Aida described is rooted in the years when the only goal of state intervention in the economy was to create jobs. Ten small candy stands or ten plastics factories created ten times as many jobs as one of each, and it didn't matter how productive they were, because competition was not allowed past the border. That world was changing fast. When I arrived in Mexico, it was not uncommon to hear a radio advertisement sing a product's praises by claiming it had *calidad de exportación,* export quality. It was an open admission that Mexico accepted mediocrity, and a cue to consumers that other countries had higher expectations. As long as there was no easy alternative, Mexicans were willing to tolerate the inequity. For example, in 1993, even buying something as simple as a box of Cheerios or a jar of raspberry jam in Mexico City required going to a small and very expensive chain of stores called Super Americano, so most people learned to live with the less attractive Mexican alternatives available at every other store. Once NAFTA paved the way for Wal-Mart, Kmart, and J.C. Penney, that tolerance quickly began to dissipate. There was little difference in price between some Mexican products and similar products from the United States or Canada. At least in major cities, Mexicans started to demand *calidad de exportación* in everything. With grocery store shelves in Mexico City, Monterrey, Ciudad Juárez, and Tijuana filling with imported goods, Mexican retailers and manufacturers realized they had to become competitive. These concepts had not yet made their way down to the small towns and pueblos across Mexico, but everything indicated that it was only a matter of time before they did.

Hand in hand with those expectations for a more competitive economy came expectations for a more open and democratic society. And change was apparent. When the deadly earthquake shook Mexico City in 1985, only a handful of civic groups existed. The government's stubborn refusal to accept help from outside, combined with its failure to provide adequate assistance to the hundreds of thousands of people in need, gave birth to an entire generation of citizen leaders and organizations. Many of those people carried the banners of the prodemocracy movement in the 1990s, and by the time the Zedillo administration ended, thousands of nongovernmental agencies were providing a myriad of services as well as acting as watchdog over all levels of government. By 1997, the mayor of Mexico City, the second most powerful government figure in Mexico after the president, was no longer appointed by the president but was elected directly by voters. The first elected mayor was Cuauhtémoc Cárdenas, but he didn't stay long. He stepped down just over two years later to launch his third run for the presidency in the 2000 elections. (He finished a distant third.) Since the ban on reelection applies to all elected officials, voters will not be able to pass judgment on the performance of the Mexico City mayor in the voting booth, but they will be able to reward or punish the mayor's party by sticking with the opposition or switching back to the PRI.

Elected officials from the president on down began to respond to that democratic dynamic and the demands of citizens, even if at times that system of accountability functioned in a way that was less than direct.

Campesinos enmeshed in land squabbles still demonstrated in front of the National Palace with placards and drums to catch the president's attention, even though the president hadn't had an office there for over a decade. But in Los Pinos, the data from poll takers influenced presidential decisions. The international spotlight also helped illuminate Mexico's newly acquired notion of accountability. Since Mexico relied so heavily on the international community, rising expectations from outside Mexico's borders forced Mexico's government to be less autocratic and more responsive to the congress and the will of the people.

But the old system that developed after the revolution was as deeply rooted as the wild corn that grows in undisturbed fields and culverts across the Valley of Mexico. Those who had profited from that system were not willing to give up power without a fight, and that tension produced a level of uncertainty that made the United States jittery. President Salinas, in a letter sent to Mexico from exile, attributed a great deal of the violence of 1994 to the intractability of the PRI's old guard, the dinosaurs who felt betrayed by the selection of another young, American-trained, economy-minded reformer. They had viewed Colosio as being too much like Salinas, and too committed to at least giving the appearance of modernizing Mexico. The old guard believed that the compact under which the spoils of the revolution had been divided meant that after twelve years of neoliberal reformers under de la Madrid and Salinas, it was their turn to occupy Los Pinos.

Mexico's demand for democracy was only one time bomb with the potential to undercut the ends of America. Countries become most unstable not when a dictator has complete control but when slight reforms are allowed, whetting the appetite for more. Many Mexicans who believed the difficult political reforms of 1994 and 1995 would end official corruption were disappointed, and their disappointment was in danger of hardening into cynicism. Petty corruption was a plague, infecting everything, from the municipal offices where my neighbors got their driver's licenses to the highest levels of law enforcement, the courts, and the army. But the specter of drug trafficking cast the darkest shadow of all. The mantle of corruption that supported the drug trade seemed to become only more insidious as prosecutors cracked down on the ring leaders. The 1997 arrest on drug charges of General Jesús Gutiérrez Rebollo, a Mexican officer President Zedillo had placed in charge of Mexico's antidrug war, seemed to make a joke of the entire antidrug effort. Even the increased border traffic that the NAFTA lobby was so proud of became tainted. Overwhelmed customs inspectors grew increasingly frustrated as the cartels discovered ways to hide illegal shipments in the long lines of transports crossing the border. The yearly ritual of certification, by which Washington passed judgment on the antidrug efforts of Mexico and other nations, became an irritant on both sides.

The escalating drug problem also led the United States and Mexico to try to cooperate more fully in certain areas. The two governments shared information that led to the arrest in Mexico in 1996 of Juan García Abrego, leader of the powerful Gulf drug cartel. He was tried in the United States and convicted of money laundering and running a drug trafficking ring that had smuggled more than 220,000 pounds of cocaine into the United States over sixteen years. The United States also continued to provide resources, including helicopters, to help Mexico fight the drug trade that pumped billions of dollars into the economy. But drugs remained one of the most damaging issues in the relationship between the United States and Mexico. Washington blamed Mexico for not doing enough, and Mexican officials constantly pushed the United States to recognize that American demand for cocaine drove the market. Some officials saw an even more disturbing problem. When the head of the U.S. Drug Enforcement Agency left office after five years of dealing with Mexico, he admitted his great frustration at the way Washington had treated the southern border. Thomas Constantine said his warnings had often been ignored and his efforts thwarted because the administration seemed to have more important objectives than fighting drugs. Constantine's comments supported the view expressed by some critics that foreign policy toward Mexico was shaped in the Treasury Department, not the Department of State. Constantine told Tim Golden of *The New York Times* that the clear priority of American officials was trade and the economy, not fighting drugs and official corruption. "The idea was, if you said those things publicly, if you release documents, you will just aggravate the situation," Constantine said. "We were not adequately protecting the citizens of the United States."[3]

As the twentieth century came to an end, the poorest, most despairing parts of Mexico continued to fight the same battles that had ignited the century's first great revolution in 1910. Violent groups in Chiapas, Guerrero, and other parts of the country were not linked militarily, but they shared the same moral vision of Mexico and its future. They always masked themselves, not so much to hide from authorities as to encourage all Mexicans to identify with them. Their goal was not to create some enlightened utopia but to return to the same rural land of small farms and big families that Emiliano Zapata had promised when the century was young. Zapata's revolution was still ongoing because, in fact, its goal remained as unreachable as yesterday itself. The conflicts were reflections of Mexico's geography, its place on the border between north and south, between Latin America and North America, between Mexico's past and its future. Octavio Paz was certain that the northerly route would make Mexico the first nation in the Western Hemisphere to leave the third world and enter the first, but our shared history made that a difficult route to take. Paz said so even though he knew he would be criticized for supporting Mexico's modernization, and for encouraging the ancient land to turns its back on Latin America by taking a place at the North American table.

Paz's dilemma was understandable, but he believed that looking northward was the only way for Mexico finally to realize the magnificent opportunity the new world offered. He believed that the absolute order the Spanish had imposed, the rigid system of racial castes and economic classes that had divided Mexican society, the limitations that reserved most opportunities for only the privileged few, would finally be lifted if Mexico became more like the north. In Paz's view, Mexico no longer needed to be only majesty and misery. Instead, the former Marxist foresaw the emergence of the same power that had long driven Canada and the United States—a middle class whose demands for transparency, honesty, and democracy would transform Mexico. Paz had undergone a similar transformation himself. By the end of his life, he held solid bourgeois credentials and a capitalist's bent. The last time I called him at his comfortable apartment in downtown Mexico City, he refused to cooperate in an interview with *The Times* unless he was paid for it. The interview was cancelled. His personal finances notwithstanding, Paz believed that the rich have no need of democracy, and the poor didn't have the tools to make it work. But a substantial working class would demand services and responsible government. That was the missing ingredient in Mexico's long-delayed transformation to democracy.

A cultural revolution seemed to be what Mexico's integration into North America would bring—not some return to Zapata's romantic past but a leap forward into an independent and democratic future. A redivision of classes, a lessening of suspicions, greater access to government, and more effective civil action all would be part of the world Mexico would inhabit some day. The consequences of that transformation for the United States would be substantial, because every one of the steps promised to be messy. Each carried risk because Mexico's past exerts such a magnetic pull on society. The factionalism that divided Mexico so often in the past could return at any time, inflamed by the new economy and modern technology. Already there were lines separating the Americanized north from the Indian south, the rapidly advancing cities from the towns still lacking potable water, the homes wired for the Internet from the pueblos where a single phone is the community's only link to the outside world.

✳

What Canadians feared most was not what continental integration might bring but what it would take away. That's why there was more than a little irony in the decision by the Canadian National Railroad—the pride of Canada—to use the NAFTA forum in Montreal to promote itself as the first North American railroad. The company handed out a lavish annual report that outlined CN's recent merger with the Illinois Central Railroad. The new CN also had entered a marketing alliance with the Kansas City Southern Railway, a partner in the consortium that took over Mexico's most important privatized rail line, which meant it could offer rail service across the continent.

CN officials said it was the growth of north-south trade that prompted the expansion, and everyone at the conference knew it was Canadian nationalism that would feel the greatest impact. In nineteenth-century Canada, building a ribbon of steel stretching from the east to the distant and reluctant west had been nothing less than a way of delineating the nation itself. Canada's history may seem thin, but its geography is rich and varied, and the need to cross great distances has challenged the building of a national identity since Lord Frontenac took his aides-de-camp in birchbark canoes to Lake Ontario to open up the fur trade. Canada's tradition of using enterprise to serve sovereignty was solidified during the early days of the railroads. The most profitable lines would surely have run from north to south and across the border. The coast-to-coast line crossed areas so vast and empty that the government had to give $25 million in cash subsidies and 25 million acres of land to investors of the Canadian Pacific Railroad to complete the project. But the nation builders determined that east-west would define Canada forever afterward, and keep the United States on the other side of the tracks.

After the first railroad was completed, the CPR company built lavish resort hotels to entice visitors to ride the lines. The railroad let artists travel free so they might be inspired to paint the splendors of the new open country. The dramatic landscapes would then pique the interest of paying customers who would want to see the country themselves. Even though the railroad struggled, the government encouraged other east-west lines to be built. In the 1920s, Ottawa assembled several money-losing railroads and formed the Canadian National, which became known as "the government railroad." The transcontinental layout of the railways thus was inscribed as a central metaphor for Canada and a way of justifying government intervention in other areas, including broad-casting, grain sales, and health care, where geography and limited popu-lation prevented the formation of normal markets.

Mexico's railroads also had been used to forge the nation's identity, but in a way that defined two contrasting faces of Mexico. Most of the rail lines had been built by the dictator Porfirio Díaz during the many years he tried to push Mexico into the modern world. Years after they were laid, those same tracks conveyed the armies of Pancho Villa and the northern generals who seized power after the dictator was forced to leave Mexico. Eventually, the railroads were nationalized and through mismanagement and a lack of resources were run into the ground. Fares were kept low to appease the poor. As time went on, only the poor were willing to sit in filthy railroad cars with cracked windows and holes in the floor. Once I traveled the 150 miles from Coatzacoalcos, Tabasco, to Salina Cruz, Oaxaca, on the single-track line across the steamy Isthmus of Tehuantepec that Díaz had once believed would become a viable al-ternative to the Panama Canal. The decrepit railroad cars rumbled slowly past impoverished villages and abandoned factories. The entire railway right-of-way was a broken dream covered in a hopeless tangle of jungle vine and rot. On several rail sidings, poor Mexicans had pirated even older railcars and converted them into crude but serviceable apart-ments. In stark contrast to the surrounding poverty, some used stolen electricity to power bootleg satellite television dishes attached to that railroad of lost hope. President Salinas tried to privatize the railroads in the 1990s, selling most to Mexican consortiums with American partners. Bombardier of Montreal bought the Ciudad Sahagún assembly complex where the company built subway cars and locomotives for the Burling-ton Northern Santa Fe Railway, using parts that had been manufactured in the United States and Canada. The massive locomotives were the first American train engines ever to be built outside the United States.

These steel symbols of sovereignty on the American continent were the backbone of Canadian and Mexican resistance to American hegemony. But in 1999, the president of CN, Paul Tellier, crowed that his new railroad would roll north and south almost without regard for the borders. Tellier, a pragmatic former civil servant who had studied philosophy, proudly declared that he only wished he had been able to make the merger happen sooner. No one at the conference knew it then, but Tellier wasn't finished with his continental dream. Not long after the Montreal conference, he announced a $28 billion bid to purchase Burlington Northern, the largest freight railroad in the United States, and add it to the North American network he was assembling. Although CN was initiating the merger, many Canadians believed that Burlington Northern would become the dominant partner and eventually push out the Canadians. Canadian columnist Peter C. Newman called the merger "the last spike in the Canadian dream," and predicted it would lead to the unraveling of Canada that John A. MacDonald had feared. In response, Tellier became defensive. "This is not the Americanization of CN—this is transforming CN into a North American company while retaining a very strong Canadian identity," he told reporters. He refused to shed tears for Canada. "I have no time for nationalists who think they can draw a gate around this country," he said.[4] But before it could ever be implemented, the planned merger between CN and Burlington Northern to create the largest railroad North America had ever seen was derailed—not by Canadian nationalists but by Washington regulators and skeptical investors on Wall Street.

For Canada, continental integration has proved to be a way to crack through the veneer of conservatism that has characterized the country for so long. Although Newman and other hard-liners consider Canada's sovereignty to be under attack, in fact Canada's system of social values was being challenged by the reality of the new continental age. "Peace, order, and good government," by now achieved, were no longer enough. Increasingly, the middle class demanded more, and it was obvious that they, like Tellier, were impatient for change. A lack of available beds and medical equipment meant waiting times for cancer treatments in Ontario sometimes exceeded the four-week maximum that doctors consider safe. Frustrated Canadians increasingly used their own money to pay for operations in the United States, while for-profit diagnostic clinics opened to offer quicker alternatives to the public health care system for those who could afford to pay. Critics saw the clinics as the first signs of an American-style competitive health care system and roundly attacked them. Yet they became popular enough to expand.

Canadians were demanding more from their government than the one-size-fits-all medicare system that for a generation had defined what it meant to be Canadian. The universal health care system began in the west and underscored the dichotomy between the westerners' fierce sense of individuality and the socialist-style comfort they sought in co-operative arrangements such as the Canadian Wheat Board. By attempting to bring private providers into the system, Alberta, the most prosperous and most American-like province in the west, showed that it essentially wanted what Andy McMechan, the jailed grain grower from Manitoba, wanted but that parts of the Canadian system had largely prohibited. Canada still cut down the tallest poppy, but in the west there was more tolerance for individual rights (provided they were not too liberal), even if such accommodation was seen as "too American." The right-leaning Reform Party, which had been founded in the west, promoted a solution for the Quebec question that was attacked as being too American and thus contradictory to Canadian history. Reform wanted more powers transferred from the federal government to Quebec and to all the provinces, so that all could be treated equally. The idea was rejected, in part because Quebec was and probably will always be unwilling to give up its position as first among equals. Canada already is considered one of the world's most decentralized nations. The federal government is responsible for foreign affairs, criminal law, and the postal service but not much else. Critics said that making the provinces any stronger would only make the federal union weaker.

It was disturbing to find that in Ottawa, Toronto, Montreal, Vancouver, and every other Canadian city I visited, Canada seemed always to be cowering before its future, a future that the majority of Canadians and their best writers and thinkers saw darkly. They feared either disembowelment by Quebec or economic and political annexation by the United States. A rare few dared suggest that tensions in Canada could be an asset, a source of creativity like the system of checks and balances in the United States. But most Canadians I met seemed to be worn down by the Thirty Years' War of defining Quebec's place in Canada. It was an intractable problem, no easier to solve than the lingering resentment of race relations in the United States, to which I often heard it compared.

One of the most telling features of Canadian character is a wistful detachment that Americans lost long ago and that Mexicans never had. It comes from being close to momentous events, but not part of them, of being members of a championship team who rarely get to play more than a few minutes in the big game. Canada's habit is to define itself by what it did not choose and what it did not become. Only in brief moments of self-confidence has it been different. One such moment came at the turn of the twentieth century when prime minister Sir Wilfrid Laurier envisioned a Canada not intimidated by its fate or fortune, a Canada that would not be kept on the sidelines. "The nineteenth century was that of the United States," he said in a speech in 1904 that was supposed to set a tone for Canada's next century. "I think the twentieth century shall be filled by Canada." He envisioned a prosperous, proud land, whose wild bounty would sustain a population of 100 million people and five transcontinental railroads—a global power to be reckoned with.

What Canada became was far different. "The country lost its nerve during the Great Depression," wrote Pierre Berton, a Canadian author who single-handedly fills the Canadiana section of some bookstores north of the border. He had been asked to assess Canadian culture in a piece commissioned by the Chapters bookstore chain a few months before the twentieth century came to an end. Berton called Canada "a cultural desert," and he attacked the joyless leaders whose small ambitions crippled Canada when it could have grown far stronger. "It has taken the better part of a century for us to learn from history," Berton wrote. "The nation is bound together by its creative artists, and not by parallel lines of rusting steel."

Although Berton is perhaps Canada's most widely read author, Chapters—a Canadian company that has benefited from government restrictions impeding the access of American book retailers to the Canadian market—rejected his column on "Canada's century." The company felt it was too negative. *The Globe and Mail* of Toronto published it anyway under the headline "Canada's Century? Not!"[5]

To most Americans, the possible breakup of Canada is almost incomprehensible. We tend to dismiss Quebec separatists and to see the rest of the country in a far more unified way than Canadians see themselves. Americans may not be clear about the politics of Quebec separation, but they presume that people as reasonable as Canadians can resolve their differences, no matter how deeply rooted the cause that pushes them apart. It is difficult for most Americans to understand Canada's obsession with questioning its right to exist. And they are baffled by the idea that a prosperous, stable democracy—and a people so much like us—could be undone because it couldn't resolve a family feud.

Sometimes I think too much is expected of Canada because it is not recognized for what it is—a comparatively young nation. Even if the quasi-colonial status that came with confederation in 1867 is taken as Canada's starting point, it is younger by almost 200 years than the Hudson Bay Company. The country's population is the size of California's, but the people are spread out over as vast and inhospitable a quadrant of the globe as exists anywhere. Canada has proved itself willing to undergo the extraordinary process of examining and validating its own existence, not something for the faint of heart. But it has done itself great damage by adhering to a single, imposed version of its history, instead of identifying and then pursuing a common national purpose. There is no question that there were two founding nations, that the great powers of Europe lived, fought, and died in North America, and that the soil of Quebec is stained with their blood. But Canadians may have it wrong when they focus on the founding nations rather than on the nation they founded, a nation where English and French have accommodated each other for more than two centuries, a nation respected around the world for its fairness and honesty, a nation that has fought many wars but is known for keeping the peace. And now a nation that has proved it is willing to stop hiding behind its borders. How different the whole unity issue would be if some Canadian leader had the political courage to say that what Canada needs most is a universal pledge of solidarity—a vow that the country will stick together no matter what crisis develops.

＊

All the nations of North America have come out from behind their borders. We have opened our markets to continental trade. And as the surging U.S. trade deficits show, Americans have become remarkably willing to buy hair dryers from Mexico, wood chips from Canada, and thousands of other continental imports that we come into contact with every day. That openness has changed the way we live. Opinion polls routinely show that a majority of Americans are blind to the rest of the world; most know little about Kosovo or Kazakhstan, Alsace or Algiers, and most don't believe anything foreign touches their lives. But even if we don't yet fully realize it, when Americans say "here," we are referring to a place that now more than ever extends far beyond the ends of America.

As our borders were transformed from fences to gateways, we struggled to keep up with the change. In many respects, the business community underwent a continental conversion far faster than politics and certainly much faster than the three societies themselves. Automobile fuses and small-screen television sets crossed borders effortlessly, but we made it tougher for our Canadian and Mexican neighbors to enter the United States. Border agents were given far-reaching powers to summarily expel people whose papers were not in order. Once expelled, those people could not return for five years or more, and there was no possibility of appeal. Congress was pushed to pass an immigration law in 1996 that required every foreigner to show some identification. The principal aim was to catch illegal Mexican immigrants, but the law applied equally to the Canadian border, which would have been paralyzed if the law were enforced. Red-faced members of Congress admitted they had not taken Canada sufficiently into account when they voted on the law. Eventually a compromise was reached when the Immigration and Naturalization Service conceded it did not have the manpower or the equipment to enforce the law. But edginess over the porousness of U.S. borders did not dissipate. And an incident in late 1999 in which suspected terrorists were caught trying to slip across the border from Canada brought demands for tougher measures, and warnings that our borders had become welcome mats for terrorists and criminals intent on hurting the United States.

Although there were no misconceptions about our basic geography as there were 500 years ago, we Americans sometimes still acted as if the rest of the world that begins where American ends was terra incognita, a scary place best avoided. When NAFTA overcame feverish opposition and was implemented in 1994, the United States turned an important corner. To fulfill its role as a world leader in the twenty-first century, the United States would have to listen to voices beyond its borders. An agreement with Canada and especially with Mexico that brought these reluctant partners so close together showed we were in the mood to listen, especially here, where it mattered most to the lives of every American.

In the years after 1993, the rest of North America and much of the world came to resemble the American realm more closely. And yet the

United States was criticized almost everywhere, including on the American continent. It was a contradictory dynamic: Even as nations fell increasingly under the spell of the United States, we Americans found ourselves more resented, and more hated, than ever. Our industry was both welcomed and denounced, our culture openly envied and violently rejected, our friendship sought, bought, and turned away. Brian Mulroney was one of the few politicians willing to look past that barrage of criticism and come up with a clear idea of how it would all turn out, even if most Americans and Mexicans did not hear it, and almost no Canadians would listen. He told me he did not fret at all about Canada or Mexico falling prey to an American *Anschluss*. "There won't be a union, and there will be no surrender of sovereignty," he told me during an interview in March 1999, rejecting suggestions that the border along the forty-ninth parallel would be erased. Mulroney thought that fifty years hence it might be possible to identify 1994 as the beginning of a new North America. "Our economies will, in the fullness of time, resemble one another more, but we'll also complement one another to a much greater extent," he said, expressing a most un-Canadian confidence in his country's destiny. And yet, he said, differences will surely remain. "You'll never change Canada, and you'll never change Mexico, not in the millennium ahead. Canadians are Canadians forever." He saw ahead more shared objectives, a greater interchange of ideas, and cooperative efforts in everything from medical research to space exploration. "The national borders will be there, but in point of fact we will float over them as we go about building this architecture of a new North America."

I had no way of knowing it then, but shortly I would be thrust into a situation that would put that new architecture, and me, to the test.

✳

About six weeks after the Montreal conference ended, I left Canada and moved back to the United States. My departure was a bit abrupt because of a nasty dispute over an arcane point of tax law between *The New York Times* and Revenue Canada, Canada's IRS. The dispute had nothing to do with journalism or diplomacy but everything to do with the unique relationship between the United States and Canada. *The Times* believed it was being charged far too much in taxes, and Canadian officials thought the paper was throwing around its weight. The editors decided to close the Canada bureau and told my successor, Jim Brooke, who had been Denver correspondent for *The Times,* to cover Canada from our Denver office, even though Denver is about 100 miles closer to the Mexican border than it is to Canada. When the dispute became public, Ottawa felt cornered and could not back down without appearing to have been intimidated by the newspaper's threat to close the bureau. Our tax squabble also got caught up in a broader debate about Canada's taxes, which opposition leaders constantly attacked for being too high. Prime Minister Chrétien, speaking at a Liberal Party meeting in Quebec, told everyone who thought Canada's taxes were too high to leave. "There's nothing forcing you to stay here," Chrétien said. "That's globalization."6 Chrétien's comments weren't directed at us, but they could have been. He expressed what was a fairly common sentiment. Many friends and some Canadians I had never met called me to express their dismay over *The Times*'s decision to leave. Since they all had to bear Canada's tax burden, none had any sympathy for the newspaper's complaint.

We returned to New Jersey, to the house we had kept during all our time away so that the kids would always have a sense of home, although by this time the meaning of home itself had changed. After six years of trying to understand the ends of America, I came back knowing how these three nations had come to be, and with a clear sense of what it meant to be an American. I had lived among Mexicans as they haphazardly went about the business of building an imperfect democracy, and I had lived with Canadians who seemed hell-bent on dismantling their nation. Back home I wanted to know what my country was made of.

Reinstalled in the house where we had raised our children, I found continental America to be a smaller place, but an infinitely more diverse and interesting place, more like Europe, where borders serve to outline countries but not isolate them. I found that same European spark of knowing there are different places and people all around you. I knew the feeling of carrying currency from all three countries in my wallet, along with a driver's license from each. Our monthly credit card statement included conversions of pesos and loonies into dollars, and our telephone bills listed calls all across the American continent.

Our children also brought back an expansive sense of America, without necessarily surrendering their national identity. One lazy summer afternoon, I drifted down a slow and easy river in a canoe with my younger son Andrés. I was in the back paddling and he was up front. He enjoyed whistling while he was out on the water. In between baiting lines and casting for smallmouth bass, I heard him whistle the national anthems of all three countries, just as naturally as if they were top-40 songs. He and his brother and sister had become fluent in Spanish and more than competent in French. Their grasp on American history was a continental one, and though they at times fell short on details of American history, they usually saw things in a more connected and continental way than their classmates. I can't tell what this familiarity will mean for them in the end. But I got a hint one Saturday when Laura Felice and I went to a football game at her new high school in Montclair. We stood while the band played the national anthem, and for the first time since she was nine, it was our national anthem. When it ended she turned to me and said, "I just don't feel like an American"—she meant at least not like everybody else in the stands that afternoon. Her home was not just a four-square colonial with blue shutters in northern New Jersey, close enough to Manhattan to see the lights of the World Trade Center from the corner. It was also a stone house on a shady street near the ravine in Toronto. And a rambling ranch squeezed between a mushroom factory and the Canada-Mexico School on a chaotic side street high above the valley of Mexico. Her friends are a block away and a thousand miles away. Her e-mail messages come to her in Spanish and in English, and a few even have some French in them.

In the time we were away, the continent had indeed grown smaller. The local bagel shop had been taken over by a Mexican family, which Miriam discovered one day when she ordered a lightly toasted sesame bagel as she used to before we left. But the counter man stared blankly, and Miriam was surprised to hear a supervisor explain the term "lightly toasted" to him in Spanish. The Irish chimney sweep who had taken care of our fireplace ten years before showed up with a Spanish-speaking helper who only understood "up," "down," and "bring in the bucket" in English. The dentist we had gone to before moved, and when we selected someone else, he turned out to be a young Canadian from Toronto. We needed something to drive, so we decided that since we were back in the states, we should have American cars. We ended up leasing two, both made by Chrysler. But we watched America's borders melt away when we compared the stickers and found out that one had been assembled in Windsor, Ontario, and the other in Chrysler's plant in Toluca, outside Mexico City.

North America seemed to have come together in a remarkable way while we had been outside the United States. I recalled a long interview I had with Lloyd Axworthy at CBC headquarters in Toronto and how he told me that the three nations of North America no longer had the luxury of dealing with their problems on an ad hoc basis, each one inventing the wheel whenever something went wrong. Our problems hadn't changed, but the approaches to solving them had because we shared so many of the same challenges. Potable water was still a problem in the American west and a touchy subject for Canadian nationalists who didn't want it exported. But now an American entrepreneur had filed a NAFTA complaint against Canadians claiming that his legally binding contract to export water from British Columbia had been voided by provincial obstructionism. The disposal of toxic wastes continued to pose a grave danger, but now an American business was filing NAFTA complaints because Mexico's less than impartial application of its own environmental laws had resulted in the virtual expropriation of the American company's multimillion-dollar investment in Mexico. And the Loewen Group, a big Canadian funeral home operator, tried to avoid bankruptcy by claiming before a NAFTA tribunal that the state of Mississippi had violated the company's rights as a foreign investor in the United States when a jury had fined Loewen $500 million in punitive damages for attempting to drive a local funeral parlor out of business. "I really do think we can talk a common language," Axworthy said. As Canada's foreign minister, he had helped arrange several meetings with his counterparts in the United States and Mexico strictly to spend time examining continental issues. "There is something distinctive about being North American," he said. "There are differences as well, but our roots are very much the same."

I have learned just how similar they are. Starting at roughly the same time, from roughly the same beginnings, on the same American continent, the United States, Mexico, and Canada became three separate and distinct nations because they found different solutions to their problem of imposing order on the wild, new land. The absolutist imprint of the Spanish crown is stamped on Mexico's highly centralized government just as clearly as divided government gives America its creative tension and the constitutional monarchy reflects the ambiguity within Canada's character. In the new American continent, it is the solutions that will draw us together because they will be shared. I have met Mexican scholars who study Canada, Canadian scholars who study Mexico, and American scholars who study both. Increasingly, there are trinational teams undertaking continental polling, and multilingual business consulting firms equally comfortable on any side of America's two borders. The big corporations have North American divisions in which managers are expected to speak Spanish and French as well as English.

This is just the lopsided beginning. What we have tended to see as economic integration Mexicans and Canadians view as aggressive American market penetration and merely a prelude to true continental commerce. "The key test will come," Gabriel Guerra told me before I left Toronto to return to the United States and he left Toronto for Mexico City, "when it's not just Wal-Marts in Mexico and Canada but when you can shop in a Canadian Tire store in Texas and a Comercial Mexicana department store in Maine."

When we entered our old house in Montclair, we realized that after six years, we had come full circle. No matter how we tried to rearrange the furniture, some things slipped right back into the places and patterns they had before we left. We put Laura Felice's bed in the same room that was hers before; the living room sofa wouldn't fit anyplace but where it had been before we left. From outward appearances, we were picking up where we were before we had left here. It was "here" that had changed for us. Now we looked beyond the edges of the weather maps to see what was happening above Lake Ontario. We stopped to read the small news reports about tremors in Mexico. Canada no longer was only Mounties and hockey. Canada had become Chateau Lake Louise on a frigid February afternoon, glacial green ice under blue skies that opened to all the north. It is the harbor at Halifax knitted with white sails and the amber hue of wooden hulls. It is the Bach cello suites and a meticulously cultivated corner of Toronto where music grows in a garden. But we also knew enough to realize that Canada is an Innu teenager so beaten by the emptiness of the Labrador icescape that he would stick his head in a plastic bag of gasoline. It is Hong Kong businessmen who bought their Canadian citizenship. And it is the sarcasm that separatists drip all over the word "Canada."

Neither language nor culture kept us distant from Mexico. Mexico was no longer merely Cancún or a small shop in Juárez. The Mexico we know is the Mexico of Sundays in spring when jacaranda trees shower the streets with vivid purple blossoms. It is the Mexico of steamy coffee in Veracruz, and the exquisite black pottery of Oaxaca. It is a Boy Scout hike through the smooth, cold water of an ancient aqueduct, and lemons the size of grapefruit and sweet as lemonade. But we will never forget that Mexico is also a six-year-old Indian boy staggering to our car window at one in the morning too tired to do the silly trick he'd performed all day for money. It is a decaying bouquet beneath the sad statue of Luis Donaldo Colosio in Chapultepec Park. It is the empty space where the Boy Scouts' trail sign that Aahren erected in the Ajusco park used to stand before it was ripped out and probably sold for scrap.

And after living with our neighbors, we were able to see the United States more the way our neighbors and allies have come to see us. America's racial tensions seemed to crackle all around us, every shifted eye or bumped shoulder laden with awful potential. Our commercial exploitation of technology—from the avalanche of new and useless products in the stores to the 906 channels on our local cable television system—seemed an embarrassing excess and a gluttonous waste of talent. President Clinton's peccadilloes made us wince.

Our journey beyond the ends of America had been a voyage of discovery. What we found was a new world, the next new world. But more important, it was a new way of looking at the world we thought we had known before. Our friends joked that we had become a NAFTA family, and in a sense we had indeed freely traded our old identities for new ones based on a different view of the American continent. We knew better than most that the trade agreement alone had not changed our three parallel nations; no single commercial pact ever could have done that. But we had come to understand how much trade and change had been a part of our history. The flimsy outposts that became Mexico, Canada, and the United States were conceived of initially as commercial ports, and the exchange of goods across the oceans and over our borders has shaped the mix of nations on this continent ever since.

✳

A few days after the moving truck unloaded our arctic carvings and Aztec calendars in New Jersey, we drove out to the American heartland to drop off Aahren at the University of Notre Dame. While I was in the Balkans earlier that year, he had surprised me with an e-mail message saying he had been accepted to Notre Dame. I was delighted, and not a little surprised. We had no connection to the school, or to Indiana, and had not even visited there during the hectic weeks of campus visits the previous summer. But as soon as his acceptance letter arrived, he and Miriam drove from Toronto to Detroit, where they stayed with friends we had known in Mexico, and then pushed on to South Bend. One look around was enough for him. After spending a good part of his young life on the ends of America, Aahren decided the American heartland was the place he wanted to come home to.

Orientation weekend at Notre Dame was an adjustment for us too after the previous six years, a reorientation to pancake houses and interstate highways and the incredible richness and diversity of America. When we stopped for something to eat at "Truckland" in eastern Ohio, we were seated next to an Amish family that had been driven to the truck stop by a non-Amish friend for the Thursday night all-you-care-to-eat Italian buffet. On the serene Notre Dame campus, we walked with Aahren beneath the golden dome, on land that had once been claimed by France, then England, and finally the shaky new United States. As we watched the fading day paint the sky over the twin lakes of St. Mary and St. Joseph with scarlet and gold, it was evident just how much we had been embraced by America's opportunity. A Cuban immigrant and the son of a dockworker had managed to bring their firstborn to Notre Dame. It was an improbable journey made all the more so by what we had experienced over the previous six years. No society believes more strongly than ours in the power of education to transform lives. Beyond the ends of America, traveling the distance from Hoboken and Havana to the University of Notre Dame would be considered a remarkable occurrence, undertaken by a few, never attempted or expected by most others. Here, it is part of a quintessential American tale.

Miriam and I drove back from Indiana in the Chrysler that had been assembled in Mexico, thinking how very fortunate we were to be Americans. We drove into the night until the only fellow travelers we had were the overnight truckers speeding along I-80 through the mountains of Pennsylvania, America's onetime frontier. Eventually, even they pulled over into rest areas, and we were alone, hurtling through the night, across the oldest part of the America we felt we were just beginning to understand fully. The lesson of it all was that the only borders that stand for anything are the ones we erect ourselves and, in so doing, imbue with authority either to keep out what we don't want or to hold in what we are desperate to contain. They are the boundaries of fear, and the edge of ignorance. They are real and will continue to be so as long as we focus on our differences rather than recognize all that we share.

For what little was left of that wondrous night, we slept in our home for the first time in over six years. Early the next morning, the movers returned to help unpack the hundreds of boxes and put things into some order. One of them had the Notre Dame leprechaun tattooed on his shin, and when Aahren called at 10:30, the man was excited to know the call was coming from South Bend. Aahren said he was feeling achy and had gone to the infirmary. The doctor thought it was first-day jitters or a flu but had done some precautionary blood tests. Aahren said the doctor would call soon with the results.

At noon Doctor James Moriarty did call, and gravely told us that something wasn't right. "We could do more tests here, but you might want Aahren home with you," he said. Notre Dame helped us fly him back immediately, and the next morning we took him to the New York University medical center on Manhattan's East Side. The doctor had reviewed the blood work from Notre Dame and did his own testing. He said there was no question about the diagnosis. Aahren's white blood cell count was being pushed out of control by a form of leukemia that usually strikes much younger children. We had to begin treatment immediately.

So on what would have been his first day of classes at Notre Dame, and our first full day at home, we were at the hospital where Aahren began a two-year regimen of chemotherapy. I felt angry and betrayed by what had happened, and since it coincided with our return to the United States, I tried to find a way to blame the air here, or the water, or something he had been exposed to years ago that had maliciously lain dormant until we came back. Or had something in Mexico or Canada been the trigger? We had covered a continent of peaks and valleys in just the hours since left Notre Dame, an expedition searching for reasons, for explanations, for some meaning that made sense of what we were going through.

There were none. Our doctors told us to stop asking because we would never know. We had more decisions to make about how and where Aahren would be treated, and with the help and advice of friends, neighbors, and colleagues at *The Times*, we brought him to Memorial Sloan Kettering Hospital and a team of specialists who had been staring down this particular disease for thirty years. Dr. Peter Steinherz assured us that although the treatment was difficult, the cure rate was high, and Aahren had a very good chance of returning to Notre Dame and getting on with his life.

In time, the disease was battered into remission. Our anger didn't subside, but we began to realize how fortunate we had been to return home when this happened. If we were still living in Mexico, we would have immediately boarded a plane for New York. And I remembered Joe Lelyeld telling me years before, as I was getting ready to take over the bureau in Toronto, that Canada's universal health care might be the best medical system in the world for somebody else's family but not for your own.

When it came down to it, we had entrusted our most precious possession—that which meant the most to us—to America. We had returned to the realm of possibility, where everyone—from the administrators at Notre Dame to the medical team at Memorial Hospital and the huge army of researchers behind them who had come up with the treatment that conquers this disease—had been touched by this same magnificent opportunity. After spending six years beyond the ends of America, we had brought Aahren back home. That miracle I had been searching for since that long-ago trip to St. Anne de Beaupré, I found right here. And we are relieved to be able to call this place our own. There could have been no clearer example of what the new American continent was going to be. Each of us will find that special place of comfort "here," that place we feel we know best. "Here" will be someplace intimate yet distant, seamless yet separate. "Here" will stem from common roots, yet it will have different trunks. It will be the place we want to be, and the place we cannot avoid. Here.

Symmetry Regained

✳

The United States is destined to have a "special relationship"
with Mexico, as clear and strong as we have with Canada.

George W. Bush, August 25, 2000

The string of extraordinary events that took place in 2000, the first full year we spent back in the United States, seemed both to affirm the mounting awareness of a North American consciousness and to bring neatly to a close the painful first years of the new American continent. The most visible and portentous manifestation of that continental conversion was the series of three almost concurrent national elections in 2000. The first was held in Mexico in July. Then, in November, both Canada and the United States elected leaders, though it was nearly the end of the year before Americans knew George W. Bush would be their next president.

The last time the electoral processes of all three nations of North America had been so finely synchronized was in 1988. The national leaders elected in that year, George H. W. Bush, Brian Mulroney, and Carlos Salinas de Gortari, shared a vision of a more integrated North America. Their awareness of the opportunities offered by working together rather than standing apart led to the signing of NAFTA. Twelve years later, the electoral calendars again coincided, and each of the three leaders selected by voters, George W. Bush, Vicente Fox Quesada, and Jean Chrétien, recognized that a strong North American identity was a vital national interest. Each made plans to strengthen and deepen relations across the continent while protecting national sovereignty. All three faced other challenges, of course, starting with the domestic divisions that had prevented them from receiving a majority of the popular vote in their countries and a clear mandate about how to govern. Bush and Fox had to work with deeply divided congresses, and Chrétien faced a parliament badly splintered along regional lines. The key words for all three men were "unite" and "compromise."

Their simultaneous start generated a certain synergy within the broad expanse of North America. Their words and actions over the course of the year harmonized the continent in a way that hadn't been possible before. United in an encompassing vision and unafraid of exploiting the advantages of the new North American relationship, the three leaders laid out plans and took initials steps that could come to be seen as a significant turning point in continental America.

Eventually, the first few days of July may very well come to be observed as a continental holiday, the communal celebration of North America's rediscovery. The Fourth of July, of course, is U.S. Independence Day; in Canada, July 1 is Canada Day, the commemoration of the founding of the Dominion of Canada. Henceforth, Mexico may be tempted to view July 2 as its independence day and the founding of democratic Mexico, because on that date in 2000, the land of Zapata had its first peaceful revolution, ending the PRI's grip on power and beginning the next stage of a true democracy with the election of Fox.

Fox's myth had already grown sufficiently to have become fairly well known across North America in 2000. A bigger-than-life rancher and business executive who once headed the Mexican division of that most American of consumer products, Coca-Cola, Fox entered Mexican politics on the side of the fiscally conservative, Catholic-indoctrinated National Action Party (PAN), the perennial runner-up during the past half century of Mexican politics. He had caught the attention of journalists and their editors early on, and no American or Canadian article about Fox failed to mention his cowboy boots, or the trucker-sized belt buckle with FOX carved into it that he constantly wore. From his earliest days in politics, Fox made clear that he was not afraid to go toe-to-toe with the PRI, and the indomitable PRI was just as clearly frightened by the combination of *pantalones* and popular appeal that Fox embodied.

Fox ran for governor of his home state of Guanajuato in 1991, but the election was marred by fraud, and Salinas appointed a substitute governor, Carlos Medina, also from the PAN. That kept Fox from governing a small state, but it didn't derail his ambitions or his party's certainty that he was the man who could defeat the PRI. An important opportunity arose when President Salinas wanted to overhaul the land redistribution provisions of Article 27, he needed the PAN's support to get the necessary two-thirds vote in Congress. PAN leaders saw a potential trade-off—PAN's support in return for a chance to remove a remnant of Mexican xenophobia that prohibited a candidate without pure Mexican heritage from running for president. That included Fox, whose grandfather was an Irish-American immigrant from Ohio and whose mother was born in Spain. An official of the highest rank in Salinas's government told me that the president reluctantly accepted that amendment in order to get his land reform passed. But he insisted that the new requirements for candidates not take effect until the elections of 2000. Having waited so long, the PAN could afford to be patient a while longer.

Even though he couldn't form an opposition alliance with Cuauhtémoc Cárdenas, the other opposition candidate, Fox overcame Francisco Labastida's early lead. His surge in popularity wasn't due to the unique appeal of his platform: Very little distinguished the positions of Fox and Labastida on economic management, social spending, and Mexico's links with the rest of North America. Fox ran a smart American-style campaign, whereas Labastida seemed stuck in the past, ignoring the political, economic, and social turmoil that had taken place since 1993. Many factors contributed to Fox's historic win, but the primary reason was that Mexicans had finally decided it was time to change. On July 2, they gave Fox the victory he, and many parts of Mexico, had sought for so long.

Traditional PRI leaders were left licking their wounds after July 2. Many blamed Zedillo, the accidental president, for losing control of the system that had served the party so well for so long. Outside the official party, Fox was hailed as a hero, the strongman that Aida Lambuth had told me Mexicans wanted to lead their country into democracy and prosperity. Few observers remembered that Mexico had been in a similar position in 1993, when Carlos Salinas was praised for having brought Mexico to the threshold of the first world. Nor did they remember that the PRI that Fox vanquished had been founded by the generals of the 1910 revolution. Fox had made so many promises during the campaign that to fulfill them would take sixty years, not the single six-year term to which he was limited by the constitution. He had style and he had charisma, but Fox also was so wrapped up in his own personality that at times he resembled the caudillos with whom Mexico has had such a long, troubling relationship. When he took the oath of office on December 1, he offended Congress, including some members of his own party, by changing the official oath and including the pledge to work "for the poor and marginalized of this country"—words not in the constitutional version of the oath he was required to recite. Although many Mexicans agreed with the sentiment, they worried about Fox's obvious comfort in doing things his way.

Even if Fox accomplished nothing else, his victory over the PRI was a historic achievement. Fox's triumph was so significant that most Mexicans, and foreign observers watching his early moves, were willing to overlook some of his more glaring inconsistencies. What he lacked in discipline, he more than made up for in courage and vision—for Mexico and for the whole of North America. With the help of President Zedillo, he managed a smooth transition that broke the thirty-year cycle of economic disasters accompanying new presidencies. During a visit to Mexico after the election, I had the chance to remind Jaime Serra about the premonition of economic disaster that he had mentioned during the Montreal conference. He admitted he had underestimated the degree to which President Zedillo would maintain economic discipline. "The markets have discipline, the Bank of Mexico has discipline, Fox has been very clear on staying the course, so I'm not as concerned as I was when I saw you in Montreal," Serra said. Clearly, Mexico had changed, and I got another small reminder of that when I met Serra in the office of his consulting firm in Mexico City. I thought the address sounded familiar, and when the cab pulled up to the front door, I realized it was the same building in the Santa Fe development where I had seen the army of Mexican laborers finishing the stone hallways and stairs with hammers in 1993. Now, in the same space, Serra was designing a website to help international corporations buy and sell under NAFTA.

During the five months between the election and Fox's inauguration, PRI officials had time to destroy or lose many records that might have implicated them in acts of corruption. But Fox made it clear he wanted to focus on the future, not the past. During visits to Washington and Ottawa, he declared that Mexico saw itself as a legitimate and full member of the North American community. "There is no doubt that NAFTA is not only a commitment for us; it is a partnership."[1] He not only supported NAFTA 100 percent but he declared it was time to deepen and strengthen the agreement so that the benefits of free trade were more equitably shared across the continent. No longer was there any quibbling about the usefulness of open borders. Fox made it clear that he believed in NAFTA as it was and as it could be. During his stopover in

Washington, he surprised Mexico's own diplomatic staff by telling President Clinton he was already looking beyond NAFTA toward the European Union, or something like it: "Really what we are proposing is an economic convergence, a holistic view of the problems and the opportunities." Fox said Mexico's goal was a "narrowing of the gap in development between Mexico and the two great nations of the United States and Canada."[2] The old shibboleths of Mexican sovereignty and anti-Americanism were swept away with one stroke. Perhaps not immediately, he said, but in forty years it would make sense for Mexico, Canada, and the United States to have fully open borders like those in Europe that allow for the free passage of people, as well as goods, from one country to the other. Perhaps it would be feasible to think of North America as a place of common interests and shared resources that could benefit all North Americans, from the Yukon to the Yucatán.

Fox also was blunt about the new reality of North America. The United States and Canada needed Mexican labor, and Mexicans needed more economic opportunity than Mexico could provide. Fox wanted Washington and Ottawa to fund a development bank that would help Mexican industry grow. In essence, he was asking that the United States and Canada take some responsibility for Mexico. The nations of North America weren't just neighbors anymore, was his underlying message. Unless Mexico prospered, the rest of the continent could not prosper: "The elections of July 2nd give us a window of opportunity to press forward a new vision of our place in the world. First and foremost, that vision is founded on a new partnership with the United States and Canada that builds on existing institutions and creates the foundation for a shared North American area of peace and prosperity."[3]

Fox's message came across loud and clear in both Washington and Ottawa. But even Mexico's friends in the capitals said it would take more than bold visions and sympathy to realize such plans. It was time to strike a new bargain with Mexico. They might have considered Fox personally honest, but critical legislators in both Canada and the United States wanted to see a real commitment from his government to fighting corruption. They heard Fox's appeal for better treatment of Mexicans who sneak across the border to the United States to find work, but they demanded that Fox do his part to curtail illegal immigration by better patrolling Mexico's side of the border. They appreciated Fox's commitment to raising the standard of living for Mexican workers, but they wanted to see Mexican labor unions organizing freely and Mexican environmental laws being enforced thoroughly. It was time, they said, for Mexico to put up or shut up. Jeff Faux, president of the Economic Policy Institute, wrote that it would take a convincing commitment from Mexico along with credible enforcement safeguards. Then, he said, "a new North American accord could have wide support in all three countries."[4]

＊

During the summer of 2000, George W. Bush also started to outline a sense of how he saw North America. He freely acknowledged that foreign affairs was not his strong point, but he said that as governor of Texas, he was quite familiar with the foreign country south of the Texas border and had visited Mexico several times. During the campaign, he said he considered Mexico a front door to all of Latin America, and although he may not have known how to pronounce the names of the leaders of Uzbekistan or Cameroon, he did consider Mexico and the rest of the Western Hemisphere to be part of "the neighborhood."

Bush promised that if elected, he would meet with Fox before either of them was inaugurated to demonstrate their shared interests and common commitment to solving problems facing both countries. He had heard Fox outline his ideas about the border, and although he saw some positive signs, Bush said the borders were there and they needed to be protected. The issue was not whether to proceed with integration, but to what degree. The vision of common interest seemed to have so captivated Bush that at one point in the campaign he mentally erased the border between the United States and Mexico. During one of the presidential debates with Al Gore, Bush combined the United States and Mexico into an ersatz unified body, albeit one no more convincing than the two-headed boy in the Cuajimalpa sideshow I had visited in Mexico years before. Bush's topic was the surging price of oil: "I brought this up recently with Vicente Fox, who's the newly elected president," Bush said. "He's a man I know from Mexico. And I talked about how best to be able to expedite the exploration of natural gas in Mexico and transport it up to the United States, so we become less dependent on foreign sources of crude oil."[5] Mexican commentators chided Bush for considering Mexico something other than a foreign source of oil, although they did not doubt he meant to import more of Mexico's prized national resource. The slip of the tongue irked some Mexicans, but generally they saw Bush as a friend whose experience on the border helped him understand their needs. "Should I become president," Bush said during the campaign, "I will look south, not as an afterthought but as a fundamental commitment of my presidency."[6]

Together, the imperfect statements of Bush and Fox carried North American identity from theory to reality, but reality rarely arrives without complications. The promised meeting between presidents-elect never took place. But soon after both were inaugurated, Bush visited Fox in Mexico—and thereafter called repeatedly for a continental energy policy that would combine the strengths and resources of all three nations. Bush had made it clear that he thought Fox was a man he could work with, and that North America was a concept he felt comfortable thinking about. Bush had predicted that the United States would be able to enter into a "special relationship" with a democratic Mexico that would be as strong as the relationship that had existed with Canada for years. "Historically, we have no closer friends and allies," Bush said. "With Canada, our partner in NATO and NAFTA, we share not just a border but a bond of goodwill. Our ties of history and heritage with Mexico are just as deep."[7]

There was no way to tell how Bush's conservative views and probusiness attitudes would influence the decisions he would have to make about relations with Mexico, Canada, or the rest of the world. He hinted that within North America, things would be different. "Differences are inevitable between us," he said, anticipating the difficulties that would undoubtedly continue to complicate the continental relationship. "But they will be differences among family, not between rivals."[8]

✳

The legal maneuvering to count ballots in Florida and complete the 2000 election in the United States took thirty-six days, the same amount of time as the entire federal campaign and election that Prime Minister Jean Chrétien had called for November 27 but that nobody else in Canada seemed to want. Chrétien was in the third year of his second five-year administration when he decided the time was right to hold another election (in parliamentary democracies like Canada, government leaders can decide to go into an election anytime before the five-year period expires). Chrétien gambled that by calling an election early, he could stave off an attack from the newly constituted Canadian Alliance party and its right-leaning leader Stockwell Day. Chrétien's intuition turned out to be on target, but the sharpest political minds in Canada doubted his wisdom right up to the time the polls closed.

I was in the control room of the CBC election-night headquarters in Ottawa when the votes were counted. The CBC had commandeered a large room on the main floor of the Canadian Parliament, a familiar place to me because it was there in 1996 that Chrétien and President Zedillo had stood side by side to denounce U.S. policy in Cuba. Although it was called the Railway Conference Room, it was dominated by a huge painting on one wall depicting the confederation meeting in Charlottetown in the 1860s. The message was clear—no railway, no nation. On election night, a bank of sixty television monitors had been arrayed below the fathers of confederation as Canadians voted in an election that would be used to confirm Canada's place in the new North America.

The brief Canadian campaign had little to do with major issues and produced few dramatic moments. Under Chrétien, the Liberals had become free trade converts and unabashed supporters of closer ties to the United States. Day, the leader of the Canadian Alliance, was a fiscal conservative with a buzz-cut and an easy smile. And he was from Alberta, the western province most aligned with American ways, from tax policy to health care. Unlike in the 1988 election in which Liberal leader John Turner had accused Brian Mulroney of selling out Canada by signing the free trade agreement, continental integration was not an issue in 2000. It was a given. The campaign was mostly about personalities and had turned particularly dirty by Canadian standards. Newspapers criticized the candidates for resorting to "U.S. style advertising."[9] At one debate, the Alliance and the Liberals traded barbs over which party was more in favor of establishing a two-tier, Americanized health care system by permitting private clinics to operate.

Chrétien won impressively, increasing the Liberal majority, destroying the Alliance's bid to win support in Ontario, and, most surprising, stealing several seats from the already staggered separatists in Quebec.[10] More than ever, the Liberals appeared to be Canada's only national party. Without effective opposition, the Liberals also were taking on the appearance of a natural ruling party, one in power far more often than not. From 1935 to 2001, the Liberal Party—whose longtime leader Pierre Trudeau once called it "the most successful political party in the history of modern democracies"[11]—had held power for all but about seventeen years. Just as Mexico was experiencing the democratic alternation of power for the first time, Canada was starting to resemble a virtual one-party state, with no change in sight.

A few days after his victory, Chrétien was in the United States golfing with President Clinton. It was a symbolic outing for two reasons: It proved how much Chrétien had overcome his earlier reluctance to be seen as being too cozy with the American president. And it tipped observers to a changing dynamic in Canada's sense of the North American balance of power. The Ministry of Foreign Affairs had tried mightily to get Chrétien to use a speech that weekend at Duke University in North Carolina to regain some of the ground Canada had lost to Mexico after Fox made his dramatic statements about North American integration in August. But Chrétien had reacted strongly against some of Fox's most radical ideas about the border and was cool to the Mexican's overall message. The reason for his resistance became clearer after the December 3, 1999, speech at Duke. In the end, one diplomat told me, Chrétien removed "the heart and a lot of the message" from the prepared text, and instead of speaking about the trilateral view of North America, the prime minister reverted to talking up the special relationship between Canada and the United States:

> The friendship between Canada and the United States is also a partnership, not only for freedom but for peace and prosperity. One that finds expression in countless ways. In the way we help each other in times of trouble. In the more than 200 million crossings of the 49th parallel that take place every year. In our championing of open markets for trade and investment around the world. And in more than one billion dollars in business that we do together—every day.

It was a defensive speech that unwittingly underscored Ottawa's preoccupation with Mexico's growing presence in the consciousness of the United States. Whereas Mulroney had originally seen Mexico as a potential ally that could correct some of the imbalance existing in North America, Ottawa increasingly looked at Mexico as a rival and a competitor—not only for American business but also for a special spot in relations with the United States. The election of George W. Bush intensified the feelings because he was clearly so comfortable with Mexico. "We have enjoyed a special relationship with the United States but we no longer have it," former foreign minister Lloyd Axworthy said. "It's gone."[12]

Axworthy made those comments at a policy conference in Ottawa where the best thinkers about Canada had assembled to highlight critical issues facing the country in the new millennium. Their meeting took place during a decisive week in North American history. It began with the Canadian elections and ended with Vicente Fox being sworn in as the first opposition president in Mexico in seventy-one years. In between, the U.S. Supreme Court got involved in determining the outcome of the wild U.S. presidential election. Two weeks later, Al Gore finally conceded and congratulated Bush on winning the tightest presidential race in American history.

The convergence of events in all three nations made it easier to think about a North American approach like the one Fox had outlined. At the policy conference, Bush's plan for a continental missile defense system revived the old conflict between security and sovereignty for Canada. Other worrisome themes, raised constantly, were the growing productivity gap between Canada and the United States and the threat posed by an economically sound Mexico that was becoming a powerful exporter and a favorite spot for corporate investment. Renée St-Jacques, director general of microeconomic policy analysis for Industry Canada, the government's commerce ministry, demonstrated the challenge clearly: Canada's share of American imports had held steady at about 20 percent during the 1990s, but Mexico's had doubled during that time, and by 1999 was about half the size of Canada's and gaining fast. Within a decade, Mexico could surpass Canada to become the largest partner of the United States. When I stopped in to talk to Gordon D. Giffin, the American ambassador in Ottawa, he was reviewing proposals for radically changing border procedures that could make the border almost seamless for both people and manufactured goods. "As trade has increased, the capacity of the border facilities has been increased incrementally, usually by adding an extra booth or another agent," said Giffin, who estimated that he spent upward of 70 percent of his time dealing with commercial issues. He said the tinkering with border procedures had gone about as far as it could go. "What we need now," he said, "is a complete rethinking of what we want our border to be."

Alain Dubuc, chief editorial writer at *La Presse* and a voice of reason in the debate over Quebec and the Canadian character. At the policy conference with Axworthy, he laid out a vision of the border as it might be. Erecting walls to keep out American influence or Mexican competition won't ever work, he said. It will be up to Canadians to find a way to exploit the advantages offered by the new market, and to use them to reinforce a new vision of themselves within today's world. He suggested a compromise like the one Montezuma had offered Cortés in the pyramid temple nearly 500 years ago. Montezuma wanted Cortés to place his holy statues alongside the Aztec idols so that both could reign together. Dubuc wants Canadians to accept a dual identity. He said they should retain whatever is their Canadian character. Alongside that he wants them also to adopt a North American consciousness. "Canadians will have to learn to live with multiple identities," he told the audience. They must stop stubbornly clinging to one identity—be it English or French—and accommodate the more complex notion of having several identities simultaneously. "In Quebec, people already must live with the concept of two identities. Sometimes it is difficult, yes, but it can also be enriching."[13]

Mexicans and Americans also will be developing twin identities, one that feels comfortable within their own borders and another that will allow them to move freely within the limits of North America. "The model we want to follow is not necessarily the European Union," Axworthy said, "but one that has a North American identity and that retains a degree of autonomy"[14]—in other words, something uniquely North American.

Almost seven years after I had headed out for the ends of America with *The History of the United States Told in One-Syllable Words* in my briefcase, I had returned to find that the map of the place I belonged to, the place called "here," had undergone a momentous change. I no longer needed always to distinguish "here" from "there" when talking about Canada, Mexico, and the United States. Whenever I fill out an immigration form at an airport, I hesitate for a moment, just long enough to consider simply writing in the word "here" for place of residence. I have come to feel like a Newlander, a citizen of North America, with all the opportunity for starting over that the concept entails. I was lucky enough to make that trip out to Notre Dame once more, this time so that Aahren, well on the way to recovering from the illness that had shadowed our return home, could begin his freshman year anew. Now I look forward to the day when he, Laura Felice, and Andrés will consider a job opening in Manhattan, Montreal, or Monterrey as just another opportunity, when they will be able to retain the singular sense of being Americans but also will feel comfortable being North Americans. Borders will continue to exist in the world they are inheriting, and some are certain to be tense boundaries mined with suspicion and hate. There will surely continue to be conflicts in parts of the world where the language one speaks or the color of the flag one salutes is reason enough to be attacked. But there will be at least one place that is different.

North America will be a far from perfect place. Our inescapable differences will ensure that we remain individual nations with unique perspectives that sometimes do not coincide. Our borders will continue to be protected, against each other and against those outside the continent who are hell-bent on doing us harm. There will continue to be economic competition and painful inequalities across our borders. The real test of these continental bonds will come not when we are forced to decide our common interest, but when we have to confront our deepest differences. But because of what has happened during this rediscovery of North America, we may be able to look past our concerns about our borders and decide that it needn't be our dissimilarities that determine how we deal with each other, but rather all that we share. There will always be issues that the United States, Canada, and Mexico would rather not hold in common, but even then North America will remain a reluctant trinity, always together, though not always in agreement.

Our futures are overlapping, whether we like it or not. The symmetry that was broken a half millennium ago will never be fully restored, but some of it was regained during the turbulent first years of the continent's second half millennium. From 1993 to 2000, North America evolved from being defined solely as three separate nations divided by two borders on one continent to being recognized as a community of shared interest, common dreams, and coordinated responses to problems that have no regard for borders. If we are lucky, in years to come the kinship formed during this initial era of the new American continent will be emulated and deepened. Our borders will not disappear, not any time soon. But what may fade away are the misunderstandings and ignorance that have plagued North America for so long. The belief that any nation can be an island and not a part of the main has been discounted. The notion that what happens across the border doesn't matter has been disproved. And the concept of all three nations being in this world together, of "there" being "here" and "here" now increasingly coming to be "there," is rapidly replacing the incomplete maps and inaccurate perceptions we have lived with until now. From "here," we can only imagine this next new world. It may be ages before this new map can be completely filled in, but now we have an incomparable advantage over the first discoverers who tried to understand North America, because we already are becoming familiar with the new continent's ends, and its beginnings.

NOTES

✳

Chapter One: American Septentrional

1. William Thorsell, "Canada Is a Country of Fences That Make Good Citizens," *The Globe and Mail,* July 19, 1997, p. D6.

2. Mikhail Baryshnikov, "My Leap of Faith," *National Post,* weekend magazine, June 5, 1999, p. 2.

3. Octavio Paz, *Tiempo Nublado,* Mexico City, Editorial Seix Barral, 1983, p. 43.

4. Morton quoted in Andrew Duffy, "Canada 'a Nation of Losers,'" *The Ottawa Citizen,* May 31, 1998, p. A1.

5. John Irving, *A Prayer for Owen Meany,* Toronto, Lester and Orpen Dennys Ltd., 1989, p. 203.

6. Salinas quoted in Larry Rohter, "North American Trade Bloc? Mexico Rejects Such an Idea," *The New York Times,* November 24, 1998, p. D1.

7. Caspar Weinberger and Peter Schweizer, *The Next War,* Washington, D.C., Regnery Publishing, 1996, p. 165.

Chapter Two: Stumbing into a New World

1. Quoted in Hugh Thomas, *Conquest: Montezuma, Cortés, and the Fall of Old Mexico,* New York, Touchstone/Simon & Schuster, 1993, pp. 327–328.

2. El Chapo Guzmán was captured in 1994 as he tried to enter Guatemala and was tried and imprisoned. On January 19, 2001, he escaped the Puente Grande maximum security prison in Mexico City.

3. Lawrence E. Harrison, *The Pan-American Dream,* New York, Basic Books, 1997, p. 18.

4. See Hernando de Soto, *The Mystery of Capital: Why Capitalism Succeeds in the West and Fails Everywhere Else,* New York, Basic Books, 2000.

5. Bernal Díaz del Castillo, *The Conquest of New Spain,* J. M. Cohen, trans., London, Penguin Books, 1963, p. 214.

Chapter Three: Pyramids of Power

1. In December 2000, Muñoz Leos became head of Petróleos Mexicanos, the state-run Mexican oil company.

2. James J. Blanchard, *Behind the Embassy Door: Canada, Clinton, and Quebec,* Toronto, McClelland & Stewart, 1998, p. 81.

Chapter Four: Old Borders, New Politics

1. Tello Macías quoted in "Mexico and Canada: The Doors Are Open," advertising supplement in *Maclean's,* August 1, 1994, p. 1.

2. Marcos and the Zapatistas, traveling in buses, finally did enter Mexico City in March 2001 to begin negotiations with the new government on a package of Indian rights.

3. Interview with Camacho, October 19, 1995, in Mexico City.

4. See John S. D. Eisenhower, *Agent of Destiny: The Life and Times of General Winfield Scott,* New York, Free Press, 1997.

5. Kelly Egan, "I Thought the Americans Had Fired a Cruise Missile," *Ottawa Citizen,* January 29, 1999, p. C3.

6. Robert Ryal Miller, *Mexico: A History,* Norman, University of Oklahoma Press, 1985, p. 229.

7. Alamán cited in Enrique Krauze, *Mexico: Biography of Power—A History of Modern Mexico 1810–1996,* New York, Harper Collins, 1997, p. 144.

8. Henry David Thoreau, *Walden and "Civil Disobedience,"* New York: Penguin Books, 1983, pp. 389–390.

9. McGee cited in Christopher Moore, *1867: How the Fathers Made a Deal,* Toronto, McClelland & Stewart, 1997, p. 240.

10. Jorge G. Castañeda, *Perpetuating Power: How Mexican Presidents Were Chosen,* New York, New Press, 2000, p. 227.

Chapter Five: The Crises That Bind

1. So-called split-run editions of magazines are primarily repackaged U.S. editions of magazines like *Sports Illustrated* and *Time* with a few columns or news articles about Canada sprinkled inside. Measurements may be changed to the metric system, and a maple leaf inserted on the cover somewhere. What bothered Canadian publishers was not the editorial content but the ads. Time-Warner Inc., publisher of *Sports Illustrated* (and the Canadian edition of *Time*), sold ads in the split-run edition to Canadian advertisers. Canadian publishers contended the advertising market was finite, and ads sold to American magazines were ads taken away from domestic Canadian magazines. After the U.S. challenge, the World Trade Organization ruled that Canada's system of disincentives, including higher postal rates for split-runs and an 85 percent surcharge, were not permissible under international trade rules. Canada later attempted to fine advertisers who took ads in the split-run magazines but finally dropped the proposal.

2. President Salinas acknowledged the assistance in his memoirs. See *México: Un Paso Difícil a la Modernidad,* Barcelona, Plaza and Janés Editores, 2000, p. 840.

3. Krauze, *Mexico,* p. 658.

4. Interview with Zedillo, August 22, 1994, at PRI headquarters.

5. Anthony DePalma, "Mexico's Financial Turmoil: Remarks by Clinton Halt Slide of Stocks," *The New York Times,* January 12, 1995, p. D6.

6. *The Journals of Christopher Columbus,* Cecil Jane, trans., 1960; New York, Bonanza Books, Crown Publishers, 1989 ed., pp. 200, 221.

Chapter Six: Goatsuckers, Mad Hatters, and
Other Demons at Our Borders

1. Tim Golden, "Mexico Party Aide Arrested in Killing of Candidate in '94," *The New York Times,* February 26, 1995, p. A8.

2. Krauze, *Mexico,* pp. 458–459.

3. Blanchard, *Behind the Embassy Door,* p. 77.

4. Jean Chrétien, *Straight from the Heart,* Toronto, Seal Books, 1986, p. 103.

5. Charles E. Roh Jr., "The Implications for U.S. Trade Policy of an Independent Quebec," Center for Strategic and International Studies, Washington, D.C., 1995.

6. Blanchard, *Behind the Embassy Door,* p. 77.

7. Charles F. Doran, "Will Canada Unravel?" *Foreign Affairs* 75, 5 (1996), pp. 97–109.

Chapter Seven:
From Conquest to National Character

1. Castro speech to the Latin American Economic System, quoted by Reuters, December 9, 1998.

2. Carlos Fuentes, *The Crystal Frontier,* New York, Farrar, Straus and Giroux, 1997, p. 222.

3. Ibid.

Chapter Eight: Hell of a Transition

1. Sam W. Haynes, *James K. Polk and the Expansionist Impulse,* New York, Longman, 1997, p. IX.

2. Ibid., p. 2; Sullivan quote at p. 89.

3. Passport figures from government estimates of all three countries.

4. Robert A. Pastor and Rafael Fernandez de Castro, *The Controversial Pivot: The U.S. Congress and North America,* Washington, D.C., Brookings Institution Press, 1998, pp. 180–181.

5. In November 2000, Aguilar Zinser was named head of Mexico's new National Security Council under President Vicente Fox.

Chapter Nine: A Border Like No Other

1. Arthur Quinn, *A New World: An Epic of Colonial America from the Founding of Jamestown to the Fall of Quebec,* Winchester, Mass., Berkley Books/Faber & Faber, 1994, p. 47.

2. Francis Parkman, *The Battle for North America,* ed. by John Tebbel, New York, Doubleday & Co., 1948, p. 744.

3. Lynn Montross, *The Reluctant Rebels: The Story of the Continental Congress*, New York, Harper & Bros., 1950, p. 124.

4. Churchill's speech in honor of Prime Minister R. B. Bennet at the Canada Club, London, April 20, 1939.

5. May 17, 1961, as inscribed in the stone of the rotunda of the new U.S. embassy in Ottawa.

6. Haynes, *James K. Polk*, p. 56.

7. Moore, *1867: How the Fathers Made a Deal*, p. 238.

8. Joe Clark, *A Nation Too Good to Lose*, Toronto, Key Porter Books, 1994, p. 54.

9. Pierre Trudeau, *Memoirs*, Toronto, McClelland & Stewart, 1993, p. 306.

Chapter Ten: Affairs Too Foreign

1. Robert Bothwell, *Canada and the United States: The Politics of Partnership*, New York, Twayne Publishers, 1992, p. 22.

2. Ibid., p. 54.

3. Geoffrey A. H. Pearson, *Seize the Day: Lester B. Pearson and Crisis Diplomacy*, Ottawa, Carleton University Press, 1993, p. 102.

4. Bothwell, *Canada and the United States*, p. 54.

5. Ibid., p. 113.

6. Chrétien, *Straight from the Heart*, pp. 99–100.

7. Ernie Regehr and Simon Rosenblum, eds., *Canada and the Nuclear Arms Race*, Toronto, James Loreimer, 1983, p. 127.

8. Trudeau, *Memoirs*, p. 214.

9. Ibid., p. 333.

10. The nuclear weapons India developed with the help of Canada's technology came back to haunt Canada in 1999 after neighboring Pakistan threw down the nuclear gauntlet by exploding its own atomic bomb, a dangerous game of nuclear one-upmanship that unsettled the world.

11. With just weeks left in his administration, President Clinton announced in late 2000 that he was reviving his Chile promise and ordered negotiators to begin work on a bilateral trade deal with Chile It was not the NAFTA membership Chile wanted, but to the Chileans it was far better than nothing.

12. In early 2001, al-Sayegh remained in a Saudi prison.

Chapter Eleven:
God Save This Sweet Land of Liberty

1. Angus Reid Group, "Canada and the World: An International Perspective on Canada and Canadians," Toronto, May 1997. The company is now known as IPSOS-Reid.

2. Ibid.

3. J. L. Granatstein, "Yankee Go Home? Is Canadian Anti-Americanism Dead?" *Behind the Headlines* 54, 1 (Autumn 1996), pp. 4–11.

4. Chrétien, *Straight from the Heart*, p. 213.

5. Ronald Inglehart, Miguel Basáñez, and Neil Nevitte, *Convergencia en Norteamérica: Comercio, Política y Cultura*, Mexico City, Siglo Veintiuno Editores, 1994.

6. For an animated profile of Frontenac, see Quinn, *A New World.*

7. Mordecai Richler, *Home Sweet Home: My Canadian Album,* Toronto, McClelland & Stewart, 1984, p. 185.

8. Charles Dickens, *American Notes for General Circulation,* Middlesex, England, Penguin Books, 1972 ed., pp. 254, 256.

9. Lord Durham's Report on the Affairs of North America, ed. with an introduction by Sir C. P. Lucas, Oxford, England, Clarendon Press, 1912, p. 270.

10. Trudeau, *Memoirs,* p. 253.

Chapter Twelve: Ant Eggs, Cod Tongues, and the Essence of Culture

1. Castro quoted in Linda Diebel, "Fidel, Mickey, Go Head to Head," *The Toronto Star,* December 14, 1998, p. A2.

2. Michael Adams, *Sex in the Snow: Canadian Social Values at the End of the Millennium,* Toronto, Viking, Penguin Books Canada, 1997, p. 190.

3. Godbout quoted in Ray Conlogue, *Impossible Nation: The Longing for Homeland in Canada and Quebec,* Stratford, Ontario, Mercury Press, 1996, p. 135.

4. Henry Srebrnik, "Football, Frats, and Fun vs. Commuters, Cold, and Carping: The Social and Psychological Context of Higher Education in Canada and the United States," in David M. Thomas, ed., *Canada and the United States: Differences That Count,* Peterborough, Ontario, Broadview Press, 2000, p. 184.

5. John Deverell, "Men's Wear Retailer Shuts After 95 Years," *The Toronto Star,* March 6, 1997, p. C3.

6. "If This Happens to You . . . ," *Reforma,* May 19, 1994, p. B5.

7. Seymour Martin Lipset, *Continental Divide: The Values and Institutions of the United States and Canada,* New York, Routledge, 1990, p. 58.

8. Margaret Atwood, *Survival: A Thematic Guide to Canadian Literature,* Boston, Beacon Press, 1972, p. 33.

9. Octavio Paz, *The Labyrinth of Solitude,* New York, Grove Weidenfeld, 1985, p. 40.

10. Henry Kissinger and Robert Thompson quoted in John Robert Colombo, ed., *New Canadian Quotations,* Edmonton, Alberta, Hurtig Publishers, 1987. McCaffrey's remarks were made during an appearance on "This Week," ABC, March 2, 1997. General McCaffrey expressed similar thoughts a few days earlier. On February 25, at an appearance with President Clinton in Washington to announce a new drug policy, McCaffrey said, "It is our belief that the United States and Mexico are trapped, economically, culturally, politically and because of drug crime, in the same continent, and we'd better figure out a way to work on it together." Quoted in Christopher S. Wren, "Two Democrats Say Mexico Is No U.S. Ally in Drug War," *The New York Times,* February 26, 1997, p. A7.

Chapter Thirteen: Nations of Nations

1. In 2000 the Liberals passed a clarity bill giving Ottawa the power to reject the results of a referendum based on an unclear question.

2. Trudeau, *Memoirs,* p. 72.

3. René Lévesque, *An Option for Quebec*, Toronto, McClelland & Stewart, 1968, p. 14.

4. Lord Durham Report, p. 127.

5. Ibid., pp. 27–28.

6. LaPierre quoted in Duffy, "Canada 'a Nation of Losers,'" p. A1.

7. Václav Havel, "Kosovo and the End of the Nation-State," trans. from the Czech by Paul Wilson, *The New York Review of Books*, June 10, 1999, pp. 4–6.

8. Octavio Paz, "Why Incite Demagogy?" *The New York Times*, November 9, 1993, p. A17.

Chapter Fourteen: Sons of the Middle Border

1. Sidney Weintraub, *NAFTA at Three*, Center for Strategic and International Studies, Washington, D.C., 1997, p. 12.

2. Paz, "Why Incite Demagogy?" p. A17.

3. Constantine quoted in Tim Golden, "Former Drug Chief Says U.S. Brushed Aside Mexico's Role," *The New York Times*, November 26, 1999, p. A26.

4. Tellier quoted in Robert Gibbens and Ian Jack, "CN Chief Slams Anti-Merger Nationalists," *National Post*, December 21, 1999, p. A1.

5. Pierre Berton, "Canada's Century? Not!" *The Globe and Mail*, July 12, 1999, p. C1.

6. Chrétien quoted in Kate Jaimet, "Canada: Take It or Leave It, PM Says," *The Ottawa Citizen*, July 23, 1999, p. A1.

Epilogue

1. Fox press conference at the National Press Club, Washington, August 24, 2000.

2. Ibid.

3. Fox speech at the Center for Democracy, Washington, August 24, 2000.

4. Jeff Faux, "Time for a New Deal with Mexico," *The American Prospect*, October 23, 2000, pp. 20–21.

5. Transcript of the U.S. presidential debate on October 4, 2000.

6. Bush campaign speech in Miami, Florida, August 25, 2000.

7. Ibid.

8. Ibid.

9. Robert Fife and Sheldon Alberts, "Leaders Get Nasty in Final Debate," *National Post*, November 10, 2000, p. A1.

10. On January 11, 2001, a disgruntled and sorely disappointed Lucien Bouchard resigned as premier of Quebec saying he had failed to keep his promise to make Quebec independent.

11. Pierre Trudeau, speaking at a Liberal Party convention in Ottawa, February 24, 1978, cited in Colombo, *New Canadian Quotations*, p. 205.

12. Axworthy remarks in an address to the National Policy Research Conference in Ottawa, November 30, 2000.

13. Dubuc remarks in an address to the National Policy Research Conference in Ottawa, November 30, 2000.

14. Axworthy remarks, National Policy Research Conference.

BIBLIOGRAPHY OF

SELECTED SOURCES

✳

Mexico

Camp, Roderic Ai. *Politics in Mexico*. New York: Oxford University Press, 1993.

Campbell, Federico. *Tijuana: Stories on the Border*. Berkeley and Los Angeles: University of California Press, 1995.

Castañeda, Jorge. *The Mexican Shock*. New York: New Press, 1995.

_____. *La Herencia: Arqueología de la Sucesión Presidencial en Mexico*. Mexico City: Extra Alfaguara, 1999.

_____. *Perpetuating Power: How Mexican Presidents Were Chosen*. New York: New Press, 2000.

Cortés, Hernán. *Letters from Mexico*. New Haven: Yale University Press, 1986.

Díaz del Castillo, Bernal. *The Conquest of New Spain*. J. M. Cohen, trans. London: Penguin Books, 1963.

Dresser, Denise. "Neopopulist Solutions to Neoliberal Problems: Mexico's National Solidarity Program." Center for U.S.-Mexican Studies, San Diego, Calif., 1991.

Fuentes, Carlos. *The Death of Artemio Cruz*. New York: Farrar, Straus and Giroux, 1991.

_____. *The Crystal Frontier*. New York: Farrar, Straus and Giroux, 1997.

Harrison, Lawrence E. *The Pan-American Dream*. New York: Basic Books, 1997.

Krauze, Enrique. *Mexico: Biography of Power—A History of Modern Mexico 1810–1996*. New York: Harper Collins, 1997.

Lafaye, Jacques. *Quetzalcóatal and Guadalupe: The Formation of Mexican National Consciousness 1531–1813*. Chicago: University of Chicago Press, 1974.

Lawrence, D. H. *The Plumed Serpent*. London: Penguin Books, 1995.

Lustig, Nora. *Mexico: The Remaking of an Economy*. Washington, D.C.: Brookings Institution, 1992.

Marquez, Enrique. *Porqué Perdió Camacho: Revelaciones del asesor de Manuel Camacho Solís*. Mexico City: Oceano, 1995.

Miller, Robert Ryal. *Mexico: A History*. Norman: University of Oklahoma Press, 1985.

Oppenheimer, Andrés. *Bordering on Chaos: Guerrillas, Stockbrokers, Politicians, and Mexico's Road to Recovery*. New York: Little, Brown and Co., 1996.

Pastor, Robert A. *Integration with Mexico.* New York: Twentieth Century Fund Press, 1993.

Pastor, Robert A., with Jorge Castañeda. *Limits to Friendship.* New York: Alfred A. Knopf, 1988.

Paz, Octavio. *Tiempo Nublado.* Mexico City: Editorial Seix Barral, 1983.

_____. *The Labyrinth of Solitude.* New York: Grove Weidenfeld, 1985.

Reavis, Dick J. *Conversations with Moctezuma: The Soul of Modern Mexico.* New York: Quill, 1990.

Riding, Alan. *Distant Neighbors: A Portrait of the Mexicans.* New York: Vintage Books, 1989.

Ross, John. *Rebellion from the Roots: Indian Uprising in Chiapas.* Monroe, Maine: Common Courage Press, 1995.

Stefoff, Rebecca. *Independence and Revolution in Mexico.* New York: Facts on File, 1993.

Thomas, Hugh. *Conquest: Montezuma, Cortés, and the Fall of Old Mexico.* New York: Simon & Schuster, 1993.

Wheeler, Romayne. *Life Through the Eyes of a Tarahumara.* Chihuahua, Mexico: Editorial Camino.

Canada

Adams, Michael. *Sex in the Snow: Canadian Social Values at the End of the Millennium.* Toronto: Viking, Penguin Books Canada, 1997.

Barrett, Andrea. *Voyage of the* Narwhal. New York: W. W. Norton & Co., 1998.

Blanchard, James J. *Behind the Embassy Door: Canada, Clinton, and Quebec.* Toronto: McClelland & Stewart, 1998.

Bothwell, Robert. *Canada and the United States: The Politics of Partnership.* New York: Twayne Publishers, 1992.

Bouchard, Lucien. *On the Record.* Toronto: Stoddart Publishing, 1994.

Cameron, Stevie. *On the Take: Crime, Corruption, and Greed in the Mulroney Years.* Toronto: Macfarlane Walter & Ross, 1994.

Chrétien, Jean. *Straight from the Heart.* Toronto: Seal Books, 1986.

Clark, Joe. *A Nation Too Good to Lose.* Toronto: Key Porter Books, 1994.

Conlogue, Ray. *Impossible Nation: The Longing for Homeland in Canada and Quebec.* Stratford, Ontario: Mercury Press, 1996.

Dickinson, John A. *A Short History of Quebec.* Toronto: Copp Clark Pitman Ltd., 1993.

Francis, Diane. *Fighting for Canada.* Toronto: Key Porter Books, 1996.

Gwyn, Richard. *The 49th Paradox: Canada in North America.* Toronto: McClelland & Stewart, 1985.

_____. *Nationalism Without Walls: The Unbearable Lightness of Being Canadian.* Toronto: McClelland & Stewart, 1995.

Houston, James. *Zigzag: A Life on the Move.* Toronto: McClelland & Stewart, 1997.

Lévesque, René. *An Option for Quebec.* Toronto: McClelland & Stewart, 1971.

Lipset, Seymour Martin. *Continental Divide: The Values and Institutions of the United States and Canada.* New York: Routledge, 1990.

MacDonald, John. *The Arctic Sky: Inuit Astronomy, Star Lore, and Legend.* Toronto: Royal Ontario Museum, 1998.

Malcolm, Andrew H. *The Canadians.* New York: Times Books, 1985.

McKenna, Marian C., ed. *The Canadian and American Constitutions in Comparative Perspectives.* Calgary: University of Calgary Press, 1993.

McRoberts, Kenneth. *Misconceiving Canada: The Struggle for National Unity.* New York: Oxford University Press, 1997.

Moore, Christopher. *1867: How the Fathers Made a Deal.* Toronto: McClelland & Stewart, 1997.

Morton, Desmond. *A Short History of Canada.* Toronto: McClelland & Stewart, 1994.

Morton, W. L. *The Kingdom of Canada.* Toronto: McClelland & Stewart, 1963.

Nevitte, Neil. *Unsteady State: The 1997 Canadian Federal Election.* Don Mills, Ontario: Oxford University Press Canada, 2000.

Orchard, David. *The Fight for Canada: Four Centuries of Resistance to American Expansionism.* Toronto: Stoddart, 1993.

Pearson, Geoffrey A. H. *Seize the Day: Lester B. Pearson and Crisis Diplomacy.* Ottawa: Carleton University Press, 1993.

Ray, Arthur J. *I Have Lived Here Since the World Began: An Illustrated History of Canada's Native People.* Toronto: Lester Publishing, 1996.

Reid, Angus. *Shakedown: How the New Economy Is Changing Our Lives.* Toronto: Doubleday Canada Ltd., 1996.

Richler, Mordecai. *Home Sweet Home: My Canadian Album.* Toronto: McClelland & Stewart, 1984.

_____. *Oh Canada! Oh Quebec!* New York: Viking, 1992.

_____. *Barney's Version.* Toronto: Alfred A. Knopf Canada, 1997.

Schnurmacher, Thomas. *Canada Is Not a Real Country.* Toronto: ECW Press, 1996.

Simpson, Jeffrey. *Faultlines: Struggling for a Canadian Vision.* Toronto: Harper Collins, 1993.

Trudeau, Pierre Elliott. *Memoirs.* Toronto: McClelland & Stewart, 1993.

United States

Baker, C. Alice. *True Stories of New England Captives Carried to Canada.* Bowie, Md.: Heritage Books facsimile reprint, 1990.

Burnett, Edmund Cody. *The Continental Congress.* New York: Macmillan, 1941.

Dickens, Charles. *American Notes for General Circulation.* Middlesex, England: Penguin Books Ltd., 1972.

Eisenhower, John S. D. *Agent of Destiny: The Life and Times of General Winfield Scott.* New York: Free Press, 1997.

Fishlow, Albert, and James Jones. *The United States and the Americas: A Twenty-First Century View.* New York: W. W. Norton and Co., 1999.

Haynes, Sam. W. *James K. Polk and the Expansionist Impulse.* New York: Longman, 1997.

Montross, Lynn. *The Reluctant Rebels: The Story of the Continental Congress.* New York: Harper & Bros., 1950.

Rakove, Jack N. *The Beginnings of National Politics: An Interpretive History of the Continental Congress.* New York: Knopf, 1979.

Roh, Charles E. "The Implications for U.S. Trade Policy of an Independent Quebec." Center for Strategic and International Studies, Washington, D.C., 1995.

Thoreau, Henry David. *Walden and "Civil Disobedience."* New York: Penguin Books, 1983.

Warus, Mark. *Another America: Native American Maps and the History of Our Land.* New York: St. Martin's Press, 1997.

Weinberger, Caspar, and Peter Schweizer. *The Next War.* Washington, D.C.: Regnery Publishing, 1996.

North America

Columbus, Christopher. *The Journals of Christopher Columbus.* Cecil Jane, trans. 1960. New York: Bonanza Books, Crown Publishers, 1989.

Del Castillo, Gustavo, and Gustavo Vega Cánovas. *The Politics of Free Trade in North America.* Ottawa: Centre for Trade Policy and Law, 1995.

Egnal, Marc. *Divergent Paths: How Culture and Institutions Have Shaped North American Growth.* New York: Oxford University Press, 1996.

Garreau, Joel. *The Nine Nations of North America.* New York: Avon Books, 1981.

Inglehart, Ronald, Miguel Basáñez, and Alejandro Moreno. *Human Values and Beliefs: A Cross-Cultural Sourcebook.* Ann Arbor: University of Michigan Press, 1998.

Inglehart, Ronald, Miguel Basáñez, and Neil Nevitte. *Convergencia en Norteamérica: Comercio, Política y Cultura.* Mexico City: Siglo Veintiunio Editores, 1994. (See also English translation: *The North American Trajectory: Cultural, Economic, and Political Ties Among the United States, Canada, and Mexico.* Hawthorne, N.Y.: Aldine de Gruyter, 1996.)

Kay, Richard, and John D. Wirth, eds. *Environmental Management on North America's Borders.* College Station: Texas A&M University Press, 1998.

McArthur, John R. *The Selling of "Free Trade": NAFTA, Washington and the Subversion of American Democracy.* New York: Hill and Wang, 2000.

Parkman, Francis. *The Battle for North America.* Ed. by John Tebbel. New York: Doubleday & Co., 1948.

Pastor, Robert, and Rafael Fernandez de Castro. *The Controversial Pivot: The U.S. Congress and North America.* Washington, D.C.: Brookings Institution Press, 1998.

Pringle, Heather. *In Search of Ancient North America.* New York: John Wiley & Sons, 1996.

Quinn, Arthur. *A New World: An Epic of Colonial America from the Founding of Jamestown to the Fall of Quebec.* Winchester, Mass.: Berkley Books/Faber & Faber, 1994.

Randall, Stephen J., and Herman W. Konrad, eds. *NAFTA in Transition.* Calgary: University of Calgary Press, 1995.

Weintraub, Sidney. *NAFTA at Three.* Washington, D.C.: Center for Strategic and International Studies, 1997.

INDEX

✳

Adams, John, 191
Adams, Michael, 264
Aguayo, Sergio, 89
Aguilar Zinser, Adolfo, 179–184
Alamán, Lucas, 81
Almada, Carlos, 182
Althaus, Dudley, 103–104
American Revolution, 197–198
   and Canada, 10–11, 191–192
Anti-Americanism, 78, 130, 203–204,
   216, 238–239, 263
Anti-Semitism, 135, 290
Arctic, the, 299–308
Aridjis, Homero, 37
Arnold, Cindy, 100–101
Arrieta, Ramón, 101
Aspe, Pedro, 88–89
Atwood, Margaret, 275, 276
Axworthy, Lloyd, 209–213, 222, 237,
   351–352
Aztecs, 21–23, 28, 33–36, 149

Baker, James A., 314–315
Baryshnikov Mikhail, 8
Basáñez, Miguel, 241–242
Belushi, John, 265
Bentsen, Lloyd, 87–90, 105–106, 174
Berton, Pierre, 331
Blanchard, James J., 51
Borders, national, 57
   between Canada and the United
     States, 185–187, 188, 196–197,
     242–243, 333
   and international trade, 332–334

   and the Mexican-American War,
     78–82
   between Mexico and the United
     States, 193–196, 333
   and the Rio Grande, 194
   and United States' expansionism,
     80–82
   and the War of 1812, 78–84
Bouchard, Lucien, 294, 297–298
Brady, Nicholas, 46
Britain. *See* England
Brooke, Jim, 335
Burne, George, 216
Bush, George, Jr., 348–349
Bush, George, Sr., 115, 129, 314–315,
   343

Cabot, John, 109, 196
Calles, Plutarco Elías, 122
Camacho Solís, Manuel, 60–65, 69–72
Campbell, Kim, 50, 245, 246
Canada
   American residents of, 185–186
   Americans' views of, 8–10, 186,
     227–228, 234–236, 240–242
   and anti-Americanism, 78, 130,
     203–204, 216, 238–239, 263
   and anti-Semitism, 135, 290
   and the Arctic, 299–308
   and Axworthy, Lloyd, 209–213, 222,
     237, 351–352
   border between the United States
     and, 185–187, 188, 196–197,
     242–243, 333